PRISONS OF THE MIND

By Kaziah May Hancock

Granddaughter of Mosiah Hancock, a Mormon pioneer

PREFACE

December 13, 1985

Salt Lake County Courthouse,
Salt Lake City, Utah

As I walked down the steps of the courthouse, the cool winter breeze on my face, I stopped for a moment with immense appreciation and joy in my heart as I thought of the courtroom scene I had just left. I burst into tears. "Thank you, God," I murmured as I looked into the heavens.

Just then a young man ran up from behind. "Uh, pardon me, ma'am. That was an incredible hearing! Do you think it possible that I could get a copy of the court transcript?"

"Well, I don't know," I replied, shaking his hand.

Some time has passed since that day, and it was only the first of such reactions. There have been many friends who have suggested that I write this story of my life. I have thought to do so but have hesitated for fear that it might turn someone against the old-time Mormon faith of my fathers and bring condemnation upon my head. However, as time has passed, I have realized that my ordeal was the result of one man's evil misuse of that faith in a way that was never intended by the scriptures. If anything, my faith is even stronger and if I have not been turned against it, why should anyone else be?

~~~~~~~~~~~~~~~~~~~~~~

The Mormon religion has always believed, since the time of the Prophet Joseph Smith, that the president of the priesthood or president of the church, has been the man who is the mouthpiece of the Lord unto his people. However, since the time of John Taylor and Wilford Woodruff, there has been much controversy over the issue of plural marriage, whether it was to be continued or abolished.

This debate has been the major issue separating the monogamous Saints from the fundamentalist Saints. Those on either side of this issue are devoted strongly to their beliefs.

It is quite common for a person to walk into a Sunday gathering conducted by the Elders of the Mormon Church and hear conversation similar to this:

A new convert seeking the truth might raise his hand and say, "I have been studying the Scriptures very carefully and have questions in my mind concerning the 132nd Section of <u>The Doctrine and Covenants</u> wherein it states:

i

1.   Verily, thus saith the Lord unto you my servant, Joseph, that inasmuch as you have inquired of my hand to know and understand wherein I, the Lord, justified my servants Abraham, Isaac, and Jacob, as also Moses, David and Solomon, my servants, as touching the principle and doctrine of their having many wives and concubines--

2.   Behold, and lo, I am the Lord they God, and will answer thee as touching this matter.

3.   Therefore, prepare they heart to receive and obey the instructions which I am about to give unto you; for all those who have this law revealed unto them must obey the same.

4.   *For behold, I reveal unto you a new and an everlasting covenant; and if ye abide not that covenant, then are ye damned; for not one can reject this covenant and be permitted to enter into my glory.*

5.   For all who will have a blessing at my hands shall abide the law which was appointed for that blessing, and the conditions thereof, as were instituted from before the foundation of the world.

6.   And as pertaining to the new and everlasting covenant, it was instituted for the fullness of my glory; and he that receiveth a fullness thereof must and shall abide the law, or he shall be damned, saith the Lord God.

7.   *And verily I say unto you, that the conditions of this law are these: All covenants, contracts, bonds, obligations, oaths, vows, performances, connections, associations, or expectations, that are not made and entered into and sealed by the Holy Spirit of promise, of him who is anointed, both as well for time and for all eternity, and that too most holy, by revelation and commandment through the medium of mine anointed, whom I have appointed on the earth to hold this power (and I have appointed unto my servant Joseph to hold this power in the last days, and there is never but one on the earth at a time on whom this power and the keys of this priesthood are conferred), are of no efficacy, virtue, or force in and after the resurrection from the dead; for all contracts that are not made unto this end have an end when men are dead.*

8.   Behold, mine house is a house of order, saith the Lord God, and not a house of confusion.

9.   Will I accept of an offering, saith the Lord, that is not made in my name?

10. Or will I receive at your hands that which I have not appointed?

11. And will I appoint unto you, saith the Lord, except it be by law, even as I and my Father ordained unto you, before the world was?

12. I am the Lord thy God; and I give unto you this commandment--that no man shall come unto the Father but by me or by my word, which is my law, saith the Lord.

13. And everything that is in the world, whether it be ordained of men, by thrones, or principalities, or powers, or things of name, whatsoever they may be, that are not by me or by my word, saith the Lord, shall be thrown down, and shall not remain after men are dead, neither in nor after the resurrection, saith the Lord your God.

14. For whatsoever things remain are by me; and whatsoever things are not by me shall be shaken and destroyed.

15. Therefore, if a man marry him a wife in the world, and he marry her not by me nor by my word, and he covenant with her so long as he is in the world and she with him, their covenant and marriage are not of force when they are dead, and when they are out of the world; therefore, they are not bound by any law when they are out of the world.

16. Therefore, when they are out of the world they neither marry nor are given in marriage; but are appointed angels in heaven, which angels are ministering servants, to minister for those who are worthy of a far more, and an exceeding, and an eternal weight of glory.

17. For these angels did not abide my law; therefore, they cannot be enlarged, but remain separately and singly, without exaltation, in their saved condition, to all eternity; and from henceforth are not gods, but are angels of God forever and ever.

18. And again, verily I say unto you, if a man marry a wife, and make a covenant with her for time and for all eternity, if that covenant is not by me or by my word, which is my law, and is not sealed by the Holy Spirit of promise, through him whom I have anointed and appointed unto this power, then it is not valid neither of force when they are out of the world, because they are not joined by me, saith the Lord, neither by my word; when they are out of the world it cannot be received there, because the angels and the gods are appointed there, by whom they cannot pass; they cannot,

therefore, inherit my glory; for my house is a house of order, saith the Lord God.

19. And again, verily I say unto you, if a man marry a wife by my word, which is my law, and by the new and everlasting covenant, and it is sealed unto them by the Holy spirit of promise, by him who is anointed, unto whom I have appointed this power and the keys of this priesthood; and it shall be said unto them--Ye shall come forth in the first resurrection; and if it be after the first resurrection, in the next resurrection; and shall inherit thrones, kingdoms, principalities, and powers, dominions, all heights and depths-- then shall it be written in the Lamb's Book of Life, that he shall commit no murder whereby to shed innocent blood, and if ye abide in my covenant, and commit no murder whereby to shed innocent blood, it shall be done unto them in all things whatsoever my servant hath put upon them, in time, and through all eternity; and shall be of full force when they are out of the world; and they shall pass by the angles, and the gods, which are set there, to their exaltation and glory in all things, as hath been sealed upon their heads, which glory shall be a fullness and a continuation of the seeds forever and ever.

20. Then shall they be gods, because they have no end; therefore shall they be from everlasting to everlasting, because they continue; then shall they be above all, because all things are subject unto them. Then shall they be gods, because they have all power, and the angels are subject unto them.

21. Verily, verily, I say unto you, except ye abide my law ye cannot attain to this glory.

22. *For strait is the gate, and narrow the way that leadeth unto the exaltation and continuation of the lives, and few there be that find it, because ye receive me not in the world neither do ye know me.*

23. But if ye receive me in the world, then shall ye know me, and shall receive your exaltation; that where I am ye shall be also.

24. This is eternal lives--to know the only wise and true God, and Jesus Christ, whom he hath sent. I am he. Receive ye, therefore, my law.

25. Broad is the gate, and wide the way that leadeth to the deaths; and many there are that go in thereat, because they receive them not, neither do they abide in my law.

26. Verily, verily, I say unto you, if a man marry a wife according to my word, and they are sealed by the Holy Spirit of promise, according to mine appointment, and he or she shall commit any sin or transgression of the new and everlasting covenant whatever, and all manner of blasphemies, and if they commit no murder wherein they shed innocent blood, yet they shall come forth in the first resurrection, and enter into their exaltation; but they shall be destroyed in the flesh, and shall be delivered unto the buffetings of Satan unto the day of redemption, saith the Lord God.

27. The blasphemy against the Holy Ghost, which shall not be forgiven in the world nor out of the world, is in that ye commit murder wherein ye shed innocent blood, and assent unto my death, after ye have received my new and everlasting covenant, saith the Lord God; and he that abideth not this law can in nowise enter into my glory, but shall be damned, saith the Lord.

28. I am the Lord thy God, and will give unto thee the law of my Holy Priesthood, as was ordained by me and my Father before the world was.

29. *Abraham received all things, whatsoever he received, by revelation and commandment, by my word, saith the Lord, and hath entered into his exaltation and sitteth upon his throne.*

30. *Abraham received promises concerning his seed, and of the fruit of his loins--from whose loins ye are, namely, my servant Joseph--which were to continue so long as they were in the world; and as touching Abraham and his seed, out of the world they should continue; both in the world and out of the world should they continue as innumerable as the stars; or, if ye were to count the sand upon the seashore ye could not number them.*

31. *This promise is yours also, because ye are of Abraham, and the promise was made unto Abraham; and by this law is the continuation of the works of my Father, wherein he glorifieth himself.*

32. *Go ye, therefore, and do the works of Abraham; enter ye into my law and ye shall be saved.*

33. *But if ye enter not into my law ye cannot receive the promise of my Father, which he made unto Abraham.*

34. *God commanded Abraham, and Sarah gave Hagar to Abraham to wife. And why did she do it? Because this was the law; and from Hagar sprang many people. This, therefore, was fulfilling, among other things, the promises.*

35. Was Abraham, therefore, under condemnation? Verily I say unto you, Nay; for I, the Lord, commanded it.

36. Abraham was commanded to offer his son Isaac; nevertheless, it was written: Thou shalt not kill. Abraham, however, did not refuse, and it was accounted unto him for righteousness.

37. Abraham received concubines, and they bore him children; and it was accounted unto him for righteousness, because they were given unto him, and he abode in my law; as Isaac also and Jacob did none other things than that which they were commanded; and because they did none other things than that which they were commanded, they have entered into their exaltation, according to the promises, and sit upon thrones, and are not angels but are gods.

38. David also received many wives and concubines, and also Solomon and Moses my servants, as also many others of my servants, from the beginning of creation until this time; and in nothing did they sin save in those things which they received not of me.

39. David's wives and concubines were given unto him of me, by the hand of Nathan, my servant, and others of the prophets who had the keys of this power; and in none of these things did he sin against me save in the case of Uriah and his wife; and, therefore he hath fallen from his exaltation, and received his portion; and he shall not inherit them out of the world, for I gave them unto another, saith the Lord.

40. I am the Lord thy God, and I gave unto thee, my servant Joseph, an appointment, and restore all things. Ask what ye will, and it shall be given unto you according to my word.

41. And as ye have asked concerning adultery, verily, verily, I say unto you, if a man receiveth a wife in the new and everlasting covenant, and if she be with another man, and I have not appointed unto her by the holy anointing, she hath committed adultery and shall be destroyed.

42. If she be not in the new and everlasting covenant, and she be with another man, she has committed adultery.

43. And if her husband be with another woman, and he was under a vow, he hath broken his vow and hath committed adultery.

44. And if she hath not committed adultery, but is innocent and hath not broken her vow, and she knoweth it, and I reveal it unto you, my servant Joseph, then shall you

have power, by the power of my Holy Priesthood, to take her and give her unto him that hath not committed adultery but hath been faithful; for he shall be made ruler over many.

45. For I have conferred upon you the keys and power of the priesthood, wherein I restore all things, and make known unto you all things in due time.

46. *And verily, verily, I say unto you, that whatsoever you seal on earth shall be sealed in heaven; and whatsoever you bind on earth, in my name and by my word, saith the Lord, it shall be eternally bound in the heavens; and whosoever sins you remit on earth shall be remitted eternally in the heavens; and whosoever sins you retain on earth shall be retained in heaven.*

47. *And again, verily I say, whomsoever you bless I will bless, and whomsoever you curse I will curse, saith the Lord; for I, the Lord, am they God.*

48. And again, verily I say unto you, my servant Joseph, that whatsoever you give on earth, and to whomsoever you give anyone on earth, by my word and according to my law, it shall be visited with blessings and not cursings, and with my power, saith the Lord, and shall be without condemnation on earth and in heaven.

49. For I am the Lord they God, and will be with thee even unto the end of the world, and through all eternity; for verily I seal upon you your exaltation, and prepare a throne for you in the kingdom of my Father, with Abraham your father.

50. Behold, I have seen your sacrifices, and will forgive all your sins; I have seen your sacrifices in obedience to that which I have told you. Go, therefore, and I make a way for your escape, as I accepted the offering of Abraham of his son Isaac.

51. Verily, I say unto you: A commandment I give unto mine handmaid, Emma Smith, your wife, whom I have given unto you, that she stay herself and partake not of that which I commanded you to offer unto her; for I did it, saith the Lord, to prove you all, as I did Abraham, and that I might require an offering at your hand, by covenant and sacrifice.

52. And let mine handmaid, Emma Smith, receive all those that have been given unto my servant Joseph, and who are virtuous and pure before me; and those who are not pure, and have said they were pure, shall be destroyed, saith the Lord God.

53. For I am the Lord they God, and ye shall obey my voice; and I give unto my servant Joseph that he shall be made ruler over many things; for he hath been faithful over a few things, and from henceforth I will strengthen him.

54. *And I command mine handmaid, Emma Smith to abide and cleave unto my servant Joseph, and to none else. But if she will not abide this commandment she shall be destroyed, saith the Lord; for I am the Lord they God, and will destroy her if she abide not in my law.*

55. But if she will not abide this commandment, then shall my servant Joseph do all things for her, even as he hath said; and I will bless him and multiply him and give unto him an hundredfold in this world, of fathers and mothers, brothers and sisters, houses and lands, wives and children, and crowns of eternal lives in the eternal worlds.

56. And again, verily I say, let mine handmaid forgive my servant Joseph his trespasses; and then shall she be forgiven her trespasses, wherein she has trespassed against me; and I, the Lord they God, will bless her, and multiply her, and make her heart to rejoice.

57. And again, I say, let not my servant Joseph put his property out of his hands, lest an enemy come and destroy him; for Satan seeketh to destroy; for I am the Lord they God, and he is my servant; and behold, and lo, I am with him, as I was with Abraham, they father, even unto his exaltation and glory.

58. Now, as touching the law of the priesthood, there are many things pertaining thereunto.

59. Verily, if a man be called of my Father, as was Aaron, by mine own voice, and by the voice of him that sent me, and I have endowed him with the keys of the power of this priesthood, if he do anything in my name, and according to my law and by my word, he will not commit sin, and I will justify him.

60. Let no one, therefore, set on my servant Joseph; for I will justify him; for he shall do the sacrifice which I require at his hands for his transgressions, saith the Lord your God.

61. *And again, as pertaining to the law of the priesthood--if any man espouse a virgin, and desire to espouse another, and the first give her consent, and if he espouse the second, and they are virgins, and have vowed to no other man, then is he justified; he cannot commit adultery for they*

are given unto him; for he cannot commit adultery with that that belongeth unto him and to no one else.

62. And if he have ten virgins given unto him by this law, he cannot commit adultery, for they belong to him, and they are given unto him; therefore is he justified.

63. But if one or either of the ten virgins, after she is espoused, shall be with another man, she has committed adultery, and shall be destroyed; for they are given unto him to multiply and replenish the earth, according to my commandment, and to fulfill the promise which was given by my Father before the foundation of the world, and for their exaltation in the eternal worlds, that they may bear the souls of men; for herein is the work of my Father continued, that he may be glorified.

64. *And again, verily, verily, I say unto you, if any man have a wife, who holds the keys of this power, and he teaches unto her the law of my priesthood, as pertaining to these things, then shall she believe and administer unto him, or she shall be destroyed, saith the Lord your God; for I will destroy her; for I will magnify my name upon all those who receive and abide in my law.*

65. Therefore, it shall be lawful in me, if she receive not this law, for him to receive all things whatsoever I, the Lord his God, will give unto him, because she did not believe and administer unto him according to my word; and she then becomes the transgressor; and he is exempt from the law of Sarah, who administered unto Abraham according to the law when I commanded Abraham to take Hagar to wife.

66. And now, as pertaining to this law, verily, verily, I saw unto you, I will reveal more unto you, hereafter; therefore, let this suffice for the present. Behold, I am Alpha and Omega. Amen.[1]

"What does the current Prophet feel is our obligation toward this revelation?" The answer most generally would be something like this:

"That has been done away with since the time of the Manifesto given through Wilford Woodruff."

"Those standing in favor of monogamy have based their position on the official declaration made by Wilford Woodruff:"

------

[1] Section 132, emphasis added.

OFFICIAL DECLARATION

To Whom it may Concern:

Press dispatches having been sent for political purposes, from Salt Lake City, which have been widely published, to the effect that the Utah Commission, in their recent report to the Secretary of the Interior, allege that plural marriages are still being solemnized and that forty or more such marriages have been contracted in Utah since last June or during the past year, also that in public discourses the leaders of the Church have taught, encouraged, and urged the continuance of the practice of polygamy--

I, therefore, as President of the Church of Jesus Christ of Latter-day Saints, do hereby, in the most solemn manner, declare that these charges are false. We are not teaching polygamy or plural marriage, nor permitting any person to enter into its practice, and I deny that either forty or any other number of plural marriages have during that period been solemnized in our Temples or in any other place in the Territory.

One case has been reported, in which the parties allege that the marriage was performed in the Endowment House, in Salt Lake City, in the Spring of 1889, but I have not been able to learn who performed the ceremony; whatever was done in this matter was without my knowledge. In consequence of this alleged occurrence the Endowment House was, by my instructions, taken down without delay.

Inasmuch as laws have been enacted by Congress forbidding plural marriages, which laws have been pronounced constitutional by the court of last resort, I hereby declare my intention to submit to those laws and to use my influence with the members of the church over which I preside to have them do likewise.

There is nothing in my teachings to the Church or in those of my associates, during the time specified, which can be reasonably construed to inculcate or encourage polygamy; and when any Elder of the Church has used language which appeared to convey any such teaching, he has been promptly reproved. And I now publicly declare that my advice to the

Latter-day Saints is to refrain from contracting any marriage forbidden by the law of the land.

Wilford Woodruff
President of the Church of Jesus Christ of
Latter-day Saints

President Lorenzo Snow offered the following:

"I move that, recognizing Wilford Woodruff as the President of the Church of Jesus Christ of Latter-day Saints, and the only man on the earth at the present time who holds the keys of the sealing ordinances, we consider him fully authorized by virtue of his position to issue the Manifesto which has been read in our hearing, and which is dated September 24th, 1890, and that as a Church in General Conference assembled, we accept his declaration concerning plural marriages as authoritative and binding."

The vote to sustain the foregoing motion was unanimous.

Salt Lake City, Utah, October 6, 1890 [2]

"We believe that we will live the law of polygamy in the hereafter, but for right now the Lord no longer requires it of us. It is more important for us to live our lives without provoking the laws of the land and raise our families in peace rather than the continual persecution and ridicule that we would have to endure were we to try to live that now. Our President has told us that we can go just as far in the Celestial Kingdom by living an honorable life with one wife as the former Saints have been able to advance with their several wives."

For those more devoted to the mother church, for the most part this is a satisfactory answer. With strong convictions those Saints stand by the leader of the Church. But for those Mormons who are not quite satisfied with that point of view, they might find themselves in one of the meetings held by the fundamentalists wherein the same question often arises from a convert. "What about polygamy?"

Then an Elder may answer, "Do you have a testimony of Joseph Smith?"

---

[2] The Doctrine and Covenants, p. 256-257.

"Yes, I do."

"Then you must believe that he was a prophet, seer and revelator."

"Yes, I think he was."

"Then do you believe that the Lord spoke to him at the time he received the revelation of the 132nd Section of the Doctrine and Covenants?"

"Well, yes, but what do we do about breaking the laws of the land?"

"What did the three Hebrew children do that were faced with the same situation--whether they serve their God or the laws of the land? They would rather be burned if the Lord had not seen fit to spare their lives than to give up their religion. Ask yourself, 'Does God change?' Should we believe that the Lord would require one thing of the saints in biblical times and not ask us to show likewise devotion even if it cost us our lives?"

At that point the elder is likely to produce a copy of a revelation given to John Taylor on September 26-27, 1886:

Revelation to John Taylor, September 26-27, 1886:

My Son John: You have asked me concerning the New and Everlasting Covenant and how far it is binding upon my people; thus saith the Lord: All commandments that I give must be obeyed by those calling themselves by my name, unless they are revoked by me or by my authority, and how can I revoke an everlasting covenant; for I the Lord am everlasting and my everlasting covenants cannot be abrogated nor done away with, but they stand forever.

Have I not given my word in great plainness on this subject? Yet have not great numbers of my people been negligent in the observance of my laws and the keeping of my commandments, and yet have I borne with them these many years; and this because of their weakness, because of the perilous times, *and furthermore, it is more pleasing to me that men should use their free agency in regards to these matters. Nevertheless, I the Lord do not change and my word and my covenants and my law do not.*

And as I have heretofore said by my servant Joseph: All those who would enter into my glory *must and shall obey my law.* And have I not commanded men that if they were Abraham's seed and would enter into my glory, they must do the works of Abraham?

I have not revoked this law, *nor will I*, for it is everlasting, and those who will enter into my glory must obey the conditions thereof; Even so Amen.[3]

If the convert can accept this revelation, then the question arises: Whom did John Taylor set apart with the keys to perform celestial plural marriages? After that has been answered, the next question is: Whom did those men set apart for this special work and calling? There is much dispute over those answers. The question of seniority and worthiness enter in like "button, button, who has the button." Who holds the sealing authority? This issue has developed into a religious jungle among the Fundamentalist brethren. A person of an honest heart and contrite spirit seeking who is telling truth may find themselves wading knee deep in evidences on the different sides of this priesthood issue, most often bringing one to prayer and fasting to ask God for guidance and a testimony. Where is the Iron Rod that I might hold on and gain celestial glory? These questions have been the major cause for the many polygamous settlements and many people are stranded at the crossroads, not knowing which path to take. Some Saints have literally spent their whole lives at this point of uncertainty, seeking answers as they sort evidence. My father was caught up in that dilemma.

---

3 "The Four Hidden Revelations," Joseph White Musser, p. 15.

My Mother

CHAPTER 1

My mother, Edith Kaziah Soderberg Hancock, was the second wife of my father, Joseph Heber Hancock. Father's first wife was married to him by the laws of the land, but she told father that she did not want to have children because she had epilepsy and was afraid their offspring might inherit the problem. Father did not want to give her a divorce but told her that he would have to remarry and she gave her consent. Now because of this, father was not able to marry Mother by the laws of the land. They had discussed the issue of plural marriage but father was not certain as to who held the keys of authority having the right to perform plural marriages, this being after The Manifesto. Father and Mother wrote up a marriage contract that they both signed and with the hope if they ever could find the man who had sealing authority, they would be married properly by him. Nevertheless, they stayed true to their covenants.

To support and keep his second wife, my mother, hopefully without incurring the wrath from the federal government, he took my mother to live on the prairie 30 miles from Short Creek, Arizona, where he had a 180-acre mining claim. Upon arrival, they gathered a little snow from underneath a bush for their water supply, and then put up their tent and began working with the tools they had brought in a wheelbarrow. Each month Father would take his wheelbarrow into Short Creek, more commonly known now as Colorado City, to pick up his government check as he was a veteran of the war. A bullet had grazed his skull while in the Army leaving him with the necessity of having a steel plate in his head.

The money he received monthly along with what he could earn by chopping wood, planting gardens, and repairing things for the folks in town would be used for supplies, including cement that he would haul three bags at a time for laying a concrete bottom for a water reservoir. The water would run in to form a little pond when it rained so they could catch it for drinking and for irrigating their garden. Through his continual trips, he built a one-room house for Mother where she raised four children. Water, however, was always a problem. During one particularly dry spell, Mother worriedly discussed the situation with my father.

"Hon, what are we going to do? We are almost out of water. It hasn't rained for almost two weeks."

"The Lord will provide," he said. "Why don't you pray about it?"

There were no clouds in the sky. "Oh, God, our Eternal Father. Please look down upon us as we are out here on this desert trying to

1

serve you the best we can. We have no more water. Would you let rain come? In the name of Jesus Christ, Amen."

Half an hour passed. There came a cloud just over their land. It rained just long enough to water the garden and replenish the reservoir, thus keeping their little family alive and well. During those years, they had been studying the literature put out by the different fundamentalist groups, mainly the truth books put out by Joseph White Musser.

After reading the news of the month, Mother said, "What in the world is the matter with Heber J. Grant saying he hopes the polygamists get the full extent of the law, then he's caught having a second wife on the side? Why, I'd just like to write him a letter and tell him what I think of him."

"Well, why don't you do it then?"

"Well, fine. I will then." So she sat down and wrote him a long letter telling him what a hypocrite he was. "There. It's finished. Will you mail it?"

"I sure will . . . but I don't know if it will do him any good."

"I don't know if it will either, but I sure feel a lot better now. Why, he needs to be told."

Far away from the rule of the Church, they believed it was better to live in the desert than in town although Father owned a house with water and one and one-half acres in Murray, Utah. He had kept this information secret from Mother, but near the end of a long illness during which he had progressively grown worse, he called her to his bedside late one afternoon.

"Hon, if anything happens to me, I want you to move to a house in Murray. Here is the deed and all the information you'll need to be able to find it. The Veterans check will be of support to you and the children. Without me there, the law will give you no trouble with our religion but I want you to promise me something. That you won't surrender so much as your little finger to anything except the teachings of Joseph White Musser."

Mother knelt beside his bed and prayed that he would be healed but her prayers were not answered. Throughout the years they had tried to locate the man who held authority so they might be sealed together in marriage. They believed they had just found one but their time was cut short and the ordinance had not been performed. Father passed away three days later, just one week before I was born.

Pregnant, Mother worked with the help of her four children--Rod, the oldest, then Jeannie, Eliza, Inesa Lisa, ages 12 to 3, to bury father and prepare herself for my birth. (Mother had another baby just before me, John, who died.) At four o'clock in the morning, May 10, 1948, by the light of kerosene lanterns and the help of her four children, Mother gave birth to her baby. Mother's heart filled with sorrow from her loss

2

and filled with joy from her giving birth. I was welcomed into this world into loving arms. Sheepherders passed through on occasion. Mother sent word to Short Creek with the news and a petition for transportation into Murray, Utah. One of the gentlemen in town came in answer to Mother's request. After loading up with all their valuables along with children for the trip, Mother then prayed over Father's grave that God would protect it from being molested. We left Arizona.

Mother settled with her little family at 4255 South Fifth East near other polygamists in the area--the Watkins, Brooks, and the Rittlings.

We became acquainted with families in the area and associated especially with Clarence Rittling and his wife, Nanas, and their ten children. They had a large old home approximately a block and a half away from where we lived. One afternoon when Clarence was taking his children on an outing, we straggly little Hancock kids were there wishing we could go but did not say much because his car was already loaded with his own kids. He came out to drive away and saw us standing there. A big smile came upon his face. "Well, come on and get in." We made a dash to squeeze in somehow. I heard him laughing as he said, "There's always room for one more even if I have to part my hair and take off my shoes." I wound up somewhere near the floor in the middle. Looking up I could see a few small patches of light.

Clarence's children and Mother's children would play together nearly every day. I could always be found following the bunch of kids searching through VaNoy's pasture with our noses downward. After rainstorms we looked for mushrooms.

"I found one, I found one," I exclaimed. We would look some more then Clarence's daughter, Laurie, would shout, "I found one and there's another one," as we both dashed for it. "Hey, there's another one." We walked along.

"What are you going to do with yours?" Laurie asked.

"I don't know. Sumpin'. Watcha' gonna do?"

"I'm giving mine to Daddy."

"How come?"

We stopped and she looked as though this was an important mission, "My daddy just loves mushrooms and my daddy is in the Priesthood Council."

"Hum." We kept looking. I was thinking to myself, "Golly, I sure wish he was my daddy, too."

When we got back to her house with our goodies, she ran to her father who was by the barn door. "Daddy, daddy. I found you some mushrooms."

He picked her up and gave her a kiss. "You sweet little thing. Thank you so much."

4

As I watched I felt so selfish and worthless with my little bag. As he walked towards the house, I got up enough nerve to look up at him as he was passing. I held out my little bag and asked, "Would you want these too?"

He said, "Why, thank you." And a smile broke across my face. Then we scurried off to a nearby creek to play in the water.

One day Mama was over at Clarence's with her wheelbarrow. Nanas said that Mom could have the pears on the ground. I was eating some when Clarence came home. He got out of his car and waved, "Hello, Mrs. Hancock," as he came over shaking her hand.

Mom said, "I sure appreciate these pears you're letting me have."

"Oh, you're welcome." Then looking into the wheelbarrow, he said, "Those don't look too hot." He dumped out the wheelbarrow. "Let's get you some good ones." He began to pick the fruit off the tree.

"My, that's sure nice of you," Mom said. "Are you sure you have enough for your big family too?"

"Oh, yes. The Lord will provide. We will be OK."

I took some good ones. "Gee thanks, Mr. Rittling."

"You're welcome, little lady. Mrs. Hancock, what are you going to have for Thanksgiving?"

"Well, I don't know," Mom replied while scratching her head and looking into the distance. "Let's see. I've got some chickens we could have." She stopped talking, as though in deep thought.

"I have a splendid idea," he said. "Why don't you bring your little bunch down here for Thanksgiving and eat with my family?"

Mom smiled, "You really mean that?"

"I certainly do."

"But you have so many to feed already."

"Nonsense. Don't you worry about a thing. I want you to know, Mrs. Hancock, that you and your little bunch are always welcome at my table."

Tears came to Mama's eyes as she said, "We love you too, Clarence. Thank you very much."

He hugged Mom for a few seconds, then he said, "Let's load this little wheelbarrow," as he continued to pick. We were soon on our way home.

Mama said, "Imagine that. He already has I don't know how many to feed, but it's quite a few he's got--Nanas and her ten children and Naomi and Sarah, and he don't say how many others. We don't even know how many children he has."

"He sure is a good man to take care of so many," I thought."

As we walked further, Mom said, "And he helps Collette and Doris too because they don't have any husband and all their children. He sure is a marvelous person."

"Mom, how come you can't marry him? Could you do that so he can be our daddy, too? Huh?"

"Now, you just pipe down and never mind now, just never mind."

While I was skipping, my little heart was swelling as I imagined how happy I would be if Clarence was my daddy. My sisters thought that he would be a good daddy because they had said so. Whether or not Mom married him, I was just happy he cared about us.

Mama took her family to the meetings whenever they were held, sometimes in one home, sometimes in another. I would look at the brethren who were talking but did not understand them much until I would get really tired and fall asleep on Mama's lap.

Winter came and with it all this talk of Santa Claus. I was wondering if we were going to get candy or an onion in our socks because Rod and Jeannie had been teasing me. On Christmas Eve we heard this singing outside our house and I jumped up and looked out the window. There were the boys and girls in Jeannie's classroom from the high school with the snow coming down on their faces, singing so. I was delighted when the door opened and in came this man in red and white saying, "Ho, ho, ho!" He brought us a bag of goodies and presents. Mama was laughing. This man picked me up and put me on his knee. I sat there looking at him like, "Is this beard real?" I wondered. I pulled on it and it came down. Oh! "It's Mr. Wright," I thought as his face went red. He was our neighbor across the way. I kept it to myself until he was leaving the door saying "Merry Christmas!" I said, "Thank you, Mr. Wright." I got a ball and jacks, a jump rope, a doll and some crayons with a coloring book.

On Christmas Day I headed down to Rittlings to see what Laurie, Erlene and Ruth got. We were in the front room playing with the toys that Sub-for-Santa had brought them when the outside door to the kitchen opened and there stood Nanas in her white uniform and coat. Our attention was immediately gained by a loud voice that nearly shook the house.

"All right, you kids. You can either shut up or go outside. Do you hear me? I've been working all night and I'm tired."

I put my coat on, chucked my crayons in the box and said goodbye to Laurie. I made it home about a block and a half away through the snow. I was so glad to get home. When I got in the house, Mama was in the kitchen where the oven door was open and her back was turned to the heat. "Oh, Mama. I'm cold."

"I'll get ya warm," she smiled as she opened up her hands for me to put my small hands into hers."

"Uhh, that feels good." We stood there for a moment.

"Let's get a chair over here," she said. Then she sat down and I sat on her lap. Mama put her arms around me. I folded my hands and wedged them between our warm bodies soaking up her warmth.

In wonderment I asked, "Does it cost lotsa money for toys 'n stuff?"

While rocking me back and forth with my feet towards the oven door, she said, "Yes. I think it did."

"How did they get the money?"

"Do you want to know. It was really cute. Jeannie took a can of beans to school for an assignment to help out a needy family, and come to find out all the things in the box that the boys and girls brought were from her classroom. Jeannie was amongst the children singing." Mom's voice choked up as she continued, "And the neighbors gave you children the toys you've got."

I sat there for sometime in silence as my little mind was trying to comprehend what she had said. Then I asked, "Mama, how do people get money?"

"Well, there are different ways. Like some people work so they can get a little money. And sometimes a person has something they can sell. Like my father, your grandfather had a farm and he would raise beets to sell for money. Now us, we don't have too much to sell, but if we had more chickens, we could sell eggs. People would buy them."

I was trying to think of what we might have we could sell. The thought occurred to me the only thing Mama had was a bunch of kids. A strange feeling came over me and I asked, "If someone had lotsa money and wanted to buy me, would you sell me to them?"

"Sell you? Why, I should say not. You are more precious than money."

"Even a million dollars," I asked.

"I should say so. You're more precious than two million," she smiled.

"Well, what about three million?"

She laughed, "Oh you're funny. Do you think I would sell my baby? Why, there is no amount I would take for you."

I was feeling so happy when she was talking. I just kinda' needed to hear it to make my day.

Then my mother would go on, "When you were born just after your father passed away, you were like a little ray of sun coming through dark clouds and I have cherished you ever since. Would you like me to tell you a story?"

"Uh huh."

"There was a wealthy woman who couldn't have children and she asked me, 'Mrs. Hancock, you have so many children, and I can't have any. Do you think you would be willing to give me that little girl? '

That was you. 'I would take real good care of her,' she said. 'Why I should say not,' I told her. She wanted you so bad and I told her, 'Give up my baby? I would never give up my baby.'"

Still sitting on Mother's lap, laying my head on her bosom, I looked up at Mama's smiling face. "I love you. I'm glad that you didn't give me away because I want you for my mama."

Jeannie, Eliza and the Rittling girls would have what they called a slumber party. The Rittling girls would sleep at our house. They were telling stories one night as I sat up listening. The one story was called "The Little Match Girl," a story about a girl whose mother was very sick and they had no money for food, so the little girl would go out in the ice and snow to stand on a street corner all day to sell enough matches to maybe get only two or three cents. As the story went on to about the end of it, I cried, "Does anybody know where they are 'cause we could take them some potatoes." Tears of sorrow were streaming down my face.

Jeannie laughed as she looked at me and said, "Poor little wire head (that was her nickname for me). You would believe anything. It's just a story."

"What do ya mean?"

"Well, somebody made it up. There ain't no little match girl freezing on a street corner."

"Oh," I sighed. She finished the story and I was sure thankful that we were not that poor.

Winter and Spring passed and Summer brought with it a day that even the small children would remember. Mother was busy making bread when the door flew open. It was Conrad, Clarence's boy, panting as he got the words out, "Daddy died."

Mama wiped the bread dough off onto her apron. "Oh, no!" she exclaimed as she began to cry. "Is this true?"

"Yes, it is," he cried as we left the house, walking and running as fast as we could, the clouds blackening the sky and the air thundering. We arrived at Rittlings only to see confusion and grief everywhere. Mama went to Nanas crying. She put her arm around her while they wept together.

Laurie was bawling and here sisters were trying to comfort her and control their own emotions at the same time by saying, "Honey, Daddy's gone to heaven. He's happy now 'cause he's with Heavenly Father." Her tears of grief continued to flow along with theirs. I knelt down in some weeds watching everyone. I cried, as I thought, "What does this mean? He died. What does it mean?" It was like they were implying that we would not see him again. I had not known anyone who had died before that time. I was six years old.

8

There were quite a few people coming and going. We stayed until after dark then Mom and I walked home. That night after supper I shook Mom's arm to get her attention. "What does it mean? Clarence died. Huh?"

Jeannie had fixed some potatoes and gravy, but no one seemed very hungry. Mama pushed her tin plate out in front of her as she rested her head in her hands. She sat in silence for some time. I ate some potatoes then stopped, looked at Mom and asked, "Ya goin' to tell me? What happened?" as I clung to her arm.

She turned to me and said, "I need to take you children to meeting more often so you could learn all these things."

"Can't you just tell me, Mom? I got to know."

"Well, his spirit left his body because God wanted him on the other side."

"What's a spirit?"

"Your spirit is what helps you think and move so you can do things. Everyone that's living has a spirit, and if you follow the priesthood's teachings, like Clarence did, his spirit is in heaven."

"You mean some day I'm gonna die, too?"

"Yes, everyone has to die."

My mind was thinking about our collie dog that got hit by a car and Rod dug a hole and put the dog in it and covered it over. I asked, "Are they going to put Clarence in a dirt hole?"

"Yes, they will bury his body."

"Oh, but it's dark in the ground."

"He won't see the dark ground because he has gone where it is light and beautiful, where there's pretty grass and sunshine where Heavenly Father lives. That's where your father is and maybe Clarence and your father are friends, like you and Laurie are friends. I showed you the picture of your father, haven't I?"

"Uh huh. I want to see it again."

We went to find her Book of Remembrance. In Mom's bedroom we sat on the bed. While I was looking at Father's picture for the longest time, Mom said, "I hope they do meet up there. Your father was a good man, but Clarence could teach him a lot about the Gospel." Mom was still crying. "If you be a good girl--and me, too--I've got to do good also so we can go to heaven, we will see Uncle Clarence and your daddy again."

After thinking a while I said, "I hope God don't take you to heaven and leave me here alone with no mama." I felt that would be more than I could stand.

Mama took me with her to the funeral. I looked out over the steps and could see people standing all up and down the stairs along the street in the parking lot when they began his funeral. They said it was one of the largest funerals that Larkin Mortuary ever had. We were standing until a man got up and gave Mother his seat. I squeezed in next to her for a little spot of the bench. We were so far back we could hear very little, almost like the people in the parking lot. They could not hear anything either but they stayed there to show reverence.

For weeks after that I would go to Rittlings to play and they said Laurie and Erlene were not there. One person said that they went to live with their sister while another said they went to live with Aunt Naomi, one of their mothers.

I ended up playing by myself. Through the summer months I often went to Pills Pond to catch polliwogs or water skeeters, along with climbing trees, going through fences or chasing butterflies so I could see how pretty they were when they landed. I was in the field one afternoon when I heard mother calling me. "Kaziah, oh, Kaziah May." The echo was sweet on my ears. It sounded just like the voice of an angel calling me, and I went running happily to meet her.

When she saw me, she laughed, "Ho, ho, ho. You look funny."

I looked at myself. I had mud here and there and everywhere. Then I exclaimed, "Look what I found!"

"Uh huh. If we had 20 acres and one mud hole, you'd find it. It's time to come in and have some supper before the others eat it all."

I passed by the table. "Ummm. Bread and beans." After half washing I sat down thinking, "Boy this is really nice of Mama to have this fixed tonight. It's so good."

Several months after the death of Uncle Clarence, an Elder came to our house. Mother said he was sent to help us learn the Gospel. He had a car that looked like a big black bug. Anyway, we could all fit into it. So on Sunday he took us to meeting held by the fundamentalist brethren in a small white house. We went into the living room and sat down. No sooner did a man get up to speak than I fell asleep leaning over on Mama. When it was over and we were on our way home, Mom and Inesa were up front while Jeannie, Eliza and I were in back.

As I sat there the two girls began talking over me. Jeannie said, "Did you hear that one guy say we're not supposed to cut our hair?"

"Yeah, and you're not supposed to wear lipstick."

Jeannie thought for a while. "I wonder if makeup is OK to cover my freckles?"

"I don't know, but we can't wear fingernail polish anymore."

"I don't care. My bottle's empty anyway."

"What about not wearing short-sleeved dresses or short skirts?"

Jeannie shook her head, "I don't have any short skirts anyway."

"Yeah, but what are you going to do with that purple and white blouse? It's got short sleeves."

10

After a while Jeannie replied, "I just won't wear it to meeting. That's all."

Walt turned the car into a Dairy Queen. His deep voice asked, "Would you girls like some ice cream?"

"Oh, yes!" I jumped up and looked over the seat, as a happy little thrill came over me. "Ummm. Ice cream. Uh, can we have some root beer, too?"

"Let's see how much money I've got." Walt was digging into a little black purse. Moving his coins back and forth, he ordered six ice cream cones and six small root beers.

"Oh, for good."

Mama laughed. "Thank you, Walt."

He nodded as if to say, "You're welcome." As we were licking our cones, we all thanked him.

When school started again, Mama seemed more concerned with just having clothes for us rather than if they were short or long-sleeved or not. Being the youngest, it seemed I would always fall heir to the other children's clothes, even Rod's T-shirts Mama put on me. My appearance left much to be desired. The dress I had was somewhat long for me, but the worst part seemed to be the T-shirts--the sleeves protruded underneath the sleeves of my dress coming nearly to my elbows. The other children, mainly boys, would make fun of me while I sat there and sweated. One day a boy called me "little witchy." I wished that Mama could find a dress that actually fit me, one with long sleeves so the T-shirt sleeves would not show. And long enough, too. One day Eliza put her slip on me, then pinned up the straps as high as she could but it was still quite long. And with Jeannie doing my hair, I was quite content. She took an interest in me most of the time, and sometimes we would skip school together.

One day Jeannie said, "May, how about skipping school with me today?"

"No, I want to go to school today."

"Oh, please."

"Nope."

"I won't do your hair then."

"OK. I'll just do it myself then." So I went into the bathroom and put some water on my hair and pushed it up a little in front as an attempt to make waves, then I stuck bobby pins in it and just let the rest go. When I got to school, the teacher said, "We are going to have our pictures taken today."

"Oh, no," I thought. "I should have skipped. Now what?" As I sat there so self-conscious, the time got closer and I was just hoping the teacher would see my predicament and take care of the situation. But she did not. Oh dear. They took my picture.

12

When Spring came, I turned eight. There was a lot of hurrying around the house the day I was to be baptized. They borrowed a white dress from one of the neighbors that was really big on me and Jeannie handed me some white socks and said, "Put these on." Then I put on my holey canvas shoes that once were white.

We all got in Walt's car and went up in the canyon to a little creek that ran next to Naomi Rittling's house, one of Clarence's wives. There was an Elder there to baptize me. When we got out, he came over smiling and said, "How are you, young lady? Do you know what this is about?"

"Uh, y're gonna put me in that water."

"Yes, and do you know why I'm going to put you in that water?"

"So when I die I can go to heaven."

He said, "I think we need to explain."

Then Walt and Mama started talking to him as I stood there listening, first to one and then to the other, and thinking to myself, "This means I can't swipe candy anymore or it will go on my record in heaven instead of Mama's."

Then the Elder said to me again, "Do you understand now?"

I nodded my head. "Uh huh."

Then we walked out into the water where he baptized me. I had looked forward to this day since I was seven. Then all the way home, shivering with a blanket wrapped around me, I was thinking to myself, "Now I hadn't better do anything wrong or it will be just terrible."

The 24th of July was coming and Walt said that there was going to be a celebration in Short Creek. I jumped with excitement. "Do we get to go?"

"Oh, that would be nice to go down there and see the old place again," Mama added.

Walt was chuckling. "There's a dance there Saturday night you might want to go to."

Mom acted like she could hardly wait. "OK, Walt. You said that. Now, I'm going to take you up on it."

"When are we going to leave?" Eliza asked.

"Well, I don't like driving at night so let's leave tomorrow morning early--about 8 o'clock. I'll be here to load up."

"Oh, goodie." I was dancing around. Everyone was happy except Rod. He was standing by the stove looking at the floor. I asked him, "You comin' too?"

He shook his head. "No, I've seen enough of those old hills. I don't want nothing to do with it."

"If he don't want to go, he don't have to," Mama said. "He can watch the place while we're gone." Rod would not go to meeting either.

"Oh, well," I thought. "I don't care. But I'm sure going."

13

Morning came and the joy of contemplation was so great that I could hardly sit still for Jeannie to do my hair. Then we were on our way. How I enjoyed the scenery in southern Utah. As we got towards Arizona, I kept seeing chipmunks cross the road and run in the sagebrush. It was a bright summer day.

"Can you stop? I want to catch one of those chipmunks."

"No, we got to get there and see where we are going to stay for the night."

As we arrived in Arizona, there were big red hills and mountains. Oh, I could hardly wait for Walt to stop the car.

"Can we go mountain climbing?"

"Well, if we go, we've got to go together so you don't get lost," someone said.

Walt stopped by a house where he went inside. he came out and said to Mother, "There's a little house that's empty over here they said you could stay in." Then he drove to the house. The little house had a pot belly stove and a bedstead with coil springs, but no mattress. We had brought blankets thinking we might have to sleep on the ground. Mama made the bed for herself and us girls. Walt slept in his car.

The next day we girls went mountain climbing to our hearts' content. When we came home in the afternoon, we washed up in a pan of water so we could change to our better clothes for the dance. That night it seemed so cute to watch Mom and Walt dance. No one would ask me to dance, so I asked Mama to dance with me and she turned to Walt and said, "You dance with her, will you?" So I danced with Walt one time. But the Virginia Reel looked fun and I did not really need a partner, so I got in on that, too.

The next day they held a meeting and the celebration after meeting. There were long tables with watermelons. Somebody said they had bought a whole truckload. There were several people cutting them as quick as kids would come and take the pieces away. I spotted Laurie. "Hey," I hollered. "There's Laurie and Ruth and Erlene." I took off towards them. "Hi, you guys," I hollered out as I came bounding towards them.

"How did you get down here?" Erlene asked.

"Walt brought us. How come you're here?"

"We've been staying here for a while."

"How come you don't live at home anymore?"

"'Cause there's this guy there and he's really mean to us. Mama let him stay there after Daddy died."

"He makes me do all the dishes," Ruth commented.

"He's not like my daddy and I don't like him," came from Laurie.

"Nobody likes him. I don't want to live in the house with him there. I think he stinks." Erlene looked so serious.

14

"He does stink," Ruth added. "Oh, oh. There he is."

"Where?"

"Over there standing by that lady in the blue dress."

"You mean that short guy?"

"No, the one in back of him. The tall man in the white shirt."

"Oh, what's his name?"

"His name is Bard Kanderhosh. We call him Stinky Bard."

"How about stink bug?"

"Yeah."

We laughed as I threw my watermelon rind into the weeds. I went for another piece. I was closer to Bard and looked at him and thought, "Ugh, don't get too close to him." I got my melon and returned.

We walked on to find Mama. Mama exclaimed with joy, "Oh, there's Ruth, Erlene and Laurie! Where's Nanas?"

"She's over there with Bard."

"Bard who?"

"Bard Kanderhosh."

"Did she remarry?"

"I don't know, but I don't like him. He's not my father," Laurie cried with disgust.

The subject was soon changed as we continued to enjoy the celebration. Most of the people we had seen in meetings were down there and Mama was shaking hands and kissing and hugging women she said were Clarence's other wives--Naomi, Sarah, Bertha--along with many other people Mama knew. Mama went over to talk with Nanas, but I went off with my friends.

A few months later after we had returned to Murray, Nanas came to visit Mama. She brought Bard with her. They talked for a while then Bard said he could get Rod a job.

"What doing?" Rod asked.

"I could get you a job nailing chests of drawers together."

"You'd like that," Mom said with excitement. She turned to Bard. "He's a good carpenter. Why, he made these tables and benches."

"Maybe I'll like it. Maybe I won't. I'll go see," Rod mumbled. "When do you want me to start work?"

"I don't know yet. I'll talk to the boss and let you know."

So Rod went to work within the week. But it was extremely aggravating to him when his boss would give him a check and it would bounce. He paid him once a month and for three months straight, his check bounced. Rod got awfully mad and would come out saying words I had never heard before.

Then Bard and Rod went to work for another boss. Rod came home and gave Mother his check to buy groceries at the store. Mama piled high two big carts full of groceries. When we went to the check

15

stand, the man called the bank on the check and said to Mama, "I'm sorry, Lady, but this check is no good."

We walked home with our tongues nearly hanging to the ground. When Rod found out, he began swearing again, slammed the door and later returned with a huge bottle of beer.

Mama said, "Now, Rod. You can't drink that in this house. This is a dedicated home."

He was laughing, "I don't care about this house. The only thing keeping it together is the termites holding hands."

Mama called up Walt and Nanas. Within a short time Walt arrived with Nanas and Bard. It was late afternoon. Rod was sitting in the big chair in the front room. He had also bought some cigarettes, and was smoking one after another while drinking. I was watching from just around the corner of the doorway from the kitchen. Rod's attitude was very scary to me.

Bard came in and said, "I'll handle him. Rod," Bard hollered, "you take your stuff outside."

Not budging an inch, Rod replied, "Mind your own f--- business. This is my home."

Walt chipped in, "You don't have the right to desecrate this house. Now, you just get up quietly and go outside."

Bard yelled, "You don't need to act like this."

Rod became extremely violent and exclaimed while coming out of the chair, "Don't you tell me what I need and what I don't need. What I don't need is you telling me anything. You and your g--d--- jobs. You set me up to work at that f--- place for nothing. Didn't ya."

"No, I didn't. I didn't even get paid. He owes me for seven months."

"That other f--- job isn't any better."

Walt hollered, "Your filthy mouth isn't going to get you paid any quicker."

Rod grabbed at Bard's shirt and said, "This f--- bastard had better get my money for me or I'll kill him." Then he threw the empty beer bottle through the window. As Rod passed by Mama on his way out. "I swear. I'll kill him," he muttered. He walked out slamming the door which shook the whole house.

Mama said to Bard, "Golly, I'm sorry for the way he acted. He just needs to cool off and get over this thing."

Bard hollered at Mama, "Get over it? Hell, your son's insane. He ought to be behind bars."

"I don't know," Mama said. "I've never seen him this bad before."

"Well, he's just getting older now to where you nor anyone else can handle him," Walt declared.

16

A few more weeks passed by. Rod slept in the garage. Mama did not want him in the house and I was glad. But he would come in to eat and every time he came in, I was scared half to death.

When suppertime came, Mama told him supper was ready. He threw open the door. We had potatoes and flour gravy, fried onions and whole wheat bread with lard spread on it seasoned with salt and pepper. Rod looked at the table and ask, "Is there anything besides pig slop?"

Mama answered in an indignant tone, "That's not a bit cute for you to talk that way, Rod, and if you don't want to eat it, you don't have to."

Rod laughed and walked off without eating. Mama was mumbling, "I don't know what's the matter with him. He didn't used to be that way." We had the blessing and ate.

A few nights later Rod came home drinking beer. The police must have followed him. As Mama was out talking to the police, they said they were going to put Rod in jail for four days for stealing. Mama cried and asked them not to but they still took Rod away.

Several days later when they let him out, Bard, Nanas and Walt were there when Rod came home. Rod walked in the door and said to Mama, "Why do you let these s--- of b-----come here? They're the cause of all our problems."

Bard said, "You cause your own problems, Rod. Nobody else causes them."

Rod went into the kitchen, then after a while he came out with a cup of something. He was laughing a little bit as he went outside. I went outside for curiosity. Rod went over to Bard's car and took off the gas cap and dumped the stuff in the cup in the tank. I asked, "What was that?"

"Sugar." He began to laugh a little. "He, he, he." Then more and louder, "He, he, ha, ha. That serves him right! Ha, ha, ha."

I had no idea what that would do to the car.

About a week later a hard, rapid knock came on the door. Mama answered it. Bard stood there puffed up with a red face as though he would pop. "Where's Rod," he demanded.

"I don't really know. I think he's out working in the garage on his car."

"I need to talk to him alone." He stomped over to the garage. He knocked at the garage door then he resorted to kicking the door. "I know y're in there. Now, come out and face me like a man," he hollered.

"What's the problem?" Mama rushed over.

Pushing Mama back, "Just stay out of it, would you. If he can play a man's game, he can take a man's punishment," Bard continued to wham at the door with his foot.

17

"What on earth did he do?"

"He put sugar in my gas tank. Wrecked the hell out of the motor."

"Rod wouldn't do a thing like that, I don't think. Would he?"

Nanas had been standing near the corner of the house, obviously not wanting to get too close. Now she came butting in, "That's what's the matter with you, Edith. You've stuck up for your kids come hell or high water. They never can do anything wrong in your sight."

"I didn't say he never does anything wrong. But what makes you think he done that?"

"Rod's a maniac," Bard hollered. "He knows what sugar would do. Who else would. Did you do it?"

"No, I didn't. Who ever heard of such a thing." Mama was scratching her head as though bewildered.

Walt came home from his Watkins route. "What can I do to help the boy?" Mother asked.

"Help him?" Bard sarcastically remarked. "I'm the one who needs help." He held out his hand. "Have you got $200 to help me get a new motor?"

"Two hundred dollars?" gasped Mother.

"Yes, $200. How would you like to come up with it like I have to just because of your damn boy," Nanas snarled.

"Well, I've tried to raise him right, but he just won't listen to me." Mother braced herself against an old tool box.

Bard was leaning over her, "The time you should have gained control is at six years old, and if you can't gain control over a child at that age, you've lost 'em. If I had that boy living with me, I'd make a man out of him. Maybe you wouldn't approve of my methods, but he'd know who was boss or else."

"Well, you act just like you'd like to kill him or something."

"Naw. I wouldn't kill him, but he might wish he were dead a few times before I'd be through."

Walt pointed at mother, "You have to admit, Edith. It would take far more force than you could give him for him to ever straighten up."

It was getting dark and the sun was setting. Just then the garage door opened and Rod came out smoking a cigarette. He stood there, looking at everyone.

Mom quickly exclaimed, "I don't know where you get that nasty habit from. The priesthood doesn't teach you that."

"I don't give a damn about their teachings. That's your religion, not mine. You're not going to force me to live the way you want me to. Just leave me alone--that's all I want," as Rod strutted by on his way to the house.

Bard was watching like an animal getting ready to attack his prey. He followed Rod. The whole scene had my heart beating 200 miles per hour. I ran in the chicken coop away from the house. I could hear loud voices for sometime, then someone ripped the drapes down. I could hear Mama's voice yelling and I just hoped nothing would happen to hurt her. A chair came hurdling out the window shattering the wooden section between the windows. I ran around the house and went through Mama's bedroom to the girls' bedroom.

"Inesa! Inesa! I was calling for my sister. I tried the bathroom door but it was locked. "Inesa, are you in there?"

The door unlocked. "Quick." She pulled on me to enter, locking the door again behind me.

"Let's get out of here before Rod kills somebody. He's so crazy. We got to get out of here. Come on! Let's go!" I was crying while pulling on her arm to come.

We took off through the back door without a coat or anything except the clothes on our back. Down the street we went as hard as we could go. We wanted to use the phone near a store to call the man who baptized me. But someone called the police on us. We stayed shivering in a phone booth trying to figure out how to make it work without money when a police car showed up. Cold, tried and confused we were huddled together near the floor to try to keep each other warm.

The policeman took us to a detention home for runaway kids. From there it was a series of foster homes, one after another for about three months. I rather enjoyed them. At the last home we were there for approximately seven months. It was a home that had ten children. I enjoyed the company. I adjusted to the home life learning all the little chores they deemed as my share. I had no complaints. The girl Martha was my age. She thought James Garner was neat. I liked Perry Mason but we both agreed upon the Beach Boys and we both liked to draw pictures of the different characters.

Mama came to visit. Mrs. Florence called, "May, there's someone here to see you." I came in.

"Mama!" I ran to hug her.

She was laughing with tears in her eyes. "Oh, it's good to see you."

"Lisa went to Mutual. She'll be home shortly." (We had changed our names from Inesa to Lisa and from Kaziah to May.)

"Could I get you something to eat, Mrs. Hancock?" Mrs. Florence asked.

"Oh, you don't need to do that," Mama paused, "unless . . . you really want to."

"I'd be glad to."

"That's very nice of you."

Mama and I sat on the couch. "How you doing, Mom?"

"Oh, I'm just plugging away. How's my sweet, little precious daughter?" Mama pulled me to her and kissed me on the forehead. I was enjoying Mama's hug.

"Just fine. Hey," I asked with excitement. "You want to come up and see all my nice clothes?" I jumped up as if to lead her to my room. "I've learned to do my hair, too." I turned around slowly in front of her feeling proud while flipping my ponytail. Mom laughed.

Mrs. Florence came in carrying a plate. "Here you are, Mrs. Hancock. I hope you like this. It's fresh from our garden."

"Whole wheat bread and fresh tomatoes. I sure do. Thank you very kindly."

"You're welcome." Mrs. Florence left the room.

"Well, it sounds like you're getting good care here anyway."

"Yeah, it's OK. I'm gonna get some of my art work I been doing." I quickly went up to my room and sorted through my stuff and took some pictures downstairs.

Mom had finished her sandwich. I moved the plate over on the coffee table to set my art work in front of Mother. While she was going over them, she asked, "Did you know that your sisters Jeannie and Eliza got married?"

"They did? Who to?"

Mama whispered in my ear. "You can't advertise these things, but you know Leo?"

"Yes."

"Well, that's who Jeannie married."

"All right!"

"Eliza married Kirk."

"She did? How come?"

"I don't know. I guess she loves him."

"Huh?" I said in wonderment. "Is Rod still there?"

Mama was looking at the floor. I was waiting. "Rod has some problems he needs help with. I don't know what to do for him. Walt and Bard hold the priesthood so I had to let them make the decision. They decided it would be better to put Rod where he can get professional help."

"What did they do with him?"

"Well, we had to put him in the Provo Mental Hospital, so they can help him to get well so we can bring him out someday. I'm just home by myself now. I've gotten off that old welfare. They're good when you need them, but the trouble is they want to know every cotton picken' move I was making. So I just quit 'em. I'm selling Dabit now and cleaning houses. It works really well. I just put a little Dabit on a rag and boy, ya' ought to see the dirt fly. Why, yesterday a lady let me clean her whole house and I made $10. That's how I got enough money to get on the bus to come up here to see you girls. Two days ago I made $3 by cleaning one woman's kitchen. The Lord has been helping me to get enough work to keep my bills paid.

"Oh, I've got to tell you. You know that white cat with the one green eye and one blue eye? Well, last night I felt something wet down by my feet. I turned on the light and there she was with a batch of kittens. It made me so happy to think I wasn't alone." Mama was smiling with tears in her eyes.

"Oh, how cute." I was tickled, too.

Mother stayed visiting until Mr. Florence came from work and gave Mother a ride home.

Two weeks later a little trouble started when Lisa came home from school. Mrs. Florence's daughter, Karen, followed shortly afterwards. When she came in she was screaming something. Next thing I knew Karen threw a fork at Lisa. Lisa took off out the door with me after her. Walking briskly away from there, I asked, "What the heck's the matter?"

"Oh, her boyfriend, Paul, asked me for a date. Heck, you'd think I had asked him the way she acts."

The more we walked the more I was thinking and asking, "How come we can't just go home? Rod ain't there no more."

"I don't know. Maybe we could call Mrs. Herzog (our case worker)." We stopped in at a house to use their phone. Mrs. Herzog could not see any problem with us going home so we packed our stuff and came home to live with Mama. It was not long until Mama had an offer on our land. They wanted to build a subdivision. So she and Walt found an acre and a half in Sandy with an old adobe house on it and we moved in.

I thought a lot about Rod being put in the Provo Mental Hospital. Walt, Mom, Lisa and I would go visit Rod. Sometimes they would not let us see him because they said he was extremely violent and they had to lock him in a nonvisiting area. I sat there looking at all these people with their strange actions. One man paced the floor from corner to corner for the longest time while another threw himself down and his eyes rolled to the back of his head. He shook while he was frothing at the mouth. Even the nurses seemed a little strange. I sat quiet, looking around me, waiting until we were on our way home. I said to myself, "How horrible it would be to have to stay there. That's what happens when a person gets really mad. They lock 'em up."

All through the summer I was always looking for something that needed to be invented as I went around the yard looking at things and thinking. After looking over the entire place, I came to the conclusion, "Gee, whiz. Everything has already been invented." Little did I know!

One afternoon Uncle Walt (who was about 70 at the time) and Mom (just in her 50s), weighing approximately 180 pounds, about 5'2", and almost as broad as she was tall, joined Lisa and I in a game of baseball on our front lawn. Mom really hit that ball. We had hardly ever seen her run. It was almost like watching a little ball bounce as she took a step. She was laughing all the way. Then Uncle Walt got up to bat, and I thought it was pretty neat to see him out there--a good old sport. Boy, they did give us kids a good game--one to be remembered.

One day when Mom was gone to work, I put some water in an empty Watkins deodorant bottle and squirted Lisa. She got the clothes squirt bottle and squirted me with more water. Oh yeah! So I filled up a cup of water and threw it on her. Ha. Ha. So she filled up a bucket with water and threw it on me. "That's what you get!"

"All right!" I went and got the hose. She saw me coming as I brought it into the house. "Oh yeah! Heehee, haha," as I squirted her royally. This was so much fun I could hardly stand it--until we realized what a mess we had made. Water was all over everything and just running out of the door. We went to work cleaning up the place before Mama came home.

I quit playing long enough to chop a pile of wood. Mama came home and paid me a little so I could buy candy for myself and dog biscuits for Turby, my little cream-colored puppy. I loved that country life. To get to our house we had to go down a lane, over a canal, then down a slight hill so you could not see the road or other houses from our place. To look around us you could see large stretches of land. There were apple trees and pear trees on our front lawn and large trees lined the driveway. I made a hammock between the two pear trees and put a mattress on it. I could enjoy a rest on a hot summer day in the shade of the trees. There was a big yellow rosebush growing next to the house on the south side, and a trumpet vine on the southeast corner of the house by the edge of the lawn where hummingbirds spent many happy hours. Large reddish orange poppies came up every year in a big patch on the east side of our house. Lisa and I were old enough now to keep up the yard. We planted marigolds and four o'clocks by the porch. I looked at our beautiful yard one summer day and thought, "Boy, this place is really nice. Even a movie star would want to live here, if they knew it existed."

I sold seeds door-to-door for the American Seed Company--well, sort of--but Mother bought most of them though so I could earn a sleeping bag. Then I slept outside on the lawn in the summertime. One afternoon Mom got a phone call. She shouted with excitement, "Aunt

Genevieve's coming! She's at the airport right now and she'll be here in a half hour."

Lisa and I looked at each other. "Wowee. Aunt Genevieve's coming." Did we fly through that house making beds, sweeping floors, doing dishes, etc. It was funny to think how fast we could work when we wanted to. We knew that if it were not clean enough, she would just stay at Hotel Utah. Aunt Genevieve came and took us out to eat and bought all kinds of nice things for Mom and us. It was through her generosity that we were able to see the other side of life. Mom had told us that Genevieve was a millionaire.

When I was 13 years of age, I began running around with girlfriends, listening to music, experimenting with makeup, and dying my hair. The year flew by quickly. I thought I was having fun. I dated some boys. Did some kissing. And drank beer once in a while. But beer tasted so horrible I could not see how anyone could like it. I was just drinking it to be stupid. Mother came in the house after working hard all day and looked at me in my stupid condition. I was 14 then. She said, "May, what are you going to do with your life? I have tried to teach you girls to be decent, not to cut your hair, or to wear makeup and do all these stupid things. You have no conception of what it is like to earn a living. I don't know what is going to happen to you if you don't straighten yourself out. That's not the way the brethren teach you to be and you know better. Why, what if Uncle Troy came to our home and seen you?"

I pretended that I did not hear. For days after that I experimented to see what swear words I could say and get by with. Also, I got hold of a pack of cigarettes and smoked them just to prove my independence. I kept running around with my friends until this one girl started to brag about how she had lost her virtue. Oh, I was sick. I left her house and on the way home I thought, "Dear God. I don't need this crazy way of living. I just don't need it. I've got to amount to something." I felt a longing for the association of the saints.

I had not been going to "group meetings" much. Lisa had been going. She soon married and left home. I found myself alone more than ever. It took a little time for me to adjust to doing things by myself all the time. But I found solitude quite pleasant.

I began to wonder about what Mother had said and knew that I had not learned any vocation or skills because I did not want to go to school any more. I dropped out without finishing the eighth grade because there was a dumb kid there who, without fail, would tease me in the hall about how he thought my nose was longer than anyone else's. I got so tired of his insults. When he would see me coming down the hall, he would stop, lean backwards a little, put one hand over his mouth to laugh and point at me with the other hand. Then he would say while chuckling, "Here comes the beak of the week."

He had humiliated me so many times that after a while, looking in the mirror, I said to myself, "Well, my nose is a little bigger than most of the other girls, but my eyes are kinda' pretty and my mouth looks OK, I guess." And I thought, "One thing is for sure though. I am not going to make it through this world with my looks. I'm going to have to make it with my brains."

My art work was not all that hot either, so I tried typing. My mother was an expert typist in her day, but it did not seem that any of her talent had rubbed off onto me. I began to feel odd and I wondered what I would really do with my life. My heart kept taking me back to my art work. I could imagine myself as a great artist, so I got the books from the library and studied Rembrandt and Titian.

One summer afternoon I had been doing a lot of drawing of faces, trying to get good at it when a knock came on the door. It was Bard and Nanas. I had not seen them for several years. I said, "Come in. Mom's outside in the garden. She will be here in a minute. She just went out to pick some beans." To be polite I sat down in the kitchen with them while waiting for Mother to come in. I could not help but notice Bard's appearance as he sat on the chair with the two back legs on the floor and leaning the back of the chair against the wall. His face was long like a poker player with a pointed nose. His skin was a mass of pimples and his hair was going every which direction. His eyes were somewhat bloodshot and his lips quite heavy. His clothes looked as though they had been slept in for days. They were quite soiled and the odor that came from his direction was something else. Nanas had not changed much. She was quite plump with a pleasant face with little rows of pinned up curls on the top of her head and a long bun wrapped in a U shape in the back. Nanas' clothes were soiled but not all wrinkled. She had somewhat of a decent appearance.

I was lost for anything to say as I looked at them and they at me. "You're Inesa," Bard said.

"No, I'm Kaziah May. I think I'll go tell Mother you're here." I went out to the garden. "Nan and Bard are here to see you, Mom."

"Oh, all right." She went around the back door to the kitchen and I went to the front door to my bedroom to return to my art work.

Mom came to the door after about half an hour and said, "I was telling Nanas and Bard that you are trying to be an artist. Would you like to show them some of your work?"

"OK." I brought out what I thought was good enough to show. They looked at my pictures, then Bard said, "Do you know how many artists starve to death? They die by the thousands. Even some better than Kaziah. That is your name, isn't it?"

24

"Yes, but most people call me May."

"OK, May. Anyway, as I was saying," Bard went on, "even if she became really good at it, there are already 30 people in line waiting for every artist's job that is available. The market is flooded with all kinds of people looking for a job." He was apparently talking to Mother.

As I sat there listening, my eyes were fixed upon the coal bucket. I felt I did not need to hear that as I was fighting an inferiority complex anyway. I looked up at the clock and said, "There is something I need to attend to. Excuse me." I quietly picked up my papers and left the room.

I heard them talking as I walked away. "May is really growing up fast, isn't she."

"Yes, she is the only one home now. All the rest are gone." I went back to my art work.

When Winter came, I spent much time walking down the canal bed when it was snowing and enjoyed the peaceful beauty. I built half an igloo on our lawn and laid down inside of it looking up into the sky at night with the snow falling in my face. I laid there wondering how I really could become an artist. I continued to spend many hours drawing objects and experimented some with oil paints.

When Mother was going to clean the Marion Hotel one morning, I asked if I could go. I did not expect any pay. I just enjoyed being with Mom and worked with her to see what that job was like. She seemed contented just to go and fill her little niche every day, happy to have a job cleaning spittoons, scrubbing floors, making beds, emptying garbage containers. But even this type of work seemed to have a sense of dignity about it as I watched my mother. She was not the type of woman to smoke, drink, chase men or do anything to make me ashamed of her. Her character was something I felt I could be proud of. I always felt good about my mother.

CHAPTER 2

One Saturday Bard and Nanas came to visit Mother. While they were all talking in the kitchen, I preferred staying in the front room. Bard was telling Mother that the things that Rod had done to reject priesthood direction in his life, along with his hatred for Bard, were the reasons why he was still in the Provo Mental Hospital.

Bard declared with a very emphatic statement, "No one can fight against the work of the Lord or the Saints and prosper." Looking at Mother, "You might love him but you've got to let him go."

Nanas chipped in, "I had to let my son go because he wanted to leave the work although it hurt me very much. He has apostatized; he has abandoned the faith and left as some of my girls have done. I couldn't hold them, Edith."

Standing next to Mother, Walt brought his finger down on Mom's shoulder while he kept poking her as he said, "You have got to decide what are you going to do. Are YOU going to obey the priesthood counsel over you? You can't worry about your kids."

Mom looked up at them, "Well, Rod would be a good boy if he could just straighten himself out. He could hold the priesthood."

Bard jumped into the conversation, "He never will amount to a hill of beans. He's a bastard child from the beginning since you and Joseph Hancock never had a priesthood marriage. You think you can go out on the prairie and commit adultery and it have no effect upon your kids. He never will allow the priesthood to guide him in anything. He has sold his soul to the devil."

"Oh, he has not. What makes you say that?" Mom asked.

"Anyone!" Bard's voice having much impact and his finger pointed at Mom. "Anyone! I don't care who they are. Whoever turns away from God joins up with the devil and his forces. There's only the two sides: God and the devil. If you're not for one, you're for the other. The only chance that boy had is if you would have handed him over to me years ago. I could have made a man out of him. But you wouldn't do it, so now it's too late. All you can do is see him go down the drain."

Mom was looking up with her finger to her mouth as if she were having difficulty coping with this announcement.

I had been watching through the doorway. I figured I had heard about enough when Bard went on to say, "All your children are bastards and you've got to give them up and let them go to hell if that is what they want to do. You can't deprive them of their free agency."

I was so full of disgust at all this kind of talk. Bard turned and looked at me and my impulse was to look right at him and pretend to throw up, then I turned, walked out of the front room and slammed the

27

door. I thought, "Boy, what an ass. Who does he think he is anyway? Calling us bastards--yeah, real bastards. Boy, why does Mama even let them in our house?" Most of the time when they came after that, I would go out of my way to let them know they were not wanted in our house. I would flip him the "bird" or walk out and slam the door whenever they would enter the house.

One Sunday afternoon they came over again and I told them to their faces, "I wish to hell you guys would stay home. Can't you see you're not wanted here?"

Nanas said, "Well, that's too bad. Uncle Walt invites us and so does your mother. They're the head of the home. You're not," and she pushed her way into the house.

I tightened my mouth, turned on my heel and walked out, slamming the door, hopped on my bike and took off. I thought, "Boy, I wished Mom would quit inviting those creeps."   As I rode away out into the country, it became rather cold since the sun was going down and I had left without even thinking of my coat. But I despised the thought of returning until I was so cold I had to return. They had finally left. I had been gone approximately three hours. I went to sleep that night with the beginnings of a bad cold.

During the night I woke up with terrible pain in my back. Mom called Nanas because Nanas was supposed to be a registered nurse. Bard and Nanas came out about 8 a.m. the following morning. The last people I wanted to see was them, but now I was in so much pain that it did not seem to matter who was there. Nanas said, "Well, her back's out of place. She needs to go see a chiropractor."

I was crying, "What will he do?"

Nanas replied, "He'll push and pull on your back until your bones are where they belong."

"Oh, no! I couldn't stand for anyone to even touch my back," I cried.

Walt said, "Well, maybe we could take her to Uncle Troy's for a blessing."

"That sounds like a really good idea," I commented. So I got dressed in my street clothes and Walt and Mom took me up to see Uncle Troy. I just knew in my heart that this was a man of God, and with perfect faith in his blessing, I kept saying in my mind all the time that he was praying, "I know I will be healed."

When he was through praying, my arm which before had been very painful to lift, just went up on its own without the slightest pain. I didn't even lift it. It just went up in the air by itself.

I stood there while they were talking then began to faint. As I was going down, someone caught me. Uncle Walt said, "It's because you're so full of evil spirits most of the time that when they are all rebuked, you don't have anything left to hold you up." What an embarrassing thing for him to say in front of Uncle Troy. I thanked Uncle Troy, as we called him, then we all shook his hand and left. All the way home I was sleeping on the side that before had been so painful. The spirit of peace prevailed and I felt very content and thanked the Lord in my heart for a blessing to get rid of all that darn pain. I thought maybe I was full of the devil.

Bard and Nanas were there when we got home, but I remained calm. Bard began to tell Mother that the reason for my back pain was because of the way I had treated him. "The Lord is trying to teach her a lesson. I hold a high enough position in the Sanhedrin, both on this side and in heaven, that that girl could lose her life over her actions. I am sent by the Lord to teach this family the Gospel and if she can't accept it, she will have more than just back pain. She will be destroyed."

Mom said, "I'll tell May she shouldn't be like that but I don't know. Sometimes she just doesn't listen to me."

And actually, I was not very happy with the ill feelings that I had been harboring. It was not like me to really hate anybody and the strong dislike I had been developing for these people was not natural for me. I began to wonder if there might be some truth to what Bard had said, as I stood there on the other side of the door in Mom's room.

"The reason people hate me is because they can't stand to hear the truth," he hollered, "and I'm not about to lie just to make someone happy."

The talk around the group was that no one liked him but I did not know why. The only thing I knew was I did not like him. I was very confused as I listened to him ranting in the kitchen.

Did God really send them? Is something radically wrong with me? My mind was in such turmoil as I felt tears of frustration running down my face. I attempted to pray while kneeling on Mom's bed, something of which I had done very little up to this point.

"Oh, God, our Eternal Father. Hallowed be thy name. Thy kingdom come, thy will be done on earth as it is in heaven." I was weeping profusely. "Give us this day our daily bread and forgive us of our debts as we forgive our debtors," thinking very carefully of every word I spoke. "Lead us not into temptation but deliver us from evil for thine is the kingdom and the power and the glory forever, amen." I laid there crying, just hoping that prayer somehow, some way would do some good. I fell asleep.

That night something kept repeating, "Ephraim, Ephraim." The next morning I asked Mother, "What does Ephraim mean?" I explained my dream. She told me that perhaps that I was of the blood of Ephraim. Then she explained about Joseph, Ephraim, and Manassa. I asked her

29

how I would know if I were of the blood of Ephraim. She told me that it tells you in your patriarchal blessing. I asked if I could have one, so she arranged it with Brother Mann. We went to his home and there in the front room he gave me a blessing.

The main thing that I noticed was he did say I was of the blood of Ephraim and had come into this world with the desire to serve the Lord. He said that because of my former state in the spirit world, the devil sought to destroy me that I might wander in the world and be lost and forgotten by the saints. I thought how horrible that would be. Also, I should seek to come under the direction of the priesthood and to labor diligently to qualify my mind and spirit to be added upon that I would have to suffer heartache and sacrifice and that I would be called upon to go through many experiences that would require faith, patience and prayer. But if I would seek the Lord in all things, great should be my reward in the end. Along with many things too precious for me to mention, but he also said that I would be blessed with children.

I felt very sober about this blessing. I felt like this was God talking to me through Brother Mann and now I must build my whole life around fulfilling this. No matter what it may lead me into, I must live so as to learn what my religion is and then live it. I wanted to go to meetings. Walt had at that time been living in our home to help Mother with bills and to supply her transportation. So he took us every Sunday that a meeting was held.

Brother Mann spoke. "Brothers and sisters. I feel it a privilege to meet with you here today. I feel inspired today to tell you that we need to clean up our minds and our homes. There are those amongst us who are worshipping idols. They are also devoting much time and monies with the gentiles."

My first thought was, "Idols? Really?" I continued to listen.

"We come here today to get the spirit of the Lord. We hear the brethren speak and we might say to ourselves, 'What a beautiful meeting I have heard today.' Then when we leave those doors, we go to our cars and upon arrival at our homes, we have put these teachings to one side while we go turn on the televisions and again we are back to our old lifestyle we had yesterday."

"What good is God's truths to us if we are not willing to practice what we have learned? Do we search out the scriptures in our spare time or are we too interested in what the national harlots are doing? Are we reading about the prophets and the saints so that we may become like them, or are we watching shows where someone is breaking one or all of the Ten Commandments?

"What the Lord wants is a broken heart and a contrite spirit for you to give up Babylon. Come out of here, oh ye, my people, that you be not a partaker of her plagues."

I was writing down what he was saying as fast as I could in my little note pad.

"When the Lord sends his destroying angel to take vengeance upon the earth, are we going to be found doing, thinking and living the same as the wicked? If we are, the angel will not know the difference."

I looked at Brother Mann with thankfulness for guidance, as a spirit of conviction ran through me.

He went on. "We are like buckets full of mud. We need to cleanse ourselves so that we can receive sweet milk."

Reflecting upon all the radio I had listened to instead of studying the scriptures, I thought, "Man, I'm guilty." I loved the influence Brother Mann had over me. It made me want to forsake myself and strive to improve. A spirit of joy filled my soul.

He went on to say, "We should show love and honor to the priesthood and those who have been valiant in the work rather than worshipping movie stars just because we think they have a cute face."

My little note pad was full so I just enjoyed the rest of the meeting. We sang, "The spirit of God like a fire is burning. The latter day glory begins to come forth. The visions and blessings of old are returning and angels are coming to visit the earth." I sang with enthusiasm. "We'll sing and we'll shout with the armies of heaven, hosanna, hosanna to God and the Lamb. Let glory to them in the highest be given hence forth and forever amen, and amen."[4]

That Sunday night Brother Mann's sermons were having such an impact on me that when we got home from meeting, I went straight to my bedroom. I collected together the pictures of movie stars I had. With a solemn mind I could see Brother Mann was right. I picked them up and walked to the front room. I opened the door to our coal and wood stove and said goodbye forever as I carefully put in one at a time. When that was done, I found Rod's hammer. Then I got my little radio, carried it to the front porch, swung the hammer down so as to shatter it to pieces. I picked up the pieces and put them in the garbage can. Then I returned to my room, pausing to think about what to do with my records and record player. I thought of someone who might want them then. I picked up the records and player and carried it over to the fourth house down the road.

I asked Carla, "Do you know of someone who would like these? I don't want them anymore. I have something more important to do with my time."

She smiled and with open arms said, "You're just giving it to me?"

---

[4] "The Spirit of God Like a Fire," words by William W. Phelps, Hymns, p. 213.

31

"Uh huh."

"Goll. Thanks."

"You're welcome." I walked home and as I dusted off my hands, I thought, "There's a little more mud taken out of my bucket. I feel better already." Then I stood again in my room. A good feeling came over me. "Oh," I exclaimed as I remembered something. I opened my top dresser drawer and took out of a round can several necklaces I had acquired over the years. I also noticed the statue on my dresser. I grabbed it, too. "I don't need you anymore either."

I made another trip to the neighbors' then on my way back I stopped at the canal to look into the water. A thought ran through my heart. "If I devote myself to finding out what my religion is and then live it with all my might, who knows--I might even surprise God."

Mama and Walt had been watching me. Walt came home one afternoon after visiting with Brother Mann. "I told Brother Mann today that you were cleaning house to get rid of the gentile influence that's been in this home for so long. He was pleased that you would do that." Walt sat in the large chair in the front room. "Can you sit down for a minute?" I was very anxious to hear what else Brother Mann said. I sat down quickly.

"He told me that you are to be my wife."

I looked at him and instead of being calm, cool and collected, a spirit of resentment was moving in fast. He continued to talk but my mind was blocked off. I interrupted him, shaking my head.

"It isn't going to work like that. I don't even love you," I exclaimed as I brought my eyes up to meet his.

"If we both love the gospel, we can learn to love each other."

I was still shaking my head. "Marry Mama!" I shouted. "She's of the same religion. Heck, pick on someone your own age. She loves ya'. I don't!"

"You need to marry who the priesthood gives you to," he snarled back.

"You wished," I said sarcastically. Jumping up off the chair then bowing before him while looking him right in the eye and raising my voice even louder, "There's no place in the scriptures that says I have to marry you, so there!" Turning on my heel, I walked out and slammed the door before he could even speak.

I marched up by the canal. I shivered to think of marrying Walt exclaiming, "Oh, yuck. The nerve of that old man. He never gives up. I'm so sick of it." I was thinking how he tried to get Jeannie and he tried to get Eliza then he tried to get Lisa. Now me. "Shit!" I exclaimed as I spit in the water. I thought to myself, "Yeah, and Mama's always behind it just because she loves him."

32

I sat staring into the water for a long time thinking. Then came Mama walking down the driveway. She had just got off the bus coming home from work. I stood in front of her. "Mama, why don't you ask Walt to marry you?"

"Well, I can't give him children. So he wants to save himself for a young girl who can." Mama looked tired so I took the bag out of her hands. "Thank you. That gets heavy after a while."

I peeked in the bag. "Ummm. Pickled pigs feet. We haven't had any of that for a long time." Upon entering the home, everyone managed to drop the marrying subject.

About a month later a strong wind had picked up the roof off the chicken coop and laid it on the ground. Bard and Nanas and Will (Nanas' nephew) came out to take the roof apart as Mom and Walt had said that they could have the lumber. I was not doing anything on this beautiful summer day anyway, so after watching them working in the sun for a while, I thought, "It would be a good idea to make some lemonade and take it out to them." So I did.

As I arrived carrying a pitcher and some glasses, Bard said, "Well, thank you, May."

"You're welcome." I poured Nan a drink.

"Thank you."

"You're welcome." Then some for Will. "I'll just set this here if you guys want more, OK?" As I looked at what they were doing, it looked like fun. "Ya' got another crowbar or hammer?"

"I don't know."

"Hey, I think we got one in Rod's tool box. I'll go get it." I hurried to the house, returned and commenced to extract the nails from the boards that they were going to take home. The sun was high and hot. After several hours we would chit-chat a little but mainly we kept working. I was getting quite hungry and my neck was red.

"I think I'll go in and make some sandwiches. Does that sound good?"

"Yes, it sure does."

I went in and made some with tuna fish and got some radishes from the garden. I returned with this platter and salt. We were all eating.

Bard said, "You're a pretty good worker, ya' know that?"

"Oh, yeah--well. What I'd like to do is get a job."

Bard asked, "What kind of a job are you looking for?"

"Well, I don't know. I've got to be good at something but I don't know what."

"Do you want to know a million dollar secret that will allow you to get any job you want?"

"A million dollar secret, huh? What's that?"

"Come here and sit down." We sat on the lumber pile under the shade of the chicken coop.

"OK. What's the deal?" as I propped my arm under my chin so as to give him my undivided attention.

"I know this works because I've done this several times. Now first of all, figure out what job you want. What do you want to be doing for the rest of your life. I don't care what the trade is. This will work. OK. Then find a place that will hire you to do janitor work or whatever for whatever wage they want to pay you--just so you are there working around those who are doing the job all day long. Then you are seeing the jobs actually being accomplished. All right?" He sat there with his fingers protruding out. As he counted he would put another finger down.

"Then third, you learn what you can at home on your offhours so you can find out all the technical questions concerning the trade. OK?"

"Yes." I was taking it all in like rain falling on a desert. I was absorbing it. "Uh huh." A thrill was going through me.

"Fourth, you have got to be willing to do extra and work overtime so that when there's little things that need to be done to help out, you just get in and do it but make sure it's done right or you will be in trouble. OK?"

"Yeah." I could just visualize how this could work.

"The manager or employer of the place will appreciate what you're doing and recognize that you have the ability to take responsibility and it's the nature of people to leave work for someone else if they think they can get by with it. So you will have things left for you to do, even though it's not your job. Those whose job it is will leave it just because they know you will do it. So what will happen is the boss will walk in one day and find the janitor, which is you, busy doing all these other jobs. Then because he is so impressed you will likely be moved up the ladder. But you have to be careful of jealousy. Because when you know enough that the manager is afraid of his position, that's about the time you're liable to be fired. But by that time you know enough to go to work for someone else."

I was confounded.

"Now, do you see how that works? You have gained practical experience--on-the-job training--and even if you need a degree, you could take the college course much faster because you already know most of thee answers."

I sat there scratching my head. "Man, that's really smart. I'm going to write that down," I said as I jumped up.

"Oh, you're a smart girl. You'll be able to remember it."

That gave a new light on things. I was very impressed that Bard would come up with something that intelligent. I could feel some vibes

34

radiating as I admired the excellent idea. Later I tried to remember it and wrote it down, as I felt that was a very important key.

A few months after that there was talk of construction in the area, another subdivision was being developed. So Mother sold our home near State Street and bought another home directly east four blocks. We had no sooner moved in there when I met our neighbor, Mrs. Ren, a little Italian lady. She was about 5' tall, 160 pounds, with curly hair and a jovial smile. I was invited to her house to have some crispy Italian treats, which I accepted. As I sat in her home, I looked around me. Here was a humble looking house from the outside. Oh, but the inside was a compilation of beauty and order. Everything was spotless. I felt myself having a love affair with the way this woman kept house.

I took her to our house and showed her my art work. I explained, "I'm trying to be an artist." We were looking at a pencil drawing I had done of the Mona Lisa.

"Why, young lady, that's beautiful. How long did that take?"

"Gee, I don't know. I just kept at it until it was done." I was thinking to myself, "Gee, you're cuter than Mona Lisa.

She must have read my mind. She said, "Maybe someday you could do me if you would like to, OK?"

I quickly replied, "I'd like that."

For a week straight I was unpacking and cleaning. Boy, after seeing the likes of her home, I resorted to cleaning some things with a toothbrush. I was trying to have the second cleanest house in all of Sandy, hers being number one. Then when I could really feel good about our home, I would go visit her.

One day she sat still while I drew her picture. When I was done, I showed it to her.

"That's very nice. How much do I owe you?"

"Not even one penny," I smiled.

"I know--I know what you'd like. I give you." She took me to her front room. Opening a door to a chest, she brought out several pieces of intricate crochet work. She had made these doily masterpieces--a set for a couch, chair and end tables. "Here. I would like you to have these."

"Are you sure?" I gasped.

"Yes. I've saved these for years for someone special and I know you would like them."

"Oh, I would." We hugged for a few seconds. "Thank you." As I picked them up to go home, I felt such appreciation for the elegance she had passed my way. "Thank you again. I will cherish these knowing who made them and all those hours spent."

"You have a hope chest?"

"Sorta' kinda'."

35

"When you get married, you can remember your neighbor, huh?"

"Yeah. I'll remember my neighbor," as I gave her another hug.

A few days later I went to visit. She was out shoveling goat manure into a wheelbarrow. "Where are we taking it?" I asked.

"I'm spreading it on the garden spot."

"OK." I wheeled it out there and dumped it and returned. "I'll do that if you like."

"Would you? Then I'll go spade that there."

"Okey dokey." I was happily shoveling and hauling manure for my friend.

The next day I was out by the side of our house where I had planted marigolds and chrysanthemums that were facing the rose bushes next to the fence. I had put my chair right there so I could read the Journal of Discourses while basking in the sun and was enjoying our beautiful yard. Mrs. Ren walked by, "Hi. How are you?"

"Fine."

"What're reading?"

"I'm just trying to expand my mind. What's ya' doing?"

"Oh, I'm dista' going to the store."

"Can I come with?"

"If you'd like."

I hopped up, "Just a hairy minute. I'll just put this book in the house."

She laughed, "What is a hairy minute?"

"Well, see it's one that might actually be longer than 60 seconds 'cause it's growing." I flashed a big smile.

"You's funny."

We walked off talking about many things under the sun. Then she said, "My grandson is coming to see me in a few weeks. He's such a fine young man and very handsome, too. I would like for you to meet him. He has just bought himself a brand new red Fiat. It's a sports car with a convertible top. He's just the sweetest boy. I love him so much."

I was thinking to myself, "Oh boy. I'd better be careful because I've got to find out who God wants me to marry and this might be tempting." With a quick reply, "I have a boyfriend already."

"You do?"

"Yes, he comes to see me once in a while."

"Oh."

Actually the boy I had referred to was just a friend, not a sweetheart, but it seemed to be a good excuse, then I changed the subject,

36

"Do you think that maybe someday you could teach me how to make some of those tasty little crispy things that you gave me the other day?"

"I'd love to," she said as we went on.

It seemed like everyone had ideas of whom I should marry. The next Sunday in meeting as I took a seat waiting for the meeting to begin, I felt a soul satisfaction to be numbered amongst the saints. I looked around me casually at the caliber of virtue and dignity of the women present: their faces with little or no makeup, their long hair well cared for, their dress modestly below their knees while their sleeves were wrist length. I felt contented to be dressed in like manner and was thankful this day that my hair had grown out and the trace of black was nearly gone.

My mind went back to a year and a half ago--my condition and frame of mind then as compared to now. I was glad I had not done anything at that time that I could not repent of. A smile settled on my countenance and my heart quivered with joy as these words went through me: "I have come home to stay. These are my people." My eyes were wet. I was prepared to hear the word of the Lord.

President Dan arose. "We'll sing as our opening song, "We Thank Thee, Oh God, For A Prophet." Then as the meeting was conducted, there were many valuable principles discussed. But my attention seemed to be focused upon President Tellason's sermon. When he got on this subject, I put my pencil to the pad I had been holding.

"You young people here today are blessed. Many of you are children of the covenant, were chosen from the other side to come down through your parents to carry on this special priesthood work and calling. Some of you young ladies are quick to run about trying to find a husband or you young men run without being sent to find a wife with little or no thought of preserving your birthright amongst the saints and the covenants you have made in the pre-existence. The Lord would have you at this time seek to bring yourselves to the feet of the priesthood, that the mind and will of the Lord may be made known as to whom you have made covenants with on the other side."

In the spirit of obedience I could appreciate his sermon, for truly we should seek God's will on something of such importance.

After a while he sat down and President Browning spoke. "Brothers and Sisters, I would like you to ask yourselves: How much do we truly appreciate having a prophet, seer and revelator to lead this people?" He paused then continued, "There is something I would like to bring to your attention. If you will turn to The Doctrine and Covenants, Section 132, verse 7:

7.   And verily I say unto you, that the conditions of this law are these: All covenants, contracts, bonds, obligations, oaths, vows, performances, connections, associations, or expectations, that are not made and entered into and sealed by the Holy Spirit of promise, of him who is anointed, both as well for time and for all eternity, and that too most holy, by revelation and commandment through the medium of mine anointed, whom I have appointed on the earth to hold this power (and I have appointed unto my servant Joseph to hold this power in the last days, and there is never but one on the earth at a time on whom this power and the keys of this priesthood are conferred), are of no efficacy, virtue, or force in and after the resurrection from the dead; for all contracts that are not made unto this end have an end when men are dead.[5]

"There is never but one man on the earth at a time on whom this power and the keys of this priesthood are confirmed." Then he stopped to appeal to the congregation.

"Here is the man (pointing to President Tellason) who the Lord has blessed and preserved that we might be left without excuse. Will we follow him as though the Prophet Joseph were here with us today? Or will we be found treating lightly those things that God has revealed to us through him? What type of rewards do we expect to have in this life or the hereafter unless we can sustain him in all things as our prophet, seer and revelator."

I felt grateful that the Lord had preserved President Tellason who was well into his 80s. Then he continued to read until he had completed verse 11:

"10. Or will I receive at your hands that which I have not appointed?

11. And will I appoint unto you, saith the Lord, except it be by law, even as I and my Father ordained unto you, before the world was?[6]

"Can you young people expect to marry without appointment and have the Lord's blessing upon that union? These things we must think about very carefully, brothers and sisters. When a marriage is sealed by

---

[5] Section 132, verse 7, The Doctrine and Covenants.

[6] Section 132, verses 10-11, The Doctrine and Covenants.

about very carefully, brothers and sisters. When a marriage is sealed by the Lord's anointed, there are angels commissioned to watch over and bless that man and his wife or wives, so long as they remain true and faithful."

He continued to talk but my mind was rehearsing what had already been said, like a sponge can only absorb so much and my mind was full.

When Brother Mann arose, he said, "We would like to ask these young men to sing for us at this time 'Glorious Things Are Sung of Zion' to the melody of 'Israel, Israel, God Is Calling.'"

Glorious things are sung of Zion,
Enoch's city seen of old.
Where the righteous, being perfect,
Walked with God in streets of gold.
Love and virtue, faith and wisdom,
Grace and gifts were all combined;
As himself each loved his neighbor;
All were one in heart and mind.
As himself each loved his neighbor;
All were one in heart and mind.

There they shunned the power of Satan
And observed celestial laws;
For in Adam-ondi-Ahman
Zion rose where Eden was.
When beyond the power of evil,
So that none could covet wealth,
One continual feat of blessings
Crowned their days with peace and health.
One continual feast of blessings
Crowned their days with peace and health.

Then the towers of Zion glittered
Like the sun in yonder skies,
And the wicked stood and trembled,
Filled with wonder and surprise.
Then their faith and works were perfect.
Lo, they followed their great Head!
So the city went to heaven,
And the world was, "Zion's fled!"
So the city went to heaven,
And the world said, "Zion's fled!"

And we hear the watchman cry,
Then we'll surely be united,
And we'll all see eye to eye.
Then we'll mingle with the angels,
And the Lord will bless his own.
Then the earth will be as Eden,
And we'll know as we are known.
Then the earth will be as Eden,
And we'll know as we are known.[7]

How blessed and sweet were the things I heard that day. The meeting closed and I went to the car. Mom and Walt were talking, but I was in a little world of my own. "That city will return," I thought to myself. "I must be careful what I am doing or what I say 'cause there might be angels around. If I can stop swearing when I get mad or hurt myself, boy, that would be neat."

When Winter came, Bard and Nanas came to visit one snowy night. When I answered the door, Bard had a box in his arms. "We brought you guys some meat."

"Come on in." I took the box. "We were about to have supper. Are you guys hungry?" I asked.

"We haven't eaten," Bard answered.

"OK. I'll make you guys a plate, too, then."

"Ya' ought to put that stuff in the freezer," Nan commented. "There's some steaks and hamburger."

"Hey, I could fry up some hamburger with onions to go with this." I had fixed macaroni, cheese and salad. I pulled out the table to add another leaf in the middle then when it was ready, I called, "Would everyone like to come 'n eat?"

When we were just finishing up the meal, Bard commented, "We delivered over 700 pounds of meat around to the different homes today and that's just today. We have been able to load up that much about twice a week."

"How do you get all this stuff?" Mama asked.

"Ya' know that Mr. Meat on 33rd South just off State? He lets us clean out the lockers of the people who don't keep up their fees."

"Well, golly. Doesn't he charge for it?"

"Well, we're paying him three cents a pound. That's what he could sell it to Byproducts for. It was about $20 for today's load."

---

[7] "Glorious Things Are Sung of Zion," words by William W. Phelps, music by Joseph J. Daynes, Hymns, p. 243.

40

"Well, we're paying him three cents a pound. That's what he could sell it to Byproducts for. It was about $20 for today's load."

Nan interrupted, "Nearly all of Willy's check from working at the Capitol Theater goes to support this work of helping the saints."

Bard was looking at the bowl of macaroni so I passed it to him.

"Well, that's really nice of you guys to do something like that. We sure appreciate it."

"This is why the Lord has brought us together--for the benefit of the saints. They work hard to support their big families, but sometimes they need extra help to make ends meet," Bard said.

I thought, "Now, there's a man who thinks about someone besides himself. That's refreshing."

"If it wasn't for the good Nan and I do to help out this priesthood work, she wouldn't have been justified in leaving Elmer (the man she married after Clarence died). But according to the laws of God, a woman can leave her husband--I don't care who he is--if she is going to a better man, so that she can elevate herself in the Lord's work. Most men won't require the service and sacrifice out of their women that it would take for them to earn their exaltation."

I began to clear the table but was still listening.

Bard continued, "A man might ask his wife to do something and maybe she does it, maybe she don't, but if it were my wife, I'd see to it that it was done. That's the only way to really make something out of her in the long run. I wouldn't put up with the damn rebellion that most men put up with. Everyone I have ever taken under my supervision to train I made something out of them."

Everyone at the table seemed to believe Bard so why shouldn't I.

Nanas said, "It's true. He trained Arlandis to where he's now the manager of the R. C. Cola Company. Bard was offered a job at Sperry Univac. They had a test that 500 men took but only eight passed it. Bard was one of them, but he turned it down," Nan said.

"Because that's not what the Lord wanted me to do. I need to be free and independent. I can't be tied down to a steady 8-hour job. When Brother Mann asks me to do something, I've got to be able to go do it right now."

"That's why I like selling Watkins products," Walt added. "So I'm not so tied down all the time."

This conversation was somewhat confusing to me but at the same time very interesting.

Will got up and imitating the Yogi Bear voice, said, "That's why they call us "The Three Mouse Catters. Yoyo yoyoyoyoyoyo hoho de do."

I snickered with a little laugh. "You guys like some Jello? Yabba dabba do."

41

"I would," said Will. "How about you?" He was still imitating Yogi Bear.

I could not see where these people were as bad as I once had supposed or they would not be doing all these good things. The bars of resistance I once had held high had now slipped pretty low, as I found myself talking to them as free as I would anyone else.

The next time Bard came over, I got him off alone. I thought to myself, "If he's so smart, I'd like to ask him something."

I began, "How do I go about finding the man I made covenants with? Do I just make an appointment with Brother Mann and ask him or what?"

"Oh, you could. That would be one way."

"Yeah, but I'm so darn bashful. I don't know if I've got the nerve yet, and besides" giving way to a little nervous laughter, "what I've been thinking is Brother Mann's the only man I know that I might not mind marrying. Ya' see what I mean. How do I approach that?"

"Yeah, I kinda' do." He paused for a while then said with a red face, "I hope I don't hurt your feelings, but I'd like to run something by you. Brother Mann is in such a high position that he can take his pick from the cream of the crop--the prettiest women with the best birthright and such. I don't know how much of a chance you'd stand so you might want to prepare yourself for a disappointing answer. But you could ask."

Boy, somehow that short statement had a way of knocking my props out from under me. I sat looking stupid for a while, trying to sort things out in my mind.

"I could ask for you if you'd like me to."

"Huh?"

"I said I could ask for you if you want. I go up to see him all the time."

"That might be a good idea 'cause Walt's got some crazy notion I'm supposed to marry him, and if there's something cooking like that, I don't even want to hear it."

"I think Mann's out of town today and tomorrow but he should be back Tuesday. So I'll make an appointment then and get back with you. OK?"

"OK."

Three days later Bard and Nanas came over. I was alone. I invited them in, anxious to know what was said. We sat down in the front room.

"Well, are you ready for this?" he asked.

"What did he say?" I was bracing my feelings to be prepared to hear whatever.

42

"Well, it was as big of a shock to me as it probably will be to you. But he told me that you are to become my wife."

My mouth fell down as I gasped for air.

He went on to say, "Brother Mann has asked me to look over this family for years, but I didn't know why. Then today he told me right out, point blank, that you made a covenant with me on the other side."

I felt like something heavy was crushing me. I rested my head in my hands with my eyes closed while trying to form a picture of Brother Mann telling them this. I had prayed all day for priesthood direction, now this heavy weight was upon me. "Will I follow it? Where's my devotion? Where's my guts?" I asked myself. "Can I bring myself to do the will of the Lord?"

Bard put his arm around me. "You could learn to love me in time, if you let yourself. If I can get you to keep your bars down so I can get a word in edgeways, you'll be alright. I do love you even when you were swearing at me and flipping me the finger. I tried not to hate you for it. The work of the Lord is more important than love." He was patting my shoulders.

Nan commented, "We need you in our family. I think that's why the Lord wants you to come this way--so you can help us in the business so Willy won't have to work so hard." (They had been washing a few glass gallon jugs and selling them for a little money.)

Nan seemed nice enough about the whole situation.

"Uh, well, I've got to think about it for a while. OK?"

"That's OK," Bard said. "Take your time, but if you wouldn't mind, maybe you could help us once in a while when we get a lot of orders so Nan isn't up so late."

"Yes, I wouldn't mind helping you once in a while, but I have this house to keep up 'cause Mama's been working pretty steady."

"Well, that will work out OK. How many days do you think you could help?"

"Oh, maybe two or three."

"OK. We'll come pick you up."

After they left I thought to myself, "Don't you dare get bitter or resentful. There must be some reasoning behind it or the Lord wouldn't ask me to do it, even if I don't see the reason right now." I wanted to throw up every time I thought about it. "Maybe I can learn to love him though because we both believe in the Gospel. He does know the scriptures more than I do. And that's something. And if he didn't love the work of the Lord and the truth, why would he study all the good books or be helping the saints?" I looked at the set of <u>Journals</u> (approximately 21 volumes), as I scratched my head. "Bard's read all of those books. Maybe he could guide me."

A few days went by and Bard had called me to see if I was ready to help him yet, but I had preferred housework until one certain afternoon. Mama came in tired as usual. I had steamed some broccoli. We sat there eating it with bread and butter.

"Ya' know what!" I said. Bard and Nanas went to Brother Mann to ask where I belong and you know what?"

"What?"

"Well, they said that Mann told them I belong to Bard."

"Oh, really!" Mama exclaimed.

"Yeah. They told me Tuesday when you weren't here. They want me to help them in their little business whenever I can."

"Yeah. I've been over there a few times helping them burn their empty boxes. So you're going to marry Bard. Is that it?"

"I don't know. Maybe. But I thought maybe at least helping them once in a while would be better than no job at all, ya' know."

"Yeah, I know. Believe me, 50 cents a day is better than nothing."

"They haven't discussed pay or anything, but I guess it don't matter."

Mama retired to bed. I came in with a wet washcloth for her forehead and rubbed some lotion on her feet as usual. Then I remembered some art work I had been doing. "Hey, I have something to show you." I returned carrying two pictures. I held the one in front of Mama.

"Oh, that's our house. Did you do that just today?"

"Yeah."

"Yes, sir. You just keep going. I think you'll make it someday."

"I've got this one here," showing her the other one I just started. "It's supposed to be a spot like the Sacred Grove where Joseph Smith's vision took place."

"Uh huh. You're making headway all right."

I bent over and kissed Mama on the cheek. "Good night, Mama."

"Good night, sweetheart."

I left the room closing the door carefully, thankful for Mom's encouragement. In another six months, I would be 16 years old and would soon have to make decisions about the direction of my life.

When Walt came home that night, he brought in three bags of groceries. As I was putting them away, he said, "Have you given it anymore thought about becoming my wife?"

Just then a bottle of prune juice slipped from out of my hands. Bang! It shattered on the floor. "Oh, man! What a mess!" I exclaimed. I began picking up the pieces of glass very quickly. "Ouch." I had cut myself. I finished cleaning up the glass and mopped up the juice. I could just feel myself brooding over the answer to his question.

"Have you thought about what I said?"

My mouth was tight, just about ready to blow.

"I'd be a better husband than half the guys you ran around with years ago."

"So who gives a hairy rat about what happened years ago," I hollered. "I wouldn't marry them and I'm not marrying you either. Can you get that through your thick skull?"

"Well, you're not obeying priesthood direction then."

"I don't believe that that came from Brother Mann. I think you made it up."

"I never made that up."

"Oh, yeah? You'd tell the same thing to every girl in the world if you thought they was stupid enough to believe it."

Walt pointed into the air and in a loud voice shouted, "You'll go to hell then."

"Fine. Then I'll marry the devil while I'm down there." I stormed into my bedroom and slammed the door. I told Mom in the morning I was going to work with Bard and Nanas, "because this house is not big enough to hold both Walt and I."

"That will be alright then if that's what you want to do. They do help the priesthood a lot." I called Bard and told him to come and get me. I was ready for work.

After I spent the day at Reclaim Bottle gluing new jug boxes together, we grabbed a hot dog and malt then went to their apartment uptown. The front room was dark, the only light being from the doorway of the kitchen, and the walls had brown wallpaper with little yellow flowers. While I sat on a chair, Bard set on the bed in front of me. While he was talking I was looking at the boxes of stuff of who knows what in piles around the room and the debris on the floors. I thought, "Well, I guess they're so busy working they don't have time to clean it up."

All of a sudden Bard caught my attention, "The children that are born to my women will be given to Nanas."

The way that came across somehow was the last straw. I already felt like a time bomb waiting to explode--and he had just lighted my fuse.

"What? What did you say?"

"Nanas being the first wife is in the position that all the children will be given to her."

I got up and thought, "What the hell am I doing here anyway?"

"Forget you" were my last words as I walked out and slammed the door.

It was 10:30 p.m. and it was pitch black outside. There were no street lights. A creepy feeling came over me as I walked fast away from there with fury running through me. As I walked I realized my condition--I was without a coat or a dime in my pocket and Mother was living in Sandy. I thought, "Now, let's see. How far away is that? I guess about 25, maybe 30 miles." I had paused to figure this then I thought, "Well, Bard and Nanas brought me here. Damn it. They can take me home." So I turned on my heel and headed back. They had calmed down somewhat and so had I. I came in, looked at them in that dreary room.

"You guys brought me here. You can take me home," I stated.

"We have been praying that you would have a change of heart and come back. I think you got a misunderstanding of what I was trying to say," Bard said. "What I was getting at is that children would need to show respect to Nanas just as much as they would their mother and it wouldn't hurt for the child to have two mothers."

Well that sounded much better and I surely was tired. They made a bed for me in the kitchen and I slept there with Nanas. Bard and Will slept in the front room. Within a few days I asked if they would take me to see Brother Mann and they agreed to do that.

Bard said on the way up there, "Even though Brother Mann told me that you are to be my wife, they are likely to try to give you to someone else."

"Why in the world would they do that?"

"They want to give you your free agency even though you are meant for me. It's because my mission is so important, they won't give you to me unless that's what you want. Women are a dime a dozen, but good ones are darn hard to find."

"I don't understand."

"Well, look. If a woman can't follow priesthood direction, then she isn't worth her salt."

"Well, maybe so, but I need to know what God wants me to do so I can start out right and hopefully end up right."   "Well,   be prepared because they might even try to turn you against me."

"Why do you think so?"

He whispered, "I'll tell you a little secret. It's my mission to correct the priesthood counsel when they are out of line and they don't like being corrected."

Well, we arrived and Brother Mann said to me, "Who would you like to marry? You can have your pick." He named five different men: Walt, Will, Kirk, Leo and Frank. But he never mentioned Bard.

I thought, "I don't like any of the choices." So I said, "I'd rather wait to know who God wants me to marry, even if I have to wait a 100 years rather than marry the wrong man tomorrow."

Brother Mann seemed somewhat surprised at my answer and said, "Well, that's all right, then. What are you doing and where are you staying now?"

"Well, I'm living with Nanas and Bard right now because they need help in their business. I left home because of Walt having some funny ideas."

"That's OK then. Just go back and stay with Nanas and Bard until the Lord reveals something in your behalf."

I thanked him and we left. Bard was excited. "See. See what did I tell you? He told you to come and stay with me. He knows that's where God wants you. But he didn't tell you that until he could see that you couldn't just be pushed around. You have passed the test. You have passed the test!" He looked up in the air and clapped his hands.

I felt so confused I hardly knew what was up or down.

About a week later Bard and Nanas needed to go south to Short Creek so I went with them. On the way I started saying, "I sure would like to marry Brother Mann," but not wanting to hurt Bard's feelings, I said, "but even if I do, I would like you guys to tell me the things you know concerning the gospel."

"Well, but if you marry Brother Mann, he isn't going to treat you very good because he has so many wives of a higher birthright, and if you marry him, I won't be able to counsel you on anything because you will have to listen to whatever he tells you."

"Oh, come on." I bumped his shoulder with my shoulder. "You're not going to get away from me that easy."

Nanas looked at Bard, "That's a proposal, isn't it?"

"Yes, it is. May proposed to me," he exclaimed with excitement. Then Bard carried on, "I told the Lord that if this was for sure right, to have May propose to me, and you have done it." Then Bard said to me, "There are very few women who can qualify to live the higher laws, the reason being they can't deny themselves of their own mind and will enough. Christ said, 'Father, thy will be done, not mine.' He is the example of the world and He is who we have to follow if we ever expect to see our father in heaven. Ever since the church was first organized, the saints have had to deny themselves. The road to godliness is a tough row to hoe and not many are willing to sacrifice their all to follow the Lord."

As I heard these words, they rang true. He continued, "A religion that does not require the sacrifice of all things, does not have the power within it sufficient to lay hold of eternal life. Most religions of the day are busy trying to give people their own mind and will. That's how they become so popular.

47

Somehow during the course of this conversation, I had managed to rip off all my fingernails as I commented, "I don't know if I can sacrifice everything or not. But I hope I can."

"You can. I have confidence in you and I know that you have above average intelligence because if you didn't, you couldn't stand to hear the truth without becoming angry."

"Well, the thought has occurred to me that those who have it easy in this life, in my opinion, don't really ever prove themselves and their loyalty to God."

"That's one thing about the principle of plural marriage. It was designed to uproot all the evil and selfishness from one's character for them to stand to live it," Bard stated.

"Can we stop and get some root beer?" I asked.

"Bard, you ought to stop and get her some."

"Yeah, I will in a minute. I'm looking for a service station so I can go to the bathroom."

We stayed at the Creek (Short Creek, Arizona) for just one day then we came back to work doing bottles. After a day's work was done in the little bottle shack, I was sweeping the floor. Bard braced himself against the rinse tub with his arms folded, watching my every move.

"All the things that I tell you about the gospel are for you to keep secret. They're for your benefit that you might understand how important this work is."

I stopped and was leaning on the broom while the orange rays of late afternoon sun came through the doorway.

"My mission is so extremely secretive," Bard continued, "that when I was given a patriarchal blessing, it could not even be written."

I thought, "Hmmm. That's really something."

"Where and by whom did you receive the priesthood?" I asked.

Seeming somewhat shocked at my question, "My priesthood? That is to be held in confidence, but I will tell you this that my priesthood and mission is like unto the Prophet Joseph wherein God told him that whatever he would bless, God would bless, and whatever he would curse, God would curse. I have been given that same blessing. Also, that before God would let me go very far wrong, he has promised me he would take me on the other side. I have already earned that right."

I resorted to a seat on a coke box while leaning my back against the wall.

"Well, why have the brethren thrown you out of meeting in Short Creek then?"

Bard took a jug box down and put it in front of me where he sat. He began expressing himself with his hands going up and down. "They don't even comprehend my mission and calling. They are to guide the people in the group, but when they step out of line or preach wrong doctrine, then I'm fast for making an appointment with them to tell them wherein they have erred. Do you think they like being corrected?"

"Well, I don't know. What have you had to correct them on?"

"For one thing, there has been several women that were meant to come into my family. I told them and also I told the girls, but they have married those women to other men. Because they have done this, I told them that they will forfeit some of their wives to go in my family in the hereafter--turnabout is fair play. And if you don't think that makes them mad, then just think again. Uncle Troy told me that I was either an extremely righteous man or he said 'You're a devil.' I told him that it was for him to take it to the Lord to find out which.

"Troy is responsible for marrying Rebecca to a Catholic rather than give her to me. If you don't think he will pay for that! But if her husband dies or she gets a divorce, I'll still try to pick her up." Bard's eyes were bloodshot.

I got up to turn on the light. "Here comes Will and Nan with a small load of jugs," I said as they backed up the truck. "That's good!" I hollered to them.

After Will and Nan came in and some general chit-chat took place, Bard said, "Sit down you guys. I was talking to May before you came in. I was telling her about how the priesthood council will be accountable to God for what they have done to me. Just the same with some of the others in the group. Like when I took the truck over to Lar Ricks. He cheated me out of $20 by putting in a used part when he charged me for a new one. And you know what happened? Three days later his whole shop went up in flames."

Nan said, "That's true. That really happened."

Then Will said, "Did you tell her about that girl, Charlotte, who was supposed to become your wife and the priesthood married her to someone else?"

Bard took over the conversation, "Yes, and the girl's mother committed suicide because she knew where her daughter belonged. In fact, I don't know of even one incident where anyone has done wrong against me where God did not step in and punish them extremely for their wrongs." He kept waving his hand around in the air to swat some flies that seemed to be having delight in teasing him by landing on his forehead.

Very soberly I considered this whole conversation and said, "Ya' know, that's what happened to Joseph Smith. There was lots of people who persecuted him and after Joseph was killed, those people all died in the most horrible forms you can ever imagine, like being eaten up by worms and their flesh rotting right off their bodies while they were still alive." I shivered. "It's really sick."

Nan said, "Tell her about your father."

"My father used to beat me all the time when I was young and not let me go anywhere, or if I had anything, he would take it from me. I couldn't even have a car when I was 17 until I left home. But before he died, the doctors couldn't find anything wrong with him, but he was starving to death on a full stomach." Bard was bawling. "I went to see him on his deathbed. He was just skin and bones. Then for the first time in my life, he said, 'I'm sorry, Bard. I have not done right with you.' Two days later he died. That's deathbed repentance and God doesn't honor it."

Nan said, "Can you guys get this truck unloaded? I'm starving to death."

As I stood in the doorway scratching my head, I thought, "I hope nothing happens to me 'cause of my big mouth."

Will got on the truck and began to throw the boxes of jugs to me as I threw them to Bard for him to stack. We unloaded the truck.

While traveling down the road, I began to reason things out in my mind. I can see why those women might not want to marry Bard, but if I have to marry him in the next life, would it not be better to learn how to cope with the situation here rather than to prolong the inevitable, if it's God's will?

I glanced over the horizon. The dark purple in the night sky was streaked with radiant orange and pink, as though it were exploding in the mountains, portraying the glory of God's art work.

After finishing work, we went to the Farmer's Daughter, a cafe. We went in and Bard asked, "What would you like?"

"Well, I don't know. What would you like to buy for me?" Looking over the menu, "All this stuff looks kinda' expensive."

"It doesn't matter. Order what you like. You're worth it."

I smiled. "Well, I've never had shrimp, but its $3.25."

"Fine. Order shrimp then."

"OK. Thank you." Then while we were eating, my eyes focused on Bard with gravy on his chin. He ate like someone would take it away if he did not shovel it in fast enough.

"My natural feelings would go on the altar of sacrifice, if I must make myself obey him," I said to myself. "You don't have to love someone in order to obey them. There's no law that says I ever even have to kiss him. But I can obey if I force myself. If I can earn my exaltation, then it will be worth whatever I go through."

That night I dreamed I was being horribly abused by a wicked man who had Bard's face with the freakiest expression. I woke up very offended in my innermost feelings. This dream shook me up so bad that for days I was trying to remove it from my memory. But after several weeks, I thought, "Well, maybe that was from the devil and he's trying to stop me from going where God wants me to go."

Nanas and Bard were able to resume possession of Nanas' old home on 5th East as Mr. Piner's lease had expired. So we moved from the old apartment to this large, decrepit house. If I had not known better, I would have thought it was haunted, but it did not worry me because this was Clarence Rittling's old home. They brought all those boxes of who knows what and piled them in the large front room. After the move was completed, no one seemed to care only that was where they would sleep. Looking at the filth that they were accustomed to, I figured, "Well, scrud, I know how to clean up any darn mess in this whole blooming place. So fine. Once I get this filth taken care of, it won't be such a hell of a mess." So I took to cleaning up one mess at a time every chance I got to where the place began to look half civilized.

CHAPTER 3

I had only lived with Bard and Nanas for three months when Nanas was hit by a car and taken to a hospital. She could no longer wash bottles. We were sitting at the kitchen table. Bard looked at me, "Can I count on you to carry on the responsibility of the business? You're the only one that can do the job now."

"Well, I'll do my best."

"We've got some past bills to pay. We've got to come up with $140 for gasoline we've charged, and $72 at Keith's for truck repair that hasn't been paid yet. But if we don't come up with some money to pay on the taxes on this place, we're going to lose it. They haven't been paid for the last three years."

"Well, sounds like I'd better get in gear. I think I know enough of everything that's been going on out there to pretty much be able to handle the orders. Do you want me to start up a batch right now, or did you want to go see Nan at the hospital?"

"Well, let's start up a batch and do about 70 for Bestline Janitorial, then we'll go see Nan this afternoon."

"OK. Oh, hey! I just remembered Mama gave me the $18 that the government sends her for my support. I've still got it. Would that help you?"

"Yes, it will. How often do you get that?"

"Just once a month." I handed it to him.

"Thanks, May. Women are supposed to give their husbands all their monies, but there's sure a lot of women too stubborn to do it. Is this all you got?"

"Yeah, that's it."

"OK. Thank you."

I filled the vat with boiling water and caustic soap. Bard put the jugs in. I got on my apron and gloves and looked at the clock. OK. Fine. I washed off the outsides then threw them on the rack to drain, rinsed and put them on a rotary brush to clean the insides, inspected then boxed them. I raced for an hour as fast as I could go, then stopped to look at the stack: 18 cases, four jugs to a case. Hmmm. I looked at the clock. I ought to be able to make it an even 20 an hour. I looked over at Bard.

"Are you ready to race? It's five after. Let's get these hummers humming."

Determined to get the lead out, I took a deep breath, grabbed the jugs, and concentrated on every move to make it count to pick up lost time. Bard was running to put jugs in the vat then take off the clean jugs to stack.

"Hadn't you better slow down? You're working the crap out of me."

"Oh no. We don't even want to slow down. Let's get this hummer revved up into third gear. I'll take them off the end. You just throw the clean case on, OK?"

We continued until five after. I stopped to count again: 18 with me taking off the end. "Hmmm. It would take about 5 1/2 hours to do 100 cases," I thought. But after six hours, we were finished.

"Boy," I exclaimed while taking off my apron. "It would be neat if someone else could take them off the end."

"Well, I'm not going to. When you're full of piss and vinegar, there's no one who could keep up."

"Ah, come on. I was teasing."

"Maybe when I was younger, but not anymore. But you're young and it don't hurt you one bit. In fact, it's good for you."

I had my hand on the light switch. "Are we ready to go?" I asked.

"I guess so but when we get back, you need to clean all these cases. And if you've got any extra time, you could go to taking the rings and lids off the ones we are going to do tomorrow right here."

"Well, can't you just do that when you go to put them in the vat?"

"Yes, I could, but it'd make it a lot easier for me to just grab them and stick them in."

We left to visit Nanas. That night when we returned, I fixed us some potatoes. At the table I asked, "Do you want to help? You could take rings off if you want."

"I would if I could but I'm just too tired."

"Well, whatcha' got to do any better?"

He jumped back sharply, "It's not for me to account to you for what I do or don't do. It's for you to concern yourself with what I give you to do. I dictate your jobs. You don't dictate mine."

I snapped back, "Well, if that's the way you feel, just don't help me. I don't care." I could not get to the shop fast enough.

As I was cleaning cases, I felt somewhat confounded as I went over the day again. "What did I do to get him going? Oh well, put it on the shelf. It's no big deal," I thought.

I worked until ten o'clock cleaning cases and removing rings and lids. Then Bard came out. Looking over what I had done, he commented, "That's enough. You can quit for the night. But you need to start getting up at five o'clock."

I sat on a case, "Why so early?" (I had been getting up at 6:30 a.m.)

54

He stood in front of me looking down. "It's like this. If you get up early, you will find that you will be able to think more clearly and be able to organize your work far better."

I was trying to make my tired brain hear him out.

"What it is is that in the morning hours, the Lord has appointed four angels to be here to help you and if you're not there at five o'clock to meet them, they will just leave and let you work out your own problems."

I was staring into the night. "Well, how do I know when they are helping and when they're not?"

"How many times have you had a problem and the answer just comes to you and the answer is such a good one you just knew it would work? That's when these angels are talking to you."

Boy, I was thinking of several times that had happened.

"Now, wouldn't you much rather have their help than not?"

"Oh, for sure!"

"Well, OK. That's why you need to start getting up early."

"All right. I'll set my alarm. Are you going to get up too so we can start up a batch first thing?"

"No. But you can finish taking off the rings and lids and I'll get up as soon as I can. But nearly every night for hours while you're sleeping, I'm communicating with the other side to find out the mind and will of the Lord on different issues. That's the only reason I can't get up early or I would. There's many times I don't even get an hour's rest, but you don't know it."

I said nothing more but retired to bed. I got up early to work in the shop, but was eating my breakfast when Bard came in. "Hi. Ya' want me to fix you some breakfast?" He looked in my bowl. "This is just oats with water and honey. Actually, it tastes better than it looks. But don't worry about this. I can fix you some 'taters and eggs."

"Naw. Don't bother. I'll get something at the hospital. I'm going to see Nan."

"Should I come too?"

"No, you got work to do here."

"Okey dokey."

Then approximately two or three hours later, I was cleaning up one of the bedrooms. I had swept the floor, made the bed and was dusting off the dresser when I looked over towards the window which was open. Bard was there. All I could see was his head looking in. It startled me.

Then he said, "So that's how you spend your time--playing around. I wanted to know what you were doing when I'm not around."

55

What a strange gesture, feeling kind of shaky, to be put on the carpet for questioning. I answered, "Well, I made the bed and swept the floor and was dusting off the dresser is all."

"If that's all you've got done this morning, that's not enough. Nan could have had all the beds made and all the floors swept in that amount of time."

"Well, I did the dishes too and had some breakfast."

"Ya' better get out here and get a batch of jugs started."

"OK."

The days flew by. The hospital was ready to release Nanas to come home, so Bard and I went to pick her up. She had to walk with crutches. We helped her to the car and out of it upon arriving home. I was under one arm and Bard under the other. Taking our time we finally made it to her bedroom. Turning so Nanas could sit on her bed, we helped her take her coat off.

"Oh. Be careful. That hip is so dang sore. It's still got a water blister on it as big as your fist."

"Is there anything you'd like me to help you with?"

"Untie my shoes and take off my stockings."

"OK." I kneeled down, removed her shoes and was taking off her stockings.

"Now, take it easy. There's a blood clot right there." (She was pointing to her shin bone halfway up from her ankle.) "Don't touch that right there."

I stretched out the stocking so as to pass the sore place without touching it, then finished removing it. Bard came back in the room chewing on a stick of celery. He plopped himself down in the chair next to her bed.

Shaking the stick of celery at me, he began, "For as long as Nanas needs help, you're to be her nurse to see to it that whatever she needs you to do, you do it. Do you understand?"

It came across that I needed to be commanded or something. My intelligence was offended. "Well, I don't mind taking care of her. It's OK."

"What I'm getting at is when you get up, you come see what she needs before you eat or anything. And when you come in at noon, I want you to see to it that Nanas has something to eat before you sit down to eat. And when you come in at night, you come and see whatever she needs before you go to bed. Do you know what I mean?"

"Yes, but I don't know what all she needs. She'll need to tell me."

"I'll tell you what I need, but you've got to be real careful. There's some liniment in the bathroom on the medicine shelf in a white bottle. I'd like that rubbed on my hip."

"OK."

After a week I knew what my duties entailed. In the morning I helped her into the tub so I could give her a bath. I brushed her false teeth, then helped her dress and put her shoes and stockings on. Then after work I helped her undress, massaged liniment on her sore spots, then took a wet washcloth to wipe her feet after which I would massage her feet and back with regular hand lotion. But she liked a lot of massaging on her back and fell asleep while I was massaging. Then when I was through, I would ask, "Is there anything else you need before I go?"

"You haven't massaged my feet yet."

"Yes, I did. You were asleep."

"No, I wasn't. You're just trying to get out of it."

"I can do it again." So I did. I would do it three times rather than argue. Then I would cover her up. "May I go now?" The clock said I had been there for nearly an hour and a half.

"I guess," she said with a huff.

Then I left for bed. I came to expect two hours of my day would go to Nanas, so I just planned to have it so. After several months she got well enough to walk without crutches, but she still wanted all the attention I had been giving her.

Bard and I were just finishing up a batch of bottles. I asked, "How many new cases did you say I needed to make up for Utah Fruit?"

"Well, their truck holds 210."

"So that's how many we make then, huh?"

"Yeah."

"OK."

Bard changed the subject. "I've been visiting a girl in Riverton for a couple of weeks now, and I think she might come this direction. Nanas and I are going out there right now to see her. Her name is Zosa Holts. Her great grandfather lived the principle so she's from good lineage. I told her Nan was my sister, so she thinks I'm single. We're going to see if we can talk her into going to meeting with us next Sunday to see what she thinks of the principle. What do you think about it?"

"Well, I don't know. What does she look like? What is her character like?"

"Oh, she's not bad looking, but she's got one eye that looks off over to Joneses when she's talking. That's about all."

"Well, what does she act like?"

"I haven't really seen her do much, except her grandfather asked her to iron him a shirt, and she went to plug in the iron and it sparked. So she started sassing her grandfather telling him to do it himself. But I wouldn't put up with that kinda' noise. I'd straighten her out in one helluva hurry."

"Hmmm," I grunted. "I think I'll go fix something to eat and do this later."

They left, so I thought, "I'll go out into the field and get me some watercress and enjoy the sunshine for a minute." I picked a handful of watercress and washed it in the water from the flowing well. I was thinking about what Bard said, and I felt a little numb. I thought, "I don't know how many women he will bring in. God said that is the law. I guess it really doesn't matter 'cause whether I fail or succeed, it only depends upon my efforts."

I sat down under a tree watching some wild geese fly overhead. "Oh, you beauties," as a thrill of joy went through me. "I'm so glad I love animals and birds 'cause when Bard gets 30 wives or more, I can always find happiness without having to have him by my side all the time." I looked over the tall green grass and wild herbs.

Laying my head back against the tree, I closed my eyes for a moment. "I'm such a tiny thing in the scope of God's creation, but I'm glad God invented all these other little things," as I was staring into a wild rose bush next to me where a little rose near the ground was almost hidden from sight. I reached out and held it in my hand without picking it.

As my mind drifted, I remembered something I had heard in meeting of how all God's creations know that God is their master and they strive to serve him to the best of their ability. This little rose has a spirit. I smiled. Here it is. It is growing to its fullest beauty, knowing that no one may ever see it except God. As a tear came to my eye, I looked to the heavens. I had never before supposed the love and nobleness of a rose. I cried a little as I said to myself, "If God recognizes a rose, then he must see me, too." Thankfulness settled in my heart as I kissed the rose and said, "You sweet little things. The Lord sees you and I have seen you. You've made both of us happy."

I hurried back to make cases so Bard would not wonder what I had been doing. I was getting used to the idea of having to account for my time. I got by that day alright. But the next day when they came home from the cafe after having breakfast, Bard asked, "What have you been doing while we were gone?" This was such a daily routine that I knew he was going to ask that. I made it a point to not only make good use of my time, but to remember what I had done. Being fully ready for this question, I would let them have it with both "barrels," like I was answering to a sergeant:

"Well, first I got the washer going to wash the first batch of clothes, then while they were washing, I done the dishes and cleaned off the table and the stove. Then I went in and took out the first batch and rinsed them, put another batch in, then hung out the first batch. Then I came in and swept the two bedrooms, front room, and the bathroom and kitchen. Then I went and rinsed the second batch and got another batch started. Then I hung out the second batch and I just got through mopping the kitchen floor. Now, I've got to tend to the third batch of clothes."

"That's pretty good," Bard commented. "Now when you're finished with that batch of clothes, go start up a batch of bottles."

"Well, I just need to do the rugs next then I'll be done with the washing."

"All right. Then come and get me and I'll put the bottles in the sink." That day passed quickly.

It was a Sunday. I had put on my best dress and hurried downstairs to the bathroom where I stood washing my face. Bard came up from behind and asked, "Here, will you wash these?"

I opened an eye and looking down saw his outstretched hand holding his false teeth that looked and smelled like they had not been cleaned for three months. I shut my eyes quickly. The thought of obedience ran through me as I said, "Uh, just a minute." I dried my face then held out my hand. Clink. Clink. Yuck. They dropped from his hand into mine. I thought, "Oh well. It's no worse than baby poop., I guess." I could feel my face pulling every which direction. I opened part of one eye to barely see the tap where I held them for water to wash off all it would, then I sprinkled Ajax cleanser on them so I could finish the job. I handed them back to him.

"Thank you."

"It's OK."

We went on our way to meeting. One of the brethren got up to speak. What he said was permanently imprinted upon my mind:

Those who are out in the world that have not had a chance to know the truth are yet in a natural territory. But when a person is brought to the feet of this order of the priesthood to where they are taught the fullness of the Gospel, once they have a testimony of the truth, then they must make a choice to either embrace it with all their heart, might, mind and strength or deny the truth and join the adversary and his forces. Those who turn against this work become darkened in their minds until they fall into the category that the Lord spoke of wherein they have ears that do not hear, eyes that do not see and a mind that cannot comprehend."

My mind reflected upon the demons who had persecuted the saints in the early days of Mormon history--the murderous mobs that were led by apostates. The realization of this sermon left me as sober as a judge. My soul was full of vibrations as I joined with the congregation to offer up my favorite song:

"How firm a foundation, ye Saints of the Lord,
Is laid for your faith in his excellent word!
What more can he say than to you he hath said,
You who unto Jesus, you who unto Jesus,
You who unto Jesus for refuge have fled.

In every condition, in sickness, in health,
In poverty's vale or abounding in wealth,
At home or abroad, on the land or the sea,
As they days may demand, as they days may demand,
As they days may demand, so they succor shall be.

Then singing loudly, as I thought the Lord would enjoy hearing the last verse:

The soul that on Jesus hath leaned for repose
I will not, I cannot, desert to his foes;
That soul, though all hell should endeavor to shake,
I'll never, no never, no never forsake![8]

Two weeks later Bard had Zosa living in the home with us. He told her she was to keep the house up, but she seemed to have a different idea. Anyway, the house needed more attention than it was getting. But all this accounting that I would do continually made me extremely sensitive of how each moment of my time was spent. Some months passed and we picked up a few more bottle accounts. One day Bard came home from breakfast. He had asked me before he had left to start up a batch and work by myself until he returned. But knowing that the bottles would go twice as fast with his help, I thought it would be a better opportunity to clean out the fridge and mop the kitchen floor. When he walked in the door and saw me there wiping off the kitchen table, he said, "Why aren't you out there washing bottles?"

"Well, this is such a mess. It needs to be done anyway so I thought I would get this done first."

"How am I supposed to pay the bills if you're going to play around in the house all day?" slamming his fist down on the table. "I don't care about this house. How filthy or how clean it is, it isn't going to keep the family and pay the debts. A business will support a family and a house, but a house and a family doesn't support anything. Now, if I have to keep you out of this house entirely to get the work done in the business, then I'll do it."

"Yeah, but, how can we live if things get too damn filthy in here?"

"That's not your problem. If Zosa doesn't clean up the place and we live in a pig pen, I don't care. But I want you to spend your time strictly on Reclaim Bottle. As long as there is one bottle to be washed that we can gain an extra five cents, that's where I want you spending your time." From the tone of his voice I was for getting out of there and getting a batch started up immediately.

So I tried to do all that I needed to in the business and still clean the house in the evenings. A week later about seven o'clock at night, Bard came home from the cafe and I was in the house doing the dishes. As he opened the door and saw me standing there by the sink, his voice raised to a horrible pitch, "I told you to stop doing this damn housework. And I mean it! If you can't be obedient," raising his hand

---

[8] Taken from the hymn, "How Firm a Foundation," by Kirkham, <u>Hymns</u>, p. 66.

61

in the air, "I promise you in the name of the Lord that you are going into dissolution. Now, let this house go and get out there and unload that truck."

There was no way that I had one word of defense. I scrambled to the door as fast as I could and ran out to the truck to unload. Bard followed me out to the shop, his railings continuing, "What good is a clean house if we starve to death? It's your duty to support my family and I can't afford for you to play around doing Zosa's work." He continued even more emphatically, "I'm putting you in the position of being the support of my family. This is the mission that the Lord has for you at this time. This is the most important thing that you can concern yourself with."

"Well, are you going to help me?"

"It's not for you to worry whether I help you or not. If I help you, fine. If I am doing more important things, then that's my business. I'm out trying to bring other women into the family. That's more important than putting bottles in the sink."

He was standing in my way. "Excuse me. I've got to put the cases right there." We were taught in meetings almost every other Sunday that the man is the lawgiver to his family. Saying no more, I continued working as fast as I could. Bard helped me for a while then returned to the house. I contemplated over what had just been said. I thought, "Well, if this is what God wants me to do, then God will help me. He'll send angels if he has to. I know he will." I asked myself, "Are you a quitter? No, I'm not a quitter. I'll do it, even if I fall over dead."

So in time I became very efficient in the duties of the bottle business. I came in the house one afternoon and looked at the filth. Zosa had locked herself in her room and had been there for hours, which was common. I felt like screaming to release some of the anger. Having to live in such filth was a real trial! A longing to communicate with Mrs. Ren was overwhelming as I went to a corner in the front room and sat down to make a little card for Mrs. Ren. It was 7:30 p.m. I had not seen Mrs. Ren in nearly two years. I folded a piece of paper and looking at one of Nanas' plates, I drew a rose on the front and put a little message inside.

When Bard and Nanas came home, Bard asked what I had been doing so I showed them the card. He hollered, "So that's what you do when we're not here. You can't be trusted alone. You waste your time and neglect your work."

I was shocked that they would be so provoked over what I thought was such a trivial thing. And it was not as if I had done nothing all day.

62

Nanas started in on me, "You could have had all this ironing done in that amount of time."

Bard butted in, "No, she could have had that truck unloaded and all the rings and lids taken off."

"Well, hell. If she has time to play around with drawing pictures, she could have done the ironing."

"She hadn't better try it again," Bard yelled while grabbing the note from out of my hand. "Oh, look at this. How nice what she's wrote," as he began to read it in a mocking fashion. "'Howdy neighbor.' She's not your neighbor anymore," he added with a gruff voice. Then he continued, "'How's that sweet little lady doing today? I miss you a bunch. I think about the times we went for a walk or was working in the garden.' Oh, pooh, pooh, pee doo," he adds. "'It was fun even when we was shoveling goat manure, just to be around your smiling face. I'm sorry I couldn't see you on your birthday or get you something, but I hope you enjoy this rose and when I'll see you, nobody knows. Love ya', Mazie.'"

Nan blurted out, "She'd rather shovel goat manure for Mrs. Ren than she would do anything for me."

Bard added, "All these damnable traditions she's got to get rid of. She thinks she's got to do something for someone just because she likes them, even if it's some old Catholic." In a commanding voice he shouted at me, "You must forget everything you learned before you came here and believe nothing or say nothing that does not conform with what I teach you. Anything or anyone that you knew or loved, you give 'em up. Do you understand? You're to love only those of my family. Why don't you tell Nanas you love her instead of this old woman?"

"Well can't I ever see her again?"

"You might see her at a distance, but the sooner you cut yourself off from her, the better off you're going to be. You can love me or Nanas. Even Zosa would like you to show her a little love." Then he ripped up the card. "Now get out there and get that truck unloaded before you're up until midnight getting the work done."

I dared not say anything. The contention was so thick in the house that you could cut it with a knife. I hurried from the front room past the kitchen table, and hitting my hip bone on a cast iron frying pan handle, "Owww." Then I pushed it out of my way. I could not get outside fast enough. As I unloaded the truck, I was thinking to myself about Bard's saying I was to give up every friend I used to have. I thought I had not called anyone or gone to see any of my old friends and they had just quit trying to make contact with me a long time ago. So, now Mrs. Ren would probably forget me too because they forbid me from even phoning her. As a last resort to communication, I said in my mind, "I love you, Mrs. Ren, and I hope you know it. I didn't forget you just because I moved away. When you're sitting in your big chair crocheting, I hope you remember me." I wiped a tear from my eye and hoped that somehow she would get my message.

I kept working in the shop until after 11 o'clock so I could bring myself to try to forget the whole mess and start over. Then I finally had guts enough to go back into the house. I took care of Nanas and retired for the evening.

That night I found myself caught up in a dream or nightmare. It was like I had a job to do in the basement of that old house. It was dark and dingy with cobwebs hanging from the bare floor joists. With the cobwebs and it being so dark, I could hardly make out anything as I walked very carefully back to the coal room about 25 feet away where I would load up my arms with something and carry it back to the bottom of the stairs. I tried not to disturb in the slightest any of those hanging cobwebs that went every which direction. As I made these trips back and forth, I noticed several huge black widow spiders as large as both fists. They were watching every move I made as though waiting for their chance to spring upon me with their deadly fate. I moved so slowly I scarcely dared breathe until I woke in a sweat.

I got up and turned on the light but the nightmare was so clear, it would not leave my mind. I knelt to pray, "Dear Father in heaven. Please remove that horrible nightmare and let peace take its place. I pray in the name of Jesus Christ, amen." I tried to concentrate on something nice until I went back to sleep. This identical nightmare would plague my nights to the extent of reoccurring two or three times a week.

One day while I was working in the bottle barn, Will came out and said that he had won a radio. "Can I have your old one?" I asked very excitedly.

"Well, I guess so."

"All right! Thank you." I plugged it in so I could have a little music. I whistled and tried to keep step while washing bottles to the tune of "The Orange Blossom Special."

Bard said, "Man, are you fast! I'm going to get Zosa to help me keep up."

I had developed a little bounce to each step for a kind of an exercise for my legs so that I would not get varicose veins or whatever I might get from being on my feet all day. The radio was a definite improvement.

64

CHAPTER 4

For two weeks every time I went in the house, Nan would bring up that card I had made for Mrs. Ren and start harping on it. I had sent all my art supplies to the dump already and I had said I was sorry several times. So I could not understand why she kept up her railing. By the tone of her voice and repetition of her complaints, one would have thought I had committed some grand crime.

I looked at her after I had endured it for two weeks straight and said, "You're trying to drive me crazy, aren't ya'? Like, that's been two weeks ago and you're acting like I can't be forgiven and start over. What the hell is the matter with you anyway? Are you jealous or something?"

"Jealous, huh! Hell, I'm not jealous," she ranted on. "You're such a baby, no wonder they always called you 'Baby May' all your life. You've never grown up yet. Now I've got the damn job of trying to make a woman out of you."

"Well, what do you want me to do that I'm not doing? Huh? Come on. Tell me. There's something aggravating you, so what do you want me to do?"

"Go mildew," was her reply as she turned on her heel and left the room.

I did not think that was very cute but it ended the argument. I started some ironing while Nanas sat down at the sewing machine. Bard came in and turned a chair around with his back to the wall and was reading a little. Then he put the book down and stated, "Nanas has done enough work when she lived with Uncle Clarence that she has earned the right to a celestial glory if she never touched another stitch of work again as long as she lives. I promised her from the day of our marriage that when I got other women that they would wait on her and treat her with the respect she deserves. That's why I won't put up with any one of you calling her a liar or showing any other disrespect. If I did, I would have to answer to Uncle Clarence, her first husband, who was a member of the priesthood council. I have to see to it that she is treated right. Not just any woman can have that place. Nanas was born of a royal birthright to start with, and that entitles a woman to a position in a man's family right there. Just like Rebecca, Clarence's daughter. When she comes into my family--if she ever does-- she will be over Zosa and May just because of her birthright. Even Zosa is over May because her father did marry her mother by the laws of the land. Also, Zosa's grandfather lived the principle."

"Well," I asked, "what about where it says that a person is not responsible for the crimes of their father or mother but for their own?"

"That's fine. I'm not saying you're condemned. I'm just saying that you never will hold a high place in my family because of it. If you were a chosen spirit on the other side, God would have sent you down here through a chosen lineage."

He was trying to make me feel like green slime on the floor because Mother and Father did not have a priesthood marriage. I remained quiet for quite some time. Then I got up courage to say, "Well, all I can do is all that I'm able to do. I can only do so much and I guess it really doesn't matter who dictates my jobs to me. If I can do the job honorably, God will judge me and say where I go in the end. I'm not going to worry about it." It took all the courage I could muster to stick up for myself, feeling somewhat shaky. I was crying a little bit inside, but would not let on that I was offended. I made an excuse to go outside and was excused. I went to the bottom of the barn and hid myself in a dark corner and plead my heart out to God:

"Oh, Father. What am I? Who am I? Am I a freak? Am I a malfunction?" As I gritted my teeth and wept bitter tears, I remained in silence for some time. As I was searching my mind and my soul, then I uttered, "Anyway, I do love You and I love the brethren and I love the truth." As I knelt there sobbing, I felt as though I had received deep puncture wounds in my soul that left me bleeding and no way to stop my loss of blood, as I weakened and fell to the floor with such sorrow to think that I might never be on the right hand of God with the Saints. As I lay there after a while, a peace came over me that seemed to erase the memory of any sting or pain as the thought came to me, "Why should I cry? It is my nature to be a servant and God will give me knowledge and strength. Why should I care if I serve all I can with all my strength and see to it that I do my best, whatever the job is, until I am dead? I'm not afraid of dying. Then God will judge and do what He wants with me. He made me so whatever my position is, it is OK."   With this thought repeating itself in my mind, I gradually gained strength. Then I heard footsteps upstairs and quickly got up and dusted the dirt off my clothes. Wiping my eyes I ran over to the boiler and blew off the steam so that it would sound like I had a reason for being down there.

When I came up to the top of the barn, Bard was standing there. The goat that Nanas and Will got from the auction was bawling wanting Nan to milk it. I looked at it and said, "I wonder if I should learn to milk the goat. It's been bawling there for about two hours. I'm going to ask Nan if it is all right. Is that OK with you?"

"I don't care."

I hurried to the house, "Nan, is it all right with you if I learn to milk the goat?"

"I don't care. Go ahead."

66

"Fine. I will," as I grabbed the milk bucket and went back to the nanny. "OK, Gretel, it's OK. I come to take care of you," as I stroked her fur and knelt down to give her a hug. "I get to milk you. Isn't that neat? OK. Now, hold still. I'm just new at this," as I began to make the milk flow. Tears again filled my eyes. "God made you and I'm doing you some good and you like me, don't you?" She looked at me and I hugged her again. "I'm so glad we got you," I said. Then I put the bucket of milk on the fence and scooped out a canful of chicken feed. I gave Gretel a handful then called, "Here, chick, chick," as the chickens ran toward me and I showered grain over the ground. "You cute little things. I'm so glad we got you too. Come on Gertrude," I called to a little pet hen who was running as fast as she could to get in on all these goodies. Then I looked up into the apple tree. Since it was dark, my little pet pigeon was not noticing that there was grain on the ground. I shook the branch a little, "Come on baby. You've got to get in on this deal too." She opened her eyes and flew down to eat with the chickens. "Thank you, God, for all my little friends." I stood there watching them as it got darker and darker.

Then the door opened at the house. A hard, demanding call was made, "May, get in here." I swallowed and stood there with a blank stare on my face as I made my feet walk toward the house. Oh dear, what now? As I entered the kitchen, there was Nanas with her hands on her hips and her frown obvious, and Bard looking like he was ready for battle.

Bard snarled, "You used the phone today without permission. Who did you call?"

"Uh, well, I didn't call anybody. Mom called. I just answered the phone. She was telling me that Walt was really sick and she didn't know if he was going to die or not."

"Is that all?"

"Yes."

"Well, Nan. Why didn't you just ask May? She'd have just told you if you didn't know who she was talking to."

"I'd rather you ask her yourself if you want to know. I don't care who she talks to. I just know she was on the phone and she didn't ask me if she could use it. That's all I know."

"Well, why don't you call Edith and see how Walt is. Maybe we ought to go see him tonight."

I spoke up, "Yeah, maybe we ought to. Maybe we can help him or take him to the hospital or something."

"Yeah, Nan. Let's go see him," Bard said. "Call Edith and let her know that we're coming."

Nan called and we went there. Walt was dying. I do not know what they were talking about in the kitchen--Bard, Nan and Mother. I was in the front room rubbing some pan oil Watkins liniment on Walt's back. I made him some orange juice and helped him drink it.

Anyway, Bard and Nanas did not take Walt to the hospital and two days later Walt died. Nanas made the arrangements to have him buried. Three days after the funeral, Bard and Nanas and I went over to see Mother.

"You know, Edith," Bard said, "if you'd turn the equity you have in this house over to us, you could just come and stay in our house and work in the business, then you wouldn't have to worry about paying the bills and living alone."

"I don't like living alone. You know. That just might be an idea. So I'd just come and work there with you guys and then it would be like a life estate, huh? Like, instead of having a life estate here, I would have one over there. I think I like that idea. I could work there with May. Yes, let's do it."

So, a few days later, Nanas got the papers together and Mama signed her property over to them. Then she came to live with us. I liked the idea, too. Mom was given the job of putting the jugs in the vat to help me wash bottles. But Mother told Bard that she had no intention of ever marrying him. She just wanted to live there and help in his family.

I turned 18 shortly after Mother came to live with us. Bard told Nanas to set up an appointment with Brother Mann to marry me to Bard. He had taken Zosa to wife just two weeks before, then he said, "Today's the day. Get yourself ready." I knew it was the day but I did not know what time the appointment was for. I had been working in the bottles.

There was no joy, no anticipation or anything to look forward to. Unlike other people, I had no desire to kiss him or sing love songs or anything of the type. How can I describe anything so dreary. But I loved the thought of being obedient to priesthood counsel. I thought by obedience I might earn the right to be numbered with the saints. My life did not mean much to me, only for the good I could do to help in the priesthood work. By that time Bard and Nan had managed to convince me that this was Brother Mann's counsel. I felt that Brother Mann's counsel was the word of the Lord to me.

I went upstairs and put on my white blouse with fancy lace in front and my green suit I had found at the Magna dump and had sent to the cleaners and shined my shoes and combed my hair with waves in front and a braided bun in back. Then I went downstairs with a feeling of sacrifice.

"To do God's will, not mine," I thought. "Christ didn't want to be nailed to the cross, but God's will was more important." A cold shiver went down my backbone as I said, "I'm ready."

Then all during the ceremony that took place in Brother Mann's living room, I was saying to God in my mind, "Please give me strength and guidance." Then Brother Mann looked at me when it was all said and done. I did not even kiss Bard then. I said to Mann, "I hope I can endure," with a very sober expression.

He laughed, "What a funny thing for someone to say who's just gotten married." I failed to see the humor as I was dead serious.

CHAPTER 5

Two weeks later Bard began to spend much of his time doing what he called "his job" to keep everyone in line. He sat in the kitchen with his chair standing on its two back legs, with his back against the wall, with his <u>Journal of Discourses</u> in his hands. Zosa was doing the dishes and I was folding the clothes I had brought in from the line.

Looking at Bard one would notice his one hand down inside the front of his pants, apparently fondling his privates as he often would do. His complexion was naturally red most of the time. He began to read on page 99, Volume 25:

> Why should we need further proof that Joseph Smith was a prophet or that his predictions are being fulfilled? Why should it be necessary to prove that the word of God has come to the world through him and that the world is indispensible?[9]

He paused there from reading and declared, "My mission is like unto the Prophet's. The Lord has given me a promise that whatever I will bless, he will bless. And whatever I will curse, he will curse. Every time I have told anyone what the Lord wanted them to do and they did not follow that command, they have lived to regret it. I can name hundreds of instances where people just refused to do the mind and will of God and they will reap damnation for it."

I came over by his side while he would find something else and read it. I was looking at the words so as to follow him and I noticed that he would say a different word than that which was in the book. Noticing it happening quite often, I opened my mouth, "Well, that's not what it says at all. You're pretending like you're reading it, but you ain't."

"Never mind. I know the way to read this book and I don't need you to correct me either. Just shut up and sit down. You might learn something."

"Well, why can't you just read it the way the Prophet spoke it? Heck, we'd like to know what they said."

"I put the words in there the way they need to be to put over a point so you get the correction you need. You don't get what was pertaining to someone else a hundred years ago."

---

[9] <u>The Journal of Discourses</u>, p. 99.

He went on. "Even when you go to meeting, it's for you to come home and come to me and I'll give you a correct interpretation of what was said so you don't get some screwy idea from something you heard in church. My family treats lightly what I tell them. That's why everyone here has so many accidents Will with his arm, Zosa with her leg, Nanas being hit by a car, and May's hand being scalded. Just because you're all disobedient and you treat lightly the things of God."

Whirling his fist in the air with a loud declaration of speech, "The whole church was brought under condemnation for the same damn crime: treating lightly the things of God, and the Lord is not pleased with it. I keep telling you over and over again. Now, what will it take to make you straighten up? Will someone have to lose their life over it?"

Similar sessions would go on regularly. We heard this doctrine so often, we all had it memorized. But I do not recall even one time when I had any type of accident a cut, a burn, stepping on a nail, or whatever that he did not remind me of some little thing that he had told me to do that I had not done to perfection and that was the reason for my accident.

I feared being disobedient, to say the least, because I heard this so many, many times. I would shake when he would even come towards me not knowing what would happen next.

I had been with the family for over two years giving all my labor without pay while all the monies were counted on Nanas', Bard's and Will's income taxes and Social Security, like Mom and I didn't even exist.

Bard was still preaching. "If anyone here desires to leave for any reason, they will walk out of here with only the shirt on their back."

"But what about if they turned over land or a house like Mama. Then what?"

"I don't care. It's the same whether they put in $50,000 or five cents. It makes no difference. I'm not going to reward someone if they choose to apostatize. I'd just tell the brethren that they had turned traitor to the work."

I looked at Bard, "It's time to milk my goats. Can I leave?"

"Well, hurry. I'm not through."

Quickly leaving the room, I ran through the yard to get my milk bucket and scrambled toward the pasture. This pasture consisted of five acres of trees, several ponds fed by flowing wells, grass, herbs and wild flowers everywhere. Stopping to take a pinch of fresh watercress by a flowing well, I noticed a friendly little frog sitting proudly on the bank. "Hi. How ya' doin', little feller?" I felt such joy to be in the field far away from the house where the sun was shining and my goaties were getting fat from the abundance of feed.

"Ah," I sighed, as I looked to the heavens. "What a beautiful day." As I walked with a little bounce to my step towards my milk goat, "How ya' doin'?" as I stroked her fur. "Everything OK out here?" as I sat on my foot behind me. The milk was hitting the inside of my bucket. She turned and licked me behind my ear. "OK. OK. I know you love me." And springing to my feet, "Thank you." whistling a tune on my way to my other little friends.

When all the goats were milked (I had five), I was on my way back to the house and noticed a mother hen that I knew had seven babies. I watched her teaching them to find little things to eat as I smiled and counted them again. There were only six! "Did you lose one of your babies?" Feeling sorry when I was passing an old lumber pile, I heard a "Peep, peep." I put down my bucket and climbed the fence. I followed the little "peep" and thought, "He's right here." So I began carefully to remove one board at a time. I think the noise scared him because I seemed to move over one-half the pile before I caught him. "There you are, you cute little thing. Let's take you back to your mommy. She's been wondering about you."

Then I returned to the house. Bard sat there still full of fire, "What the hell takes you so long to milk a few goats?"

"One of the little chickens was lost under the woodpile. I had to find him."

"Well, you should be here hearing something that will help you to get your exaltation, if you will just follow it. The only reason the Lord has been blessing us as a family at all is because of my prayers. I petition the Lord day and night to forgive you for treating lightly what I have been telling you, but I don't know how much longer I can hold back the wrath of God from coming on this family. The prophets since time began have been treated with impunity while they alone held the keys and the powers of heaven over their dispensation."

I thought on that statement and sure enough, that's the truth. And the people didn't like the prophets either. I thought, "But they should have been obedient anyway so that God would have spared them from destruction."

Bard went on preaching while I sat there silently, then I blurted out what was on my mind, "Well, what if your leader teaches you something and you follow him and it's wrong and you're doing it 'cause you don't know it's wrong?"

"Huh," he grunted. "You can't judge your leaders. God put them over you, not under you. Can the lesser judge the higher? What kind of order would God have if everyone was doing their own damn will instead of God's? It's for you to follow your leaders and God will hold them accountable. Even though you may be learning and steadily going up the ladder, your leaders are learning also and they are going up ahead of you still, so that you never can catch up. Where I am now, you may be 20 years from now, but I will be just that much higher. Now if everyone were allowed to just do their own will, heaven would be made into a hell in a hurry, wouldn't it. The order of heaven always has been and always will be: God speaks to the head of the house and then man speaks to the tail. God doesn't ever come directly to the tail. You get it? If I were to lead you wrong and you followed me, you would go into heaven for obedience and the fault, if any, would be on my head. What you need to worry about is being obedient. You never will be able to judge me. Never," his eyes seeming to drill a hole through me.

Then he started hollering, "Now because Edith has come to live with us, I want everyone here to know that just because she is older than Nanas, that doesn't make her on the same level," turning to Mother with his finger pointing at her. "Don't you try to boss anyone when it's not your place."

"Well, Bard. I don't try to boss anyone. I just do my own job and that's it."

Nan blurted in, "Yes you do. You try to boss Zosa when I'm not here. And you always get May to do your work for you. I'm the boss over these women, not you. You get out of my position and stay out."

Bard stared at me, "I want you to quit obeying your mother. You are to obey Nanas, not Edith. For the adultery she has committed on the prairie to have her children, she doesn't deserve any praise. She needs to be recognized for what she is. She never had any more of a marriage than a dog or a cat, and she thinks God will accept it?" shouting at Mother as he slammed his fist down on the sideboard. "HE WON'T! He won't accept nonesuch." He turned to look at me, "I want you to call Nanas 'mother.' She is worthy of the name. But this old bitch is not. Do you understand?"

The impact of his voice almost nailed me to the wall. I stood there with my mind blank and did not know what to say. I always had wished Daddy would have grabbed Mother and taken her to the priesthood to get married. I had wished that all my life, but I had never thought of Mother as a bitch. A quivering, sickening feeling came over me as I had to listen to everything that he had to say about Mom. As he continued to rail on, "You call her 'Edith.' That's a good enough name for this old slut. That's what the Lord would call her. She can go on lying that God will accept her marriage just because she done it in sincerity. Why even the devils in hell are sincere. You know it?"

"Well, Bard, we tried to live honorably. But it was hard to know where the priesthood keys were. Joseph was studying to try and find that out. Our intentions were good."

74

"Hell is full of devils that had good intentions like you. God doesn't honor it in the least degree. May never will be free from your sin until she can put you down and recognize what you are, but as long as she thinks you're a somebody, she can't advance herself. The first step to perfection is to repent of your sins. Now how are you going to repent of a sin if you can't even recognize it? You first have to recognize it then you've got to be sorry then admit it and then forsake it, and never pick up that sin again."

Bard looked directly at me, "You have got to first recognize what your mother is. She is an adulterous woman. Then you must feel sorry over it. If you don't, you should. If you had any idea how your exaltation is hanging by a thread of whether you can recognize these things, you would feel damn sorry. Then you need to admit it. Quit telling yourself that you love her."

Then with his fist slamming down again on the sideboard, "THEN FORSAKE HER!" He pulled out The Bible and began reading where if a branch is dead, you cut it off lest the whole tree go into the fire. "If you don't cut yourself off, you will go to hell with her."

"Well, uh, what about the part where a child should honor their father and mother?" I asked.

"That is referring to a mother worthy of honoring, like Nanas. Her children can call her mother all day long, and that's just fine, but Edith is not a fit mother because she has denied the priesthood by taking authority to herself to marry herself to that old boy she had affairs with on the prairie (meaning my father)."

Mom tightened both her fists and stamped her foot on the floor, "I have not denied the priesthood, Bard. You lie when you say I have. I have always loved them and tried to do what they say. I wanted the priesthood to marry Joseph and me, but he couldn't figure out if they had the authority or not." Mom's voice dropped quite low, almost a mumble. "I don't know. Maybe he was kinda' stupid in that respect. If he had just taken me, we could have had things right and it would have saved us a lot of problems." She boldly declared then, "But he studied the priesthood's teachings and he told me before he died for me not to surrender so much as my little finger to anything except the teachings of Joseph White Musser, and I haven't. So there! Now, if you'll move yourself, I'll get the pig bucket. I've got to feed the pigs." Bard stood up and moved his chair. Mom took the bucket and went outdoors.

"All of you, with the exception of Nanas, are outcasts from the priesthood work. I'm trying to redeem you, even if the priesthood council has given up. Brother Guy has told me many times 'if anyone can do anything for them--meaning you people--you can.'" Bard was twiddling his thumbs while his hands were resting upon his belly with his chair leaned against the wall. Out of the corner of his eyes, he looked at Will as he said, "The priesthood had given up on Will because of the trouble Will stirred up with several women in Short Creek. They were ready to kick him out of town. And if I had not taken him in, he'd most likely have apostatized."

Will said nothing. The room was somewhat quiet for a time, then Bard, looking at Zosa, said, "No one would want Zosa. It's plain to see she's not all there."

Zosa had a frown on her face a mile long. "Gee, thanks. Thanks for letting me know what you think," as tears formed in her eyes.

"Well, it's true. I didn't say that I didn't love you," rubbing his hand across his bald head. "But I can't lie just to make you happy. If you weren't half cracked, you'd get in and do something in a day rather than sit around sulking. You'd also take a bath once in a while instead of being so damn filthy. But I'm glad you're here. I just know that no one else would put up with you. You'd probably end up in the nut house."

At that Zosa flared up and barked back, "Why should I do anything? If I do something, Nan says its wrong and if I don't she's mad. Hell, Bard. How would you feel if you were getting beat all the time?"

"That shouldn't stop you from doing your work if you wanted to."

The door knob turned. Mama came in from feeding the pigs. Holding her hands out away from her dress, she said, "Excuse me," as she walked in front of Bard. "My hands stink."

He looked at the muck on her hands and arms from the chore. A smirk crossed his face as he said, "That's a good job for you. It's one pig feeding another."

"You just pipe down. That's not a bit cute," Mom said while washing her hands.

Will got up. "Nan and I are going to a dance. There's a couple of girls there I been watching pretty close. Maybe the one girl will become my wife or both. They seem to like me."

Bard leaned forward as the two front legs of his chair hit the floor. "Well, if they come towards this direction, you'd better let me meet them before you get your heart set. Because you're better looking than I am, it would work well for you to get the fish on the line and then let me see if I want them or not."

"I don't know if they're that far along. I haven't said much about religion."

"Well, take your time with them. Get them to fall in love with you first or you'll be dead in the water."

This went on until after 11 o'clock. I left the room thinking, "What IS right? I know Mom has taught me to uphold the priesthood all my life. She has preached to me time and again how valuable they are to us." I tried to put it from my mind, placing it on the shelf and asking God for understanding that I might know what truth is in time, as I sure can't change the past.

About this time I had been married approximately three months. One day after all the work was done, I needed to sew a rip in one of my skirts and had settled down in a recliner in the front room. It was 9:30 and I felt the need for more rest. Bard approached me with a gruff voice, "Are you ready to go to bed?"

"Actually, I'd rather sleep by myself. There are enough beds in this house. I'd really rather not sleep with you tonight. Is that all right?"

"Oh. You don't want to sleep with me, huh? Well, you'd better get something in your head, the sooner the better." His breath was beating down upon me in such a way as I would never forget. "You WILL sleep with me and anytime you get to where you don't want to, I will put you down as the LOWEST person in my family and you will be made to feel it. You will be put down lower than a concubine." I was already put down lower than anyone except Mama. He considered her to be a concubine.

In my understanding that meant that anyone could beat me that wanted to and I would be deprived of food, anything that was good, and I would be made to clean up all the filthy jobs (like when Bard would mess his underwear). Also, I would be made to do the heavy lifting like carrying the water out of the basement in buckets just because he wanted it done like that because that was just the way he treated Mother on account of her refusing to marry him.

I said nothing while picking up my sewing and making my way upstairs to the attic to his bedroom. Totally shocked at his answer, heartsick and confounded, I laid myself down in the bed. Then Bard snuggled up to me and in a low voice, as if attempting to apologize, "Just don't ever defy me, honey. I'll be good to you. I'll let you have a little more rest. OK? You can go to sleep now, but I want to wake you up later. Is that alright?"

Bard would demand that I take care of him sexually three to five times per night. He would sleep during the day while I worked. So at four in the morning, after he became somewhat satisfied, he turned to me, "Well, you'd better get up and get the cases cleaned." It was my job to go through the boxes to clean them up before we put clean jugs in them. I lay there in silence. How nice it would be to get a little more rest.

His voice became sharper, "Get up. Come on. Get out there and get your work done." Then pausing a moment he added, "I'll get you up." Coming across with a much quieter tone accompanied by a hideous giggle, he swung his legs up so as to place his feet in the center of my back and applied steady pressure, and as I was pushed from the bed, I caught myself from falling. There was no use. I did need to clean the cases.

So I got dressed quickly and scrambled downstairs to meet the day. As my face was embraced by the fresh morning air, I breathed deeply. The joy of leaving the jobs of the night and beginning a new day put a slight smile on my face, as I hurried to the bottle barn to get every necessary thing ready for cleaning jugs.

When Bard came down to the shop approximately four hours later, I had started a batch of bottles. Mother had gotten up and was putting them in the vat for me. I was wondering but I did not know if I dared ask. After a while I turned to Bard, "You know, sometimes I wonder why you treat me the way you do."

Sensing what I was referring to, he replied, "Well, any man that had you would treat you exactly the same way I do."

"You think so?"

"I know so. Women are a dime a dozen. The only thing that makes them of any value is if they can be obedient."

I stopped washing jugs to pay attention to what he was saying.

"If a man never required anything of his women, he would be held responsible for their being worthless. No real Saint ever did have an easy life. So, do you think you are going to go to heaven without ever earning the privilege of being there? You're not. The early pioneers went through more than anything you've been asked to go through, and if you're not obedient enough, I can't take you where the Saints are. Take Edith over there. She is so damned disobedient. She's as worthless as teats on a boar pig. She isn't even worth her salt."

He walked towards Mother then grabbed her by her hair on the top of her head and gave it a few yanks, just enough to make her holler, then let her go. While staring at Mom with his beady eyes, "I'd be just as far along if I didn't have her."

"Now, Bard. You just keep your hands to yourself," Mom said as she threw her hands up to stop him. "I'm trying to help May anyway."

"Yes, and a very damned little bit of help at that."

After a while I interrupted throwing a word in edgeways, "Bard, before we came here you didn't used to treat us the way you do now. So how come it's different?"

Bard began to laugh, "Ha, ha, ha, ha, ha! That's a good one. Let me answer you in this way. Have you ever heard of a man trying to catch a fish that he has already caught? He uses the bait for those who are yet swimming around, doesn't he. Ha, ha, ha. What a silly question."

"I pondered on that a moment then said, "Yeah, I guess that's true." Mom and I stopped talking so maybe he would leave, and he did.

As the day's temperatures increased, Mom and I had been working over the boiling water for nearly five hours and were nearly finished with a batch. The bottle barn had all the windows boarded up. There was an inspecting light we could see by and also the double doors were open. It still seemed somewhat dark in the shop, but straight ahead about 10 feet of the rinse tubs was a large solid picture window. Nearly delirious from the heat and fatigue, I glanced up and looked through this window that was facing the street (5th East). A young man was riding his bicycle with his swimming paraphernalia across his shoulders, casually going by, eating an ice cream cone. I stopped working to watch him pass. I stood there with sweat running from every pore of my body. Staring as though I had been hit in the face with a steel frying pan, a feeling of hopelessness took over as I found myself caught up in a daydream. Then a lump began forming in my throat as I began to cry inside, while the thought came across my mind, "Someday, someday I will be considered valuable, like a prize, and I will be paid a decent wage for my efforts, too."

Mother, noticing I had just been standing for some time, said in a sweet voice, "Come on, May. Let's finish."

"Yeah. Let's get this over with."

We went in the house for a bite to eat. Mother and I were sitting at the table eating a bowl of Zosa's fresh rice pudding, hot from the oven. Nan was sitting in the front room on the couch crocheting a doily. Bard asked, "Did you get all those through?"

"Yeah, we did," I answered. "Will can deliver that load anytime. The truck is all loaded ready to go."

"How many is there?"

"One hundred and five."

"That's pretty good. I wished everyone was as obedient as May. Boy, I'd really get somewhere."

Mom spoke up, "Well, what about me? Don't you appreciate what I've done?"

"Ah, hell. You're not much help."

I jumped in, "Well I betcha what. She saves me one-third of my time anyway."

"Well, hell. If she amounted to something, the system would go twice as fast, but she doesn't."

"Well, I appreciate her anyway. I'll tell you that."

"Yeah. Just because she's your mother, you stick up for this lazy old bitch."

I had heard enough. It seemed as though Bard would delight in railing on Mother's adultery until it was just the most obnoxious thing. I left the house. Pester, my cat, met me in the driveway, rubbing her body against my legs. "Hello, you sweet thing," as I bent over to pick her up. I carried her to the goat shed stroking her fur while I sat on a bale of hay brushing my face against hers. "I sure do like you, Pester. You know that? You're a darling little kitty spirit." I closed my eyes for a moment while I leaned against the haystack as I went into a daydream. It was late afternoon and the sun was setting.

I was remembering a dream where I had heard beautiful music. I wanted to sing something so I started singing a hymn,

> There's surely somewhere a lowly place,
> In earth's harvest fields so wide,
> Where I may labor through life's short day
> For Jesus, the crucified;
> So trusting my all to thy tender care,
> And knowing thou lovest me,
> I'll do thy will with a heart sincere;
> I'll be what you want me to be.
> I'll go where you want me to go, dear Lord,
> Over mountain, or plain, or sea.
> I'll say what you want me to say, dear Lord;
> I'll be what you want me to be."[10]

I hugged my little friend, "Thank heavens for kittens. I sure do like you," I repeated, while setting her down so I could give the goat some hay. Then I picked her up again while I whistled the music to that song on my way back to the house.

Over the days and weeks the contention was continual. One morning Mother and I were in the front room. I had combed her hair and was braiding it. Bard came in and saw us. Being quick to rebuke me for showing any kindness to Mother, he yelled at me with fire in his eyes, "What are you doing her hair for when I've told you not to be doing anything for this woman?" He walked up to me and slapped my arm, knocking my hand off Mom's braid. "You let her do her own hair. You shouldn't want to do anything for her or even touch her any more than you would want to do it for the devil in hell."

My heart was going like crazy. Mother's hair was finished. I backed against the wall. The force of his word was so loud, it just about knocked me over. He was hovering over Mother, the saliva flying from his mouth making Mom blink her eyes, while her upper lip was pulled down tight toward her chin. As he continued his railing, "You're just as bad as Lucifer, and that's what I'll call you. I don't want

---

[10] "I'll Go Where You Want Me to Go," text by Mary Brown, music by Carrie E. Rounsefell, <u>Hymns</u>, p. 75.

anyone in my home thinking you're a Saint or patterning their life after you. And I don't want you talking to my women, teaching them to be a devil like yourself, Miss Lucifer."

"Now, Bard. You just pipe down. I don't go around calling you names. You act just like I go around making trouble. I don't."

"Well, I want you recognized for what you are so you don't go around deceiving anyone by your pretty face." He grabbed her by the cheek shaking her head. Mom's hand went up against his in an attempt to get his hand away.

"You don't need to touch me. I don't want you to touch me."

"I'll do anything I feel like to you. And so will anyone else, you old devil."

"You act just like you don't have anything better to do than to rail on me and I'm sick of hearing all this."

Bard's voice heavy in rebuke, "It will be shouted from the housetops before you're through, and everyone will know what you are, Miss Lucifer."

"Why do you keep calling me a devil? I'm not the devil. I don't want a thing to do with him. Just get him away from me as far as you can."

"You have betrayed God the same way the devil did. If a person does the same thing as the devil, doesn't that put them in the same category? It does. God's no respecter of persons and you're not one bit better for your wrongs than he is for his. Until you can hate your wrongs enough to where you can atone for them, you never can be forgiven. You have got to recognize the sin you have committed on the prairie that God had nothing to do with it. That it was just you and the old boy you shacked up with out there having a screwing good time. And that's all it was in the sight of God."

"Well, we had children, and I raised them the best I could anyway."

"Oh, pooh, pooh. That's nothing that any dog or cat couldn't do. So where are you any better? You have got to atone for your crime before you can ever be forgiven." He was still hovering over her and hollering with such impact that he almost lost his false teeth a couple of times. "And for you to atone, you would have to take your son, Rod, who you love so much, and put his head on a chopping block. And you, Edith, whether you like it or not, would have to swing the axe. Then after you had done that, you never would go around telling anybody that what you done out there had anything to do with God. And until you can bring yourself to do that, all your words of how you've repented is just a lot of hot air. It doesn't mean a thing. If God allowed you to walk into heaven without atoning for your damnable crimes, he would be showing partiality. Why not just let the devil walk in scot free. He just as well as let you in."

I said, "Can I go? I got work to do."

"NO! You need to hear it as well as she does so you don't go treating her like some kinda' saint instead of the devil she is. If you don't quit it, you will carry the same curse on your head as she has on hers."

This type of preaching ran rampant. Every spare moment that Mom was not helping me, he would park himself in front of her and begin the same old thing again. Whether Mom was sleeping or eating or whether she was helping me, to say anything or do anything against his frame of mind would prove outright defiance.

I felt there was some truth to what he was saying but how much, I could not say. He claimed to have read all the Journals, the truth books, Joseph Musser's teachings, The Doctrine and Covenants, and The Book of Mormon. He said that he knew the laws of God forwards and backwards and that God had chosen him because he was not afraid to tell the truth like it is without beating around the bush. I knew I was unlearned, but I could sure see why Mom would not want to chop Rod's head off. I was fighting to keep down my resentment towards Bard's horrible attitude. I told myself, "I must not hate. If I ever do, it will destroy me."

I had found within myself an outburst like Rod had had. I did not want to ever have that type of character, for if I ever lost control, I could see myself maybe killing someone, which I never wanted to happen, no matter what.

I worked on my feelings to try to keep calm and level headed. "Uh, can I go now? I think I've heard enough."

"All right. You can be excused."

"Thank God," I said to myself, as I fled out the door. I could hardly stand it another second. I went straight to the bottle barn where I found a quiet corner and began to pour my heart out to God.

"Oh, Father in heaven. Please help me to control my feelings. I must have your help. Oh, please help me to remove this evil influence I have. I mind Bard and I know I have to do it, but I can hardly stand this tension. Please bless Mom, if you can, 'cause I'm glad I was born. I hope I don't have a curse on me. I pray for help in all things, in the name of Jesus Christ, our Redeemer, amen."

I got to calling my mother Edith to make Bard happy, but when I was to refer to Nanas as "Mother," I could not seem to make the words come out.

CHAPTER 6

A few weeks later one beautiful summer morning, I stepped outside of the house and breathed deeply some of that good country air. I walked over to where the apple trees were to see if I could find a nice one that the little worms had not polished off. I found a couple of good ones. While sitting on an old log next to a small pond near the house, I began to daydream, looking at the mud around the edge of the water. I had been thinking for about a month how it was a shame that all the clean jugs that I washed that had flaws in them. Why could they not just be broken, crushed and remelted, saving the glass? As I pondered over the idea, I thought, "Well, heck it would probably cost more for the gas to get the temperature high enough than it would be worth."

Nanas and Bard had said that the ground around there was clay. I was thinking about how I had seen a show on the Indians making pottery with clay. I wondered, "Is this the kind of soil?" So I bent over and took a handful of the thicker mud and formed it into the shape of a bowl, then wet the surface so it was slick and finished, then I placed it on an old board. Bard came out just then and walked over to me, he asked, "What are you doing?"

"Well, I was just wondering if this clay is the kind they use for pottery."

"Ha, ha, ha," he went on. "You've never grown up. You're still making mud pies. Do you still play with paper dolls, too? Ha, ha, ha."

I went in to wash my hands and Nan said, "Mr. Mullen called. He needs your help at Old Mill Packing (a local food packing plant) today."

"All right," I shouted with glee and jumped for joy. I ran in to change into my better clothes. "I'm ready to go," I exclaimed.

"Well, Micron Chemical wants 30 cases delivered tomorrow so you'll have to do them when you get home if you want to work over there."

"OK. No problem."

So after working at Old Mill until 5 p.m., I came in the house. Nan was standing there with a pious expression and in a commanding tone, started saying, "Bestline Janitorial needs 50 cases first thing in the morning. So you have got to get 80 done tonight."

"Well, are you sure they can't wait until the afternoon or Friday?"

"NO, THEY CAN'T!" she screamed.

Then Bard chipped in, "The bottle orders come first. You're the one who wanted to work at Old Mill now you can do this too."

I was looking at Nanas and had a feeling, I really wouldn't put it past her to not even ask the company if they could wait a day, but it wasn't worth the argument. Besides, if they got mad, they would likely not let me work over there anymore, even though I was giving them all my earnings.

"Well, OK, if that's what I need to do, I will. But who's going to put them in the vat for me?"

"Bardell (Will's wife) can help you when you get started up until about 9 o'clock then Edith can help and maybe Willy will. We'll see."

Bard had been sleeping during the daytime as usual. Being fully refreshed and strengthened, he came out when Mother was helping me. Looking at me, Bard referred to my mother and asked, "Is this old devil doing her job?"

I was silent as I continued to work. While Bard would rail, it just seemed the best way to handle the situation would be to let him carry on without any contradictions in hopes he would become bored and eventually leave or maybe I could change the subject.

But Mother quite often would bear all she could then she would give him a piece of her mind which would prolong his being there.

"You're slower than cold tar in January," Bard pushed Mom. "Move over. I'll put them in. You take them off the end." (That meant stacking the clean jugs.)

"Well, that's all right, if you think you can do better than I can."

"I know I can do anything better than you can. Don't compare me with yourself. I'm not on your level, Miss Lucifer. I'll show you how it's done. You never do keep up with May. She always ends up doing half your work for you 'cause you're so damn slow."

"Well, I try anyway."

"The devil could try, too, and he'd be about as good--maybe even faster--than you are."

"Well, I'm not the devil and I resent you calling me that nasty name. I just resent it." Mom stood there with her fist doubled up with her arms by her side and slightly stomping her feet as she expressed herself.

"You're in the same category. You live the same life as the devil. So that makes you one, too."

Mom started interrupting, "Well, in Joseph's patriarchal blessing, it said he would accomplish much with his own two hands, so we would get by with the marriage we had until we could do something better. We were trying to learn about these things."

"That's just your justifying devil talking trying to justify your damn devilmentary. You thinking you're so great just because of a patriarchal blessing. God won't have anything to do with it." Bard raised his hand in the air in an attempt to put his hand to the square, "And I promise you that in the name of the Lord, Jesus Christ."

Oh dear. I looked out into the blackness of the night. The workings of Mom and Bard had stopped. All this kind of talk was sapping my strength. Mom was standing there braced against the end table leaning over backwards while looking up at Bard. He was hovering over her with his hand still to the square with hell fire written all over his face.

"I can't help what you say. I'm here and I'm trying to do the best that I can under the circumstances."

Then Bard grabbed a handful of Mother's hair on the top of her head and was shaking her head back and forth, "Well, your trying isn't good enough, Miss Lucifer," as he spit in her face.

Mother's hands flew up against him, "Oouhh, get away from me you filthy thing doing such a dirty trick, spitting on me." Mother started crying as she went for the water to wash it off.

Ugh. A creepy feeling that sent cold chills running down my spine. I turned and attempted to make peace, "We have a job to do. If you don't want to help us, why don't you just go back to bed. I don't mind taking the cases off the end. It'll be faster than we're going, whether she's a devil, I'm a devil, or who's a devil. It isn't going to get the work done if we don't get busy."

"She'd better get it in her head and not tell me how it is. I know how it is. I don't need this old devil to correct me."

"Bard, if you don't get out of here, I'm quitting. And you two can stay here and argue all night, but I'm tired."

He turned to me, "I'll tell you when you can quit and when you can't. I'm the boss here. You're not. And you'd better quit sticking up for your damned old mother."

I paused, "Look, Bard, are we getting anything done?"

"It's up to me whether we get anything done or if we stand here all night. I'm the priesthood over this home."

We stood there looking at each other, then in a gentle voice I said, "Well, that's fine, but would you please leave us two devils alone so we can get this job done. You're probably tired and we can do it OK."

Then Bard softened somewhat and said, "Well, if you're going to be so damn nice about it, then OK." He left.

I sighed with relief. Talking it over with Mom, I said, "You know what?"

"What?"

"If you could just stand to listen to him without saying anything back, he might feel like he's talking to himself and leave quicker because it would be boring for him."

"Yeah, I know, May. But I just can't stand the way he treats me." She shook all over. "He needs to be told."

"True, but you ain't goin' to change his mind. He'll have his way anyway."

"I know it."

The next day I went with Nanas and Bard to make the delivery and the first thing out of the manager's mouth when he saw us walk in the door was, "Oh, gee, that was really quick. I didn't expect it so soon."

My heart sunk and I thought, as I looked over at Nanas out of the corner of my eye, "This lady appears to be so sweet, but why would she do that to me? Is there any logic?" Then I asked the manager, "Oh, I thought you needed them in a hurry."

"Oh, tomorrow would have been fine, but it's OK. Let's unload them over here."

A feeling of sorrow filled my heart. I could not imagine why she would want me to work into the night until two o'clock in the morning when it was not necessary.

Several months passed and I went to work at Old Mill again. I was hurrying in my usual rush at the factory. There was a little wad of mayonnaise base on the cement floor. I stepped on it and my right leg slipped sideways at the knee. As I came down, those working around me noticed the accident and came to help me.

"Owo! Owo! Owooo!"

"What happened?" everyone asked with excitement.

"I slipped. Ow. Ow."

They could see my leg was out sideways. I was suffering excruciating pain. One asked, "Should we take you to the clinic just down the road?"

I nodded, with tears flowing down my face. They took me down there as fast as they could. I was waited on and the knee was put into place, wrapped up nicely, and the doctor told me to stay off my leg and apply ice packs. Then a fellow employee took me home.

When Bard and Nanas found out that I had gone to a clinic instead of coming home, even though an insurance company was paying the bill, they became furious.

"You should have had them bring you home," Bard yelled at me. "Nanas could take care of you. You had no right going to someone else for your care."

In an attempt to defend myself, I stated, "They took me there. I couldn't say where I should go. I was too busy screaming and crying trying to stand the pain. Heck, I didn't know where I was going."

"Well, if it ever happens again, you'd better call home. Do you hear me?"

I sat there with a bleak feeling then murmured, "Well, I'm kinda' glad they took me there so the doctor could put it in place."

"Nanas could put it in just as good as any doctor. She's a registered nurse and THIS is where you belong. The only reason this happened is because of your sticking up for your damned old mother. You need to learn obedience or I don't know what God is going to do to you."

I was sitting there in pain and all he could think was that it was my fault that I got hurt. Not one ounce of kindness or even pity did he offer. I was so confused that I was sick to my stomach. I said, "Can I please lay down?" And because I could not get up the stairs, I went in the other room and laid on Will's bed, since he was gone.

I could hear Bard telling Zosa from the bathroom where the washing machine was that she was to wash all Mom's clothes, even her temple garments, in the last batch after everyone else's clothes were through. With the oldtime washer we had, the wash water was used many times before being dumped. A feeling came over me that was rather scary. I was remembering the priesthood brethren's teachings in meeting that the garment was not to even touch the floor, if possible. Now they are going to be washed in mop water, just because Bard said Mom was a devil and her garments were null and void in God's sight.

I lay there thinking about the crime of adultery and how important marriage was. My mind was in a turmoil, as I began to petition heaven, "Kind and good Father who is in heaven. I'm told to despise my mother but I don't feel good about it, and I know that Mom is not perfect, but she could have been lots worse than what she is and I'm thankful for her and I'm thankful she's here with us. I also ask for Your blessings to be upon the priesthood over this home that they will be inspired to know what thy mind and will is concerning us and that they will be able to guide us according to correct principle. This I humbly ask in the name of Jesus Christ, amen."

Three days later I was still hobbling around on crutches. I could not do a whole lot of work anyway, so I was resting on an old chair by the side of the house enjoying the sun. I heard a lot of yelling going on in the house, but I enjoyed the thought of not getting involved. After it seemed to have died down, I came in the house. I could see Mother in the bathroom crying, bent over the sink, washing her face. I hobbled in there and she turned towards me as I came closer. The whole left side of her face was black and blue. Her left eye was totally bloodshot.

"Awh! What happened?" I exclaimed.

"I was just sitting on the toilet when Bard came in and kicked me just as hard as he could to the side of my head."

"What the hell for?"

"He said he didn't want me talking to Zosa," she continued to cry.

"Oh, how sick." I went to find Bard. He was in the kitchen harping at Zosa while she was frying hamburger for supper. The table was cluttered and messy. His chair leaned against the wall as usual while he held The Journal of Discourses in his hand.

"I am your Lord," he shouted at Zosa. "If you think you will ever get to God by bypassing me, you're crazy. You have to go through me to even get to God. He recognizes the head of the home, not the tail."

"Bard," I rudely interrupted. "Why did you kick Edith?"

"I've told her a thousand times to quit talking to my family," he said, getting off his chair. I moved to one side to get out of his way. He was going toward the bathroom. "And here she is in there having a gab session with Zosa." We were now in the bathroom standing next to Mom. "AND I WANT IT STOPPED," he yelled to Mother at the top of his voice. Then he slammed his book on the top of her head.

Mother screamed, "Oh shit."

I yelled, "Give me that." Then I reached for the book and my crutch fell on the floor as I hopped toward him. Now yelling at the top of my voice, "WHAT IF SHE DIES FROM THAT DAMN INJURY? A BLOW LIKE THAT COULD KILL HER."

"Well, it would be her own damn fault for her disobedience, not mine."

"Well, for God's sake, will you just quit."

"I'll never quit until she gets it in her head. I'm the boss around here. She's not."

"Well, can you just get the hell out of here. She is in the bathroom! She ought to at least have some respect and some privacy." I pushed him to get him out of there.

"Well, you quit sticking up for Miss Lucifer."

I locked the door and holding onto the washing machine, I hopped over to Mother and wrung the cold water from a towel and placed it gently against her face. She was still crying. I felt so sick I nearly threw up.

"Mom," I said quietly, "just don't even talk to him. It ain't worth it."

Mom's broken voice replied, "I was just asking Zosa if maybe she could help me carry some of the buckets of water out of the basement. It's really hard for me to lift those buckets, May. But Bard said it was my job and I shouldn't be trying to get Zosa to do my work."

Sympathizing, I said, "I know. The whole damn thing of carrying that stupid water out of the basement is all for nothing anyway. It will just be back there tomorrow." I hobbled out of the bathroom. Bard had gone to the shop. I went out there, looked at Bard with fury still running through me, "Why can't we just have someone come out and unplug the drain in the basement? That's all that's the matter."

In an insinuating tone, "Have you got $70 or $100? That's about what they charge. I don't," like it was all my fault when we didn't have money. "And even if someone did clean it out, it would be plugged up again with roots in about three months."

I left the shop confounded and hobbled out to the fence by the pasture, leaned against a post, and looked at the threatening gray sky. It seemed that no matter how much I earned, no matter how hard I worked, it was always the same.

I was trying for all I was worth to suppress my feelings, to keep my cool. When I would get to the stage where I was about ready to blow, my body would quiver with emotion begging to be released but then I would remember Joe again. I would tell myself, "Cool it. Just cool it."

Bang! The thunder rumbled through the sky, lightning flashed. I stood with rain drenching me, my mouth clenched tight. I repeated in my mind, "I must never lose control. Never. Never. Never!" After a while, I hobbled back to the shop. Bard was sitting on a stool looking out the window and waiting for the rain to stop. I stood there like a drowned rat.

"Ya' know, Bard, just because ya' have the priesthood and stuff, that don't mean ya' can commit murder to any of us and get away with it. Ya' got to know in your own mind it ain't right to kick an old lady in the head. How would you like it if someone done that to your mom?"

He glared at me, "I've told you but you are like those who have ears that don't hear and eyes that don't see and a mind which doesn't comprehend." As he came up off the stool, he hollered at me with real violence in his voice, "That's nothing to what God is going to do to the old devil when she gets up there. He's going to destroy her. And if you stand up for her, he will destroy you, too."

I said no more.

Some time elapsed. My leg had healed and I had resumed work as before. One evening I went in and asked Nan if she was ready to go to bed. She answered, "In a few minutes."

Fine. If it was just going to be a few minutes, I thought I would lay on her bed and wait. I fell asleep. Then, obviously, she went upstairs and told Bard that I had refused to wake up and put her to bed. When I woke up, I was screaming. Bard had hold of the front of my blouse and had just slapped me across the face as hard as he could. I was shaking, screaming as he was hollering at me, "You wake up and put Nanas to bed."

"What? What the heck is the matter?"

"She said she tried to wake you but you would not wake up."

After a while I quit shaking, calmed down, and did my job.

The next night I was leery, to say the least. I purposely told Nanas, "I'll just lay on your bed until you're ready to be put to bed. OK?"

"OK."

Then I laid there pretending I was asleep with my eyes shut just enough so as to deceive her. She tiptoed to the door, barely peeked in, saw that I was, what she thought, asleep, went upstairs and Bard came running down just as fast as he could. He turned around the corner, and I sprung upright instantly.

"What's the matter?" I asked.

"You wake up and put Nanas to bed."

"I'm not asleep. And I'm here to tell you Nanas did not even ask."

"Is that right, Nan?"

"No. She's lying. I did try to wake her."

"Bard, I'm perfectly willing to take care of her the best I can but I can't see for the life of me what in the world she gets out of seeing me get my head knocked off."

Everyone was still for a few moments. "Well, Nan, you'd better let her put you to bed."

Not wanting to prolong the contention, I went about doing my work.

One Saturday night Bard was going with Will to priesthood meeting and had left his instructions for me to follow. I came in the house and was eating a bowl of Zosa's delicious chili.

"Ummm, Zosa. This is yummy. You know it?"

Nan sitting next to me said in a very sweet tone of voice, "May, could you help clean up the kitchen? The fridge needs to be defrosted and the floor needs to be mopped."

I looked at her, pausing for the moment and thinking of all the things Bard had told me to do in the shop, and yet here is Nanas being so nice. I knew if I didn't, she would get really mad and liking to be on the good side of her if possible, I replied, "Well, OK. If I hurry 'cause I got all this other stuff that I've got to do, too."

So I hustled and emptied the fridge out quick and got it to defrosting while I swept the house and mopped the kitchen floor, all except where the fridge and sink were, while Nanas was in the front room sewing and singing a beautiful hymn, something about how the wheat and tares together grow and how the Lord "shouts the harvest home." How I loved that song. She seemed so happy and contented. So fine. I finished the fridge and then cleaned the rest of the floor.

Then I went to the shop. Bard came home and as he walked into the shop, he said, "Well, are you ready to come to bed?"

"Well, I don't know. Do you think I need to finish this tonight?"

"What in the heck is taking so long?"

90

"Well, Nan needed a little help."

"With what?"

"Oh, just a few things in the house. But I can still do this, too, if I need to."

"You helped her with what?"

"Well, the place needed cleaning up a little bit."

He began to holler again, "What the hell's she got you in there doing Zosa's work for? I've told you to stay out of the house a hundred times and tend to the business."

I said quickly, "Well, it ain't that big of a deal. I can still do this just fine. OK?"

"No, it's not OK. I want you to come to bed right now. Now I find out you've been playing around in the house again. You get in here right now. I'm going to have this out."

My heart was beating fast as I followed him. We went in and Bard blew up again at Nanas and said, "What have you got May in the housework for when I had her in the shop?" She gave me a look as if to say, "Damn you. You shouldn't have told him."

Nan quickly answered, "She came in and started cleaning the house. I don't know what she was doing."

You could have knocked me over with a feather. I looked at her like, "Am I hearing right?" Bard turned to me for an explanation, I said, "Uh, no. That's not so. I was sitting here and Nanas asked me very nicely if I would help her, so I did. I figured fine, it needs to be done anyway. I can hardly stand the mess myself."

Nanas turned to me with her voiced deep and convincing, "You're a liar."

At this gesture I bristled, "You're the liar and you know it."

Bard was quick to correct me, "Don't you call Nanas a liar."

"Even if she is one?"

"You're not to correct her." He raised his hand as if he were going to swing it. "Do you understand?"

"Well, hell, Bard. Do you think I would just volunteer to do this work and mine too if it wouldn't make someone happy? Just think about it."

The argument became one big shouting match that lasted until 2:30 a.m. Sunday morning. Nanas was crying a little while hollering at Bard. "You told me that when you got wives, they would serve me."

"Yes, and they will, too." Bard turned to me and declared, "You better forgive and repent right now or you will carry all of Nan's sins upon your head."

I thought, "Nan's sins upon my head? Heaven forbid. She ain't worth me going to hell over."

Bard repeated, "You apologize to Nanas."

"For what? For her lying?"

"Don't you say that again, damn it. I'll knock you so hard you won't know what hit ya'. Now you say you're sorry."

I was reflecting upon Zosa's battered face. I stood still, looking at the situation. "What am I saying I'm sorry for?"

"Because you lied to get Nan in trouble. Now, admit it."

So very politely like a soldier answering to a sergeant, I said, "I'm sorry."

"What are you sorry for?"

"For calling Nanas a liar."

"Why?"

"Because I'm the one who lied."

"OK. You kiss her now."

I gave her a peck on the cheek. Well that was enough and the session broke up. I never could see getting my face remodeled over someone who would never change their mind anyway, but I thought to myself, "Strange. I wonder if there is any truth to that about my taking Nanas' sins if I don't forgive her. Boy, I would forgive anything rather than have all her hell on my head. So maybe I'd better get over being so stiff necked about it."

As my feelings settled down, I began pondering some of the priesthood brethren's teachings I had heard in meeting. They said, "Blessed is he that is persecuted for righteousness," and I was crying inside as I thought to myself, "I sure don't feel very blessed."

I continued having two bosses until one day Nanas was chastising me for something and after listening to her for about two hours, I figured she was trying to drive me crazy again. She would follow me around while I was working, just continually yelling at me. I was doing the washing with our old Maytag, so I began to whistle. I often whistled as I worked.

Then Nanas became furious. She started in on me, "Don't you whistle while I'm talking to you." She grabbed some dirty socks that were floating on the water and quickly crammed them into my mouth. I pried her hand down and went to find Bard.

Bard told Nanas that if she kept up that kind of thing, he would have to move me out from under her direction.

Will had found a young lady, Bardell, who married him. But even so the amount of groceries brought into the house was limited, just so much of this and so much of that. Bard and Nanas seemed to have little concern for what we had at home to fix in the way of food because Nanas claimed she needed a cup of coffee to kill the pain twice a day after her accident. Bard said, "Well, it's not good to bring coffee into the home, so I'll take her to the cafe for a cup."

While they were there, they would both order delicious meals. While Will was on the bottle route picking up gallon jugs from the cafes, he had money to buy the jugs so he would get whatever food he wanted also. My mother, Zosa, Bardell, and I had no way to go buy anything to bring it home, so we were dependent upon Nanas and Bard. We got very tired of bread, bottled fruit and milk. The meat goods had not been given to them for a long time now. We asked if we could have some hamburger this day and they brought home some coarse ground meat they said they got a really good deal on because it was coarse ground, and said, "See how you like it."

So I fried some up and made some hamburgers and I got deathly sick. Three days later I fixed some in some Spanish rice and again I got sick. Then when we went to Glen's on 45th South to deliver him empty jug boxes, as I passed by the meat counter, I recognized these patties, and it said "Dog Patties."

I went out by the truck and said, "Damn it, Bard. You guys bring home dog food and expect us to eat that kinda' shit. No wonder I got sick."

"Well, Glen said it was really good meat. That's all I know. Because government regulations won't allow anything but real good meat to be used for animals."

I shook my head and thought, "Oh hell. I've heard of everything."

Because I was raising goats for milk, I also raised baby goats for three months for some Italians to barbecue, but they only wanted to pay me $5 tops and I had to talk like a Dutch uncle to get that out of them. They would always try to get them for $3. In the meantime, we girls were really wishing we had some meat, so one time I thought, "Heck. I'm not going to sell that thing for five bucks. Why in the world can't I kill it so we can eat it?"   I told Bard of my plans and he said, "I don't care."

So I thought, "Fine. I'm going to do it."

I had never done anything like this before. The only knife I had was from saving bubble gum wrappers as a child. That's how I got a knife from the Bazooka Bubble Gum Company. I sharpened it on a hot wheel the best I could, and then caught the little goat and tied a rope around its back legs and pulled the rope up over a beam in the basement of the bottle barn, which used to be an old cow barn, so that the blood or whatever could go in the trough in the floor.

I blocked the door open so I could have more light down there, then I said a prayer as I was trying to brace myself for what I was contemplating. "Please forgive me for killing this little goat." Then I grabbed hold of its head and took a deep breath, and stabbed it in the jugular vein. Oh dear. That thing let out a scream that made my blood curdle. Oh. I sawed and sawed on its neck as fast as I could. Golly, this thing was bellowing and struggling and getting loose and I would keep losing my exact place and I was so nervous and it seemed like this knife was too darn dull. I kept working at it until I finally succeeded in killing it.

Dear me. I stood there with blood all over. I was coated from head to foot and my heart was going 90 miles an hour. Shaking like a leaf, I sighed and leaned against the wall. If I never went through another experience like that again in all eternity, it would be just too soon.

Then I took another deep breath and commenced to skin it. When I was all through, I took an old meat saw and cut the goat into pieces. I put the pieces in plastic bags and put them in the freezer, all except one piece, which I cooked. All the time the meat was steaming, those bloody screams were running rampant through my brain. I suffered hours and hours of mental torment.

Then when the meal was cooked, we all sat down. Mother said, "Oh, this is really good."

"Well, I'm glad you like it. You can have mine."

"Are you sure?"

"Yeah, I'm positive." I ate my asparagus and bread and butter and a glass of milk and sought some quiet place where I knelt down. With my broken plea, I asked, "Oh Father, please forgive me. I am so sorry. I can't even say how sorry. I don't even care if I eat nothing but vegetables for the rest of my life. Please take the screaming cries out of my head." I stayed there crying and ended it "in the name of Jesus Christ, amen."

CHAPTER 7

The arguments continued to get worse and I struggled to discover ways to please everyone just to avoid the tension and bickering. There was no way to stop the arguments, but somehow, if I could just be left out of them, how happy I would be. On a particular Sunday morning, I got myself ready to go to meeting, then wet Bard's hair and combed it so he would look half civilized. Feeling anxious to hear the brethren, I hurried to the car. While we were on our way, I was thinking of different questions that I hoped the brethren would answer for me. We arrived and I took a seat on Bard's left side. A sweet spirit prevailed and the meeting began.

One brother talked about wives following their husbands and the husband following the priesthood and the priesthood council following God. "If you women want to be treated like a queen, you have got to treat your husband like a king." What a beautiful concept. Then they began to read from The Bible on charity. As I listened I was consumed by a desire, oh, how I would love to acquire that attribute. The thought was going through my mind, "That is the spirit of God. That's what we came to this earth to learn, I'm sure." Joy was radiating through me like small volts of electricity.

The meeting closed and we returned home. I was so happy for the Gospel I had heard. Later, when I could be unnoticed, I went to a little spot in my closet where I could not easily be found and poured my heart out to my Father in heaven.

"Oh, Father," I began with tears streaming down my face. "I'm so thankful for the teachings of the brethren this day. I pray that I, too, may acquire the attribute of charity wherein it suffers long and is kind and is not easily provoked and seeketh not her own. If I have nothing else, may I leave this world with that in my character. Help me to overcome myself." I was thinking as I paused in my prayer that I must renew this plea and continue to strive for this goal that it may guide me through every hour of my life.

"Thank you, Father, for the gospel that has been preserved down through the ages for our benefit. I pray that you will help me to overcome my imperfections. I give you all the honor and glory for all that I have, and I look to you for all that I hope to obtain, I pray, in the name of Jesus Christ, amen."

As I brushed the tears from my face, I thought I must remember these things no matter what happens. I got up and walked into the hall.

Nan shouted, "We've been looking for you to get in here and help me. Zosa's baby is ready to come."

95

We hurried into Zosa's room. She was having labor pains. Sure enough. In about ten minutes, the head appeared.

"Come on, push," Nan shouted. "Push. Each time you have pain, push with it."

Zosa was crying, "It hurts!"

"Quick. Get me a bowl of water." I took off to get the water. When I returned with some, "Hand me that string." I felt really good watching Nanas sweat. She was very diligent in her labor.

"Give me the scissors. I need another pad. Now that piece of material." She was trying to stop Zosa's bleeding. "Gimme those safety pins. Now hand me some cotton balls. The olive oil." She was holding a black-haired little girl. "Now the baby blanket and a diaper." I smiled looking at this tiny lady. Everyone was so excited and happy over this little addition to the family.

The discussions of a name went around and Bard said, "I think we ought to call her Nanas."

Nanas said, "Well, we could call her another name, too. What do you think about Sherrie?"

"Yeah, that sounds good. Let's think about it and if we don't come up with a better name, then that's her name."

Bard and Will left the room. I left shortly. Bard was talking in the hall to Willy, and I overheard them on my way into the kitchen. Bard was speaking, "I would like to see you take this little girl for your wife when she becomes of marriageable age."

I thought to myself, "Did I hear right? Yeah, I did. I heard right." I went out in the hall to stand there and listen to all this. I commented, "Well, goll, how do you know who she wants to marry? Heck, she's just barely arrived on the scene."

"Oh, she'll want to marry Willy, if he treats her right." Will had a somewhat pleased expression on his face. Bard continued, "Will is a good man, as good as she could find anywhere else. So what is wrong with it?"

I could not say what I thought was wrong with it. But I figured, who knows, that's a good many years down the line.

A few days had passed by since Sherrie's birth when I walked in the house from the shop. Here were Nanas and Bard hollering at Zosa and Zosa not able to get out of bed yet. Bard was giving this baby of Zosa's to Nanas over some crazy excuse they used of why Zosa was not a fit mother. I looked at Zosa, her face was all red from bawling.

Nanas declared, "You're so filthy and slothful, the baby would die anyway. You don't even have enough brains to care for yourself properly, let alone a baby." Zosa's hollered at Nanas, "Well, hell, Nan. I haven't even been given a chance. You just want to steal my baby."

Bard chipped in, "Well, we don't want the child growing up to think a mental retard is its mother."

"Well, damn. Do you think that Nanas is any better?"

"Yes, I think Nanas is a whole lot smarter than you ever thought of being, or ever will be," Bard walked over to Zosa and grabbed hold of the hair on her head, shaking her head a little then throwing it back as he let go.

Zosa's face was twisted in agony. "WELL, I'M GOING TO TURN YOU GUYS INTO THE LAW FOR TAKING MY BABY."

Nan laughed, "It's not your baby. It's Bard's baby. You're just like a Coke machine. A man puts in a dime and the Coke comes out. Would you say that the machine owned the pop? Or the man who put in the dime?"

"Well, it's my baby too. Hell, Nanas, do you think it's easy having a baby?"

"I know what it is. I've had ten." (Nanas had had ten children with Clarence, her first husband.) "If you report this to the law, we'll just send you off to the Provo Mental Institution. You're nutty enough they'd take you right in."

"Well, what about yourself. You think you're so damn smart. You're not."

"Yes, I think I'm smart and if you say anything, I'll just tell them it's my baby with Bard."

This argument lasted for hours. During the course of this conversation, I had managed to bite off all my fingernails. Several nails were torn off into the quick. I imagined how that would be if I were in Zosa's shoes. I had heard enough. As I walked away a creepy feeling accompanied me as I sought tape for my bleeding finger. I told myself what Bard had pumped into my head a thousand times: It ain't my place to try and judge those who are over me. I'd better keep my nose in my own corral.

It was obvious that Zosa lost after four days of arguing. Along with the insults Bard had put some black and blue marks on her face. The child was registered on the birth certificate as Nanas' and Bard's.

That night when I retired for the evening after taking care of Nanas, I found myself wrapped in the midst of a nightmare. It was like I was confined in a room. It was so dark I could hardly see anything around me. There was the light of just one small candle. I was hovering around the candle which seemed to be my only hope for light. There was a small breeze coming from several different directions that would continually threaten to blow out this candle. So I cupped my hands around it to protect it the best I could. The thought of this little light going out was very heavy on my heart as I felt if I ever lost this tiny thing, I would be left groping around in utter darkness, as in the blackness of hell, and there would be no way to light the candle again.

This nightmare seemed to last for hours, teasing and tormenting my soul to where I sweat so bad and the agony was enough to wake me. I turned on the light and Bard said, "What's the matter."

"I just want to sleep with the light on."

"Why? It just wastes electricity."

"I can't help it. I just hate being in the dark."

"Whatever."

I laid down and tried to put it from my mind. I was so glad to see the morning come, so everywhere there was light around me. As I looked at the inspecting light in the bottle barn while washing jugs that day, a good feeling came over me. How happy I was to have a nice light to look at all day.

While thinking about trying to improve our miserable surroundings, it occurred to me that I had been there approximately four and a half years. All the things that were working in the house when we moved in were broken down or worn out and neither Bard nor Will would make even the slightest attempt to fix anything.

The bathtub drain was plugged. We had to scoop the water out and throw it down the toilet each time anyone took a bath. The kitchen sink was also plugged. We had to bail the water out and throw it over the fence. Then the water heater in the house went on the blink and we had to carry hot water from the shop over 300 feet away for all the needs, dishes, laundry, bathing, etc.

I did not have the slightest idea of how to use a pipe wrench, but I decided to attack the plumbing under the tub in the bathroom to see if I could unplug it. How could I wreck anything if it did not already work? So I thought about it for a while then took a pipe wrench down in the basement and studied the plumbing under the tub.

I adjusted the wrench. While standing on an old orange crate and holding a bucket under the goose neck of the drain with one hand so that hopefully whatever was in the pipe would not go all over me and the wrench in the other hand, I tried to undo the pipe. When I got both sides of the fitting loose, it started to drain into the bucket. While I was continuing to loosen it by hand, the fitting, being full of dirt, suddenly landed in the already heavy bucket. The sudden jar caused me to lose my balance. I kept the bucket from spilling but the drain water from above went all over my shoulder and down the front of me. Hell. There I stood with this black, smelly crap all over me. I

went upstairs and walked outside to the hose by the house and washed myself off, clothes and all. The water was cold so I washed off just the worst.

OK. Now I needed a hanger. I got one and undid it so I could stick it down the pipe. I went back downstairs and felt thankful the sewer water did not go on my head instead of my shoulder. Then I commenced trying to stick this hanger down the line. The thought occurred to me if I just had a hose and ran water down there, that it might do the trick.

So I went for the hose and told Zosa, "OK, now. When I holler, turn on the water. OK?"

"OK."

I wrapped an old rag around the hose that I had stuck into the pipe as tight as I could. Then I said, "OK. Turn it on."

She turned it on. It was all I could do to hold it in there until water was running down both arms. I was hoping it would break lose and it did. "Whoopee!" It was a triumph that would save us girls from all that darn work.

Then I cleaned out the goose neck and put it all back together. But I had cracked one nut and both rubber gaskets were shot. So I told Bard what I needed to fix it.

"You're always messing around with something," he said. "You should have used a crescent wrench on the fitting, not a pipe wrench. That's why you cracked it."

"But can't we just get another one? I got the drain cleaned out. It runs good." I stood there looking like a proud, drenched rat. "It'll work just like a charm when we get this fitting and two gaskets."

"Yeah, but that's such an old style that we just might have to buy the whole goose neck and that's going to be some money."

"It wouldn't cost that much, would it?"

"You bet. They don't give those things away." So the project was left unfinished because he did not even try to find the parts. I found an old baby enema bottle that I shoved up the pipe in the basement so that we could use the tub as we had before.

I got cleaned up and Bard said, "Come on. We're going to make a delivery to Plastiform Company."

I always tried to keep myself clean and decent looking. My clothes were nothing to brag about but at least my body was covered. I was always wearing either a long-sleeved blouse or sweater with a vest and a skirt which came below my knees and stockings one could not see through. I generally wore shoes I had got at Deseret Industries or found at the dump (mostly they looked like something one would see on a boy) or my bottle boots. Such was the appearance of "Mazie." Oh well.

Anyway, when we got to Plastiform, a really nice lady --I don't know if she felt sorry for me or what--but she told Nanas and Bard to follow her to her house that night. So we waited for her to get off work. Then when we got to her house, she gave us a whole bunch of really nice clothes. She said they would fit me, that her daughter had grown out of them. I thanked her very much and was really happy going home.

When we got the clothes in the house, Bard said, "OK. Nan you decide where they go."

I stood there hoping I might get a few things anyway. But I knew Zosa and Bardell needed clothes also, so I was glad to see them get some, too.

While Nanas was deciding on each piece, my mind wandered back to when Zosa and Bardell came into the family. Bard said that because we believe in the United Order, I was to share what I had in my closet with them. And I had said, "Fine. I will."

So both girls came upstairs and as I stood back while each one went through my clothes and took what they wanted, Zosa took my Sunday blouse and best sweater. Bardell took my green Sunday suit that this same lady had given me before in a box of clothes. It had shiny, fancy designs, much nicer than my other green suit.

I smiled as they said, "Thank you."

"You're welcome." I really did not care only that Bardell never did wear the suit and Zosa wore the blouse and sweater for working every day and they were both wrecked in no time. Well, that's all right.

I sat there on a chair in the kitchen, watching Nan, and halfway falling asleep while she was making up her mind. Then she put three blouses and two skirts on my lap. By the time she had distributed all the clothes, I took what I got and wanted to save them for best, which I did. Two weeks later when we went to Plastiform again, this lady looked at me--actually I was wearing the same old clothes I had worn the last time I was there. Her face had an expression of hurt, wonderment or disappointment. I could not tell which. I was lost for words and did not know what to say. So I busily unloaded the truck and then went and sat down in the cab feeling quite stupid. I was too timid to even tell her "thanks" again and that I really appreciated what she had given us, but they were all too good to wear for bottle clothes.

As I sat there, I wished that I had the courage to explain my feelings and my appreciation; somehow I could not bring myself to say anything.

I had been in the family now for approximately five years. One day Bard and I were upstairs in the bedroom and I brought up the subject of when it be my turn to have children.

Bard said, "Well, I'm praying continually for other women to come into the family so that they can take over the work that you're doing. Also, I need to have a woman to take care of my sexual needs so that you can have your children. When the Lord wants you to have your children, he will send those women that belong in my family."

The thought crossed my mind, "It's kinda' hard to imagine how a woman would ever come into a family like this unless they had no idea of what they were coming into." It surely was not how I had supposed it would be. Now I did not mind working so that Zosa could have children and my supplying an income to keep the family fed, but the thought of another woman doing that for me--boy. I could hardly believe that that would be the case.

I pondered this for a while, then I asked, "Well, what if women don't come into the family?"

"Oh, they will. Nanas and I are working on a couple of girls right now, but I don't know how long it will take them even after they come into the family before they can do your job. I might let the 'fillies' have a little time running with the reins before hooking them up to the plow."

I contemplated on that statement for a while. Then again I said, "Well, what if they don't?"

He threw an answer back as though to chastize me, "It's up to God when women come in the family so that you can have children."

"Yeah, but who knows how many years that would take."

"Look, if God wanted you pregnant, you'd be pregnant already."

"How could I be when you won't let it come off inside?"

"That's OK. You'd be pregnant with just the seed that's on the tip of 'johnny.'"

I said no more and decided to put the question on the shelf until the Lord might give me a better understanding.

As the months went by, I became quite used to my role of supporting the family and felt that I had been given an important responsibility. It made me happy to see the family enjoy the fruits of my labors. I felt glad that Nanas, Zosa, Will, Bardell, Mom and the babies were there. I thought, "Wouldn't it be terrible if it was just Bard and I? It's surely a good thing that we believe in the principle."

I had Mom's help and Will would make the pickups and deliveries most of the time until he got a job working for Fred and Kelly's, an eating house, as a cook. I would work as long as necessary to accomplish as much as I could because it might make the difference of whether we ate chicken or feathers.

On one occasion I had a dentist appointment to have an infected wisdom tooth pulled and told Bard it was for 11 a.m. Tuesday. They went away and were not back, so by 11:15 I was beside myself. The dentist might make me wait all day now. Not having a driver's license but impatient to go, I drove the truck over there.

While I was being waited on, an hour and a half later, Bard, Nanas and Will showed up. One would think I had committed the crime of the century and here came the forces to take me away. "Good grief," I thought when I got outside the dentist's office.

Nan and Bard both started in on me at once. "What the hell do you think you are doing stealing the truck? Bard could have you thrown in jail."

I smiled, "That's kinda' a pleasant thought actually."

"You have no business taking off."

Bard said, "I could have you reported to the priesthood. Now, you leave these trucks alone. Do you hear me? Don't you ever, ever do that again."

"While you promised to be back in time to take me and you weren't, so that's why I had to do it."

"I don't care if you're late or not for anything. You'd better not leave the yard," his bloodshot eyes seemed to drill a hole through me.

"Here's the prescription for pain pills."

"Forget it. Just get in the car." He opened the door and shoved me in. I fell to the seat and climbed in.

They left there without getting any pain pills for me. I could not figure if it was because he just was mad or tight because they cost $3. When we got home, Bard snarled, "Are you going to wash any more bottles today?"

"I don't know. My head hurts so bad. I feel like I've been stabbed in the side of the head with a knife. I'd like to rest."

"Well, all right, if you have to."

The pain was pulsating with each beat of my heart. I needed the medicine to kill infection, too, but I used salt packed in the hole instead. I tried to rest for about an hour. It seemed hopeless so I got up and went down to work to try to concentrate on something constructive.

I started repairing the end table for holding clean jugs. I was thinking to myself, "Heck, it's only three stupid dollars. Big dang deal. Maybe they would have bought it if I hadn't made them so mad. I don't know. But if they don't give a hairy rat what I suffer, then fine. They can just keep the cockeyed money. I hope they enjoy it." I was hammering to drive nails in the old wood with tears of pain and frustration. The nails were too big and the 2x6 split. I should have known better. Everything just seemed crazy.

Shortly after that day came a change. The workload demand

increased immensely. Nanas and Bard contacted a company, Spring Hills Distilled Water, that wanted 200 cases washed two or three times a week. That would bring in $32 per day at 4 cents per bottle whenever we worked for them. That sounded pretty good to us but it meant extra work on top of handling our regular accounts. I had been washing, with Mom's help, 100 to 120 cases of easy to clean jugs and making about $20 to $25 per day at 5 cents per bottle. This would be a good opportunity to get some bills paid. We could do 200 cases for this company in a day because all we needed to do was to remove the lid and label, run them through the water, rinse them and box them, removing any heavy dirt, as they intended to run them through their bottle wash again.

Bard said that I could handle the account by switching around my sleeping hours. He said if I would work six hours, then sleep for two, then work another six hours, then sleep another two, on and on, I could go 'round the clock that way. So, we agreed to handle this account. But it took seven hours to run the batch. Then by the time I would eat and rest for two hours, then work for another six to eight hours and have two hours rest, different ones of the family took turns to help me to run during the night hours. In the morning I would load the truck ready for delivery.

When we arrived at Spring Hills, I would throw the cases to the back end of the truck to one of their employees. He would stack them then after the 200 were unloaded, he would put their returns on the truck, which I would stack. When we got home, I would unload the truck, rest for two hours then get up and start up the batch. Somehow between putting Nanas to bed at night, doing whatever I had to do for Bard sexually, for the months of that summer, I was averaging four to five and one-half hours of rest per day.

My arms were not used to doing that much handling of the cases. When I would lay down, they would sting and burn and I would cry from pain that was so bad. I tried laying on my arms, holding them up in the air, putting them in a bucket of cold water--anything. The only thing that would stop the pain was for me to go back to work.

I was so extremely tired and delirious from the heat in the building, fatigue and long hours, I would continually feel myself falling asleep with my eyes wide open standing there working although I was moving in as fast a momentum as I could. But the constant fear of the cement floor in back of me and the boiling water in front of me would keep me awake until the job was done.

When I had loaded the truck, I would no sooner sit down in the cab after telling them that everything was ready than I would fall asleep in less than a minute.

One morning I told them the load was ready and I sat in the truck to go. I woke up when Bard began hollering and shaking me as he said, "You've got something radically the matter with you. Why can't you stay awake? Every time you sit down anywhere you fall asleep. Whatever it is you've got, it's bad. Brigham Young prophesied that the people in the last days would have a sleeping sickness come over them." He grabbed my arm and was shaking me. "Wake up and listen to me!"

"I am awake."

"Yeah, but are ya' listening? For every crime there is, there is an evil spirit that enters into one's body and takes over. And what you have got to do is rebuke it if its a sleeping devil that's got a hold of you." He was still shaking me. "Do you understand? I have prayed in your behalf but you're the one that needs to plead with God to get rid of this evil spirit."

As the weeks and months went by, I fought and struggled with myself, praying, "Oh, Father in heaven. Please help me overcome this sleeping spirit."

When I went to meeting sometimes, I would wake up, my head bowed, only to notice I had been drooling on my hymn book. I would quickly wipe it up with my hankie. What a cut low. I could just feel myself blush. But the next thing I knew I was asleep again. This problem was seven days a week for four months, May through August.

I fought with myself to try everything and anything I could think of to make myself stay awake: throwing cold water on my face, slapping myself, singing out loud. But the moment I stopped, zonk--I would be out like a light.

As I sat in the truck ready to go on another delivery, Bard woke me up again, shaking me, "Wake up. Are you awake? Now listen to me. Are you listening?"

"Uh huh."

"There are all kinds of devils. There are laughing devils, crying devils like Zosa has, justifying devils like your mother has. For every crime there is, there is an evil spirit and you've got this one awfully bad. It's so damn bad I can't even wake you up at night. It's like you're dead. I shake you, kick you, pinch you, and it scares me. You just act like a dead person and I don't know what to do about it, but if you don't control yourself, you're not going to wake up. You'll just die."

I sat there feeling like a soggy piece of bread. "But Bard, I have prayed about it many times. I have tried to rebuke it for all I'm worth and it doesn't seem to help."

"Well, I'll tell you one thing. You can be glad that you're not living in the days of Brigham Young. If you lived in those days and you fell asleep when he gave you something to do, he'd do with you like he did with one man that fell asleep on his horse while he was on guard

104

duty. Brigham Young came along, slapped the horse on the ass driving the horse out of camp and the guy was never seen or heard of again."

"Well, I'm so tired I could fall over on my face even while I'm working, and I've even thrown cold water on my face but it doesn't help."

"Well, you've been getting four to five hours of sleep. You should be able, if you're any good at all, to go on two or three hours per night, and you're getting twice that, so you should be fine."

"But I read in a magazine a long time ago that the average person needs from six to seven hours of sleep to be well rested." I looked up at Bard as his eyes were beating upon me.

"Well, they're talking about lazy bums. That's just what people want to get, not what they actually need."

With every day being so heavy with such a dredge of work upon my head, I became somewhat delirious. It was as if I could not even remember a time when I was not exceedingly tired. And I made a comment to Bard, with a sincere desire to know the answer to this question, "Why did God make us to come down here and to suffer so." Every day I believed that it was right for me to push myself so that I could not be blamed for neglect of my duties. I really could not see the purpose of life.

"Well, some people don't get their rewards in this life," Bard commented.

But in my mind I could not imagine how even in the next life the Lord would let me off the hook. With all there was to be done and so few people willing to devote themselves enough to do it, I just figured at least when I get on the other side, I will have the joy of knowing that I am building God's kingdom and maybe He might allow a little bit of sun to shine on my corner of heaven.

Two nights later when I laid my body to rest, I found myself wrapped up in a dream. I was in a canyon-like environment. The autumn colors were in the trees--the temperature was pleasant. There were many different types of beautiful plants amongst the trees. A meadow with flowers, not many rocks but green stretched out before me, landscaped as if by God Himself. I noticed a canal with the water very clean and clear as I put my foot into the water. The canal was approximately 8' wide and 4' deep. As I slipped in for a swim, I saw exotic fish pass by me every now and then.

Then I swam to where a few ducks were. I was laughing and just loving it. I swam around with the ducks as though we were friends or something. Then I came to a flat landing that looked something like a golf course with flat stretches of green grass, an occasional tree here and there. I stepped out of the water to explore this environment.

I walked in the grass for a little ways then went towards a grove of trees. On the lefthand side of the trees and bushes, I turned as my attention was captured. I had never beheld such beauty. I gasped at the view which nearly took my breath away. I had stumbled onto a flower garden surrounded by a slight mist, each flower in its radiant glory portraying beauty to its fullest potential.

I was standing on a path that led through this garden. Oh! My attention was captured by a lovely white flower, with blossoms about 5" across. I touched the petals which were almost as soft as the dew. It was like some type of rose bush standing 5' tall. There were some plants that stood 4' here and there and they were spaced so as to have other flowers growing between them according to color, size and height. Surrounded by such splendor, I just stood there in awe. They were all coordinated together so as to create a masterpiece. Oh. You sweet things, as my eyes focused upon glory after glory of the flowers, giving me a spiritual uplift like I had never known before.

The joy was vibrating through my body to such an extent that I woke up with a thankfulness that I had seen a glimpse of heaven. With tears in my eyes, I whispered a prayer, "Oh thank you, God. Now I understand the reason for living that we might someday be worthy of dwelling in your kingdom."

I could look upon the duties placed before me in a different light now, with a more firm determination to strive to deny myself anything that God did not want me to have.

That night after the day's work was done, Bard was talking to his family in the front room. "I fell in love with a girl when I was 17. This was Caroline. She had beautiful red hair and a lovely body. I took the matter before the Lord and I was told to leave her alone, to let the Lord have time to work with her. She would be given to me. I was in such a hurry. Instead of waiting upon the Lord, I went to see her again after I was told to leave her alone. I read her the 132nd Section of the Doctrine and Covenants and told her I intended to live that principle."

His head dropped into his hands as he stared at the floor. Then in a whimper like a child, he cried, "I kept going over to see her. She wouldn't even answer the door. I wanted her so bad. Three days later my papers came to ship me off to the Army."

I listened as compassion was taking over. Bard looked at me and said, "I'll never love any woman like I did her. I love you because you love the Gospel, but not like I loved that woman. I've learned obedience by the things I've suffered. When God speaks, I obey. I could have lost all the women I have in this life and in heaven just over that."

I bent over and put my arm around him while he continued to sob.

106

I felt so sorry. After a while he gained control of his emotions and said, "She will be amongst my women in heaven."

"How many wives do you have in heaven?" I asked.

"There are approximately 500."

"What do you mean 500 approximately? Don't you know how many you have?" I gave way to a little laughter.

"Well, some of them get tired of waiting for me to return. They leave to marry other men, but that's how many I had the last time I was there about six years ago."

I sat down by the vanity somewhat confounded. "Now say that again. You went to heaven and what now? Did you say 500?"

"Yes. I have 500 women over there."

"How in the world did you get 500 wives?"

"There are thousands of good women over there whose husbands are not worthy of them. There's seven women being born to every one man right now. But all men are not worthy to take them, so what few good men there are have to, according to God's laws, take more than one. I could have more than that if I wanted them, but 500 is about all I can handle. They do the work. But my job is to organize them along with teaching them the Gospel and keeping them in line. But they mainly keep themselves in line. It's a big job for me just having affairs with all the ones who want to get pregnant. I only visit them once every seven years. They continually plead to the Lord for me to come over there. Just as soon as my mission here is done, I'll be gone. That's why I keep trying to train you to take over the responsibility here. If I can get it to where you are doing it all, then you won't miss me when I'm gone."

I sat in silence then asked, "Can I be excused? I think I left the light on in the basement of the barn."

He glanced out the window and seeing it was on said, "All right. Go on."

I stepped outside into the cool evening air as I slowly walked to the barn in a daze, trying to sort out my thoughts. I stopped to rest on a bale of hay near the stack. I leaned over one so as to relax and closed my eyes. As I was trying to visualize all these women, something was saying, "You're just a number with no more significance than a speck of dust."

Then the spirit within me struck back as I sat up, staring into the darkness, as I shook my head and said out loud, "Oh, no! I'm not just a number. I've got a brain." With feelings running rampant through me, "I'll do the work so that their suffering will not be upon my head of why he is not with them." I was thinking of what the brethren said in

meeting of living so that the blood and sins of this generation are not upon our heads that I might stand blameless before the Lord at the day of judgment.

A strength filled my body as a spirit of conviction entered in. I will do my part--all that is asked of me--for I know God will help me. How do I know that? I know that because I have not rejected any of his laws, ordinances or principles. My life is his to ask what he will of me. The Lord will judge all. This is where I want to be found in that day.

Half an hour passed quickly while I renewed my covenants with God and contemplating the priesthood's teachings. I got up and turned off the lights. then on my way back to the house, I was singing,

I think of his hands pierced and bleeding to pay the debt,
Such mercy, such love, and devotion can I forget?
No, no, I will praise and adore at the mercy seat,
Until at the glorified throne I kneel at his feet.

Then with tears in my eyes,

Oh, it is wonderful that he should care for me,
Enough to die for me!
Oh, it is wonderful, wonderful to me![11]

Renewing my covenants with God to do his will and forsake my own, I looked forward to hearing the brethren more so than before. When meeting time came Sunday afternoon, I took a note pad with me. When the brethren spoke I would jot down everything that I felt was pertaining to me so that I might not forget it.

I appreciated the sweet attitude from one of the speakers who said, "Jesus set the example that we must do good, even for those that would do evil towards us."

As I heard these words, my whole soul was consumed with joy. I could see why God would love Christ for he truly did do that. Then they spoke upon the principle of forgiveness. They said that we must learn how to forgive seventy times seventy, as I jotted that down in my

little pad. I thought, "How well fed my soul has been this day," as we

---

[11] "I Stand All Amazed," music and words by Charles H. Gabriel, Hymns, p. 80.

sang the song, "God Be With You 'Til We Meet Again,"[12]

During the following week, everything that anyone would say to me that would tend to rile my nature, I would go off by myself as soon as I could and seek for strength to overcome my rebellion.

I thought about this principle of forgiving "seventy times seventy," and it occurred to me, "Let's see. Seventy times seventy--how much would that be? That goes into the thousands, doesn't it? Heck, who could ever keep track of all that."

Then the thought struck me, "Well, maybe that's the point. You're supposed to forgive and forgive and forgive until you don't know anything else but how to forgive. Yeah, I bet that's what he's getting at. OK. Fine.

I remembered what someone had said a long time ago. They said if you want to like a person, then what you do is keep repeating in your mind every good thing that person has ever done, but all the stupid things you have seen them do, don't even think about that and try to forget it. Then after a while, you could begin to like that person.

I thought to myself, "Heck, I gotta' work with them anyway. If I can just be a friend somehow . . ."

Will backed in the load of jugs and started walking towards the house. "Hey, how about giving me a hand?"

He started clapping his hands.

"Very funny," I said. He turned to keep walking. "Darn your potato hide. Get back here."

"In the morning," as he waved his hand to say goodbye. "It's 5:30 and I'm tired."

I stood there looking stupid. "Oh, just like that," I thought to myself. "Well, what has tired got to do with the price of rice in China? We need to unload them tonight just in case it rains so the cases won't be ruined."

He shut the door. But I thought, "Well, that's all right. I'm not going to be judged according to what Willy does, so I'd better get over my hangup as fast as I can."

I seemed to have some kind of crazy drive in my mind. It was like I felt anything I can possibly do today, I'd better get it done because God will have tomorrow's work for me to do tomorrow. I felt myself on a time schedule that was very pressing. It was so demanding but I could not explain why, even though I had worked through the night, I told myself a little trick like, "OK, May. Now just pretend, just think you're waking up now. OK? This is the start of a new day, right?

---

[12] "God be with You," words by J. E. Rankin, music by W. G. Tomer, Hymns, p. 47.

Now, get busy.

Seeing the family get by on what little bit I could earn, I felt very deficient in what I was able to bring in for their support. I always thought, "There's gotta' be a better way. Heaven help me and we're goin' ta find it."

I worked to unload the truck by myself as I thought, "It really doesn't matter. 'Cause I'm going to do all I can whether he helps or not. It's just that we would get more done and I'd feel better towards Will if he would get off his tuther end." Feeling like a rag, I went to bed and fell into another dream.

I found myself in a mansion next to a park. In this lovely room I felt so natural standing there in a lovely white gown. Beauty, order and cleanliness surrounded me. The wood furniture had a deep walnut stain. The carpet was a cream color with a slight purple cast. It seemed to be a simple touch of elegance. Delicate white lace curtains graced the window. The walls were covered with a white wallpaper with light silver designs. I was standing alone in this bedroom.

Feeling very content as I glanced out the window, I could see the tops of the trees because the building was three stories high. There was a lawn, so rich and green. The grass was not like it had been mowed but more like each blade knew how high it needed to grow and then had stopped growing at about 3". I could appreciate an occasional little white flower here and there amongst the grass.

It seemed very fresh outside like a rain had just cleansed the air. The sky was a light gray-blue. There were no clouds in the sky but no sun shining either. The peaceful stillness that prevailed left a permanent impression in my memory.

As the morning came and my dream was over, I left the bedroom, taking with me the peace in my heart. I stepped into the hallway of the attic and could see all the junk that Nanas had saved for years: an old trunk with broken leather straps, a bunch of old chairs with the backs broken off, her old quilting frames with a half finished quilt still on it, some old bedsteads and a dresser with the mirror broken up, and boxes of all sizes with old clothes, and raw material pieces, then a couple of old carpets, one with a big ragged spot on one side. Oh dear. This is a fair description of Nanas' precious junk coated with layers of dust and cobwebs.

Bard had said that because of the filth in that area, it was a comfortable home for evil spirits to dwell. As I looked at the mess for a moment and then hurried past it, how thankful I was, indeed, that I could comprehend a more blessed realm than what I was living around.

As I entered the kitchen, everyone was talking around me but I was wrapped up with the thoughts of my own mind. All I could hear were sounds. A feeling came over me that even though there were all

110

these people around, "I am alone." Then as I began frying some eggs, Bard distracted my attention by singing "It Is No Secret What the Devil Can Do," to the tune of "It Is No Secret What God Can Do."

"What he's done for others, he can do for you," singing to Mom with both arms flying up, whirling around in the air while Mom was sitting there looking up at him.

"With arms wide open, he'll pardon you." He stopped there and shouted, "The devil's the only one that's going to pardon you."

I thought to myself, "Here we go again. I've just got to get out of here. I'm so tired of all that crap and I've heard it so dang many times. Just let it go in one ear and out the other."

I ate my breakfast and went to work.

Bard always claimed to have a bad back and said the doctor told him that he was to get more rest and quit working or the work would kill him. Will had brought back a 50-pound box of staples on the truck that needed to be moved into the shop. Bard told me to carry it in. I tried then dropping it back down, I said, "I can't. It's too heavy."

"Can't is a coward too lazy to try," he commented.

So although I only weighed 110 pounds myself, I picked it up and moved it in. Bard, being large in stature, approximately 6 feet tall and weighing 230 pounds, he did not even offer to help. His attitude was obvious. I thought to myself, "Fine. If ya' don't want to help, don't." I already had a hernia and serious back problems.

With the demand for jugs for our regular bottle accounts for root beer stands and fountain syrup, along with Spring Hills, I knew that it would not lighten up through the two remaining summer months until August. We had handled that account for two years, but there was soon to come a drastic change.

The Spring Hills Distilled Water Company decided to use plastic bottles to replace the glass for over half of their orders. During the same time period the Coca Cola Company switched from a glass gallon jug to a gallon carton, like a milk carton. Spring Hills no longer needed us to recondition their jugs. I was not bothered anymore by supposed "sleeping devils." I was able to relax to the extent of getting six to eight hours rest.

Because of the scarcity of jugs due to what the Coca Cola Company had done, we picked up other accounts, more root beer stands who had jugs returned to them to be cleaned. Those jugs were somewhat unpredictable and could not be run through at the fast pace of a regular syrup jug. Many of them were dusty from sitting in someone's garage or basement, and most of them had large water rings and lime deposits.

The method that Nanas had showed me for cleaning water deposits was to pour a little hydrochloric acid in each bottle, then dump it back out into a little cup, put a little rinse water in there, and a piece of 3M pad, then insert a long wooden stick, shaped in a V, at the bottom so as to fit the bottle. By chasing the pad around the bottom of the jug while applying pressure with the stick, this is how we removed water rings.

Then I removed the pad and put the jug on a rotating brush hooked up to an electric motor that had bristles fastened into a metal shaft by a thin wire.

The most I could clean by working all day was 30 cases, that being only 120 jugs. I looked at the situation and at that time we had gone down to where I was only making $7 a day to support the family. I thought to myself, "Boy. This is sick. I could do better than that at Old Mill."

My mind was constantly striving to come up with a better way. Then I got an idea. I had thought this over in my mind pretty carefully as to the things I would need to make an improvement. I found almost everything by searching through the debris at the dump. I found a 7 1/2-gallon plastic acid container and sawed the one side off with a skill saw, then I drilled holes in it near the top so as to fasten some 2x4x4' board legs to make this little vat waist high. Then I took some old angle iron from the basement of the barn and with a dull hacksaw blade and dull drill bits, I made a rack and bolted it together so it would hold six jugs in the draining position. I lined it with wood so the jugs would not break and fastened a plastic skirt around the bottom of the rack so as to avoid any acid splashing on me. Then I directed the skirt into a half of a 55-gallon plastic container to catch the acid for recycling purposes.

I experimented as to how much I could dilute the acid and still have it clean the jugs. Then I had also found some old plywood at the dump and brought it home, too. I cut it up into pieces approximately 3'x5|' to stack jugs on. I was ready to try my experiment of rolling the jugs into this acid solution, rinsing a little bit around the inside, then placing them on this rack as fast as I could move. I was doing this one afternoon when Bob and Bev came to the door of the shop. They were some friends of the family.

Bob said, "Boy, is this Speedy Gonzalez or what! I've never seen anyone work like that woman, but I'll tell you Bard, if she doesn't slow down, she's going to have a burn out."

I was sure happy that I had made this improvement because now the jugs could sit overnight, soften the dust and dirt, remove the water ring, and I could run them through in the morning just as fast as I could go.

I also thought of using a plastic stick instead of wood, so we got a

1/2" plastic rod 17" long. It would last longer. I fastened a pad right to the end of the stick so I could grab it, insert the pad and stick, give it a swift whirl and out.

I started making my own bottle brushes since those from the factory had bristles coming out two sides through only eight holes tied by the fine wire. The wire would break sometimes within 15 minutes of use, causing the bristles to fall out. These brushes cost $7 a piece, so I saved the shafts and figured that by drilling eight more holes so that I could have them coming out of four sides instead of two, then I had Bard get me a new push broom with nylon bristles which I would carefully remove so as not to damage them. By inserting the bristles in these holes in sequence and by shoving an old darning needle up through the center so as to catch the bristles and hold them secure, and the end bristle I secured with a nail. Then I cut a small piece of nylon hose, heated it up and put it over the tip of the shaft so I could throw the bottle on quickly without fear of chipping the top. Boy, that worked slick.

Between all the little things I had improved, the amount that we could put through then of these hard-to-clean jugs was up to 120 cases per day. I was very encouraged because the bottles could not be cleaned to that extent in the back of some cafe. I raised the price to 10 cents per jug. Then our profit margin was $48 per day.

One time when we were down visiting Bob and Bev, Bob said in a casual way, "May's just about taking over down there. Is there anything she can't do?"

"Well, she's doing pretty good. 'Bout the only thing I haven't really let her do is talk to the companies on the phone much."

"Why?"

"Well, she's just not got the personality for it. I'm afraid customers will quit us."

"Oh, I dunno about that. I think she'd do all right. She's got a mouth, doesn't she? And ears, doesn't she? So, what's wrong with her?"

"Well, nothing really. I just don't like the idea."

While listening to them, the thought occurred to me, "It might be 'cause he just don't want me using the phone, as though I'm going to call someone up and tell everything I know. But why would I do that? No one would believe it anyway."

Then one day a company called up that I had contacted. They ordered 200 five-gallon plastic buckets. Nanas took the order. I asked Nan, "Is the order for Bennett or Roper buckets?" I had both styles but their lids would not interchange.

Then she called them and asked. The man said, "I have some lids for the Roper but I need 175 buckets with lids and just 25 without lids.

I asked her again. "Does he want all 200 buckets Roper or can he use some Bennetts?"

She said, "Oh hell, call him yourself."

Fine. I did. After that Nan did not seem to mind my contacting the companies on the loads incoming and outgoing.

I called Mountain Beverage to see if we could pick up a load of jugs and the man said, "I have not been paid for the last 104 cases that were picked up."

"Oh, really! Well, I'll check on that and get back with you, OK?"

"OK."

I sat the phone down and walked in to see Nanas. I asked her, "Hasn't Mountain Beverage been paid on the load we picked up over a month ago?"

"What's it to ya'?" she snarled. "That's none of your business."

"Well, that's fine but they are not going to release another load until they're paid. So, whatever. But Miller ordered a load and we don't have a load for them."

"Just get off my back."

Bard walked in and hearing the commotion asked, "What's the matter?"

"I was just telling Nanas we need to pay Hill for their last load so Will can pick 'em up so we can put them out for Miller."

Nan piped up, "No she's not. She's trying to boss me and tell me how to spend the money."

I looked at her and thought, "Good night. Of all the stupid things." Then I said, "Look, if you don't care about what money we have in here or the customer, then that's your problem. But I can't do jugs I don't have."

I went back to the phone and said in a whisper, "Just hang onto the jugs until you're paid. They'll pay ya'. OK?"

"OK."

I went to the shop. Bard followed. I turned to him and asked, "Why does she do that? What the heck's the matter with her? She's always mad over something stupid. I can't figure it out for the life of me."

Well, May, ya' got to understand. Before you came into the family, she was washing the jugs. It wasn't much but she worked hard. And everywhere she went on a delivery, people would show her love and praise her for her work. Then you come along. Some young whipper snapper that does three times as much and everyone knows you're doing the work. Also, you've been talking on the phone and she's so damn jealous of you she can't see straight."

"Oh, come on. How in the world would be anyone jealous of

someone with just a lot of Chinese labor? For what little bit of praise I get, you've got to be kidding."

"No. I'm serious. If you want her to like you, just praise the daylights out of her. She laps it up like a cat laps up cream."

I plopped myself on a jug box and tried analyzing that statement. I could recall for the first three months when I had started washing the jugs before Nanas' accident how Bard had told me to shut up and not tell anyone that I was washing them--to let Nanas get the credit from the customers. It did not seem to amount to the ashes of a rice straw so I went along with the idea--anything to keep the peace.

CHAPTER 8

I was in the shop one afternoon when all of a sudden I heard Bard yell from the house, "MAY, GET IN HERE."

I started shaking as I took a deep breath. I walked toward the house. The way he hollered I had no idea what I would be facing. I opened the door. There stood Bard, his pot belly and poor posture with shoulders slumping over, with his bloodshot eyes and deep wrinkle lines in his forehead. His face had a look of agony as he commenced to "jump" all over me.

"Nanas told me you were talking to your sister Lisa this morning."

"She called and just wanted to know how I was."

"What did you tell her?"

"I just told her I was fine."

"I want to know everything that was said."

"Well, she said she had a new baby girl, that being her fourth child."

"What did you say?"

"I just said I was happy for her." I looked at Bard and he scared me half to death with his expression.

"You know better than to talk to anyone without my permission." He leaned over me and hollered at the top of his voice. "You're to talk to business customers only and if you don't quit talking to everyone else, I won't even let you do that. DO YOU UNDERSTAND?"

"Yes," I muttered.

"Well, you'd better."

"Can I ask you something? What should I have done? She called me, I didn't call her."

"You should've just hung up. If you'd keep hanging up when she calls, she'd quit calling. Now, wouldn't she?"

I looked over at Nanas crocheting on the couch. She looked up with a smirk as though she was delighted in the scene. I said nothing to provoke him further, and after a while he quit hollering and I was excused. Oh dear me. I was glad to get outside to get my mind off the hell. But I would remember what I was told. Oh yes. I would remember for how could I ever forget even if I wanted to.

I dreaded to even go in the house and I would not even go in to eat until I was about ready to die of starvation, if there were contention going on. I would rather wait until whatever battles there were would die down so I could eat in peace, if possible.

I had just come in from the shop again when Bard said, "Get in the truck. We need to go after a new carburetor."

117

A friend of ours, Bob, told Bard that when we needed parts, we could buy wholesale from Genuine Auto Parts. By telling them that we had an exemption number, we could buy at wholesale prices. Bob then gave us his tax exemption number to use. But Bob said, "Be positively sure that you pay the tax because if you don't, they'll come at me for it." I thought I understood that pretty plain.

So when we got there, Bard had picked out the parts that he had gone after and the salesman asked, "Is this taxable?"

Bard said, "It's wholesale and here's the tax exemption number."

Standing there by him, I said, "But we want to pay the tax anyway."

Bard turned to me gritting his teeth, "Shut up."

"But Bob said for us to be sure and pay the tax."

He turned to me again with a horrible look on his face with a little saliva running down the corner of his mouth, bringing his hand around, applying a blow to my head as hard as he could hit. "Get to the car," he commanded.

I stood there for a few seconds then said, "Bard, I'm telling Bob."

He turned to the salesman, who was surprised at all the commotion, and said, "I'll pay the tax this time." It was under $2. Then all the way home, he screamed and hollered at me telling me how I had no right to correct him on anything. It was a horrible thing to ever cross his path.

I remembered the many times I had seen Zosa beaten, once or maybe twice a week. Her face would be black and blue and all puffed up with bruises all over her body. I saw no point in having my body put through that type of treatment. Therefore, one could say I was very obedient.

Zosa was, by nature, a rather easy person to get along with. She liked to be somewhat quiet and off to herself. I asked Bard in private why Zosa always wore the same clothes day and night with scarcely ever a change.

"Well, I'll tell you. But don't tell her I told you. When she was in her teens, her grandfather came up to her room and caught her in the nude without a stitch on. He beat her for it so bad that since that time, she has had a real complex about getting undressed for sleeping, sex or anything."

Nanas and Bard would try to impress upon Zosa the necessity of bathing and taking her clothes off to go to sleep at night. There was much railing that continued along those lines.

On one occasion when Zosa had not bathed for over three months, Nanas got awfully mad. Between her and Bard they held her down on the couch. Nanas pulled one of Zosa's stockings off. There was black muck on her feet and between her toes. Zosa liked to wear dresses that almost reached the floor and heavy wool socks.

Zosa had a leg injury that Nanas took care of rather than take her to the doctor. If Zosa did not bathe often, this sore on her leg would become infected and full of pus and rotting flesh about 3" in diameter. Much of Zosa getting beat seemed to be over this problem.

The house seemed a little quieter most of the time after Sherrie's birth because Nan would insist that Bard not holler so as not to wake up the baby. Autumn was upon us and the children next door were selling pumpkins. I came in from the shop and commenced to get something to eat for myself. About 15 minutes later Nan came in with Bard behind her. Zosa was also in the kitchen feeding Sherrie in the high chair.

Nan said while standing next to Zosa, "Have you changed that baby?"

"A little while ago."

Nan inserted her finger between Sherrie's diaper and her bottom, "You haven't changed her diaper." As she came around with her hand slapping Zosa's face, Nan turned to Bard, "She's trying to feed that baby with her diaper full of shit. No wonder the baby doesn't want to eat." She then turned to Zosa, "You nut. How would you like to sit down to eat in shit up to your waist?"

Bard butted in, "Change that diaper or I'll change it, and if I do, I'll mop your face with it."

"Well, hell, Bard. Do you think it was my fault that she just messed?"

Then Nan yelled, "Yes, I think it's your fault because you never check to see if she needs changing or not. Her little bum is so damn raw now just because you don't give a damn."

Bard then grabbed hold of Zosa's hair, "You change it right now." He yanked her hair for a little bit and then let it go.

Zosa was bawling, the baby was crying and had knocked the food all over the floor. Nan said, "How come every time I check her diaper, it needs changing. If you were doing your job, you'd have it changed already."

Bard again stated, "If you don't take to changing her more often when I come in and find a messy or pissy diaper, you will get it in your face." He grabbed hold of her hair again and shook it. "Do you understand?"

Zosa screamed, "Yes!"

I was sitting there watching everything like a church mouse. I had heard quite enough so I put my dish in the sink and said while leaving the door, "Thanks, Zosa. Those potatoes were delicious." Then I went back to the shop.

Will could always pick up and deliver bottles in one-fifth the time it would take me to wash them. I asked Bard if it was fair for Nanas and Will to run around visiting relatives, going to dances and shows, while I was just stuck with the work that went on and on.

Bard said, "Don't worry. The Lord sees who does what. Just don't concern yourself with what Nanas and Will are doing. It's what you're doing that you should worry about. God will see that you will have rewards far and beyond what Will gets if you do your part regardless of whether he does his part or not."

"I understand that, but Will thinks it's cute just to leave the truck for me to unload all the time. He's such a goof-off. When five o'clock comes, he acts like he has a perfect right to quit. He doesn't care if it rains during the night and ruins all the cases or what. But if I talk like a Dutch uncle for half an hour, then sometimes he'll help me. Heck, if this is supposed to be United Order, then shouldn't he do 50 percent?"

"Yeah, but Brigham Young said that a person isn't worth his salt if he couldn't support ten others besides himself."

"Well, doesn't that apply to Willy, too?"

"What do you care what rewards Will gets?"

"I know but you're talking 100 years from now. I'm not worried about all this reward business when I get in heaven. The Lord will probably say, 'Here's what I need for you to do,' and I'll have work over there, too. So heck, I'm just wishing I had some help now."

"Willy does give you some help, so be glad for what little bit he does, that he doesn't just leave it all to you."

"Yeah, but you know what? Just to show you what I mean, when we have to take a load for Adria Maintenance Company and I'm the one to load the truck, Nan says that I need to take each bottle out of the case and screw a lid on it and put it back upside down. But when Will is going to load the truck, he just loads the bottles on and puts the lids in a box, and tells Nan they can put the lids on up there. And she says nothing. But if I try that, I get the third degree. She tells me that I'm just damn lazy, that I'm not doing what the customer wants. I really don't care one way or the other, just so it's the same. You know what I mean? I wish you'd ask her about it."

There was silence for a while then he said, "Well, the customer likes it that way so it is better if you do it, that's all."

I got a bright idea. The next time I was delivering a load I said to the manager, "Would it be all right if we brought your lids in a box or do you need to have them screwed on each bottle?"

"Oh, a box is just fine."

"OK. Thank you."

Bard heard it so that took care of that.

On our way home I asked if we could stop to get me a candy bar. "If you want us to spend a dime on you, then you should see to it that you earn an extra dollar, so that nine other people in the family besides you can have a dime also." That seemed only right. But even though mine was the only money coming in, they would never say what they spent it on, only that if I wanted something, I had better work harder.

We would save lids. If I sorted through five boxes in an hour and a half, separating the aluminum from the tin, we could sell the aluminum for $4. So I would do this in my spare hours, rather than waste the time even though it was not much. Also, between the demand of incoming and outgoing loads, I had a huge stack of bottles in back--approximately 2,000 cases--that I would work on cleaning up in slack time.

Between that and working at Old Mill, or babysitting, I liked to think that I brought in as much income for the family as I could, just as a working man would feel trying to support his family to the best of his ability.

Even so, I hesitated to ask even for a candy bar or anything else. Rubber thongs cost $1 back then, but rather than ask for a $1 to buy a pair, I made some out of wood. Ha! I cut the wood in the shape of my foot then drilled holes where my big toes were and on the side of my foot so I could run a rope through them. I put them on and wore them a little while and had a good laugh at myself: all the work I had done and they were too uncomfortable to wear.

Bob and Bev came to visit us one afternoon. We were standing there in the yard and Bob was telling me that he knew the famous artist Robert Wood personally and that he could get me into taking lessons from him if I wanted to. Knowing Bard's attitude, I said to Bob, "Maybe if you could talk to him and see if there's any way of talking him into it."

Bob said, "OK." So he approached Bard off by himself. I came up and joined the two of them after a few minutes.

Bard said, "No way. There are too many artists starving to death now. She already has a job. She needs to be here to help the family and keep the business going."

I thought that was an opportunity of a lifetime, but Bard could not have cared less. When I was talking with him in the house later, he started railing at me, "The religion that doesn't require the sacrifice of all things doesn't have the power within it to save. You need to be concerned with what the Lord wants you to do, not what you want to do. There's a billion people out there all sending themselves to hell because they want what they want, and there's no way they'll allow the priesthood to guide them in anything."

"Look, Bard." I thought I would change the subject. "I know were supposed to sacrifice everything, but is it really that big of a sin to have a vacation once in a while? I mean, what can it hurt?"

"What do you mean--a vacation! You get a vacation every time someone dies down south. So what are you complaining about?"

"Well, let's put it this way. Who would work as long as I do without vacations--like it's been nearly nine years. You'd think I was abnormal or something."

"Well, you're not normal," he laughed. "If you was, you'd be coming after me for more sex instead of wanting to do all this dang work."

I thought when he walked away, "What a stupid statement. I've got a family to support and that's far more important. But, boy. What a godsend it would be if I just could have one day by myself just to think."

One afternoon I noticed Will and Nan talking to a gentleman in the yard. After the man left, Will came in and said, "That was Nanas' brother, Leo. He asked us if you were mentally retarded."

I wondered how the man could say such a thing when he didn't even know me. I had never talked with him, but I had the strong feeling that Nan and Will would prefer people to look at me as a nut. But I told myself just to forget it. It did not amount to the ashes of a rice straw anyway.

CHAPTER 9

Mom and I were in the kitchen. I had fixed some supper for us and we were eating. I could hear Bard, Will and Nan in the front room. Bard was telling Will that he needed to be more diligent in helping with the business and Nan chipped in, "Well, Will just figures why should he. You say May's doing it all anyway. So if he doesn't get any credit, why should he give a damn?"

Then Bard hollered at Nan, "I didn't say May was doing it all. I said she was doing most of it. So just shut up while I'm correcting Willy, will ya'?"

"Yeah, but he's told me many times that he wants to leave and get a house of his own. He doesn't tell you everything that he tells me."

"Well, I can't help it. What he needs to do if he is going to be worth something is either help May to build Reclaim Bottle or he could even start a business of his own, if he thinks he can make more money."

Nan said, "Well, he feels like it's just a bunch of shit. You've got your wives and he wants to marry more women, too. He feels like he's just not getting anywhere."

"Well, hell, that's what I'm telling him." Bard slammed his book down, "If he is ever going to gain influence in the eyes of the priesthood council, he's got to be making good money so they'll give him recognition if he wants to influence them to give him any more women."

Mom and I were still eating our sandwiches when Will said, "What I would like to do is start raising cows. I can get calves for about $30 sometimes in the auctions, and I can get a cow for about $150 if I watch the ads and then feed the calves--we have all this pasture."

Bard thought for a while. Nan said, "Anyway, if he doesn't get something, then he'll leave and I know it."

"Well, go ahead and get him a cow then, if he is sure he wants all the work of raising calves."

I jumped up and butted into the conversation, "Even calves do good on goats milk."

Nan said, "Yeah, they do."

Bard said, "Well, you're still going to have to help May in the business or we won't have enough money to buy the hay or grain."

I thought, "We might have a little meat to eat now and then."

Will worked long and hard to get old lumber he could get free to build sheds. Then when I got inheritance money from my Mom's old estate that totaled $2,500, Nan used it to buy hay for the cow and the goats, also for fencing materials and posts. Will fenced the whole pasture--four acres. I thought it was kind of neat to see Will care about something. They also got some sheep and some more cute little

123

baby pigs. It was my job to feed these little pigs, at least I took over the job because they were always hungry and I did not see anyone else feed them. Feeling sorry for them, I saw to it that they got fed.

Anyway, one day I was adjusting the portable picket-like fence that was around the pigs when one little red pig got out. He was only about a foot and a half long, but boy, did he take off. Heck, we paid $3 for him. I could not just let him go so I took off after him. I was not far behind him on his trail. He ran through the front yard, across the street, through Mr. Pill's fence, and into a huge pasture. I thought, "Surely I can outrun this little twerp. Oh dear me." He just kept going. I was about 20 feet away from catching him. He ran clear to the end of the field then over and through the fence again, and across the street and over towards the canal. He seemed to have got out of my sight, so I carefully looked around and then I spotted him in the canal hugging the embankment. So fine. I got in--shoes, clothes and all--went across and got him. Then I got out and commenced walking home.

I noticed a girl from a wealthy family whom I had known when I was young passing me on the same side of the street. She was dressed very nicely, her hair all pretty and everything. There I was, if you can imagine how I looked. I swallowed and breathed deeply as we passed. Oh dear. I would have liked to have been spared that.

As I walked home, it was just a lovely warm summer day. I enjoyed the walk home even if I was holding Mr. Piggy.

I was soon to get a little pet. The sheep that Will had picked up at an auction was having a baby lamb. "Easy, gal, easy. It's OK," I whispered. But she was so wild, spooky or nervous that when the little thing had only its head out, she turned quickly and caught the lamb's ear on a nail sticking out from a board in the hall and ripped it. I let her go into a pen in the back of the goat shed and took her some feed and water. She was so darn rambunctious that she accidentally stepped on the little lamb's front right leg and broke it. Two and a half hours later when I came back to check on them, she had stepped on the back left leg and broken that one, too. That was just enough.

I said, "To heck with you. You ain't goin' to have this baby no more." So I took the little thing to the house and commenced putting some splints on its legs and some salve on its ear. I held the little thing in my lap and petted it, "What a sweet face you have with pretty blue eyes--just so innocent. Poor little thing." I felt so bad. I made a box of straw for him and fed him goat milk from a pop bottle with a nipple.

The days passed by quickly and he was standing on his legs. I was so happy. But the sore on the lamb's ear had not healed completely and I saw maggots on it. That made me mad. I went and got some

124

tweezers and picked them all off, then I washed his little ear and put a bit of Vaseline on it, just enough to make powdered golden seal, an herb, stick to it. Every day I packed it with more golden seal until it healed up.

Then this darling little lamb was fat, well and healthy. I staked him on the front lawn every day under the huge shade trees that lined the driveway. "Have a good day," as I gave him a hug. "You darling little thing. I will see you later."

Now we had cows, goats, pigs, chickens, geese, my cat Pester, and Will even bought a few ducks. What a joy to see a Mama Duck take her four babies into the pasture, down the hill, through the grass, and into a small pond fed by a flowing well. The sunlight glistened through the trees and sparkled on the water. Those ducks had the time of their lives. While in the rapture of those moments, I could forget much pain.

I had no objections to bottle money supporting Will's cattle farm, but what would irk the hell out of me, and I felt it just was not right, was that Will was always running off to auctions, sitting on his butt, or going to his dances claiming he was going to find another wife or off to shows just because he had connections with friends who would let him in free. I would think, "Where is there justice?" I would work on my feelings to keep them from cropping up like a weed in the soil. I would keep stomping them down.

Over and over I would try to ignore his sluffing his work, leaving it for me. I had the hardest damn time with myself not to get mad when he would go off to play. He would always have some fun thing going on. If it was not a free show, it was watching TV or going swimming. I just could not see it. Heck, I liked to watch Mission Impossible and Red Skelton once in a while. That was like two hours a week compared to his playing everyday. I liked to hear Red Skelton's jokes so I could repeat them to make Mom and Zosa laugh. To this day I like to remember all the good jokes I dare repeat.

But seeing Will quit at five o'clock every night like he was better than I or something, I just could not swallow that. I felt to seek my God all the more for truly, if there were anyone who might care, I felt it would be the Lord. I did not know of one person on this earth that would give a care. My mother cared, but even she figured that I was just doing my duty. That's fine.

I began to sing in the shop one night with the rain beating against the glass on the shop door:

Put your shoulder to the wheel push along.
Do your duty with a heart full of song.

We all have work, let no one shirk.
Put your shoulder to the wheel.[13]

I would keep on until I choked up with a lump in my throat as I tried
to continue singing.

Come, come ye saints.
No toil nor labor fear.
But with joy wend your way.
Though hard to you this journey may appear,
Great shall be as your day.
'Tis better far for us to strive,
Our useless cares from us to drive."[14]

As I would look at a stack of about 200 cases that would take me
until two o'clock to clean, I could find peace and comfort in the hymns
of my religion. Then the pain was not so great and I would think about
all the fun times I would have in my dreams because in my dreams I
would go skiing or sleigh riding up in the snowy little villages. There
were only about 12 other skiers. Or all the various times that I had
gone swimming in beautiful locations and all the different lovely
environments I had enjoyed. It would just send my soul thrilling.

I dreamed many times that I could fly. I could go anywhere
without my feet touching the ground, and my body would move with the
command of my mind. I could be standing, then when I wanted to go
through the air without walking, I would tilt my feet up in back of me.
I would be about four feet off the ground and just move ahead. When I
wanted to turn, I would slightly turn my head in the direction I wanted
to go and I would go in that direction. Boy. What a way to travel.
But that was a dream and it seemed like I was always dreaming, as I
leaned against the cardboard boxes behind me.

Then the pain of reality would give me a jolt, and I could not help
my eyes becoming wet again. I thought, "This life will never hold
anything for me." I could see before me a scene of myself being a 90-
year-old woman still washing jugs. I told myself, "My mission is to
prove myself and my worth before God, and that's the only prayer I
have." For truly, my mind was so darkened with servitude that I could

---

[13] "The World Has Need of Willing Men," words and music by Will
L. Thompson, Hymns, p. 206.

[14] "Come, Come, Ye Saints," words by William Clayton, music from
an old English tune, Hymns, p. 13.

not even imagine one day--24 hours--where a person in my position could get up and do anything or go anywhere that I wanted to do or go. I could not see how that could ever be, as I began to slap the side of the box I had just tipped upside down to knock out the dust.

Then as I pulled out the liner and flipped it to its clean side and reinserted it into the box, I again looked at the stack and thought, "I'd better hurry if I want to get any rest tonight."

We were into the coldest months of the year. Bard and Nanas took me to the University Hospital to see why I had not had a menstrual period for about four months. The doctor discovered that I was hypoglycemic. He said that I had either been working too many hours, had spent too much time in the cold, or had been wearing heavy boots. Any of the three, he said, could have caused my periods to stop. I was doing all three!

The shop had no heat in it and the floors were icy. I found a pair of old fishing boots at the dump. They were big enough that I could wear several pairs of socks, although that made them quite heavy. So upon the advice of the doctor, when we were at the dump again I sorted through the old boots. I found a pair of ladies boots that fit me. There was a little hole in one. So I put four plastic bread bags over the one foot and then put the boots on.

I liked that style of boot really well and asked Bard if he could buy me a new pair.

He said with a big grin, "Do you think you're worth a new pair of boots?" He was joking of course.

I started breathing heavy and being very sober about the whole situation.

"Yeah, I'll get you a new pair. You're worth it."

It was just like ripping open an old wound and then throwing sand in it. I said, "Don't be in any great hurry. I can get by with these for some time." A few weeks later we found a local connection where they bought me a new pair.

My neck hurt so bad for want of a chiropractor adjustment from tilting my head back to look at the inspection light so many thousands of times that I could hardly stand it. I devised a little contraption to hang myself from to try to put my neck in place so they could save the $3 chiropractor fee, but it did not work very well.

Even though my neck was killing me, I started up a batch of jugs. The water was straight from the boiler, approximately 210 degrees. I had just added the caustic and Bard was putting the jugs in the sink filling them with the water being pumped through a hose from a submersible pump. Suddenly the hose slipped out of Bard's hand and caustic was spraying all over the ceiling, I hollered, "Shut it off." Without thinking, I ran around the vat and ran right through the spraying water as I grabbed the string that controlled the switch.

"Awghhh," I screamed.

The boiling caustic water had sprayed all down one side of my chest, shoulder, neck and face. I screamed as I ran towards the house. Running to the kitchen through the front room pushing objects out of my way as I headed for the bathroom, Nanas and Zosa, seeing me run past them, followed me. Nanas hollered, "What's the matter?"

"It's caustic water. Wash it off," I screamed. I was shaking as I was trying to turn the water on in the bathtub so that it could come through a hose we had hooked up to the faucet.

"Quick grab the mineral water," Nan said.

I was washing myself off then Nan threw mineral water in my face, then that started my eyes to burn.

"Where's the olive oil?" Then she threw that on me as I was jumping and screaming. Then my vision was blurry. All the time I screamed to the top of my voice.

Bard hollered, "Get some of that milk outside. That's supposed to neutralize caustic."

Someone ran and brought some in and they threw it on me. That felt good. "More," I cried. They kept throwing milk on me and I began to calm down a little.

"Ohhh, wrap some cotton on me and pour some milk on it. Can we do that?"

Nanas wrapped gauze around me with large pieces of cotton over my burns and poured milk over the cotton. This would ease the pain but as soon as the cotton started to dry out, it would sting again. I laid on the couch in Zosa's bedroom and had someone dump milk over me every little while.

Bard came in and looked at me after I had settled down and said, "I knew something would happen to you for the way you acted at Genuine Parts store. I didn't punish you enough or God wouldn't have took a hand in the matter. Joseph Smith said we learn by the things we suffer. You can't defy me and get away with it."

"Well, goll. That's been weeks ago."

"I don't care. God might not punish you for years. He gives you time to see if you're going to repent."

If he was trying to scare me, it worked for I had no answers. I was suffering with so much pain. I stayed there about ten days with third degree burns and huge water blisters hanging on me about an inch and a half in diameter. It was about two weeks before I went back to work.

Someone had offered to buy the five acres in Murray where we were. Nanas and Bard were working with a realtor, Kent Long, to try to find us a new location. It seemed like once or twice a week, they would take me with them to go look over a place to see if it would be suitable for relocating the business. This went on for about six or eight months. We saw a lot of nice places, but they finally located a property in West Jordan with a three-bedroom home, large basement where there could be other bedrooms, and a large building in the back which the former owners had used for light manufacturing. It had several other old buildings that we could utilize--chicken coops and what not. They were able to purchase this property of an acre and a half for $35,000. They were selling the home on Fifth East for $70,000. So they located a six and one-half acre farm with a nice home in South Jordan and used the other $35,000 for a down payment. The total price was approximately $65,000 with the balance to be paid approximately at $200 a month. Will could have his cows on this six and a half acres, and of course, I would use the buildings in West Jordan for the continuation of Reclaim Bottle.

Zosa had four children, Sherrie, Don, Skip and Lee. Will and Bardell had three children, Gary, Katie, and Bonnie. Seven adults and seven children totaled 14 members of the family that made the move.

The City of West Jordan approved our license for reconditioning jugs in that area because it was similar to what had been done there for years.

129

CHAPTER 10

I really liked the new home. It was a 100 percent improvement over what we had. A trumpet vine grew next to the house, crawling along the wall so as to protrude a few branches close by the bathroom window. I could see little hummingbirds come to nurse on the flowers there. We spent a lot of time hauling junk from the premises so we could move the bottle business in. With one of the last loads, I took Pester. We were in the back seat. As I stroked her I said, "You're going to like this new place. It's much nicer." I hugged her and petted her all the way so she would stay and she did.

After the move was completed, I could concentrate on working in the business. I spent a lot of time on the phone contacting anyone for whom we could do some type of washing, whether it be bottles, glass or plastic, one gallon or 15 gallons, five-gallon buckets, head pack or cubatainers, or 7 1/2-gallon acid carboys.

I felt eager to begin each day to learn more and do more and try to expand my capacity, hopefully to bring a higher income into the family so that our lifestyle could be improved. However, I could not seem to locate enough work. Then one day when Will and I were at an eating house picking up jugs, I noticed about 15 cases of one-gallon cans, six cans to a case, in their dumpster. I thought for a minute as we were carrying out jugs. When we got loaded there was a little room on the back of the truck. I said, "Hey, let's put these cans on, too."

"What for?" Will asked.

"Well, I'd like to see if maybe I can sell them to the nurseries. I mean, look, Will, if they have thrown this many away at one time, we have to come here all the time anyway to get their bottles, so depending upon how much we can sell them for, that just might amount to quite a bit. You know what I mean?"

"All right."

So we took them home. The next day I called around to every nursery in the valley. I found some sales for them at 6 cents per can, but they wanted holes punched in them, so I asked Will if he would keep bringing them in and he said he would.

I rigged up a little jig. I took a flat piece of metal, 1/2"x1" that was approximately 2 feet long and cut a notch in it, 3/4" wide, 3/4" deep, so as to bend a U shape on the end of this flat bar. I inserted a short bolt that I had sharpened to a point into this notched groove so the bolt would be pinned in the U. Then I took a peg that would normally be used for a hinge on a fence post to swing a gate and I looped the end of the U over it for my hinging action. Then I placed a platform just the right height with a stop on the other side so I could place a can into position very quickly and work the handle to punch holes in the bottom of the can. By turning the can three times, I would have four holes. As fast as I could grab another can, punch holes and pitch it, I was just counting the money that I was making. I started to laugh then I shouted with glee, "All right!" I looked at the clock and waited for the second hand to get into position, then I worked as fast as I could doing this while timing myself. In five seconds I could have one can with four holes punched in it and the other one in place ready to be punched. That was approximately 60 cents per minute. Hey, that's all right. It came to about $15 to $20 an hour for my time and the rest for Will's time to pick up and deliver. It was better than washing jugs because we could wash bottles all day to do 120 cases at 40 cents a case gross income, if the jug belonged to the customer. Then if it was our jug, we were selling them for $1 a case, which was much better. But I was determined to capture the market on this little deal, too, for whatever we could do without going too far out of our way to pick up the cans.

But even then with all the money I could make on doing whatever, I looked at my mother. She was still wearing rags all the time and it hurt my feelings. It seemed like no matter what, I could never do good enough.

When Mom and I would wash 5-gallon buckets, we could do 200 per day including the lid. I would pay $1 per bucket and sell it for $1.50, clean with the lid. So when we had buckets to do, we would make $100 per day.

I was desperately looking for more work to do and went to a place I had contacted over the phone that had 2,000 buckets he wanted cleaned up. He said they only had a little bit of fruit juice and they would wash out really easy. Seeing as how they were his buckets, I said, "Well, I'll do them for 30 cents each."

"That's way too much," he said. "How about 20 cents?"

I hesitated knowing how badly I needed something to do, "Well, let's try a few at 25 cents."

"OK."

So we took 800 of them. When we got home and unloaded them, they were stuck together so bad I had to put sections of them about ten at a time in the vat of hot water to soak them loose. As they came loose, all this rancid peach juice would go into the water. After pulling apart 100, I had to drain the water and start up fresh. But it took so long to pull them apart, that by the time I had washed 100 buckets and lids, that was the most we could do in a day. The worst part was getting them separated.

One night I was using the old water that we had used to wash in that day to pull apart the buckets for tomorrow's running. My clothes were soaked with sweat and the sticky, brandy smelling liquid from the buckets all over the floor and me. Just then a knock came on the shop door. I answered it. It was one of the members of the priesthood council in his suit. I told him Nanas and Bard were at the house. He thanked me and left. I stood there a moment looking at the deplorable condition he had just seen me in. I felt somewhat forsaken and ashamed, then I said to myself, "Good grief. Of all the days to show up. Oh well, it can't be helped right now." So I just finished what I was doing.

After a week and a half when I had them all cleaned, it had rained but now the sun was shining so I went to Will and told him they were ready to load for the delivery. He said he did not want to deliver them, he wanted to do something else.

So I went to Bard and said, "Are you and I going to make the delivery?"

"Why? What's wrong with Willy?"

"I don't know. He said he had something else he wanted to do."

Bard jumped up and went into the other room. "Like what? Why can't you make the delivery?"

"Nan and I were going to look at some turkey feeders."

"Well, you make the delivery first and then you can run around on turkey feeders." Will sat there for a minute looking disgusted. "Come on. Get up and make the delivery," Bard demanded as he nudged Willy in the arm.

Nan walked in the room and Willy said, "Well, I guess we can't go."

"Why?"

"Because I've got to deliver those damn buckets uptown first."

"Well, I guess we'd better do it first then," Nan commented.

So Will went out and backed up the truck. It had mud on the bed from Will picking up old produce from the stores and taking it out to feed his cows on the farm. He started to load the clean buckets without cleaning off the mud, then he shoved them ahead and a stack fell over. I heard the noise and went out. Here were these beautiful white buckets that were such a pain to clean, were all muddy down one side of the stack and on the bottom of the others.

I stood there a minute, sick and forlorn with the fury of disgust running through my veins, I yelled at Willy, "You didn't even clean off the truck. Why the hell didn't you just tell Bard you refuse to do it rather than do this kind of crap? Now, I've got to wash them over, thanks to you. You don't even care. I'd rather make the delivery myself than have you wreck them all just because you don't give a damn."

"Well, why don't you then?"

"Fine. I will."

So I went to the house and told Bard that now I had to wash a lot of them over just because of Willy's dirty, rotten trick. "I'd just rather deliver them myself to see that they get there all right."

Bard said, "OK."

So I cleaned off the truck. Mom and I loaded them, then when Bard and I got up there, the boss came out, looked over the load, "Well, you done a beautiful job, kid."

"Thank you."

"Would you like to take the rest of them and clean them up?"

"Not really."

"Well, what would you charge me to do the rest of them?"

"One dollar per bucket."

The guy gasped, "A dollar?"

"Yep. That's right."

"Well, I can't afford a dollar."

"Well, that's the cheapest I can do it for, so whatever."

We unloaded and I handed him the bill, got the pay and left, with a hopeless feeling running through me all the way home, the thought repeating itself, "There's got to be a better way. There's just gotta be. God help me, we're goin' to find it."

So, in addition to trying to find new accounts, whenever I could spare the time, I would have a few minutes fun with the children. Even though I was not allowed to have children, I sure was glad that Zosa and Bardell had the children that they did.

I took some old chains that we had around the place, climbed up in a tree, sawed off a few branches, and bolted the chain securely so the children could have a little swing.

At the supper table I was going over Don's spelling list while I was eating. Bard came in and hollered, "You're playing with the children again. When you get through eating, I want you in the bedroom. I took as long to eat as I dared then I would go to the bedroom to comply with Bard's demands.

It really confounded me one Sunday afternoon, as I sat with Sherrie in the living room. I was reading a story to her about the life of Wilford Woodruff, how he walked 30 miles through mud and swamp land to preach the gospel. Bard came in, "How much longer you goin' to be?"

I lied to him, "Well, I'm not quite through."

"Well, hurry up." He left.

I went on to read another story about Joseph F. Smith about his mission to Hawaii. He told of an Hawaiian lady that took care of him when he was deathly ill and brought him back to health. Twenty years later he returned to Hawaii. This woman, though very old, came to greet him bringing a cluster of beautiful bananas. She was blind. Joseph hugged and kissed her with such love and appreciation that she had come to meet him.

Sherrie and I loved these stories, but Bard kept awful close track of me so I could not read another one. But I thought, "Goll, if that isn't strange. I can't even read the gospel to his own daughter."

Then on another occasion, Bard was sitting in the kitchen when Lee, his youngest son, came in and in a fun, loving mood, Lee jumped up on Bard, throwing his arms up to put them around Bard's neck with the biggest smile on Lee's face. Bard grabbed Lee and threw him half way across the room, slamming Lee into the wall. Lee's expression was one of shock as he gasped. He looked at me, puzzled, so I put out my arms and went over and grabbed him. I smiled like "come to me," since he was looking at me not knowing what to think. I said, "Oh Lee. Come and give me your lovin'. I just love it and you can just love me all you want to," as I kissed him and held him to me.

Bard said in a heavy voice, "I don't like all that mauling. May likes it. Go to her for your kisses."

I said, "Yeah, I really do."

Lee was sitting down now as I continued to hold him. Bard got off his chair and walked into the bedroom. I rocked Lee in my arms loving every minute of it. Then Lee was fine and went to play. I walked into the bedroom, closed the door and looked at Bard with daggers, "What the hell is the matter with you that your own son can't come up and give his father a hug?"

"Well, I don't like it."

"I don't care if you like it or not. Just suffer it for his sake."

Bard said, "You love him, if you want to."

"Well, I sure will." That made me so sick. Lee was the most loving little boy; anyone could enjoy Lee. Lee and Katie were the "lovers" of the family, always hugging each other and kissing each other, although they were only four years old.

It seemed like Zosa, Mama, Bardell and I were always trying to do what we could to get along with Nan. Bardell, Zosa and I would pretty much do the cooking. It was like whoever started on it first would do it.

Nan came home around noon from going with Willy on the fruit route to pick up the old vegetables for the cattle. Zosa had fixed some lunch for everybody. I was sitting in the kitchen along with a few of the children eating a little bit when Nan walked in. She went to the stove, looked in the pot. Zosa had fixed vegetables with stewed tomatoes with a little macaroni in it. It was OK if you put a little margarine or cheese with it.

Nan turned to Zosa with the children watching, "What did you fix this garbage for? Do you expect the kids to eat that? They won't." Some already had.

Then Zosa being hurt over the statement hollered, "Well, at least it's better than nothing. If you don't like it Nanas, you don't have to eat it."

Nan, still hollering, said, "You're always fixing some kind of garbage. Look at all the things you've wasted that's went into that. It's just a bunch of pig slop."

"If you don't like it, then fix something for yourself. See if I care." Zosa was crying.

"Don't you holler at me," Nan raised her hand and struck Zosa on the side of the head. Then the battle was well on its way. Zosa put up her hands to keep Nan from hitting her head. "Get your arms down." Of course, Zosa kept her arms up. "You get your arms down or I'm going to get Bard."

Nan walked into the other room. "Zosa's got her arms up again."

Bard flew off the bed and grabbing the belt from out of his pants, came in, "You get your arms down," and whacked her across her arms. "Come on. Get them down."

"I will if you'll quit hitting me."

Oh dear. I just wanted to leave the room. I was so damn sick of this scene. When I returned, Zosa had Bard in a clinch. Bard could not moved. Bard looked at me standing there and said, "May, come and give me some help."

I looked at him and shook my head a little bit and said, "If that's the only way you have of communicating with your wife, then that's your problem." Then I walked out. When I was far enough away from his view, I burst into a giggle. That was the neatest thing I had seen in a long time.

As the months went by, Nanas seemed delighted in making people mad at me and would continually sow her discord. Because she would accompany Will on the fruit route every morning, which generally took about four hours, Will told Bard that he did not know what to do with Nanas because she would say all kinds of things about May.

Will said, "I don't know if they're true or not, but if I tell Nanas to shut up that I don't want to hear it, then she gets mad and starts mistreating <u>my</u> wife. But if I don't say anything and just listen, then I find myself believing her and I have to work with May and this makes it very difficult for me."

Bard said, "Well, tell Nanas that if she doesn't stop her damn discord, that you'll leave her home. Then do it a couple of times, if you have to. She'll quit."

Then in the house she would say things while talking to Bardell like, "I've seen May take some of our brand new towels and wipe off her muddy boots." Bardell's job was to do the washing as well as go through the produce. Why Nan would just say such an ignorant thing to try to make Bardell perturbed at me is unknown, but she would.

Strange enough even after I had been there ten years, I was still taking care of Nanas every night. Somehow I was such an "horrible person" but yet I was the only one that she wanted to put her to bed at night and give her a bath because she said that anyone else was not careful enough with her sore spots. Although Nan never asked for forgiveness, I would forgive her anyway, and continued to do the best I could for her. But I always knew that if Nan ever really had her way, it would be my throat.

I had thought about this situation and took my line of reasoning before Bard. "You know what, Bard. Even after all these years that I have been here working to support your family, still if anything happened to you, I'd be kicked out without one dime to show for ten years of hard labor. You know how you're always saying you're on borrowed time and you know how Nanas is always sowing discord."

Bard said, "Yeah, I know what you mean."

"I just feel like it's hopeless. You can't put appreciation where there isn't any."

Bard went to Nan, "We ought to put something in May's name for all the years that she's been here supporting the family so she'll have something if anything happens to me."

"Well, hell. Willy's worked too. You act like May's been doin' it all and she hasn't."

"Well, if it wasn't for May's labor supporting the family, and Will's cattle farm, we'd probably have to live off welfare."

They discussed this situation for several days. Then Bard said, "If you don't want to give May anything, then I'll give May my share."

As Nanas had put everything between her and Bard, then Nanas decided, "Well, fine. I'll give my half to Willy then and they can work to take care of us."

So the papers were drawn up although the business property of an acre and a half on Redwood Road was half Will's and half mine, the same as with the 6 1/2-acre farm in South Jordan with half Will's and half mine. It was a general understanding that if "cuts ever come to cuts," Will would take the farm and I would take the business. I had no idea what would have been fair but I thought, "Let's see now. For ten years' labor and they paid $35,000 for this place, that would be $3,500 per year for my wage. Well, that's OK. That's better than a poke in the eye with cigar butts." I felt somewhat enthused now because I had something concrete to build upon.

There was enough money to make a downpayment of $5,000 on a $21,000 dollar home next door. The neighbor had passed away. And we figured that between renting it and what I could make, we could make payments of $186 per month.

As the months went by I continued trying to locate work. Florence Titian from the Titian Chemical Company asked me if I knew where I could get 55-gallon metal drums. I said, "No, but if I hear of any, I'll let you know." Shortly after that I was calling around to some of the bakeries to try to locate some 55-gallon cardboard barrels for Will to use on his fruit route. I called a local bakery and they told me they had three metal, open-head drums they would sell me for $3.50 each. I asked how often that I could get that many and they said once a week. I talked to Bard and Nanas about them. I told them I thought some of the people in the group could use them for wheat storage.

Bard said, "Well, why don't you call them and ask." So I called around to several of the large families and several wanted them. Will picked them up. I cleaned them out by laying the drum on the shop floor and reaching in with a pad and detergent, remove the lard. I rinsed them with a hose then I would sell them for $6 cleaned.

I called Florence Titian to see if he could use open-head. They were blue and white and the paint was still pretty good after I finished washing them. I told him they would be $6.50. He told me he could use all I could get. I thought to myself, "All I can get? Oh, boy!" That statement got my adrenalin going. I sold all we had and began looking for more.

I called around to some of the dairies and sure enough, we picked up another source for drums. Then we began picking up 15 a week from the dairies. That was approximately 20 drums a week that I had to clean. I had to figure a better way to handle them, so I made a rack out of 2x4s and a pipe. An angle iron was bolted to the 2x4 on the bottom. To look at this rack sideways, it had the shape of a triangle. I could clean the drums out much easier, then I contacted an even larger dairy in Ogden and started buying all their open-head, approximately 70 per month. They said, "If you don't take the closed-head, we can't sell you the open-head."

"OK. I'll take them too." But I had no way of cleaning out the closed-head drum. After I had accumulated 25 or more drums, I told Nanas and Bard we would have to buy a submersible pump to wash them. It would cost $60.

I went to work making a rack to go over the bottle vat by using 1/2-inch pipe. I borrowed a cutter and threader and got the Ts and elbows I needed to put it together. A drum weighed approximately 35-45 pounds each. I made a step shelf on each end of the rack to rest the weight on as I could not just lift a drum.

I took a pipe cap and drilled holes in it for the nozzle to give the water somewhat of a spraying effect. With this screwed onto the pump discharge, I could then flush closed-head drums. After washing the closed-head drums, if they were bare metal on the inside they would rust immediately if they did not get dried out fast enough, so I hooked up a little contraption to the natural gas line and put a pipe on the end with a flame shooting out of it into the drum. But after the oxygen in the drum was burned up, the flame would go out. So I had to develop a better way of drying them.

I found a little 5-gallon barrel in the junk pile out back, flushed it out, then I put it on top of a little natural gas burner. I built a little skirt around the drum so the flame would not blow all over with the one side open so that it would get enough air to continue burning. I then drilled a couple of holes in this little barrel with a circle saw, inserted a vacuum hose on the one side going up to the barrel, then the air from the vacuum going into the little drum which was being heated on this little burner, then that would dry a drum over a period of time. But it was not nearly fast enough.

I called up a friend, Joseph Mandley, who had been in the plumbing and heating business for years, and we discussed how we might make something more efficient for drying the drums.

I was also thinking about what a man who worked at VWR was telling me about a little machine that would hold two barrels, tilt them from their tops to their bottoms while rolling sideways, with chains in the barrel to scour out rust, as some of them were too rusty to sell even after washing.

I took some plans of what I thought a chainer might look like to Bob, who was a welder by trade, to see if he could make me one. I continued to wash mainly open-head and save up the closed-head until we could have a decent dryer and a chainer made.

Without painting the drum, I could do about 20 open-head a day from start to finish. I was still working on bottles two to three days a week. When it came time to license, I said to the lady while handing her my money, "What do I do to change the name of my business?"

"Just tell me what you want me to put down here."

"OK. Put Reclaim Bottle and Barrel."

After approximately a year's time, Bob had what we figured would work for a chainer: a little frame with wheels on each side and a shaft with wheels in the center and a motor with a sprocket attached with the chain going to the center shaft to make the center shaft turn. This is what would cause the drums to roll. But the only way we could get the barrels to go on their top was to go on that side of the chainer and push down, then put blocks under both sides to hold it in that position.

Different blocks were used when we wanted to hold it level and the same for the bottom, but this was quite time consuming.

Then the little chainer developed some serious cracks in the frame. I asked Bard, "What are we going to do to fix it?"

He said, "Well, load it on the little pickup truck and we'll take it over to be welded."

So I unhooked the electricity that went to the motor and rigged up a skid braced with the little truck and figured out how to use a come-along winch. After working the better part of a day, I had it loaded and ready to go. Bard drove it over to be welded. After 20 minutes welding we were on our way again. I said to Bard, "We're going to get a welder."

"Why? Nobody knows how to weld."

"That's all right. I'm going to learn."

So we did. I started out doing a lot of "turkey pucking" with a little buzz box. My horizons had expanded and I loved doing it! The work was not a masterpiece, but man, I could make all kinds of little things to assist me in creating more effective equipment.

I had put together another 20-gallon barrel with a flame under it for drying closed-head drums. I welded a few baffles on the inside to restrict the air from just whipping through for a better, hotter drum dryer. I bought a commercial insulation blower and hooked that up for my air supply. That worked fairly decent for drying a closed-head drum. Then I asked Wayne at Centron Chem if he wanted to buy some of my closed-head drums. He said, "Sure. Send me about 20 of them." I had washed glass gallon jugs for that company for years.

The only thing I had for painting was a paint brush but Wayne said he wanted them painted. I did not know the difference between latex and oil base paint, so I got some latex paint and tried thinning it down with turpentine. I mixed and mixed--this was the strangest stuff--it just would not act right. After about half an hour stirring, I thought, "What the heck." I took the brush and commenced to paint the drums. Boy it looked really strange. It was not covering or anything. So I painted them again. I used black oil base paint for the sides and this white latex for the tops. Well, needless to say, the tops looked like they needed to be painted again. So I gave them a third coat. I thought, "Well, that's about as good as they are going to get, I guess."

We loaded them on the truck and made the delivery. We unloaded them at Centron and Wayne looked at the drums, with an observant eye. I said quickly, "Do you have a bung wrench? We can unscrew the plug and you can look inside."

"Oh, if you washed them I know they're clean." Still looking at the drums, "But boy," he exclaimed, "You're sure one hell of a painter.

Next to me, standing on pallets, were other reconditioned drums. I gulped with envy looking at the product my competition was producing. Boy, they looked almost like new. I thanked him for the order and we left.

I asked around with some different people on spray painting equipment. The best deal I could find was at Sears. They had an offer of a little compressor, the hoses, canister and gun for $70. So I told Bard we needed to get that. The little cup would hold one pint of paint and I learned all about the difference of latex and oil base so as not to have that problem again.

Soon after that I got a 30-drum order from Flo Rep to be painted orange for anti-freeze. My mother would bring the drums to the doorway for me to wash, then after I had washed them she would put the drums on a 2-wheel cart and take them to the old chicken coop which we called our paint shed. It took all day to do 30 drums, so at ten o'clock that night Mother and I were ready to paint.

Orange is a rather transparent color. The painting set-up consisted of two turntables made out of 3/4" plywood with some casters which I had bolted on the bottom of the plywood with a pipe flange bolted in the middle. The pipe from the plywood would drop in a bearing block bolted to a flat steel plate on the floor. I could sit on a little stool I had made out of grocery cart casters bolted to a little piece of plywood and a cushion glued on that. I would kick the tables with my foot to turn them while I painted. I had no exhaust fan at that time and the fumes were heavy.

After I painted the drums, Mom and I looked at them and the original color of the drum was showing through the paint really bad. There was orange paint all over the floor and there I was half stoned from the fumes. I looked at Mom and started to cry. It was an orange nightmare. Mom said, "Come on, May. Can't we just forget it for the night? We can't kill ourselves just because we have an order. You look tired and I'm tired."

"But we need to deliver them in the morning so we've just got to do them over."

"OK. Let's hurry then and I'll help you."

So we began to paint them again. Bard came down to the shed. He started railing at Mother, "You're supposed to hurry so that May isn't waiting for you instead of being so damn slow."

"Well, Bard. When you get as old as I am, then we'll see how fast you are."

"Well, I'm sure I'll be faster than you. You're slower than cold tar in January."

I stood up half stoned, "Well, she is helping me and I appreciate it. Heck I don't see anyone else around that even gives a damn 'cept Mom. You're too busy watching the boob tube to even care what's goin' on."

"Don't get smart with me. I'm the one who allowed you to go into this barrel business to begin with and I can just as easily stop it if you don't show me more respect," he yelled as he hit me on the shoulder.

Standing on slick paint with my footing not being too sure, I fell and landed on my bottom. I picked myself up off the floor, my head spinning, "Well, yeah, but it's benefiting all you guys too because of what we're doin'."

"I was benefited just as much and more by the bottle business."

I stood there and a hopeless feeling came over me. I just wished he would leave. I stood there saying nothing. We were looking at each other. I said, "Well, can we please just finish."

"Well, I'll go but you'd better get your head screwed on straight." He watched us for a while then left. We finished about 2:30.

CHAPTER 11

I wanted to drop the bottle business and go strictly into reconditioning drums. I approached Bard with this thought one afternoon. We were in the kitchen sitting around the table, and I said, "You know, I think I can get enough barrel accounts to where we could just flat out drop the bottles and do pretty well."

"You're just barely starting into something. You really don't know hardly anything. You could have OSHA, or West Jordan City, or anything shut you down. You'd better not drop the bottles until you are positively sure of what you're doing."

So I continued on for approximately another eight months doing both bottles and barrels. It was such a disgusting thing to me to continually set up to wash bottles for a day or two and then switch back to my barrel set-up. I wanted to locate more accounts so that I could wash their drums.

There were a couple of oil companies that I thought were large enough that I could work steady for. One afternoon after washing a batch of bottles, I said to Bard, "I think I've got enough accounts to work for to make a decent income that we don't need the bottle business anymore."

His comment was, "I'd rather you stay with the bottles. I know you want to go to the barrels. I knew you'd come to this someday, but I think it is a job for a man, not a woman. You'll probably spend the rest of your life putting back all the money that you make into building the business and never live long enough to enjoy the fruits of your labors. I think it's way too damn much work."

"Hey, work I already know. But at least it's got a future."

"Well, I'll tell you one thing right now. If you feel that you can do well enough on the barrel business to support my family, plus the cattle operation along with the fruit route, and still have time to take care of me, then OK. But if any of those things need money, you're not having any to build your barrel business. But after those things are taken care of and if there is anything left over, then you can use it to build your business."

I thought of all the shows I had seen on Mission Impossible. My body tightened like I had gravel in my guts and spit in my eye. "Let's go for it," I said to myself. My time would be extremely well organized to accomplish the most amount possible. I thought to myself, "It's a matter of getting the right contacts. If I could get some half decent drums in here and get set up for better production, I'd have something."

But I had to pay more so that my incoming contacts would sell me their drums. When selling I would have to sell for less to have the

143

customers take my barrels, which were not as nice looking as my competitors' drums.

I contacted a paint company and arranged to buy a load of about 80 resin drums for $3 each. They told me the resin would wash right out with hot caustic water. But when I tried running them through, they would not come clean. I had tied up $240 on that load and had no idea of how to clean them. I went to bed that night after trying to wash them and perspired from the pressure, searching with my mind going through space trying to pick up any particles of light on the subject.

Bard was already threatening to make me stop on the drums. If he knew I was at the pit of despair, he might try to stomp out my dream of someday having something worthwhile. Where could I go? Who could I ask for the knowledge that I desperately needed? I shook, tossing and turning, in a cold sweat until morning.

I got up and built a rack that would hold five drums. I held the drums on a tilt so the resin would drain towards the big bung hole. I took a cream scoop from the house and bent it so that I could extract most of the resin that had settled there. Then I took the drum and put thinner in it, put the plug back in, let it sit for a day, then put them through the wash. They came out clean enough for me to sell. I painted the load. Titian Chem said they would buy them for $8, but after getting the load, they said they were slightly sticky inside and that they had to rinse them with acetone before they could use them. So they only paid me $6 per barrel. Anyway, I learned that that method of cleaning worked fairly well.

I contacted another paint company for their resin drums for $1. One hot summer day while I had drums on the rack, I forgot to screw out the small bung on top before I unscrewed the large bung on the bottom. The pressure from the heat of the day built up inside the drum so that when I unscrewed the bottom bung, it went poof! It blew resin all over my face and eyes. There were some nasty words that crossed my mind. I had to wash myself quickly with paint thinner.

Mother was doing most of the chaining--that is what we called it when we put drums with chains inside on the little machine Bob had made. After I had extracted most of the resin, Mom would put thinner into the drum--about one gallon--and put it on the chainer. Then after they had rolled on that for 15 minutes, the drums were tipped upside down on a rack outside the door to drain into a sludge holding tank underground.

One morning for some unknown reason, the rack was not there outside the door and Mom put a drum over for me to wash that was right side up and had been chained with thinner. I brought it inside without thinking much about it. After I washed the outside then boosted it to the washing rack, the thinner splashed out onto the floor which quickly caught fire from the flame underneath the vat that heated the water. This caused an explosion that blew out the shop windows. Fire was all over the floor. It was a wonder that drum did not blow up and kill me. The hose was in the middle of the fire. Standing there, Bard yelled to me, "Grab the hose!"

"I can't. It's in the fire."

"Grab it anyway."

So I did and commenced to spray water everywhere. I was able to put out the fire from all the things that were burning around me, but I got third degree burns on my arms between my gloves and the short-sleeved sweater. I no sooner had it under control when Bard, with a smokey face, started hollering, as if I needed chastisement, "You're going to kill all of us before you're through." What could I say. So I did not say anything.

Bard got a small burn on the ankle and Bardell had a small burn. I was glad that I had gotten the worst of it, if someone had to be burned because it was my fault. The whole shop was black and smokey inside, but I was thankful to still be alive.

After several months of working to earn all I could, I finally made enough to buy a few improvements. I had installed a small exhaust fan in the paint shed and bought a couple of 3 1/2-gallon paint pots along with a paint gun. I now had a 10-horse compressor. One day I was in the paint shed switching the material line from one paint pot over to the other for a different color. The bleeder valve that releases the air acted like all the pressure was out, so I commenced to undo the quick coupling. "Oh, hell," I exclaimed. The pot had full pressure. It shot paint all over me from head to toe. I was dripping with blue paint. I stumbled past whatever to get to the bathroom where I had to use thinner to clean myself up. Bard walked in. I had one eye opened. He began to laugh. "Ha, ha. That's the best thing I've seen all day. Oh, I shouldn't laugh, but you ought to see yourself. Ha, ha, ha, ha."

"I hope it makes ya' happy." I was glad I had free thinner which had come in the drums because I sure used a lot of it.

I had figured that I could do possibly 50 drums a day instead of 20 if I had a high pressure sprayer to wash off the outside of the drum, which would increase the income to $200 per day. I bought a pressure sprayer, but I needed 3-phase power. I proceeded to try to get the power company to install 3-phase power on the property. Everything was approved, the date was set when they were to come to do this. I called up in the afternoon to find out why they had not shown up. The man in charge said that he had a note on his desk that morning from the City of West Jordan that said there was to be no 3-phase installed for Reclaim Bottle and Barrel.

I asked who signed it. He just said, "The City of West Jordan." Oh dear. I called an attorney and explained that I had put "barrel" on my business license along with the "bottle" and that if they were going to shut me down, why did they not do it then, because now I have spent several thousand dollars on equipment to recondition drums. I told the attorney that for every day my high pressure sprayer was not in operation, I was losing $200. I have no idea what he did, but the next day the power company was down there putting up the 3-phase.

With appreciation I thought, "Whenever they want drums for something, they'll be happy I'm here, because I will just give them a heckuva deal."

Mom was out chaining drums on a wet, drizzly day. I was washing trying to get a rush order through. Mother came over to me and said, "May, the chainer's on the blink again."

I came out and looked at it and said, "Oh shit." The motor mount frame had cracked on the side and the motor had dropped in the mud, ink and oil below. "Heck, I just welded that thing half an hour ago." But I never could know where the next breakdown was coming from, because this thing was so coated with crap. I felt like I was under such tension. I looked up in the air as I clenched my fist and gritted my teeth, and just wished that I had a nice little room I could go into that had a foot of insulation all around the walls so I could scream bloody murder to my heart's content, and then come out and go back to work and fix it. But I had no such room.

I looked at it and looked at Mom, rain dripping off the plastic bag she had on her head. The feeling of hopelessness running through me, I slid down against the shop's outside wall. I sat there looking at my problem, then started to bawl. I just kept crying with the rain washing my face, along with my tears, my arms braced on my knees as I sat there in the mud. Then I began to think. "That's an explosion-proof motor. All I have to do is hoist it back into place and spray the mud off. It'll be fine."

I looked back up at Mom as she said, "Oh, come on, May, what are you going to do about it? Let's hurry."

"Would you please help me up?" I held up my hand for a lift. She helped me up. "OK. We've got to move all these thinner drums so I can weld after we wash off the motor with the high pressure sprayer."

I got the welder out to secure the motor rack up in place. As I was standing in the muck trying to weld, I kept getting shocked. I felt like everything was after me to blow my mind.

I got it repaired and felt much better. Mom said, "You know, May, we're just like pioneers."

I smiled. Huh. I had never thought of that but I thought that was cute.

146

Mother was always willing to help me. I would gladly let her rest if I thought she would get to rest, but it seemed like every darn time she was not with me, I would find Bard had her cornered somewhere, either railing on her or slapping her around or some damn thing. It just seemed a lot better for her to help me at whatever pace she wanted to go. I needed her spiritual strength and encouragement. She was the only one that maintained confidence in what I was trying to do. I never heard even one discouraging word from her.

Mother's Day came and that was one thing Bard could not stop: my sisters would come over and bring my mother something. Previous years Bard had tried to stop the girls from taking Mom to Chuck-a-rama on Mother's Day. My sister Esther said, "I'll call the cops. I'll just tell them you've got my mother locked up and you won't let us see her." Bard did not like that idea too well, so fine. Twice a year--Mother's Day and on Mom's birthday--Mom and I went with my sisters to Chuck-a-rama. Nanas was welcome to come with us so she did. Sarah and Esther, my sisters, had bought Mother a new blanket, three new dresses, and a new sweater.

The next day Mother was in the kitchen when I walked in. Bard had a hold of Mother's hair and was screaming at the top of his voice, "I don't give a damn who gives you what. Anything that comes in this house comes into the family and Nanas will decide where it goes." Then he let go of her hair as he shoved her head back.

Mother put her hand up so as to straighten her hair a little bit, "Well, I'd like to keep those things that my girls brought. But if you don't want me to, it's OK. I like Nanas."

With all the railing that was always going on, I said to Bard, "You know there's one thing about it that you have to admit. Of all the things that people do to Mama, I've never seen her, not even one time, take revenge or say anything bad about anyone."

"Yeah. Yeah, that is one thing that's good about the old devil," he commented.

I thought about how Bard was always forcing people to do what he wanted. I asked him, "The brethren said that force is of the devil, that God don't force anybody."

"Ha," he said. "When an angel stood before Joseph Smith and said, 'You either do this or I'll run the sword through you,' now tell me that's not force."

"Yeah, but don't you think you'd get more by showing people love?"

"Are you kiddin'? That's a joke. If you let people do what they want, they'd just sit around and do nothing and I'd have nothing but lazy bums on my hands. I'll tell you, before I'd have a wife like that, there'd be some serious ass kicking. Zosa is lazier than hell, but I see to it that I punish her for it, too."

147

"Yeah, but have you ever thought of just being sweet and asking nicely?"

"If you're so smart, why don't you try it and see if it will work?"

"Well, it'd be better than all that damn beating. That's not going to make her work harder." I turned to go about my own business. I had no more to say and left the house shaking my head.

The blanket ended up on Nanas' bed, the new sweater on Nanas' back, and the same with two of the dresses. Nanas gave mother her old clothes since they were the same size. The one dress that Mom got to keep was black with orange flowers and white and purple designs. I think that is why Nan let Mama have it.

Cleaning drums was still a problem. I asked the man at the paint company if there was a way they could drain the resin drums better. Some had as much as a gallon left in them. "Boy, May, if I could, I would. That stuff's valuable."

"Well, it don't have no value to me."

"The only thing you need is the paste, which is for color, along with lead, cobalt, and ASA then you could use it to make paint."

"Oh, yeah? Well, why don't you write down the recipe for me. Do you have all the ingredients there I could buy?"

"I sure do, and I'll make you a heckuva deal, too."

"All right. Let's go for it."

So I saved the resin and got to making my own paint. The ingredients cost approximately $2 a gallon, so I really appreciated the savings over our having to buy paint already made. Bard came out while I was making some blue paint for Amoco Oil drums and asked, "Are you going to come in the house and take care of me?"

"Well, I need to make some Phillips gray, too."

"You're always doing something, and I'm getting neglected. I told you when you first started the barrels that you had to take care of me. I'm not going to suffer over your damn business. Now come on. Get up to the house."

"Well, let me finish with this first."

"How much longer will it take?"

"About 45 minutes."

"Well, hurry up."

He was gone for about an hour and then came back. "You ready to come up to the house?"

"Well, not quite."

"You said 45 minutes and it's been an hour. Now come on. Get up there. I mean it, now quit," as he took the stick out of my hand and put it on a barrel, giving me a nudge in the shoulder. "Come on."

"Now, just a minute. I've got to put a lid on this thing so it won't dry out."

He stood there while I fetched a lid, secured it tight, then I went to the house with him following behind me.

Bard had his ideas of exactly how he wanted to be, as he called, "taken care of." He had this hang up about exactly how I should undress, that being when I walked into the room, I was to go over, fetch a pair of see-through pants from under the mattress, slip off my stockings and boots with my skirt and blouse still on, then slip the pants on underneath my skirt and turn towards him showing him my behind while dropping my skirt, then removing my blouse, stand up on the bed while he was fondling his privates while watching me, and I would turn around for him to see my body, then he would say, "OK. That's enough. Lay down now."

While having intercourse he would pull out just before he ejaculated, lay there and rest for a few minutes, long enough for him to relax, then he would say, "OK, get up and show yourself again." This would continue for about an hour and a half, then I could go to sleep.

He would wake me up at two o'clock in the morning by shaking me and kicking me, "Come on. Get up and take care of me again." After this went on for approximately one hour, then if I slept until five, he would wake up again and I would have to proceed for another hour before I could go to work. But if I did this, he would pretty much leave me alone all day long while he slept and watched television, coming down to the shop occasionally to check on me. He would never allow himself to have a natural climax until three days before my period. Then after he had had a climax, three hours later he would want me to work him up again. He would allow himself to climax once a day. Then during my period, I would not have to have intercourse, but rather I would have to work him off by hand while being in a position so that he could look at my body.

As we lay there, I asked Bard, "Why do I have to be the one to take care of you sexually?"

He turned and looked at me, "Because you're the one that God has blessed with a beautiful body and you don't get pregnant."

"Well, why can't you sleep with Zosa? She wants you to sleep with her."

"Ah, hell. She's too damn filthy. She stinks so bad, I can't even stand to go in the room let alone lay down beside her. I don't mind having it with Zosa if you want to pose [for him to watch me in the nude while he is having intercourse with Zosa]. If you want me to have it with Zosa, that's fine, if you're ready to have three times as much when I get through."

"No way." I could not figure that out.

Zosa came to me in the bathroom on one occasion and said, "May, will you show yourself so I can have intercourse with Bard?" I replied, "Look, Zosa. I have no problem with showing myself so you can have it, but the hell of it is, Bard's told me that I have to have three times as much when I get through and I know that this is the way it has been in the past. What is hard for me to explain is I don't want to have intercourse with him for one damn minute, let alone for hours. I'm sorry, Zosa, but I can hardly stand him."

"Oh, May. I'm sorry. I didn't know."

"Please don't tell Bard, because I have to do what he wants or he'll fight me on every turn I make." I left the bathroom and walked outside in the fresh air trying to sort out my mind.

I would try to do just enough for Bard to keep him happy. So I was then free to run the business as I saw fit--pretty much. Being determined to rise above the poverty level, I dedicated my body, mind, and soul to build Reclaim into something.

The little chainer that Bob had made for us was all together too light. Having to repair it anywhere from three times a week to four times a day, I gained quite an education on mechanical engineering, also metal stress and strain, by oversizing to adjust for the continual shaking and hammering on the carriage. By the time I had repaired the little chainer as many times as I had, I thought to myself, "I could have built a whole new machine three different times."

As the months went by, I could afford bigger air compressors and I came up with a design for making my own paint pots of an approximate 20-gallon capacity. I ordered ten pieces, three feet long, 12 inches in diameter of 1/8" pipe, also 20 convex end caps that would fit snugly inside the pipe. I then welded the bottom cap inward and the top cap round on top and made ten tanks. I welded a pipe going down from the top just up two inches from the bottom for a material line and an air supply coming in from the top and a bleeder valve to the side on top, and I rigged up the plumbing so that by merely turning a few valves, I could stir the paint with air. Shut off some valves, turn on others, and I was ready to paint. This allowed me to have many customers' colors on tap to expand our abilities.

I felt that I had enough air pressure from the compressors that we could dedent drums if we had a dedenter, that is, a cage that secures a drum so that air pressure can go in the drum to pop out the dents. I knew where I could locate approximately 100 drums a week I could get just for hauling because they were so dented. They were an 18-gauge bare metal drum that I figured I could sell for $10.50 after dedenting and washing them. That was approximately $1,000 extra a week gross if I just had a dedenter.

I asked Bard about making a dedenter. "Save up your money until you have $12,000 then buy one."

I was not contented with that thought. "It will take me forever to save up 12 grand."

"If you start messing around with air, you don't know what you're doing. You could kill yourself."

That ended the conversation but it did not stop my mind from wishing. When I was off by myself, I drew little sketches of what this thing might possibly look like in order to do the job. I thought of the size and height and just how possibly it could be put together so that it would actually work. I considered all the materials I had on the yard that Willy had accumulated from who knows where. Then I waited until Nanas and Bard went somewhere for about three hours.

I dragged the materials in and began measuring and cutting as fast as I could. Bard came home, walked into the shop and asked, "What are you doing?"

"Well, I'm trying to make a dedenter."

"I told you to forget that crazy idea. Now get that crap out of here and get back to doing something you know how to do."

So I dragged the materials out, pretending that I had repented and listened very earnestly to every word that he said, until I overheard another conversation of when they were going to be gone for five hours. Oh my. I had that day pegged. I made sure that at the moment they left, I ran as fast as I could, dragged all that material in, and began welding it together.

With the worry of Bard catching me, I hurried so fast that I had not done as good a welding job in one corner as I should have. I was ready to test a drum when Bard returned. I saw him coming. I had a drum in this cage with air inserted through a fitting I had welded into a bung, but this cage had no shield around it. I hollered to him, "Stand back. I'm trying this thing out." As I inserted the air pressure, I was 30 feet away watching this set-up through a plastic window in the paint shed. Just guessing, I thought it had enough air so I uncoupled the connection, waited for it to release, then went to check it out.

"All right," I hollered. "Look at that. Look at that! Hey, I can sell that drum now. Just a minute." I grabbed at another dented drum, rolling it towards this cage. "Here. I'll show you." I took the one drum out of the contraption as quickly as I could, put the other one into position. "OK. See that--how bad that is? Now just watch. Stand back." I went over to add pressure again. Then I came back after the air had exhausted, "See that? Whoopee!" I hollered. Thrills of joy were running through every part of me. "Isn't that neat," I laughed. "That really works."

Bard stood there with a bored looked on his face, "Well, it is a little bit better."

"Little bit better heck. Now it's good enough I can sell it. Before it was a piece of junk. You're looking at $2.50 straight profit right there every time I do that," as I removed the drum to insert another one into position.

After doing the third drum, we noticed the frame that I had made out of 4-inch eye beam--the top part being a 2 1/2-foot span--had a 3-inch rise in it. I talked Bard into taking me to get a 5"x 1/2" steel plate that I welded on both sides of the eye beam, top and bottom, also some other necessary improvements, like a metal cage with a door to secure a drum from killing someone if it should blow apart. And I rigged up a motor and gear box bolted to a plate that was welded to a couple pieces of pipe with bearings inserted in the pipe that would run up and down vertically on a polished case-hardened shaft.

I had fastened the motor shaft to a 3-inch threaded shaft that I had made specially by a machine shop along with a nut which was welded underneath the top part of the frame. The threaded shaft went through the nut with a bearing secured on the bottom of the shaft, fastened to a one-inch solid plate the size of the top of the drum. By working the controls, the motor would take the plate up and down so as to allow us to insert and remove the drums very quickly.

We had a 1/2-inch thick metal round--like a pipe--2 1/2 feet in diameter, 3 feet tall. I cut it down in two places, and put heavy hinges on one side and a lock on the other side. Then I torched 2" holes at random in the round so as to allow 10 cubic feet of air under 100 pounds pressure to exhaust in a split second. By using the machine to generate a higher income level, I would make improvements on this piece of equipment as time and finances would allow.

One summer day Boyd Huntsley, Jr., was operating the dedenter when a heavy drum blew. There was a flaw built in at the time I originally threw the frame together that I had not detected. The pressure was so great that it pulled a piece of metal apart 1"x 1/2". In a split second the bottom part of the dedenter blew open sending the machine like a rocket up to the ceiling cracking a floor joist then down again breaking a huge hole in the cement floor. If Boyd had been on the other side, he would have been killed instantly. I was sick at heart at the thought that my invention almost killed a young man. At the same time I was so thankful to God that he was all right. My mind tracked through time as I remembered how fast I threw that frame together.

As I stood there looking at the mess, Bard walked in the door and began to holler at me, "See what I told ya! You don't know what the hell you're dealing with when ya start dealing with air." He did not need to say that. I already felt like two cents worth of dog meat. I looked through the scrap pile and found several lengths of 1 1/2" pipe, approximately 4 feet long. I dragged them in. By using a wrecking bar to tilt the dedenter so I could put the pipe under it, I could roll the dedenter on the pipe and rotate the pipe. With the help of Bard's boy, Don, who was about 10 years old, I managed to get the machine to the other side of the shop. Then I drilled a hole in my office floor directly above so I could lay a steel bar across the floor and bring the hook up from a come-along and hook it on the bar so I could jack up the dedenter.

I did not know how I was going to fix it, but the next morning I was up at four o'clock because I knew my clean stack of drums was limited and companies were depending on us. I knelt down and asked the Lord to please inspire me to know how to fix it right so that I would never have to worry about it again and to give me the strength to do it.

I walked out, sat down on an old cinder block in the shop and stared at the mess, still not knowing what to do. Then I decided to cut off all the twisted metal junk and hope for some ideas. Sure enough, I did figure out as I went along how to repair it and then to reinforce any possible weak spots, then to reinforce as a third precaution. I went entirely through the machine and reinforced as a fourth precaution anything that could possibly have a chance to give way. By the time I was nearly done, I really felt good that this was five times the machine that it was before. No matter how many drums blew apart, I would know that everything was fine.

Joseph Mandley was out of town and Bard would not help me. After two weeks working from 4 a.m. to 10 p.m., the dedenter was almost finished. I had built an all new undercarriage for it and the locks worked like a charm. The top part where the bearings were mounted so the motor could go up and down was lined up perfectly. I had tried to finish it totally that night but my strength would not allow me to.

I came in the house. The scene that hit me as I entered was filthy walls. The kitchen floor had not been cleaned for at least a month. The sink and sideboards were filled with dirty dishes and the table was a filthy mess with baked-on crap like it had not been cleaned for days. No supper was prepared. I was very hungry since it was 10 p.m. and I had not eaten since 1 p.m., doing cutting, grinding, and welding all day. I went over and got a bowl to put graham crackers and milk in. I moved enough on the table where I could put my bowl

then sat down. As I sat there, I had hardly enough strength to feed myself.

When I was finished, I crawled along holding onto the walls to make it to the bedroom. I opened the door. Bard lay there with watermelon juice on his underwear and the sheets, the plate still on the bed with the rind on it. Candy wrappers and peanut shells covered the floor and some were on the bed. Bard sat there with buffing dust on his face which he had gotten from going down into the paint room while my help was buffing drums earlier in the day. I looked at the watermelon juice on his chin as I entered and took the plate off the bed, and set it on the dresser next to a six-pack of pop. I pulled the blanket over the watermelon juice and fell on the bed.

Bard said, "Well, come on. Get up and take care of me."

I lay there in silence. He raised his tone of voice. "Come on. Get up. It's your own damn fault you work as hard as you do. I've been waiting for you all day and I'm not goin' to suffer just because you want to work like a fool. Now, get up!" He shouted, "Come on, get up!"

I lay there while he was kicking my leg with his foot. He had hold of my arm and was shaking me then he grabbed my nose and shook my head back and forth, "I'm not going to let you sleep until you've taken care of me."

I laid there as long as I could and then said, "Bard, I should think you would appreciate having a wife that would work as hard for your family as I do."

"Well, I do appreciate it. But I'd appreciate it a whole lot more if I had a wife instead of an old work horse."

"But if I don't get the dedenter finished, pretty soon we will be losing orders 'cause our stockpile is all gone."

"Well, I can't help it. I'd rather you lose orders than neglect me."

What could I say. I remained silent and lifeless.

"You're not going to sleep," he hollered as he continued to shake me. Then he commanded, "Get up and do something for me or I won't allow you to work at all tomorrow, if you don't take care of me tonight. Now, come on, get up. You could've come in sooner but you didn't. So it's your own damn fault."

"I'm so tired I feel like I could die. I just can't."

"Oh, yes, you can," gritting his teeth, "and you will. You're not going to make me suffer anymore." He put his foot on my hip and kept shoving until I fell from the bed. I put my arms and legs out to break my fall, then I lay there on the floor.

"Come on. Get up," as he grabbed my hair. Accelerating my disgust for what seemed to be a nightmare rather than reality, it took all the constitution I had to hold myself like a lump of coal without flying apart. I stood up, looked at him, crying inside, and dropped my clothes. My mouth was closed tight.

"Come on. Put some life into it. Don't act like you're dead." Just as he said "dead," I fell back on the bed. I could hardly hold myself up anyway and I was not about to entertain him if I did not have to. He grabbed my nose again and shook my head back and forth.

I raised my hand and hit his arm and said, "Do you think all this is going to help you Bard? Whatever love I ever had for you in all the world, you're killing it. And once it's gone, I don't think I'll ever be able to bring it back." While I lay there enduring his loud voice, in my heart I made a covenant with myself to never do anything for him that I did not absolutely have to do.

He kept kicking my leg while pushing me out of bed again, as though I meant no more to him than a warm piece of meat. Where are the answers? What is it? I can't even think. There is an intelligent solution to every question.

I was confounded to see such inconsideration. Somehow I had supposed that he appreciated what I was doing. In the shadows of the darkness, the thought kept repeating itself in my weary mind, "He wouldn't care if it killed you."

"Come on. I'm not going to wait all night."

With agony of body and spirit, I lifted and moved my body thought I felt no more stamina than a soggy piece of macaroni. "Can I lay down yet?"

"No. Not yet. Keep going."

As I turned, my body was shaking while my stomach was threatening to relieve itself of graham crackers.

"I can't," I exclaimed as I fell onto the bed.

"Damn it! You're going to pay for this."

The next thing I knew, the clock said 5:30 a.m. Bard was asleep. I quickly got dressed and left to start a new day.

CHAPTER 12

I was beside myself over the memory of Bard's inconsideration that was more horrible than anything I had ever known up to that point. I sat in the kitchen while having some breakfast and Nanas began to rail at me, "I know you can't keep that business going much longer. It's going to crash. If Will doesn't get more than $5 an hour, he'll just quit bringing in the drums for you."

She had been telling me two days beforehand that the reason Will had been charging diesel fuel on my account and having the attendant give him cash with it appearing on the receipt as fuel was because I did not pay Will enough. But I paid him $5 per hour even for the time he was on the fruit route to pick up cattle feed as well as barrel pick ups. The good produce that Zosa and Bardell would take out from the barrels that contained cattle feed and set aside for the Saints to pick up and utilize I felt was a very worthwhile project. I seemed so vulnerable to Nanas' and Will's tactics of stealing money from me. They would always come up with different ways that I would not suspect.

I sat there while she continued, "He's going to quit and get another job. Douglas Excavating would hire him tomorrow at $7 an hour, if he wanted to work for them." Her words were like drums pounding in my ears.

I walked outside and Bard hollered out the window, "You'd better quit early tonight, if you know what's good for you."

I just walked to the shop with a blank stare on my face. It seemed as though I was trying to forget so much that I was beginning to feel like even the space around me seemed to be coming closer at times so as to squash me. My spirit was slowly dying as I was slowly but surely becoming somewhat demented. I had little faith in myself and as I worked and things were accomplished, I would stand back, look at the project, and exclaim, "I did that? But how did I do that?" I would look with amazement at my own accomplishments and say, "Could I do it again? I don't know. It looks kinda' complicated. I can't even remember how I did it." I seemed to get more stupid every day.

I went upstairs to the office and sat down to dial Dillard Oil to see if they had a load of drums we could pick up. I was half way through dialing when it occurred to me that I was dialing their address. "Scrud!" I exclaimed. "How stupid." My head dropped into my hands while I listened to the ticking of the clock keeping time with my fast pulse. My mind was racing a mile a minute--Bard's demands, Nan's demands, Will's demands. Somehow I must please them all.

Brrring. "Reclaim Barrel."

"This is Union Pacific Railroad. We need 50 open-head drums

157

delivered to Store 240 in Salt Lake City. Use the same order number as last time, as soon as you can."

"OK."

"Thank you."

As I hung up I exclaimed, "Oh, for good. Man, that's neat. I've got 65 out there all ready to go." Just two days before I had had it out with Ron Delsey at Delsey Honey Company on a load I had sent to him two weeks ago.

Bardell was doing the washing for 14 people and the oldtime Maytag had broken down leaving her to wring all the clothes out by hand. I looked at that and said to myself, "This is a bunch of bull. There's no dang sense in it. You need an automatic washer and dryer and by crackie, you're going to get one." So I called up and asked to talk to Ron to see if they could pay us the money they owed.

"Hello. This is May at Reclaim. Uh, do you think it's possible we could be paid on the load we delivered two weeks ago? I'd sure appreciate it."

"I don't think we can pay you until after 30 days at the soonest. That's the best I can do."

Bang went the receiver. I sat there looking stupid holding an empty phone. I quickly dialed him again.

"Could I talk to Ron again?"

"He's on another line right now. Would you like to hold?"

"Yeah hello. I'm sorry to bother you again. If I didn't need the money just really bad, I wouldn't ask right now."

"You mean you called me back again just to tell me that? I was on a long distance call," he retorted in a loud voice. "I've got more to think about than you and your damn barrel business." Bang.

I sat there for a while thinking. After about ten minutes, I decided. "It ain't right. I don't think he'd give a hairy rat if I was cold, hungry and in the dark. He wouldn't want to pay me one day sooner. So, what am I going to do about it?"

I called again and left a message. "Could you please tell Ron that the driver from Reclaim will be in there tomorrow to either pick up a check or pick up the drums. I'm sorry but this is just really important that I get the money. And if we pick up the drums, then he can find someone else to do your reconditioning."

"OK. I'll give him the message."

"Thank you."

So the next day Will ended up bringing back the drums. We unloaded them in the paint shed, as I thought, "A lot of good that done. Now I won't even get paid in two weeks. Who knows when I'll sell them."

"Thank the Lord!" I said out loud, as I quickly raced through the invoices to find the blanket order number for Union Pacific with gratitude running through me. Here it is. I began to copy the heading: Union Pacific RR. P.O. #---. Delivered to Store---, SLC. For reshipment. Shit. To Pocatello, Idaho. What? "Oh, no! Mercy sakes a living. I don't believe I did that. That invoice has already been sent off for payment. Heck. I hope they pay it. Oh, May. Wake up!" I said to myself. Gheez.

I ran downstairs to the house. "Will, do you want to back up the truck and load 50 of the open-head in the shed to go to Union Pacific? Here's the invoice."

I went to find Bardell. "Ya know what? We just sold those drums. I'm going to use the money from them for your washer and dryer. We could start looking around to find a deal."

"I'll be so glad to see that." I was looking at her smiling face. "Yeah, that will sure be nice."

Within a couple of weeks, the new set was installed and working. We were all happy.

The water line coming to the shop was also hooked up with the house. I had started up a batch of drums. While trying to rinse one, all of a sudden my pressure was cut down to a tiny stream of one foot high, making it impossible to continue. That along with all my other agony, I stood there and bawled. I just wanted to cry and kept crying. Somehow it made me feel better just to be a boob. Day after day after day every time anyone would use water at the house for anything, it would shut me down. Deeply frustrated, I felt like screaming, pulling my hair out or bawling, all of which did not help. "I either have to get some decent water flow or go nuts," I cried. "I've got to get this hummer fixed."

This was happening way too often. So I called up some friends in construction and asked them what the price would be for them to run a 1 1/2" line back to the shop. The price was high but I would just have to do it. I had them start installation immediately.

Several months later with that improvement of having plenty of water pressure, I decided to hire a little more help. I already had two guys working part time helping buff and paint. If I could find small jobs that Bard could do to help me make better equipment, I asked if he would come down and help.

He answered, "I'm not goin' to help ya'. You're the one that wanted all that damn work. I don't. Why don't you go get Joseph Mandley to help ya'?" When Bard was in a good mood, he would help for maybe an hour--until something good came on the television.

Even though Joseph Mandley was an expert in his field, his wage being from $20 to $50 per hour depending upon the type of work, Bard felt that Joseph would help me without charging me anything. I did not like to impose upon Joseph but he had such a sweet, willing attitude that I called and asked if he would come help me.

Joseph was 72 years old. Bard was only 48. When Joseph came, he would grind off slag from the pieces of steel that I cut and he would help me measure things and line things up for whatever piece of equipment I was working on.

We were working on the development of an even more efficient drum dryer. After he had helped me all day, we sat up in the office kitchen.

"How much do I owe you?" I asked.

"Don't worry. I'll send you a bill."

"But you've been saying that for over the last two years now."

He wore a big smile as he gave way to a jovial little laugh.

I said, "How would you like some fried chicken? Zosa's cooking some."

"That sounds delicious."

"Fine."

I ran to the house, made a quick salad, and grabbed three plates with salad and chicken. I took one into Bard and went to the shop with the other two plates. As we sat down, Joseph asked the blessing. While we were eating, I said, "You know, Joseph. Seriously, I realize you charge $20 per hour when you work on other jobs and I don't have any idea how many hours you have worked here. You know, I have to be able to pay this bill and I expect it's pretty high already."

There was silence for a while. We looked at each other and he began to answer in a very tender voice, "I have never in all my life seen anyone work so hard to support so many with so few rewards for herself as you have. I decided years ago that if there was anything I could do to help you, I was going to do it."

I sat there thinking of what he had said with tears in my eyes then said, "Thank you."

He continued, "You've really got a head on your little shoulders."

I had always looked at Joseph as a highly intelligent man. What a statement coming from him. He was such an expert in his field. These sweet words lay so gently on my soul. I smiled and said, "Would you like to see a drawing I done of the air dryer we're making so the man from the gas company can see how it works?"

He smiled, "Sure."

I quickly got it and brought it to him.

"Uh huh. That's pretty good. And that's a very efficient design we've come up with, too. They ought to like that."

"I couldn't have done it without your help," I said.

"That's OK. Anytime you need any suggestions, just call me."

We were walking down the stairs from the office now. I walked down to his truck as he was about to leave. There was a longing in my spirit that was saying, "Oh please don't go." So I talked about everything under the sun that I could think of so he would not go. But after about two hours, the sun was about to go down and I said, "Well, thanks again."

His hand was on the door and I put my hand down on top of his as I applied a little pressure while looking into his eyes, what a humble expression his face contained. "Thanks," I said, again coming from the bottom of my heart.

"You're welcome."

I removed my hand and backed up to allow him to leave. As I worked in the shop I was thinking of the lovely words of encouragement he had given me. Something inside would say, "Joseph thinks I'm smart." I would smile as gladness filled my soul.

I would call Joseph and discuss new ideas and all kinds of things. Just talking to him was such a spiritual strength. I soaked up his encouragement like a sponge. When I went to make an improvement, Bard would say, "That's not the way you're going to do it."

I would go in, get Joseph on the phone, and explain my plan to him and he would say, "That's really a good idea."

"Could you please talk to Bard. He doesn't want me to do it."

So Joseph would talk to Bard and he would tell Bard (I would know because I was on the other phone listening), "The girl has a good idea. Let her do it." I noticed Bard would never argue with Joseph because he knew that Joseph was such a well educated man on many things.

Whenever Joseph came, I could not help but notice his clean, neat work clothes of navy blue and a smell of Old Spice pleasantly arraying around him. Even though he was helping me with dirty jobs, somehow he would manage to keep his glasses clean. I also noticed every time that Joseph came on the yard, Katie and Lee, the two youngest children, would come and hug him. Seeing this, I tried to control my feelings but was wishing inside that I was getting a hug, then I looked away.

As the days went by I felt a force coming over me more and more. I could not seem to control my innermost feelings. "Could I be falling in love? I wonder." I had never felt this strongly about anyone before. As I fought with my feelings, I said to myself, "Golly, May. He's in his 70s and he's got a big nose."

No sooner had I thought that than the other part of me said, "And I think he's darling."

The only time I was happy was when I was talking to or was around him. Then when he was gone, I would contemplate his return. I

161

thought to myself, "That's what's the matter. By George. It's true. You're falling in love, Mazie."

I told Bard one afternoon while we were in the buffing shed, my two part-time employees were listening. "Do you know what, Bard? I love Joseph."

"Oh, you don't love him. You just appreciate him."

"Oh no. I love him."

"Well, I don't care if you do just so you love me more."

Every day my mind and my heart were upon Joseph, remembering the good times we had enjoyed working together and the great expectation of when he would come again. The thought crossed my mind over and over, "How would it be if Joseph died and I never did tell him what I think or feel?" Oh, that would be so horrible.

One morning when Joseph came to help me, the sun had just peeked up over the mountains at the start of another beautiful day. I quickly walked to the shop. I threw open the door. Joseph was standing by the chime straightener. Oh, my soul felt as though I could melt. He looked better than a million dollars to me. As I proudly walked up to him, opened my arms and he opened his, we hugged as I gave him a great, big kiss. Wow. What a kiss. The thrill from that went through every part of my body. I felt like hot wax that was about to puddle on the floor. I was starved for affection I had never known. As we kept kissing, I experienced something like I had never even had the wildest dream possible. The feelings that I had tried to keep confined now were exploding with joy.

"I love you Joseph. Do you know that?"

"Yes. I can tell. I love you, too, little darlin'."

To try to keep my head straight and think about accomplishing work that day was next to impossible. My mind was on him. That is all there was to it.

After that heavenly day went by, I thought I should have another discussion with Bard about children. Not that I felt any desire to have Bard's children but I knew that Bard did not believe in having intercourse with a pregnant woman and it would stop me from being abused. Also, I thought it might be better for me to be pregnant than to have my feelings run away with me because of my love for Joseph.

I said to Bard that night, "What if I tricked you into getting me pregnant by me moving ahead when you go to pull out?"

Bard said in a most horrible tone in his voice and cruel expression, "Don't you ever, ever do a trick like that." I sat on the bed with a blank stare on my face.

I thought, "Oh, how sick. Has he been lying to me all these years?"

Bard had a cold. Ka, ka, ka. Splat--as phlegm hit the wall.

162

"Oh, hell. Can't you spit in the garbage can?"

"It's on your side of the bed and I'm not going to hold it in my mouth and take a chance of swallowing it again. Just get busy and clean it up."

Oh, yuck. It was enough to make me sick to look at all this crap running down the walls. He had spit there for days. I had put newspaper on the floor but not on the wall. With Bard's body odor lingering in the room, I closed my eyes to think of Joseph's sweet kiss and perfume. Just as I was falling asleep, Bard demanded, "Get up and fix me some spuds."

"Right now?"

"Yeah, right now. Come on." His foot pushed against my hip and I got up.

I said to myself, "Bard might have my body and all my earnings and the labor that I can accomplish, but Joseph has my heart and I can't help that."

With Joseph's help, my interest in improving the equipment in Reclaim Barrel was accelerated. Joseph came to help me again one morning about six o'clock. I had been working since 4:30 a.m. on a jig to make the washing nozzles over the vat to rotate so that it would clean the drums better. I nearly had it finished by the time Joseph arrived. Being in the shop alone, he walked in, came up to me and grabbed me. Then he gave me one powerful, loving kiss. Oh. I thought that was the end of my knees. Wow. The thrill went through me like a streak of electricity. I went for another then another one.

"Oh, I love you," he murmured low. "You're so sweet." He glanced over at my little project and smiled, "And versatile, too. You're everything a good man would want in a woman."

Joseph truly had all the right words to say. As I stayed there in his embrace, I looked up at his pale blue eyes. They held an expression of innocence and gentleness. His sweet smile had caused deep lines in his cheeks. His cute nose--it looked just like Jimmy Durante's. I laid a big kiss on the end of it as I gave him another squeeze. I stood there just holding him for a moment while my soul seemed to receive a rejuvenation as a light bulb would if the cord were plugged into an electric socket.

After we had worked that day, the drum dryer was perfected. I had located a blower that would force seven pounds pressure through a 1 1/2" line. That air was forced through this heating chamber. After two minutes the drum would be so hot it could not be touched with bare hands--and perfectly dry inside.

That night after Joseph had gone home, I thought how Mama loved Daddy and his name was Joseph also. Here was I, madly in love with a

Joseph. The magnetism that brought us together was extremely powerful. Like a gnat being burned up on an open flame, I could not resist the fire. Every day I was so full of desire to see him again.

I remembered my statement as a child telling Uncle Walt, "I'd never marry an old man. Ha!" Now the laugh was on me for I truly felt a fulfillment of a longing when he arrived.

I had a dream that night that Joseph came to the house and I told him that I would get him something to eat. When I went in the kitchen and returned with a meal for him, he had gone. I looked at the family and asked, "Where's Joseph?"

"He left. He said he had to go on a mission."

"Well, when will he be back?"

"He didn't say. He said that he might not come back."

I flew out into the night and ran down the street. I came to a cross in the road. Not knowing which way he went, I ran down one part of the cross as fast as I could. Then I ran back up and down another part of the cross. I was asking people, "Have you seen an elderly gentleman go past here?"

A man answered, "Yes. I seen an old man go into that white house over there."

I ran to the house, opened the door without knocking, and there was a man lying on the couch with his back towards me. I quickly turned him over. It was someone else.

"Oh, excuse me," I gasped, and backed out.

I was heartsick, forsaken and forlorn. I gave up as he would likely be far away by now as I slowly walked back to the house. I opened the door and the family asked, "Did you find him?"

"No, but if I ever, ever see him, I'll never let him out of my sight again." I sat and wept.

When I woke up to find it was only a dream, I went straight to the shop and called him at 4:30 a.m. I told him the dream, "Oh darling," I cried. "I hope to God you never leave me."

Joseph came as soon as he could to soothe my hurt feelings from that nightmare. When I was in his arms, I said, "Honey, there is something I need to tell you."

"What's that?"

"Well, I'm not Bard's daughter. I'm his wife."

"What now?"

"I don't know. But I love you with all my soul." I wanted just to stay in the security and joy of his loving arms around me. It dawned on me that after Joseph came into my life, I no longer had the dreams of heavenly places nearly as often and that was all right. For now, I was living in reality like as if it was a dream and loving every single day.

164

"Joseph," I said while looking in his eyes, "what if something happened and I could marry you? What do you think about having children?"

"Hummm," as he gave me a squeeze. "I can't think of anything sweeter than having children with you. I would probably spoil the little things rotten or just love them to pieces."

What a gorgeous answer. I imagined what our children would look like--little cottontops with pretty blue eyes. I said, "They'd sure be cute with big noses on every one of them."

"Now, if they took after their mother," Joseph said, "they'd be saints. But if they took after their father, they would be holy terrors."

"Oh, come on," I laughed. "You're as sweet as they come."

"Hmmm. But not as sweet as you, my little darlin'."

We decided to get to work.

He helped me for about three and a half hours then he had to tend to other business. My mind was a furious confusion over the whole issue.

What kind of situation was I in and why? I did not know. Bard refused to give me children and I am married to him under the covenant. "When can I have my children as I am getting up in age now?" I asked myself. I am 34 and my patriarchal blessing says I would be a mother in Israel. All this turmoil and arguments I had heard for years about Mom shacking up (as Bard called it) with my father on the prairie. The shame of my illegitimate birth that I had lived with.

I went to the shop storage room and put this question before the Lord. As I pleaded before Him, "Why am I going through this? I don't understand, Father, if there is a way that I can marry Joseph, please bring it about. I'm so happy he has come into my life. Please don't ask me to give him up. I'll do anything, anything you want me to. But please don't ask that of me." I whimpered while trying to speak. "I don't want to have a baby out of marriage but I do so want to have Joseph's babies."

As I knelt there, I had ceased praying for a moment while my mind was thinking, "What a hypocrite I am. Here I am telling God I want His will while all the while I'm begging for mine." I felt my prayer was likely in vain but the disgust in my feelings declared, "If I never have to have intercourse with Bard again, it will be too soon."

Then I raised up from my knees and sat on the floor crying. I thought, "I wish to God I had to go to Joseph's bedroom every night then it wouldn't be such a hell."

I began to daydream thinking how it would be to have a few privileges like going to the canyon on a picnic with Joseph where there is beauty everywhere you looked. Or to be by the side of someone I loved and who was so sweet to me, and then to have some nice goodies in a basket. Ummm. I was just seeing it all in my mind. Oh yes. I have Joseph's head on my lap so I can gracefully kiss him while he is resting. I loved this thought. "Dreamer," I said to myself. "You'd dream your whole life away if you didn't have so much work to do." Oh dear. I got up. "Heaven help us," as I kicked an empty box out of my path.

CHAPTER 13

Joseph began to study plural marriage diligently. He had a wife but did not want to lose me. It was late afternoon when Joseph arrived. I ran to the shop. We went where no one could see us if they walked in.

"How's my darling?" Joseph whispered.

"I've been missing you. I'm so happy you got here OK." He held me while I melted into his arms. "I have been waiting for this privilege ever since you left, just living and counting the seconds until you are here--holding me again. Oh, Joseph. It takes every ounce of strength in me not to upchuck and to say 'to hell with it all' and leave."

"What about the business though?"

"Even if I did lose it, you're far more important. We could make it doing something. Heck, even if I was a scrub woman, I'd be happy. Besides, between my guts and your brains--you know--I'm sure we'd do OK."

Then Joseph said, "But you've sure worked hard for all this, little sweetheart."

"Yeah, but you just don't know what I have to live with to keep it. Bard come up to me this morning and said, 'May, I saved your life today.' And I said, 'Oh, yeah? How?' And he said, 'There was a shit-eating dog headed this direction and I killed it.'"

Joseph reacted, "Oh hell. What a dirty, rotten statement. You know, honey, I just can't figure out for the life of me how in the world a man like him ever got you for his wife. I just can't comprehend it, you know?"

"Yeah, I know what you mean. What I can't figure is how he has the audacity to tell people that he loves me and to tell me that he loves me, when he's all the time slandering me in front of other people for some kind of kick he gets. For whatever reason, I don't even know."

I continued, "Oh, you know what, honey? I made the neatest salad. I think you'll like it. Do you want to wait here for just a minute and I'll run and get you some, OK?"

"Hurry up," as he gave me a little slap on my behind.

I brought back a salad that had pig weeds, watercress, mustard green, boiled egg, and little pieces of cheese topped with thousand island dressing. We had the blessing and Joseph began to eat.

"Ummm. Now that's what I call a salad. I really like this."

"I got almost everything from the field right next to us."

"Man, this is delicious."

"Well, I'm glad you like it. Whether anybody else does or not. Should I tell you what Bard said just now when I gave him a bowl?"

"What?"

"He said, 'What the hell you got in this? Some damned old weeds again? You're always trying to feed me weeds and I hate it.' So I said, 'OK. What would you like?' He said, 'I want grilled cheese sandwiches.' So I made him some, but I'm sure glad my little sweetheart likes it."

Joseph finished eating and I went over and sat on his lap and looked into his sweet face and said, "If I had to give you up knowing now what joy is, it would be like turning from the light back into the darkness. Years ago when I would see someone run to hug someone and they would seem so happy, I was so confounded. I never could figure it out. Oh, but now I know. I look at the world through different eyes than I used to. You're like a reward for years of hard labor."

Joseph's eyes were wet. With the sweetest smile and a heavenly look of innocence in his eyes, he said, "Oh, May. I would give anything to have you. Like Jacob worked 14 years for Rachel? I would work 14 years for you."

I put my head on his chest and wept as I whispered, "I love you so."

We worked on repairs for approximately two hours then Joseph had to go.

Every other Sunday I took Bard's and Will's children into the office and taught them Sunday School. As I was teaching the children, I thought, "Here I'm discussing religion to help these children become better and yet I wonder if my life has a stain because of my love for Joseph. What in the world are we going through all this for?" Perhaps it was to prove to me that I was not perfect. Not that I thought I was ready necessarily for the celestial glory, but I would pride myself in the control of my mind, my thoughts, my appetites that I might do God's will over my own. But this was different. How could I fight something that I wanted so badly.

I dismissed Sunday School with the children. As they all ran downstairs to play, I sat there for a moment contemplating on what Joseph had said the day before. He told me that he was impotent and did not know if he could give me children or not. I thought, "If God wants us to have children, we'll be able to have 'em. Besides," I said to myself, "I'd rather go through eternity just holding Joseph's hand than anything Bard had to offer with his big prick."

I had enough money saved up ahead that I could buy a diesel tractor if I got a really good deal. So I bought an old clunker that was barely hanging together along with a trailer that would haul 144 drums. I had a larger vat built and with Joseph's help we insulated it to keep the water hot. This new vat was long enough that we had two nozzles washing instead of one and a large gravity flow pump, so that I could have two people washing drums. Boyd Huntsley, a good friend of mine, had a son, Kevin, who was just out of school and looking for work--a very fine young man. I saw an excellent opportunity to hire a very trustworthy, hard working young man, who later became my manager.

It expanded our procedure from the 30 to 50 drums per day that I was able to do by myself to 140 per day with two men washing the barrels. My being able to answer the phone so that they could continue to wash was far more profitable.

Joseph and I built new paint tables. They were square racks made of angle iron. We bolted four pillow bearing blocks that had two shafts running through the block bearings with cone-shaped metal pieces welded on the ends so that the drum could roll and the top and bottom shim would be the only thing that was touching. Then we hooked up an air ram that expands and contracts that would tilt the one end down so we could take the drums off when they were painted. The rolling was done with an air motor. We made two tables but the first motors we put on were way too small. They were supposed to be a horse but they acted more like a mouse. So I got some larger motors installed. We felt that we had the set-up pretty much perfected. We were ready to time ourselves.

I postponed doing the painting until Joseph arrived because he wanted to see how fast we could do this. I had some good guys help me take one barrel off one table and put another barrel on while I was painting the drum on the other table. Then I would swing around on my pivoting chair and paint the one they had just put on. I had one paint gun in one hand for black paint and the other paint gun in the other hand for white paint. With the paint pots I had built, I could put 100 pounds pressure instead of 60 recommended pressure on a factory pot. Also, with making my own paint, I was able to add more color for coverage so it could be just a drat bit thinner to come out quite fast. Joseph was standing by the door with his stop watch out of his pocket. We were all in position. Just raring to go, I said, "Tell me when."

"OK," Joseph said, while flipping the paint fan on, "Go!"

Boy, I concentrated on every second to make the most of this deal. The guys would grab hold of the painted drum with a set of vice grips, flip the handle, the table would tilt down to drag the drum off. They would put on another drum, flip it up, while the other kid would drag the drum across the room. It took three guys to keep the two tables supplied and me going lickety split.

When we got through with the 144 drums, "Stop!"

"All right. What did we do?"

"Nineteen and a half minutes."

"Let's see. What does that figure?" I asked.

"Well," Joseph scratched his head, "I think that's around 7 1/2 drums per minute, isn't it?"

"Boy, are you sure?"

"Yeah, that's about right."

"Wow. Are we good or what!" We all stood around laughing. "Wahoo! Can you believe it! That's so neat I can hardly stand it. Do you know what that means? Course, we was just showing off, but heck, realistically, think how fast we could do 300 drums if we needed to. Man, that's so neat."

As the days went by, I tried to locate more business, but it seemed like all the accounts that I ran into had quite a bit of chaining to be done. Our poor, little two-barrel chainer could not keep up with the demand. Mama was working nearly day and night chaining drums. It seemed like there was only one answer. I checked into the cost of a 6-barrel chainer. The man quoted me $45,000, 1/2 in advance, the other due when the chainer was finished, and they could not promise a completion date. "Forget that," I said to myself.

I went to Bard and said, "I'm going to have to build a 6-barrel chainer."

"Are you sure?"

"Yes, I'm positive. There's no way that I can get enough business in here without one. Just like Centron's account, we could do all theirs but they've got over 75 percent chainers. I mean, we're talking 300 drums a week to be chained and there's just no way in all the world that I can ever pay $45,000, half in advance, and they don't promise a completion date either. So I know what I've got to do."

"Do you think you're smart enough?"

"Well, there's only one way to know and that's to try, and if I screw up, I try again. But I've got to figure this thing out before I make a move to know just exactly what the heck I'm doing."

"Well, OK. It's fine with me, if you think you can."

I was getting approximately 150 drums per week that had large dents so I got them for nothing. With the dedenter perfected and the washing system adequate, I could sell them for $10 to $11 a drum. This was producing enough income with what accounts I already had to where I felt I could afford the chainer parts.

I had never had any experience in mechanical engineering except for all the work I had done in repairing the little 2-barrel chainer along with fabricating several pieces of equipment for Reclaim. But this was a monster of a job as far as I could see. "That's all right," I thought. Joseph had such confidence in me, I had to give it all I could, no matter how difficult it was. I could not disappoint him.

So I measured, calculated, drafted, and drew plan after plan with different ideas, taking the best from each idea and applying it to another one until I figured that what I had drawn would actually do the job. Then I showed the drafting papers to Joseph. He approved. I continually went over my drawings pinpointing each intricate part then drawing a line out to a large circle then drawing that part out to scale so that I would know exactly what it needed and how to put it together--what needed to be done first and so on.

I spent hours on these plans. Bard came upstairs where I was drawing, looked at me, and said, "You're just wasting your time." He pushed my drafting papers away from me. "If you'd just get down there with a torch, I'll show you how to build it."

I was offended by his ignorance and while pulling my papers back to me, I said, "I can't just do that. I have to know exactly where every single part goes and what size it is. It's a whole lot easier to erase a mistake on paper than to have to weld metal back together because it was cut in the wrong place."

"Well, I don't think all this is necessary. I think you're just wasting your time."

"Look, man, I'm the one that's got to work to earn the money for the parts. Right? And if my plan is wrong, then I'm the one that's got to correct it. Right? So, I would at least like the privilege that seein' as how it might be a screw up, at least it'll be my screw up. OK?"

"Well, all right." He left me to myself.

When I felt confident that I knew exactly what I needed, I ordered the chainer parts. Some things needed special machining so it took nearly a year for all the parts to arrive. During that time I also fabricated a water vat for testing the drums for leaks. We filled the drum with air then a pneumatic ram was fastened above the vat with a bracket that pushed the drums under water.

Also, I located a machine that would straighten and reseal the top and bottom chimes of the drums thus improving their appearance considerably. Our reconditioning methods were approved by the Department of Transportation and a DOT number was issued to Reclaim Barrel. We were then able to have DOT certify our drums and therefore picked up more accounts.

171

When all the parts arrived for the chainer, I was anxious to begin construction. But between managing three employees, organizing the loads coming in and going out, secretarial work, cooking for the children, taking care of Nanas and meeting Bard's demands, I could only spent one to three hours a day on the construction. So to allow more time towards this project, I designated all of Saturday and Wednesday of every week toward working on the new machine.

All during the project, Joseph would give me whatever time he could spare. After seven months I looked at the monster machine and thought, "Will I ever get this hummer built?" But every hole that was drilled, every weld, every bolt that was sunk put us that much closer to the completion date.

After a full year of untold hours and $20,000 spent for the many parts, the project was finally done. Joseph was so proud of me that he just beamed, "Boy, I know of a lot of men who would not believe me if I told them a 108-pound young lady constructed that machine!"

We had professional movers remove the machine from the shop, take it outside and put it in place. Joseph and I hooked up all the lines from a hydraulic motor to the tank. We had a man come to wire the electricity, but even after it was running, I still had a few problems that I had to fix.

It ran about a month when the main shaft broke in half. It was 1 1/2" thick and there was just too much work load on it. "Oh, hell," I thought. "We have all these companies waiting for us to recondition their drums, and this will take some time to repair."

I had my help remove all the flammable drums from the area then we sprayed down everything with water so I would not catch the place on fire. I got the torch out there and cut away all the old shaft and removed the bearings. I went to town and picked up the bearing blocks and shaft with three new chain sprockets for drive. Everything was being switched to 3".

Several months passed and the business did fairly well. In addition to paying the bills so Nanas would not need to worry about them, I also gave her $120 per week to do whatever she wanted to with it. At that time I was buying the groceries, hay for the cattle farm, paying for the diesel to go after barrels for the barrel business as well as barrels of produce for Will's farm, and I was also paying $186 a month on the white house next door and all of Reclaim Barrel's debts. We had never been better off financially.

One day I walked into the house and went over towards the sink, thinking that I would make some soup for lunch. I took some vegetables and washed them, cut off the bad spots, and was dicing carrots to put in a kettle. The children were running up and down the stairs as usual when Gary, Will's boy, ran up from the basement into the front room. I moved the kettle of vegetables over to the table so I could sit down while I was preparing them. I saw Gary whisper something to Katie, his sister, then they ran downstairs together. A moment later, Katie ran back upstairs and into the front room then into the bedroom to find Bonnie, her sister. They were very happy over something. Then Katie whispered to Bonnie and they went running by me to go downstairs.

I stopped Katie and being anxious to know what they were so tickled over, I bent over and whispered to Katie, "What's the secret?"

She looked at me and smiled. "Well, I'm not supposed to tell you."

"I won't tell anybody. I promise." I tickled her under the chin. "I tell you my secrets."

Then she said, "Well, Nan found some candy in one of the barrels and she said not to tell you or you might want some."

The smile dropped from my face and the kids rushed down the stairs. I sat there in shock. Sick to my stomach, I was totally confounded. There was not a thing that I had that I would not share with the children. But this was Nanas. I wanted just to forget what I had heard and pretend I did not know about it, but I could not. It offended me to such an extent that I was weak and felt a little faint. I sat, resting my head in my arms on the table, whimpering like a baby. Even all that I gave and did for Nan, I had done it willingly because I did have some love for her even though I never could comprehend or understand her actions.

I did not know what to do. I just sobbed. Bard came in and went to his bedroom. I thought to myself, "I don't know if I should say anything or not."

I went in and sat down and said, "Can I tell you something?" Then I told him.

Bard jumped up. "I'm not going to let her get by with that. She's so damn selfish, she stinks." He went downstairs and sent for all the children. I was standing there listening. He said to them, "I want to tell you something. For as hard as May works, she is the one that has earned the fuel for Nanas to even go to get the candy. Nanas is just so damn selfish because she is jealous of May. That's the only reason she doesn't want May to have anything. Do you understand?"

I looked at the children and said in a soft voice, "I want you to have the candy because I love you, not because I didn't know about it. OK?"

I was thankful for Bard's sticking up for me, but it took a long time to get over the hurt. It seemed so unreal.

It was a cold, drizzly wet day. I was in the paint shed with three of my employees. They were standing around waiting for me to replace the worn pulley belt on one of the paint tables. Because the employees were all waiting for me, I was hurrying as fast as I could to undo the bolts, replace the belt, line up the wheels, and tighten the bolts up again.

Bard walked in. Bard started hollering at me with these employees listening. "Why don't you ever look over the equipment to see how it's doing to avoid some of these damn breakdowns around here? If you were doing your job the way you ought to be, you'd have seen that hose wearing where it was rubbing against the steel long before it wasted all the hydraulic oil. If you'd put a bend in the middle of that metal line so that the hose would have been far enough from the side of the chainer, it wouldn't have worn a hole in it."

I looked at the guys. They seemed somewhat uncomfortable at what Bard was saying, but he did not care. He just kept on hollering. Then one of the guys who was timid by nature spoke up and said, "I don't see where it was May's fault. Actually, I don't see where it's anybody's fault."

I appreciated his words but Bard continued to rail on anyway. Then Bard left because we were ready to paint. When the drums were painted, one of the guys, while walking out of the paint shed, slapped the "No Smoking" sign on his way out and said, "May, how the hell do you ever stand that man? You must have nerves of steel. I couldn't put up with that for five minutes. Boy, I'm afraid I'd kill the sucker."

Just two months before that time, I had an employee doing the chaining who was continually perturbed at Bard. He threatened to kill Bard--flat out--to his face. With the fury of that fight, I hated to dismiss such a good worker, but boy, I did not know if he was serious or not. So this more recent statement came as no surprise.

On another occasion I was in the office and I had just gotten off the phone. Kevin stood waiting to talk to me when Joseph poked his little nose in the door. My spirits picked up. "Hi," I smiled.

His deep voice came across the room, "How ya' doing?"

"Just absolutely fine." I rose from my chair and turned to Kevin. "Can I help you with something?"

"Did you want to paint that load for Hart's Oil or do you want me to?"

"Would you? I'd sure appreciate it."

"OK. What colors are they?"

"Let's see. There's 40 hex bung--the plugs--, black, white, and 60 round bung Amoco blue and white. OK?"

"All right."

"Thank you," I said and Kevin left.

Joseph pushed me against the door giving me a greeting kiss.

Knock. Knock. I opened the door. There stood a delivery man.

"My, what good things you bring me today?" I asked.

175

"It looks like 200 rings from Theadon Drum Ring Company."

"Oh. OK. Yeah, let's just unload them right there." I pointed to the cement platform at the bottom of the stairs. Bard was coming up the stairs with one of the employees behind him.

The employee said with a worried look on his face, "Uh, I was dedenting and I accidentally had the control switch in the "up" position when I pushed the power button and the top plate is wedged against the frame and I can't get it to release."

"OK. What we'll have to do is get the 36" pipe wrench and that 6-foot pipe for leverage there in the corner of the tool room by the door. If you can get a good hold on the threaded shaft, you might need to have someone help you to break it loose. But be sure you're turning it the right way to unscrew it, OK?"

"OK." The young man left.

I hurried to my desk to make out a check to pay for the delivery of rings when Joseph said to Bard, "May is handling the business pretty good, it looks like. She knows how to keep things running." There was a slight laugh in Joseph's voice.

Bard responded rather loudly, "Yeah. It's May's job to run the business and my job to run May." Then he cracked up laughing.

I hurried out the door to give the check to the driver. Upon my return Bard was saying as he looked at me, "She could never run this place without me. Someone has to keep her in line."

I turned to Joseph, "I need to inspect just a few more drums outside so they can bring them up to run. But weren't we going to plumb in a bypass with a ball check valve in the hydraulic line?"

"Did you get the ball check valve?"

"Yeah."

"OK. I'll start working on that right now."

"I'll be there to help you with it in just a couple of minutes." I picked up my overcoat uniform and gloves to protect my clothes from the greasy oil barrels. We walked down the stairs.

Bard said, "Well, I'll leave you two. It sounds like you've got your work cut out for you." The three of us went in different directions with Bard returning to the house.

As the weeks went by, it seemed that we were doing rather well in many ways, but I would keep looking at Mom in her rags--the damned old stuff that Nan would give her--and it really bothered me. I thought to myself, "How in the world can we get some decent dresses at Deseret Industries to make Mom look and feel better?" A faded memory came to my mind. Mama would love wearing white nurse's uniforms like she used to wear many years ago.

I went to Nan to hand her $120 and I mentioned, "I wonder how much extra you would need to get Mom some decent dresses from Deseret Industries."

"She doesn't really need anything nice to work in with those old greasy barrels. She's got a best dress."

"Well, heck. It shouldn't really cost that much. Can you at least see if you can find her something and then tell me how much it costs?"

"Yeah, I'll see what I can find when I'm over there."

So as the weeks and months went by, I would ask her, "Have you been able to get Mom something yet?"

She would reply, "No, not yet."

I knew if Bard got involved that would be "all she wrote." I could only wait upon Nanas' mercy, which never did prove fruitful. I was sure that Daddy would roll over in his grave if he knew how Nanas and Bard were treating my mother. Mama would sometimes come into the house with grease on her clothes from working in the barrels. She wore an apron but her clothes still got dirty.

One night Nanas came at her and said, "Don't you come up here, you filthy old woman. You get downstairs." Nanas struck Mother with the side of the knife she had in her hand, as Mom was going downstairs as fast as she could. "May can bring your food down to you. You're not coming up here to touch anything."

Then when I commenced to fix a plate of food for Mom, Bard shouted, "Don't you give her anything but leftovers."

"Why?"

"Because I don't want her having any of this good food while the stuff in the fridge is going to waste."

"Well, the things we're having today will be leftovers tomorrow, so why can't she have it today while it's fresh? It isn't her fault that Zosa cooked too much of this stuff yesterday. Why should she be punished for it?"

"You quit trying to give your mother the good food and never mind."

Mom was standing on the stair landing waiting for me to hand her a plate. Bard walked over and said to Mom with a sick grin on his face, "Oh, Edith. I'm sorry. I forgot you needed to eat. I flushed the toilet already."

I heard Mom reply, "Bard. Can't you get your mind out of the toilet?"

Then as we sat down to ask the blessing, he said to Mother, "You get downstairs. I don't want the devil present while we ask the blessing."

I took Mom's plate downstairs to her room. My eyes went over every nook as I glanced around her little room. Approximately six feet wide by eleven feet long, it had been painted with silver gray paint. There were fruit shelves around the sides with old bottles of fruit that had been there for years. The window on the north side was about 18"x30" with a dirty, old piece of material hung up by two nails. The pattern was gray with large pink roses on it. There were little cracks in the walls and larger cracks in the floor growing a black moly fungus where water would trickle in.

Bard and Nanas had taken all of Mom's chests of drawers when she came to live with us. She was left with cardboard boxes in which she kept her old ragged clothes. Her little cot was pushed against the wall on the south side of the room under the shelves of fruit with about 2 1/2 feet of clearance between her bed and the shelves. If she got up quickly, she would hit her head. When Mom stepped out of bed, she would either have to step into her boots or step into the water. I had brought in a board about 2'x3' so that she could step on it when getting up.

I saw this deplorable condition every day. A desolate feeling came over me that night as the stench of mildew added to my disgust. I stood there organizing thoughts as I looked over this mess by the light of a 40-watt bulb. What would it take to change this condition without a lot of money? I figured I could take all the fruit bottles and stack them in boxes in the furnace room. Then I could pull out Mom's cot, rip out all the shelves with a wrecking bar, and sweep the dirt and cobwebs down off the walls and ceiling. Then if I had some of the stuff I had heard about that you can shove in cement cracks that is supposed to swell and seal to keep the water from coming in, that would take care of the walls. I could get a paint roller and some of the barrel paint and just paint the whole thing white. Now let's see. If I could get eight redwood 2x4s, 12 feet long, and three pieces of 3/4" plywood, I could put paint resin, like varnish, that I got out of the drums on the plywood to waterproof both sides. I would use this to make a false floor. I figured that this would take me a day if I really hurried. But how could I do it without Bard's sanction?

I went to him, "Bard, I have an idea that won't take much time or money. What I'd like to do is go to JB's Home Center and get some redwood 2x4s and some 3/4" plywood to make a false floor in Mom's room so she doesn't have that damn water all over ruining stuff. And I figured I could take out all those fruit shelves and if I hurried, I think I could clean it up down there and paint everything white and it wouldn't take me very long."

He sprang up quickly, "If you've got so much time, why don't you take care of me? I need a helluva lot more of you than I'm getting. You only give me two hours a night when I need five. I go around being neglected so you can get work done, but to hell if I'm going to suffer if you're wanting to spend time with that. You get in here and take care of me first like you're supposed to."

"Well, maybe I'd better forget it. I really need to fix the motor mounts on one paint table before I get another order."

"I want to see you in here early today."

No comment. I went down to the shop then drilled new holes in a new motor mount. It looked good so I put it in place. It worked slick. I washed 100 lids and rings for open-head drums, swept the shop, made 50 gallons of green paint for V.W.R.

Bard came down about four o'clock. "Are you going to quitn' come upun' take care of me?"

"I need to take out the plugs and inspect this load of drums that just came in before it gets dark so we can bring them up and everything will be ready to run first thing in the morning."

"Yeah, hell," he grabbed hold of my arm and shook me. "You wanta' take time for your damned old mother but when it comes to taking care of me, you can't spare the time. I've been waiting for you now to come up and take care of me first, then if you want to come back down and work on this, OK. Or you can leave it until tomorrow."

"If I don't get these inspected tonight and get them turned upside down by the door, it might rain. That would just make a lot of unnecessary drums to be chained."

"Well, hurry then."

When I came in the house at approximately 10 p.m., I was having some milk and crackers when Bard came into the kitchen in his dirty long-john underwear with three center buttons missing and his hairy belly sticking out. What a hopeless, dreary outlook I could see for the rest of the night.

"It's about time you came in. Saved me from goin' after ya'. Ya'd better get Nan put to bed."

"Is she ready to go to bed?"

"I don't know. I'll find out. . . She says she's not quite ready, so you come lay down until she is."

I did the least I could get by with and yet not provoke his anger more than I already had. Then I went in to take care of Nanas. As I sat there massaging lotion on her feet, my mind went downstairs where Mother was. I was sure her feet needed massaging but I dared not think about it. Such thoughts were like pouring salt on old, festering wounds that could not heal.

Several months later as I was coming up from the shop, while opening the door to the house, I heard a horrible, blood curdling sound come from the front room. I ran into the room just in time to see Bard kick Mother in the leg then swing his arm down to give her a hard blow to the side of the head. As Mother let out another scream,

Mother's face showed evidence that this had been going on for sometime. Her jolly, plump face had black and blue marks all over it. Her hair was in a snarly mess with blood trickling down from the top of her head from his having slammed something heavy down on her head. "Oh shit," I thought. Then I hollered, "What the hell is goin' on?"

Nanas blurted out, "Bard wants her to sign over power of attorney and she thinks we are supposed to put up with her around here for nothing."

"What does she have that you haven't already gotten?"

Nan answered, "If I've got to be the one handling her damnable papers and all this legal crap of hers, I'm not going to have her tagging along with me telling me what to do everywhere I go.

Mother's broken words came across, "I don't know why you need power of attorney. I sign everything you want me to."

Bard stomped his foot, "We're not taking you in there to tell everything about my family."

"I don't talk about your family to them." She was referring to the Social Security Administration.

"You damn right you're not. You're not even goin' there."

"Well you guys act just like Nanas owns me but she doesn't," Mother looked up at Bard with her eyes somewhat fluttering as though she feared she might be hit again.

Nanas interrupted, "I have to handle your damn mess. You'd just love to work the shit out of me, dragging you around wherever I need to go."

Mother looked as though she were contemplating. The room was silent for just a moment although the tension was so thick, one could cut it with a knife. I knew they would win--they would always win over all of us--they had all the chips in their corner. I was physically sick over the oppressive, domineering methods they constantly used over Mother who was now in her 70s. She did not have a prayer to stand up against them. They would beat her senseless if they had to just to get their way.

I turned to Mother, "Why don't you just sign it? They have all of yours and my money anyway?"

"I know, May, but then they can do just anything they want."

"Don't they do anything they want now? What can it hurt?"

She sat there scratching her head with her eyes upon the floor. Bard and Nanas remained quiet thinking Mom would do it. Mom looked up at Nanas, "Well, I'd like to see the things you sign of mine before you sign them."

"Well, if you have to see every cockeyed little thing . . .," Nan snarled.

180

Mother said, "Well, OK. I'll sign it then." So she signed the paper. I have no idea where Nanas got it notarized but she did.

I helped Mom to the bathroom where I washed her face and combed her hair very carefully. There was a little lump on her head with a small cut. I fixed some lunch for us, and after eating I went outside.

A dreary, hopeless feeling weighed heavy upon me. I sat down on the cement edge which circled the driveway in the back yard. A thought scrambled across my mind: What am I? Who am I? I was sick with myself as I said a silent prayer. "Dear God, help us--Mom and I-- to let us know what you want us to do. Give us knowledge and strength." I felt so weak and sick that I could have collapsed.

The thought occurred to me that anyone else would come up with a way to stop somebody like Bard from beating up their mother. I just felt like a damn wimp. I was totally at a loss as to how to combat him and keep him from abusing everyone.

I sat staring at the rocks while the sun beat down upon my already hot body as I wondered why they wanted power of attorney when Mom already signed over her checks and gave them to Nanas. It did not make sense.

I found out months later that Bard and Nanas had taken the deeds to a 180-acre mining claim in Arizona my father had left to Mother. Also, she never again saw her Social Security checks after that time.

Whenever I said anything about the way Bard, Nanas or Will treated Mother, they would say, "It's just May sticking up for her damned old mother again." I heard that so many times but now it is like music to my ears to think that I did stick up for her sometimes. But I feel like it was not nearly enough.

Bard also had a hang up about Mom talking to anyone that came on the yard. He would say to her, "When anyone comes on this yard, I've told you to hide 100 times and there you are out there talking to them." He would slap her and pull her hair over and over again while he said, "I'll teach you to hide." Then he would get on the rampage. One could hear it on the other side of the house: Mother screaming while he kept hitting her.

On one occasion some people brought some barrels on the yard. After they left Bard sent word by way of Skip to tell Edith to get up to the house. When she got there, I was in the kitchen.

Bard yelled, "I've told you to hide when anyone comes on the yard and there you are out there talking to 'em."

As he grabbed hold of her braids, he had a pair of scissors in his hand, obviously contemplating what he had in mind, as he quickly cut off her braids. Mother's long hair meant a lot to her as mine did to me.

"What are you doing?" Mother cried. "Oh, you stupid old thing! What did you do that for?"

"I've told you to hide. You'll learn. You just insist on letting everybody see you that comes on the yard."

"I wasn't even in the yard," Mom whimpered and began to cry.

"I seen you out there," Bard hollered at the top of his voice. "Out there with that man unloading those barrels."

"Oh, you stupid ass. That was his wife. That wasn't even me at all. Now look what you've done." Mom sat down, picked up the braids that were thrown on the table and wept.

CHAPTER 14

Mother mentioned having pain in her privates and as the weeks went by, she talked more about it. One day while she was sitting on the couch, she asked if I wanted to look between her legs, so I did. There was a big "ball" about 3 1/2" across coming out of her uterus. It had come out approximately one inch.

"Oh hell." I went and got Nan.

Nan looked at it and said, "We'd better take her to the hospital." So they did.

Many times I had seen Bard and Will kick Mother and I could not help but wonder if that was the cause. Along with the kicking, the heavy lifting they wanted her to do probably contributed to her problems. They seemed to fix her up at the hospital by reattaching the uterus and she came home.

After Mom's operation, I thought, "Maybe I oughta' have a doctor look at my hernia." I talked to Bard about it and he said, "Well, we can go ask and see how much it would cost."

When the doctor saw me, he said, "Young lady, if you can't afford to pay me, I'll just do it for you anyway."

I thought that was so sweet. I asked, "Well, how much would you normally charge?"

He said, "Well, if we did it in a clinic, it would be $500 for the clinic and $500 for me. But if you need to go to a hospital so that they can give you something strong to kill pain, then that would be another $1,000."

I said, "I can suffer a lot of pain to save $1,000."

He said, "If you do decide you need to go there, we can send you from the clinic to the hospital."

I said, "I wonder if we should try to afford it or just keeping going with it the way it was since I have lived with it so many years."

The doctor said, "No, you ought to get it fixed immediately."

So I said, "I would like to pay you. Is $100 a month OK?"

He said, "Sure."

So we arranged to have it taken care of. When I went to have my operation, it was really sweet because Joseph went to the clinic with me. Bard said it was OK. When I came out from being operated on, although I had a lot of pain, Joseph was there holding my hand.

"How's my little sweetheart?" he asked.

"Kinda' weak. I'm so glad you're here."

"You're sure going to have to take it easy now for a while. You can't just run down there and give them guys heck for a while." He was referring to my employees. I started to laugh, but quickly stopped as I noticed more fully the pain the doctor had told me to expect.

"I wonder if Bard would let me take you home to my house so I can see to it that you are taken care of."

Oh man. Just hearing that, my heart just thought that was the neatest idea in the whole world.

"I'm going to ask him," he said. So he got Bard on the phone.

Bard said, "She can rest in my bedroom."

I told Joseph, "He lies. He won't let me rest." I was praying and hoping that Bard would have at least one ounce of compassion.

Joseph hung up and called his wife and asked her if it was OK to bring me over there. She said, "Yes." So Joseph called Bard again and talked him into the idea.

"Oh! Thank the Lord. What a blessing!" I said.

Joseph helped me into the car so carefully as the snow was gently falling down upon us. When he got me home, he made the couch into a bed. Although his home was simple, it was clean and peaceful. He waited on me hand and foot. After a good night's rest, I woke up slow and took a look around me. There were Joseph and Heidi, his wife, being so quiet in everything they were doing so as not to disturb my rest. For me to see such consideration filled my soul with appreciation.

Joseph noticed I was awake. He smiled and said, "I thought you'd be coming around pretty soon. I have some nice breakfast for you," as he set down a bowl of hot oatmeal mush, milk and honey with margarine in it for me. I wanted for nothing for three days, even an occasional hug and some tender kisses. Everything he would do said "I love you" without words.

The thought of returning home was distasteful but the business needed me and in a few days, although I had to walk slowly, I went right back to managing everything.

Several days later the kid that lived across the way came over with an old bike he wanted to sell for $5. I bought it and when I got to feeling better, I straightened the sprocket a little and put a thicker washer on one side so the chain would not keep coming off. The children were so excited. We went to the back of the property. There was a dirt road where they could ride. Skip, smiling from ear to ear, declared, "I'm first."

"OK. You can go three times up and back." He did.

"Now it's Don's turn." Then when he returned, I said, "Sherrie, would you like a turn?"

Watching she replied, "Well, I don't know if I can."

"I'll help you. We'll go slow."

Skip said, "Heck, that's no fair. Sherrie's taking forever."

"That's all right. You had to learn one time too. OK. Now it's Lee's and Katie's turn." I picked up Lee and put him on the seat in front of me to give him a ride. Bard was wondering where I was. He came out, "You're out here playing with the kids again. Every time I turn my back, you're playing. If you don't have any work to do, you'd better get up to the house and get some rest." A sick streak ran through me as he continued.

"They can have fun without you."

"Katie needs a turn."

"Well, let Skip give her one."

"I don't think he can. Let me give her a turn then I'll be right up."

"Well, all right."

When Katie had her turn, Lee cried, "Don't we get any more turns?"

"Well, I have to go right now but I'll give you some the first chance I get." He was sobbing.

That evening I heard the kids and everybody talking about how "The Sound of Music" was going to be on television at seven o'clock. "All right," I thought. The family had a large color television in the front room that they watched it on. I had never seen it because, of course, if I had had time to watch TV, Bard would want me in his bedroom. But he did not like the show so I would never get to watch it. So I kind of figured that I would be doing some fixing of supper and take my sweet time whenever Bard was not on my case. While standing in the kitchen and with the door opening into the front room, I could see it.

Bard came in the kitchen, "Boy, it's sure taking you a long time to fry just a few potatoes."

"Well, the kids have been eatin' them as fast as I've been frying them."

So he left. In an instant he returned. He came into the kitchen again and saw me standing there in the doorway holding a potato, "Yeah, hell. You're standing there watching TV. If you want to watch it so damn bad, come in my bedroom."

So after I had taken as long as I dared to fix supper, I went into Bard's room. All the time the show was going on, he was making mockery of the lady's singing. He would say, "I don't know what you see in a silly show like that." All of his comments and distractions made the show almost impossible to enjoy. He kept asking, "Have you seen enough?"

So I said, "Fine. Move it to whatever you want. I don't care." I never did get to see it all the way through.

185

A new day of work began at Reclaim. Seeing quite a few drums that needed to be welded, I began to weld up the holes while Kevin tested them under the water for leaks. I noticed a drum that had "hole" written on the top, but it had a fresh paint job. It looked somewhat suspicious so I stopped welding and went for a bung wrench and removed the plugs. Oh hell. Someone had put this drum to be welded without being washed first. It had acetone fumes in it. I was furious. I gathered my help around me.

"You see this drum?" I asked. "Someone put that there without it being washed and that's just like a bomb. If I hadn't stopped to remove the plugs, my body parts would be blown all over this building. You know what I mean?"

They stood there looking at each other like who could be that stupid. It seemed that if it were not one thing, it was another. We all went about our work again. Boy, the thought was horrible. If someone else had done the welding and had not stopped to question that drum, how could I live with the thought that this place had killed someone.

I was also trying to figure out what to do about the IRS wanting to audit me. I ended up having to spend a lot of time digging up old receipts for the auditor. Then when he finished with the audit, he told me I owed $7,493. I about died on the spot.

"What do you mean?" I exclaimed. "Why, if I didn't have guts enough to run this place, there wouldn't be any money to argue over."

"I know. But since you did make it, the law says you have to pay income tax and this is what you owe."

I had been paying my three helpers in cash, so it looked as though I had kept all that money. I felt like I could chew nails. I went about setting up the pay for the guys so I could take out FICA, state and federal taxes and arranged to make payments on that huge sum with extremely high interest.

As if that were not enough, a week later I was plagued by another run of bad luck. A customer had placed a rush order for 240 excellent lined drums with a baked on enamel finish inside. Not all lined drums when they are reconditioned turn out in the "excellent" category, so I had Will bring in over 400 lined drums.

When we got the paint shed full, I got a phone call and the customer said, "Cancel that order."

"Are you serious? This is a joke, right?"

"No, not really. It was an Army order that canceled out. I'm sorry."

"Well, OK." The customer is always right and there is no use making them mad. So I went out and told the guys they had canceled the order. They were the only account I had at that time that would use that type of drum, so I had the guys stack the drums back out in the yard.

Shortly afterwards, Kevin came to me and said, "May, the air ball has a crack in it and it's hissing air."

John, the compressor man, saw that I had been using an old Army buoy for an air holding tank. He had told me some time ago that if it burst, it would go off just like a bomb. He told me it could wipe out half the shop by blowing it into kindling wood. I ran to the compressor room and turned off all the compressors.

I had hoped to get enough money by now to have replaced it with a regular 500-gallon air storage tank made for the purpose but could not afford it yet. So we moved the drums away from the area and I welded up the crack. I asked Kevin if he would set the pressure controls down a little, which he did.

I got busy checking prices on an air tank and ordered one. That was too close for comfort.

Then Will came to me, "I'm going to need another load of hay. It'll cost about $215."

"Well, OK, but they might need to hold the check a little while."

I was supporting 16 head of cattle at the farm now. The cost of hay and grain was approximately $250 per month. I was coming undone. How could I pay for everything when I did not have many orders?

I locked myself in the shop bathroom. I wanted to scream but I knelt there and began to bawl. After having a good cry, I started to pray.

"Oh, Father in heaven. Thank you. I'm sure glad that this whole place didn't blow up. Please help us to get the orders we need so we can meet our debts and obligations. I need guidance and strength. I humbly pray, in the name of our Savior, Jesus Christ, amen."

I leaned against the wall staring at an old rag underneath the sink as I sat there on the floor. Then I remembered that I had been working on plans to build a bung washer (bungs are the plugs that go into a closed-head drum). I wanted to build this machine so, hopefully, I could wash three 5-gallon buckets of bungs at one time, instead of washing them by hand in a bucket as I had been doing.

I jumped up and quickly went to the phone and called Joseph. I asked if he had time to discuss plans for a bung washer and he said, "Sure, come on over."

I hurried to the house. It being around 5 p.m., I went to Bard's room, "Can you take me to Joseph's? We're going to design a bung washer so I can wash a whole bunch at a time."

"I want some fried potatoes," he said. "And you need to take care of me before you go."

"Can't I do that when we come back?"

"No, because then you'll claim you're too damn tired."

I hurried to the kitchen, got the pan of grease heating while I peeled and diced the spuds. I fried them in a hurry and fixed him some grilled cheese sandwiches. Then I hurried to the bedroom, got undressed and did enough of what he wanted so we could leave.

When we got to Joseph's, Joseph and I sat down to look over my drawings.

"Well, that looks as though it's all right. But instead of using an open-head drum, why couldn't you just use a closed-head drum on its side held by a shaft running through the drum and bearings on each end? Then mount the bearings on a rack."

"OK. Just a minute. I need another piece of paper. Now you said the drum was sideways," as I began to draw out what I had understood him to say, while scratching my head. "OK. What if we use a pipe instead of a shaft? You know what? Hey, look, I got an idea. Why in the heck couldn't we just drill holes all along the pipe and then put a plug in the middle of the pipe and you know what? Heck, we could just use the one side for the water to come in and then when they're through washing and rinsing, we could turn it around and use the other side for the air to come in to dry 'em."

"Yeah, now you're getting your little noggin' to working," Joseph laughed.

"I was thinking that we probably need to use Schedule 80 pipe so it would be heavy enough. That way we could have the ends machined to where we can put the pillow block bearings to mount to our frame."

As we drew the outlines, it looked like a brilliant idea. Then Joseph said, "Yes, I think we have it now. That looks good." Joseph winked at me with the usual sweet smile on his face.

I said, "Let's see now. What are the materials I need," as I began to look over the drum drawing for a parts list. "I'm going to start rounding up everything I need to put this together first thing in the morning," I stood up from the table.

Since Joseph and I were alone in the kitchen, he pushed me gently against the fridge and gave me a big kiss that went right through me. "I'm so proud of you," he whispered. "You sure have a head on those little shoulders." I hated to leave.

We stepped into the front room where Bard and Heidi were watching television. Bard looked at me, "You got it figured out?"

"Yeah, I think so."

"Are we ready to go then?"

"I guess," I looked at Joseph. There was love written all over his face. "Thanks for your help."

"Good luck," he wished me, while I shook his hand before leaving.

I worked on this "little" project off and on for nearly two weeks before it was working. I had to get the sprockets, bearings, couplings, what-not. When it was finished and I tried it, man, it worked so slick. Wow! I could not wait to get on the phone.

"Oh, Joseph. Man, you oughta' see these bungs now. They're as pretty as new. And perfectly dry, too."

He laughed, "Yeah, I'd like to see 'em when I come down there."

"It only takes me one hour from start to finish to do 3 1/2 5-gallon bucketsful. But you know, I think if we had a heavier motor and gear box to where it could pull a heavier load, I think we could do five buckets slicker than a greased pig," I laughed.

"What size you got on there now?"

"Three horse. But I think I need a five horse. But I don't want to worry about it until this thing wears out."

"Well, that should do you a good job for quite a while."

"Yeah, really."

Going to the house I noticed the children were running around full of excitement and anticipation talking about how Will was going to take them all to the canyon for a picnic. Sherrie came up to me all excited and said, "Do you think Bard would let you go with us?"

I smiled, "That would be fun, wouldn't it. I don't know. Do you want to go ask him?" I knew what he would say if I asked.

So when we were in the house and Bard walked by us, Sherrie said, "Will's taking us to the canyon. Can May come with us?"

"No, she's got too much work to do to be running off to the canyon."

I followed Bard to his bedroom, "What do you mean? Don't you think I've done enough that I could go with the children once in a while?"

Since the door was open, he dropped his voice to a creepy whisper. "Well, if you have time to go to the canyon, why can't you come and be with me? That's not as hard for you to do as work is."

I might have known. "Well, I've got to tighten up the bolts on the dedenter and the chainer along with adding more oil to the hydraulic tank."

I left the room. I walked by Sherrie sitting in the kitchen and just shook my head as I walked outside. While walking to the shop, my mind reflected upon a few weeks ago when Bard's family called a family reunion to be held in the canyon. Bard took everyone except Zosa and Mother, but I had long ago given up hope for any happiness around Bard.

On the occasion of the family reunion, I had to stay in his sister's tent for two hours with Bard before I could go play with the children. There was definitely more joy in greasing the chainer.

Every time I had a few spare moments between secretarial work, organizing loads coming in, loads going out, repairing breakdowns and painting, my mind would drift off on a daydream. I would find myself wrapped up in a memory of Joseph's sheltering embrace, filled with the joy that would make the memories of everything distasteful disappear while sweet contentment and peace took its place.

I always thought of myself as an extremely strong-willed person that could suffer just about any torment necessary and still keep my mind on what I was supposed to. But here this 72-year-old man had me in such a dither, it was almost unbearable to go even 24 hours without his presence. It seemed as though everything I would do was just a means of passing time until I could see his sweet face again.

Working around all the equipment with back problems that continually worsened, one day I commenced dressing and all of a sudden my back muscles tightened. I had a vertebra out of place so far that it was now pressing inward toward the middle of my back between my shoulders making even the slightest movement of any kind extremely painful. As I walked into the kitchen, it became more intense and brought tears to my eyes. What could I ever hope to accomplish in this condition?

Nan said, "Today Bard's sister wants all of us to meet her family in the canyon." Being Saturday, she said to me, when I told her of my problem, "You're probably faking so you won't have to go." She was certainly right about my not wanting to go, but there was no way that I was faking.

I called Joseph. There was no answer. He had been doing the chiropractic adjustments on my back. He was good enough not to charge me although I would offer him a few dollars each time. I called his daughter. She said he had gone to the cabin. He had a cabin in the mountains 50 miles from Salt Lake near Kamas, Utah.

I begged Bard to take me as I was no good to anyone in my condition. He finally consented and Nanas, Bard and I headed for Kamas. Some of the bumps we went over to get there were almost unbearable. The pain would nearly take my breath away, but as I watched all the turns and the roads, then up one hill and down the other, turning to the right, then turning to the left, I was smiling. For truly Joseph wanted to hide away so that he would be hard to find.

We finally arrived. Seeing us arrive, Joseph came out to greet us. Just stepping from the car my focus narrowed to a beautiful person with a red plaid shirt and suspenders fastened to his navy blue Levis. His silver hair with delicate waves was gleaming in the sunlight. He looked so handsome, cute and dignified. I felt much lighter just to be near him again. He bid us welcome.

He could see I was in pain. He said, "Has this little gal got a problem?"

"I think so," I said. "My back hurts really bad and I don't know what in the heck is the matter. Your daughter said you were up here."

"Let's have you lay on the couch." In a few moments his loving fingers were carefully moving over my back so as to define the problem. "Ah ha! It's a duzy. This time the vertebra is going in towards your chest and a dickens to push that kind out. Now, if I could just roll her over so as to expose her backbone, I could just go pop with a little hit, if I could just put my fist through the front of her rib cage, then her back would be all straight." Joseph was now laughing. "But it tain't done quite that way. I'll do all I can for her but she'll need treatments every five hours if she's going to be able to manage the place by Monday. Is there any way you can leave her here?"

"Well, we do have a family outing to go to. I wanted to take May with us."

"What this gal needs is rest, peace and quiet, not an outing."

"Come on, Bard. Let's just leave her here. Can she stay overnight?" Nan asked.

"Oh yes."

"OK. Let's go."

"May, are you sure you can't come with us?"

"I'm sure. This is where I can get my treatments so I can work Monday."

"Well, I'll leave you then." They left.

Heavenly days, can you imagine that! What a beautiful thing. Although my back was stabbing with pain, my little soul was so filled with joy. This was just the neatest thing.

Joseph said in his low, manly voice, "Would you like to take a hot bath, little darlin'? It would relax your muscles."

"That would be nice."

"OK. Let me help you up the stairs," holding me as we walked halfway up.

It was a pleasant room, the walls a dark honey-colored wood with little knotholes here and there, the wood grain an intriguing display of individual patterns. A chandelie, I noted, was a wagon wheel with little lamp lights arranged in it. As I reached the top stair, my eye was caught by a white bear hide spread out on the wall. A little pot belly stove stood in the corner and delicate curtains graced the windows.

"What's this? An old time wind-up record player?"

"It works, too."

What beautiful furniture. The silverish, cream-colored velvet material on the couch and chair with little flowers arranged among larger flowers reminded me of the pretty little things I had seen coming up there.

The table with a glass top and exquisitely beautiful wood carvings on the legs was truly a complement to the environment. As I turned around, "Oh, and you have a fireplace, too. Isn't that nice."

Joseph wrapped his arms around me tenderly from behind, then kissed me behind my ear. "You're what's nice." His voice went much lower now. "I'd give anything if you could live here with me."

Turning to look into his blue eyes with such love and tenderness, "Oh, Joseph."

We wrapped together like one body, one heart beating for the two of us. His kisses set my soul afire. Can it ever be? It would be worth waiting for.

"If there was even one chance that my prayers could be heard, I would be your wife."

We stepped out on the balcony. Ummm. What beauty. Tall aspens stood among pine trees with the blue sky piercing through. A little squirrel, running down the tree, bounced with delight across a patch of wild flowers. Joseph's loving arms were still around me. My pain was forgotten in that moment.

"Have I died and gone to heaven?" I asked.

With a little bit of laughter and him kissing me on the neck again, he said, "I don't know, but I think we're still here."

How would it be to love someone that much and be allowed to marry them. I could not even comprehend such joy. I took a hot bath and laid down in the bed upstairs. He called it the "honeymoon suite." Everything was so clean, orderly and fresh. I soon dropped off to sleep only to be awakened moments later with the sweetest kiss.

"It's time I was working on that little back again. Don't you think so?"

I pulled him down for another kiss, "I think so."

Each time he worked on my back, there was less pain. When he was through, his treatments were working and so was everything else!

"Can I play some of your records?"

"Help yourself. I'm going to go fix you something to eat. I think you may be pretty hungry by now."

When he returned with a sandwich and a bowl of delicious homemade soup, I asked, "May I have this dance?"

I put the Blue Danube Waltz on the record player. As his mighty arms swept me across the floor, I was lost in a joy that I could never imagine, the strongest force I had ever known taking over.

That day and night flew like a light flashing through space and the darkness descended all too soon. With Bard's knock on the door, the brief moment of happiness ended. I had dreaded the thought of his return and when I saw him standing there, I was filled with an overwhelming depression.

"Are you ready to go?"

The thought traveled through my mind, "If I stayed here over a million years, I would not be "ready to go."" My heart sunk.

"My back feels better. It's not normal but better."

"Well, let's go then. You can't stay here forever just because your back hurts."

I thanked Joseph and Heidi and went to the car with a vacant stare on my face, but a memory of joy was a part of my soul hidden where no one could touch it or mar it or steal it from me. There was not a day that went by that I did not pray, pleading to God for a way to open up wherein I could be free, if possible--to deny my feelings would be hypocritical and to change them would be impossible.

CHAPTER 15

The following Monday in the shop, I went through the motions of working, but my mind was 50 miles away. I could not take it anymore. It was in the afternoon when I went upstairs to the office where there was an old closet I went into. I shut the door so that I was in total darkness where I could be alone with the miseries of my mind. I had no sooner shut the door than I burst into tears.

I knew better than to commit adultery but I was coming undone in my feelings. I would much rather commit marriage than commit adultery. I looked at myself as being as honest as they come and this was a form of stealing, lying, cheating. But I would never steal anything, at least so I thought. How can I marry the man I love when I am married and so is he. The Doctrine and Covenants says if a woman is found with another man, she shall be destroyed. Oh, hell. I cannot help my feelings. It was like a matter of survival, like a starving person being thrown bits of food. Although stolen, I devoured it, as I looked forward to each ounce of love or kindness Joseph could spare me. I tried to look at how one might judge the situation as I wept bitterly.

"They're going to call it adultery," I said to myself. "I've committed everything in my mind, so what's the difference. And if Joseph wasn't impotent, I'd probably have had it by now." Not for the need of a sexual relation, but just for the wanting so badly of having children with someone I adored, and knowing that he also wanted children.

Before all this I had thought of myself so morally clean that I would squeak. Now, here I was. It was the hardest thing I had ever tried to control, but God help me. It took all the strength from every fiber of my being to control my thoughts, words, and actions. It seemed like I was battling with myself every moment of the day wondering which would win--my intelligence or my feelings. I would ask myself, "Why in the world am I fighting myself? I know why I love Joseph. There isn't a woman in this world that wouldn't love a man like that." But I did not feel that I could condemn Bard because he held the priesthood and my religious convictions dictated that I should uphold him.

I hated to put myself in the judgment seat over Bard or anyone else because first of all, what if they repented? If I did not have forgiveness, then I could be worse than they are because I cannot forgive them. Besides, who says that the Lord might not just put that person into a position to take care of me if I have an accident or something. I would just never know. So it would not pay to be hasty in setting myself up thinking I am so smart.

I really had no way of knowing how God would look at Bard and his actions. I knew how Bard made me feel and it was exceptionally difficult to try to uphold him in the position of a husband the way a woman should treat a good priesthood man.

What's going to happen? Am I going to hell? I can force myself to be an obedient wife but I cannot force myself to give up all hope for anything better.

When the council of judges comes into a session to consider my situation, I hope they will consider everything. Am I going to be in the same predicament mother is in? Bard had said that because of her sin, she would be a servant throughout eternity. What should I do? I would be a fool, a total fool, to give up the only sweetness I had ever known.

I continued to cry, the tears streaming down my face. I thought, "It's a good thing I'm in the dark so God can't see what a mess . . . Well, he already knows what a mess I am. Oh, God. Have mercy on my wretched soul." I could not help but have more compassion for Mom. I had thought so much about where it says in <u>The Bible</u> that the sins would go from the fourth and fifth generation, and boy, I did not want that to happen. Just because Mom and Dad did not have a priesthood marriage, then here I go and do not give it any thought. Then along come my kids and they do not give it any thought, and we end up on the bandwagon with nobody giving a damn. That cannot happen because, God help me, I know better, kind of like "the buck stops here." Whatever suffering it takes to be clean of such a thing, I am the one that has to stop it here and now.

"God, please show me what to do."

I got up from the closet, went into the bathroom and threw cold water on my red face. I wanted to center my mind on things that were constructive. I was so thankful to have the business. I made the statement many times, "If I didn't have all this work to do, I'd go nuts." I began sorting out my secretarial work.

The certified public accountant I had contacted told me that it would be better to incorporate Reclaim Barrel. So I began looking into that situation. I told Will I would need to have him be more diligent in getting and saving receipts for every single thing. He was headed to Dillard Chemical in Wyoming that night. He had always told me that the trip cost $80. The next day when he returned, he had $29 worth of receipts. I asked him for the rest of the receipts.

He sat there on the couch and hung his head and said, "There isn't any."

"What? What in the heck do ya' mean?"

"I've been pocketing $50 every load since we started."

"Oh." My stomach began to churn. I could understand him wanting more money. I could understand everybody wanting more of everything good in life and I wanted them to have this as fast as I could possibly give it to them. What did I ever have that I did not share with all of them anyway? Why, why do this to me? It could not have hurt worse if someone had kicked me in the stomach--to think he would do that to me! Just several weeks before then, I had questioned Will and Nan on $3,000 worth of missing checks out of the mail. I noticed over a month ago that several outstanding invoices had not been paid. I asked the companies for proof of payment and copies of the returned checks and when they arrived, Will had endorsed them. I asked Will and Nan at that time what they did with the money.

Nan said, "Oh, we paid bills with it."

"Don't give me that because I know what bills were paid because I paid them."

But Nanas kept rattling on. It was obviously hopeless to expect to see that money. But like the brethren taught in meeting, returning good for evil, I was determined to make myself forgive them. Will continued to have full rights as my partner in the business. Now I caught him doing this. He did act like he was somewhat sorry. I just assumed that he was sorry. I thought to myself, "He probably feels like an ass," so I just dropped it.

For the next several months I was considering the incorporation and getting it set up with my bookkeeper. The papers of incorporation were being discussed and who was going to be the president of the company. Bard and I were sitting in the kitchen.

Bard began, "I think you should let Will be the president."

"Why should I give him that position when he won't help me half the time unless he just happens to feel like it? I don't think I should."

"I know, May, but he does hold the priesthood, and if he doesn't have a position that is over yours, he will probably just quit and leave it all to you. Then you'll be making the deliveries too. But if you give him the presidency, he might feel like doing more because he is more a part of it."

As I sat there, trying to be open minded on the whole situation, I just had an uncomfortable feeling. I said, "You know very well that if you wasn't pushing Willy, he wouldn't do anything, except maybe take care of cows. I was asking Willy yesterday if he would learn how to weld to help me a little. You know what he said? He said, 'If I learn how to weld, then you'll expect me to do it.' And I told him, 'Well, I guess that's fine for you to have that attitude, but if I had that attitude, wouldn't we be in a helluva mess.' I just get so sick trying to get him to do anything. It's worse than just doing it myself."

197

"But that's the point. That's why you ought to give him the presidency so he'll take an interest."

I sat there for a long time. "Well, what the hell. It's just a name. He needs the flattery. OK, let's do it. Maybe it'll make him feel like getting in and doing something."

When Will came home, we told him what we decided. We set it up the next day with the bookkeeper then it was written up that way. We also set up a new account for the corporation with the bank and closed out the old account.

Two days had passed by. Nanas and Will were doing a lot of discussing. Then Will came to me and said, "I've decided to set it up with the bank so your signature alone will not pass on a check. Mine must be there too." By the look on his face, I assumed he was not joking.

I called the bank and sure enough. That is what he had told them. Is there any end to the shit this guy will pull? It was like I had been hit by another flying brick. I was stunned.

I went to Bard and said, "Will has fixed it with the bank so that my signature on a check alone will not pass anymore. He wants two signatures so I can't do anything without his approval. I've had it Bard. All my incentives are shattered. Every dang time I turn around, he stabs me again. I can't work under those conditions. I built the business without much help from him and now he wants to sit like a little tin god over the top of me and dictate my every move. I wanted to give him some incentive and that's what I get." I rambled on, "If he thinks that he's going to sit there and be my lord and master while I work all my life just to feather his bed, he's nuts."

Bard went to Will and Nanas. Will was down in his room. Bard told Nanas to come down there. "What are you doing so May can't sign checks and have them pass? What's the purpose of it?"

"Well, that way I'll know what the heck she's spending the money for."

"Hasn't she done well on her own? You haven't been hurt."

Nanas butted in in a high pitched voice, "Well, Will has worked just as hard on the deliveries and cattle. May can account to Will. He wants to know everything she's doing?"

"Why?" I asked. "What have I ever done that I should come under Willy to that degree? Why should I have to account to him for every little time I turn around? What has he ever done to deserve that position over me?"

"Ha. You're the one that gave him that position," Nan said with a proud look. "He's the head of the company now and he wants to know what you're doing with the money."

198

"Everybody and their cat and dog knows that I built Reclaim Barrel."

"Well, you used my lands and buildings that Bard gave you."

"Don't give me that baloney. If I hadn't earned it, he'd never have signed it over to me."

"It's not just signed over to you. It's Will's too. You just act like you're the owner and Will's nothing. Will will show you he's something and you're going to have to account to him, like it or not."

I sat there by the door on an old milk carton turned upside down while all their words were like jangling noises. I sat there for the longest time trying to sort out my mind and come up with an answer. This went on for better than an hour.

When I looked up and as soon as everyone shut up so I could get a word in edgeways, I said, "I've got an idea. If Will wants that position, he can have it. He can have all of it. I'll run Reclaim Barrel for two weeks and then I'll hand it over to Willy to run without my help for two weeks. If he hasn't had enough and handed it back to me to be the full owner, 100 percent, without him as partner, without him on my account, it will be so far run down, even I won't be able to redeem it. If that happens, I'll just go look for another job."

They all stood there in silence as I walked outside. Bard followed me. "Are you serious?"

"You damn tootin' I'm serious."

So for two weeks straight I ran drums through like mad and sold them for C.O.D. prices plus I called in all the money that I could get in that was outstanding. I paid up bills to where all the bills I had incurred under Reclaim were paid. Then I explained to my choice customers what Will was trying to do and what I was doing.

Leon at Centron said, "May, that's nuts! What does he know about the company? Do you think he could run it?"

"I don't know and I don't care. One thing's for sure, I won't continue on with him having any part of it."

"Well, I won't deal with him."

"I really appreciate that, Leon."

Then I explained to my help what was going on. They all said, "Oh, that's fine. We'll just quit 'til you call us back to work."

One man said, "I wouldn't work for that lazy bum for ten minutes if I never worked here again."

"Thanks."

Then Friday night September 26, 1981, I said, "OK, Willy. As of Monday morning, Reclaim Barrel is yours. Good luck!"

Things were silent all day Saturday. No one talked much and silence prevailed Sunday. Then Monday morning at 3 a.m. Will came knocking on Bard's bedroom door. He was crying.

"I got to talk to you," he said. "I haven't slept the last two nights. I've thought about this over and over," as he continued to bawl. "Nanas keeps trying to get me to take over the business, but I can't. I just can't. I don't know anything about it. It's May's baby. I'd rather see her have it than see it go under. I'll sign off my half."

I had tears in my eyes, too. I was thankful that he would rather give it to me than to see it destroyed. With a feeling of compassion, I told him that I would finish paying off his debt to the IRS which was approximately $1,400. I wrote up an agreement and we had it notarized to that effect. I then owned 100 percent of Reclaim. I removed his name off my Reclaim Barrel checking account. He was then an employee working for wages.

A few months later Mother stepped on a nail. It went through her work boots into her foot. We were in her bedroom in the basement where I was putting a diced onion poultice on it. I noticed that her toenails needed to be trimmed. Mother had a difficult time doing that job with an old paring knife she had found in a barrel because of her large stomach, dim lighting and poor eyesight. There was no one she could ask to do this for her because of Bard's teachings. No one wanted to even touch her. The horrible neglect that had taken place was making my stomach churn. I knew if I was caught taking care of this, I would likely be knocked from here to kingdom come.

I was quivering and thinking. In a whisper I said, "I've got an idea. After I put Nanas to bed tonight, I'll get the toenail clippers and scissors and hide 'em in the bathroom. OK? Then if I drink a lot of water, it will make me wake up in the middle of the night without waking Bard. Then I'll sneak down here and do this. OK?"

Mama started to cry. "That would be so sweet of you to do that for me. I'd really appreciate it. I can't seem to do it and they hurt me every step I take."

I finished taping the bag of onions around her one foot. "Maybe it's kinda' a good thing you stepped on a nail, huh?" I smiled.

Mama wiped her tears away and smiled. "Maybe the Lord had me step on it just so I could get this other taken care of."

"OK. I got to go."

"Thank you, sweetheart," were Mother's words as I was leaving her room.

Choking up with tears on my way upstairs, I stopped there with the scene of injustice before me. Then I went about getting Nanas taken care of. All the while I was thinking as I washed her feet with a wet washcloth and massaged lotion on them. I had trimmed her toenails last week. Mother would think she had died and gone to heaven if I could give her this much care. I massaged Nan's back and legs with lotion, and pulled down her nightgown.

"Is there anything else you'd like?" I asked.

She moved over to the side of the bed, "Yeah. Adjust my neck."

Carefully massaging her neck so as to relax her then giving it a slight twist to one side bringing her chin up--like the chiropractor had showed me years ago--we heard a pop-pop.

"The other side needs it, too."

So I did the same on that side. Then she swung herself around into her sleeping position.

"Is there anything else or may I go now?"

"I guess."

"Good night," as I turned out the light and shut the door with the toenail kit and some medicine for sores in my pocket.

Then at 2:30 I woke up. I quickly sneaked downstairs and woke Mama. I thought, "I should have grabbed a brighter light, too." But I managed.

After cutting the nails and doctoring a few sores, Mama said, "Can you raise up a little closer? I want to kiss you."

I smiled. "Well, OK." Then I quickly made my way back to Bard's bedroom. But for weeks after that I had a gnawing feeling inside of me.

After 13 years of caring for Nanas' personal needs, occasionally my mind would ponder over this situation. One morning I had given her a bath and was dressing her. She was sitting on her bed with all but her stockings and shoes on. I dared to speak.

"How come you hardly ever thank me for taking care of you?"

There was silence as I stretched the stocking wide to put over her foot.

"Why should I? You're only doing your job," she replied sarcastically.

"What do you mean by that?" I waited for an answer.

"You wouldn't do it if Bard didn't make ya'."

I stopped right there leaving one stocking halfway pulled up her leg. I carefully lowered it to the floor. I got up and went to Bard's room. Bard was laying on his bed partly asleep.

"Bard." I shook him a little. "I need to ask you something."

"Huh? What's the matter?"

"Is there someone else who could take care of Nanas instead of me?"

"Why? What's the matter?"

Nanas was standing at the door. "I told you May didn't love me," she cried. "If she doesn't want to help me, I'll go live with my kids.

201

She was bawling while raving on, "May begrudges every little shittin' thing she does for me. I don't have to live here and put up with it." She slammed the door.

I was shaking my head. "That ain't it at all, Bard. All I ask for is a thank you. You'd think her face would crack or something. It ain't going to kill her." I sat there dumbfounded. How in the world could she say all that crap when all I asked for was a little appreciation? I hung my head to collect my thoughts then looked at Bard.

"I don't mind doing for her. But if she does appreciate it, why can't she just say so? It would be so much nicer. Maybe I'm wrong, Bard. But I've got just enough gravel in my guts to the point where if she can't afford a thank you, then I can't afford to do it for her. I've got work coming out of my ears, and you figure $10 to $15 an hour for three hours a day, that adds up in a hurry. Hell, if I handed someone $500 or a thousand dollars, I think I would at least get a thank you. Don't you?"

"Maybe I ought to have Zosa or Bardell take care of her so you can earn more income."

"What about Sherrie? She's old enough. I think she could learn to do a good job. She's got more time than Zosa or Bardell have."

"Yeah, why don't she get Sherrie?" Bard commented while raising up off the bed. He went into Nan's room to find she had put her own shoes on and finished pulling up her stocking when she had always claimed that she could not bend over.

"I want you to get Sherrie off her butt to learn how to take care of you. May's time is too valuable at the shop." I could hear Bard talking as I left the scene.

There was continual contention for about a week. I could hear bits and pieces of the arguments but stayed out of it as much as possible. The next thing I knew, Nan was moving to the white house next door.

One day I asked Sherrie, just out of curiosity. She told me Nanas was taking care of herself over there. Hmmm. Maybe it was just as well.

With Nanas moved next door, Will helped her fix up the house she was in but Nanas left all her boxes of what not in the red house. After months of having them sit there, I said, "Look, Nan. Tell me what you want me to do with this stuff."

"I'm trying to sort it as fast as I can."

"We've been hearing that for 15 years. Now that you live in a half decent house, we're still in a dump. These boxes are depressing because of the clutter. And there couldn't be anything very valuable in them

202

because obviously, we are getting along just fine without whatever they contain."

Nanas flew into a rage, "You're always trying to boss me and tell me what to do." She raised her hand to strike me across the face. I caught her arm before it made connection. I stared her right in the eye.

"I wouldn't try that if I were you. I don't want to hurt you," I said very sincerely.

She lowered her hand and went into Bard, "May's trying to boss me and tell me what to do in my position. I've been working on sorting those boxes in the front room as fast as I can." I could hear her hollering clear in the kitchen.

Nanas and Bard came walking toward the front room. Bard hollered at me, "You stay out of Nan's territory. Nanas will get it cleaned up."

I said, "Look, Bard. We've been hearing that same damn story for 15 years. She's left this territory and we girls don't intend on living with this crap for another 15 years. The only thing I asked her to do is come with me and we would mark out whatever was valuable so that whatever boxes she wanted taken to her place, we'd carry them over to her. Then whatever was left, I'd sort through them. OK?"

I stood there with Will, Nan and Bard, all hollering at me at once. It was such a massive jangle I could not make any sense out of it. As I stood there listening to this jangling mess, I said, "Yes. You are all right. You're right for each other. I'm the only one that doesn't belong. But I don't care if you beat me, if you get mad, or what the hell you do. This crap is leaving. Now, she can decide whatever she wants over there. If it's not valuable enough for her to clutter up her house with, then it ain't very valuable, is it." Then I left.

Within a week Nan came over. She knew damn well that if she did not do something, I was going to. Very nicely we went through and I marked a little mark on each box she wanted carried to her house, and I had my guys from the shop carry them over there.

Skip, Bard's second boy, was wearing a pair of pants with a broken zipper. He had a piece of string from a bale of hay around his waist for a belt. I looked at him and said, "Skip, can't you find a better pair of pants than that?"

"No."

I took his hand, "Come on. Let's go see."

We went downstairs and I looked, but neither of us could find anything better for him to wear. For the next three months I spent long hours sorting through the heaps of boxes that were left. Anything that was halfway decent, I threw into a big pile in the middle of the floor to be sorted later according to size. Everything else we loaded up for the dump along with keeping the dumpster from the business chuck full every week. They charged me for dumping 5,000 pounds of garbage by the time I had sorted all there was upstairs and downstairs.

I had all the children trying on clothes and marked their names on the ones that fit. Then I took all the extra clothes that were nice and stored them in a couple of fiber drums in the upstairs of the shop. Then I went to work building a table about 2 1/2 feet high, 12 feet long, and 3 feet wide. I put plywood dividers on it, along with a back, so as to make little bins. Then I put each child's name on the front of a bin.

I had been teaching Don, Bard's oldest son, to do the washing. He would take the clothes from the dryer and put them in two old grocery carts. Skip would sort the clothes and pitch them into the bins so the children could find their clothes. They were not ironed, but what the heck! They could at least find what they had.

"Sherrie's job was doing the dishes and tidying up the kitchen. Will's boy, Gary, had the job of sweeping the floors. Katie and Bonnie, Will's children, since they were the two youngest, cleaned the bathroom and helped sweep the upstairs.

I began remodeling the kitchen. I textured and painted the ceiling, painted the woodwork, put up wallpaper and wood paneling about four feet high with moldings on top. My manager and I ripped out the old sink cabinets and had Fashion Cabinets make new ones. We got a formica counter top from the lumberyard that I installed myself. Then after scrapping all the old flooring, I laid down ceramic tile. The children were so happy to see all this happen. They helped to keep things as good as one could expect from kids who never before had the slightest conception of cleanliness.

Will became worried that the people from Welfare or Social Services would investigate the house. Nanas told the Social Services that she was undergoing a separation from Bard. Also, she had been claiming that Bard's children were living in the white house with her so she could collect Social Services for them, but the children were still living in the red house. So when Bard went in to talk to Social Services one day, the Social Services people found out that Nanas had been fraudulent without Bard's knowledge.

Will did not want his family to be caught living there in the red house, so he moved his wife and children over to her father's house to stay for a while. Will did not know that Bardell had wanted to leave for a long time, but her only reason for staying was because Bard and Nanas had told her that if she ever left, she would have to leave her kids with Will. Now she found herself out of all the mess and with her children, so she immediately filed for divorce. In an effort to protect my business from being involved in a lawsuit, I asked Will to sign off his half of the business property and I would sign off my half of the farm. I agreed that I would give Nanas and Bard a life estate in the white house and that I would finish paying off the balance of over $8,000. They were glad to have it done and we recorded it.

I continued to remodel the red house. The stairway and bedrooms were done. I was glad to have my time occupied as much as possible so I could stay out of Bard's room as much as I could.

With Nanas gone I moved Mom upstairs from the dingy little room she had stayed in for years. But she caught a cold and developed pneumonia. For three days she did not eat much of anything. I asked Kevin to help me lift her into the tub as I wrapped a sheet around her to prevent any embarrassment to Mom or Kevin. When I had her cleaned and dressed, we took her to the University Hospital. Kevin and a acquaintance of mine assisted me. Bard did not even care to help.

While Mom was in the hospital, Bard had an automobile accident and he ended up in the hospital at the same time. Boy, did I see a golden opportunity while Bard was gone. My mind was working a thousand miles a minute. I worked as fast and hard as I could to fix up Mom's room, Nan's old bedroom, upstairs.

I redid the ceiling, sanded and painted the woodwork, put all new wallpaper on the walls and a special wall mural on one wall--a scenery of trees, flowers, beautiful environment with a pond, like that of a canyon with the leaves turning pretty colors as in the Autumn. I thought of Mother as being in the autumn of her life and I thanked God for Bard's accident. I knelt down in solitude with tears blurring my vision. "Thank you, Lord. Just, thank you." Now Mom would have things nice at last. I worked with a feverish passion and determination to complete this before Bard came home. I bought new curtains and painted her bedstead and bought pretty new rugs and a new set of sheets and blankets with a new bedspread.

When Bard came home from the hospital, I was not quite finished as he stepped to the door and looked in. "What the hell is going on? What's all this for?"

I stood there like a little tin soldier and said right back to him, "It's for my mother. I don't know how much longer she will be here but I want it to be nice for her." What could he say. He went to his bedroom with disgust written all over his face. I had done too much and I had gained too much control over everything for him to stop me.

I went to the hospital to see Mother, but my sisters had found out that my mother was there and they all agreed that "No way is she going back to Bard's."

I asked Mom what she wanted to do. "Well, May, I have lived with you for quite a while. Now the other children want me to live with them."

I looked at Mother lying there with her silver-gray hair adorning her stunningly beautiful face. I bent over and kissed her as tears distorted my vision. My mind rolled back in time over all the years I had wanted to see my mother have better things. She was with me all that time and I had never managed to make her living conditions better until now. And now, it was too late. She never would live there again. With the bitter memories that had scarred my soul, I lay across her bosom and uttered, "Whatever makes you happy, Mother. Whatever makes you happy."

I returned home and over the days and the weeks, Bard became more and more sexually obsessed so that beyond any shadow of a doubt, I could hardly stand him. Zosa had acquired a book called The Sensuous Woman. Bard had read it and said to me, "You ought to read this. It's really good."

"I'm not going to read that damn thing."

"This woman enjoys her man. You would too if you didn't have something wrong in your head. I want you to read it."

"NO!"

"Come on." He kept shoving it in front of me. "What can it hurt?"

With fury running through me, I grabbed it and threw it into the garbage container and shouted, "I'm not going to pattern my life after some fucking whore."

"Wait a minute," as he grabbed hold of my arm while I was leaving the room. He went over and pulled out a girlie book from under the mattress. He showed me a picture that about made me throw up. "This is what I want you to do for me."

"I'm not going to do that."

"If you don't do it, it will end up taking you three times longer to take care of me than it would if you would just do it."

"Shit," I exclaimed as I slammed the door.

I continued to work extremely long hours in the business and in the house to stay away from him. I was so tired I could just drop. I felt deliriously sick to my stomach as though I was going to pass out, but I could not lay down anywhere.

One might ask: Why could you not just find a nice little corner and curl up and go to sleep? How could I explain? Bard would never allow me to rest in any other room or place except his bedroom. If I did lay down anywhere else, I would surely get caught. Bard kept a constant watch on me.

One Sunday, a bright, warm beautiful day, I had the children in the shop teaching them Sunday School. Bard knew that this would last approximately one hour. The children asked questions and it looked like we would be over ten minutes or so. But after an hour's time, he called. Then he kept calling every five minutes. "How much longer?" "Not much."

He called three different times in approximately 15 minutes. Then after the closing prayer, the children went to play. Being very fatigued, I fell asleep instantly on the couch. When he saw the children at play, he came up promptly to see why I had not come to the house like he had told me to do when I was through. He saw me asleep.

His loud voice woke me up. "What the hell are you doing sleeping up here when I'm waiting for you? You know you're not supposed to sleep anywhere except the bedroom. I knew I should have checked on you sooner to see what you were doing. How long have you been sleeping?"

"I don't know."

In a demanding tone, he said, "You get up to the house and take care of me."

I just sat there bearing up under the heat and impact of his voice.

Several weeks later I went in the kitchen and picked up two oranges then walked outside where I sat on the cement edge that encircled the lawn in the back of the house. While I was sitting there, Bard came out, walked up to me and asked, "What are you doing out here?"

"Just eating an orange."

"Why are you eating it out here?"

"Well, why not?"

"Are you enjoying yourself?"

"Yeah."

"Huh." And he walked back into the house.

Less than two minutes went by when he came out again and a similar conversation ensued. He went back into the house and came out again--three times while I was eating those two oranges. "Hell," I thought.

I shook my head, as I stared off into the weed patch next door. I looked at the cat running over in the field and thought, "Goll, that cat has more freedom than I do. That's right." Then I thought for a minute. "What in the heck. Lincoln freed the slaves a long time ago."

The long hours continued but I dared not pass even one hint how fatigued I was. My body felt like it was made of marshmallows and wax waiting to melt under the workload and heat of the day.

Bard came down to the shop while I was working. "Aren't you tired?"

"I've got all this that's gotta be done tonight." I was so tired I could have fallen over right then, but I tried to put momentum in my movement.

"Yeah. You're so damn tired. You'd better get up to the house and get some rest."

I avoided going as long as I possibly could. I went up there but there was no rest to be had. I took the pillow and put it behind me as I sat up in bed to ask Bard a question.

"Why do I have to take care of you just because you say so?"

Highly provoked, his eyes had a nasty glint. "What do you mean, 'because I say so'? That's a stupid question. The woman is meant for the man, not the man meant for the woman. You're to do what I want, not me having to do what you want. You get that?"

I looked away from him toward the window. "No, I don't get it. I don't get it at all."

"Let me show you something," he said as he pulled out The Bible. "The woman's desires should go to her husband and he should rule over her," he shoved The Bible in front of me with his finger pointing to the word "rule." Then he put The Bible on the dresser and pulled out The Doctrine and Covenants and read where the Lord told Emma Smith that she should administer to Joseph Smith and be a helpmate to him. "You're in the same position to administer to my wants and needs and these are my wants and these are my needs, whether you like it or not."

"I don't care about Emma Smith's position. I don't want that position. Can't you get someone else?"

He grabbed my shoulder and shook me then yelled so loud they could here it across the street, "NO!. You belong to me and you will never get away from me. Never. Never. No never, unless you break your marriage covenants and I'm the one who will say whether you are allowed in the celestial glory or not. I hold the keys over you and I'll tell you right now, if you don't bring yourself into submission, you'll go into dissolution."

I was so damn sick of hearing all this stuff. I sat there with a blank stare on my face and thought to myself, "I don't know that I won't go to hell." With tears filling my eyes, "I believe I'm at God's mercy anyway. But before I get there, I'm going to do all the good I can for people. Who knows? If I can do enough good, maybe God might decide to keep me."

Later that day after being with him, I went over the statements in my mind that he had made. Feeling bewildered and sick at heart, when I lay myself to rest, I went into a dream or a nightmare. There was a large room--it looked like a cave. The ceiling was about 25' high. Some of the rocks were broken out on the one side close to the ceiling so that some daylight came through a small opening. The cave looked about 40'x80' and the opening about 4' wide and 6' high.

I was toward the back of the cave with a steel ankle bracelet fastened around my ankle and hooked to a chain that was fastened to an object in one side of the floor underneath the top opening. I could look out toward the entrance of the cave and see beautiful fantasy-like country scenes of the kind that Walt Disney created: a town, beautiful green hills, trees and flowers and everything nice so as to promote happiness.

Bard was walking around in the cave near me. He would do whatever he wanted to do to me. I could not see any way to free myself but even so my attention was focused toward the entrance. It seemed that there was so much darkness between me and the opening and that I could never escape. I woke up. I had that same dream for several nights.

I contemplated over the things of the gospel and what they meant to me in my life. I thought of the sufferings of our Savior. He suffered for God and his religion to save the world. The early Saints, too, suffered for God and their religion. Now I was suffering for God and for my religion but there was no good to come of it--just continual humiliation and the disgrace of my innermost feelings by having to do things below my dignity. I always believed that if I kept my mind looking toward the Lord for answers and not give up, He would help me find them. I was just totally confused.

One Sunday afternoon I called up Joseph when I got home from meeting and told him what the brethren said, also some of the things Bard would say and do.

Joseph, with a very sober tone, said, "I know he's not justified. And boy, I know what I'd do if it was me. I'd take a sharp knife and chop off his dick."

Two weeks later I went to Sunday meeting and a man, Alfredo Chykosky, whom I had much respect for, was talking and he said that it was a correct principle that when your file leader tells you to do something, you should take it before the Lord. If the spirit of the Holy Ghost does not bear witness to you that it is of God, do not accept it. He said that Joseph Smith taught that people place too much confidence in their leaders instead of finding out what the truth is for themselves. Then he picked up one of <u>The Journal of Discourses</u> and began to read from it.

> What a pity it would be if we were led by one man to utter destruction? Are you afraid of this?
> I am more afraid that this people have so much confidence in their leaders that they will not inquire for

themselves of God whether they are led by Him. I am fearful they settle down in a state of blind self-security, trusting their eternal destiny in the hands of their leaders with a reckless confidence that in itself would thwart the purpose of God in their salvation and weaken that influence they could give their leaders, did they know for themselves, by the revelations of Jesus, that they are led in the right way. Let every man and woman know, by the whisperings of the spirit of God to themselves whether their leaders are walking in the path the Lord dictates or not.

Then he continued,

Let all persons be fervent in prayer until they know the things of God for themselves and become certain that they are walking in the path that leads to everlasting life.[15]

"Did I hear what I thought I heard?" I sat there numb. "Is this the truth? Is this our religion? Whew! That's quite a statement. I want to read that again when I get home."

Then Alfredo went on to say that one person should not want to lord it over another. It sounded so good I could hardly stand it.

We came home from church. I rode with Will because he would drive much faster and I could make a phone call first thing. Bard came in the house while I was talking to Joseph and I quickly changed the subject.

"Who you talking to?"

"Joseph."

"Well, hang it up or I'll hang it up for you."

"Well, I best be going. Good bye."

"You ready to go to bed?"

"No."

"Why?"

"I need to go to the bathroom."

"Well, hurry."

While I was in there, I knelt down and prayed quietly. I poured out my heart, "Oh, God. Don't you see me? Don't you hear me? How long must I suffer this ungodly oppression? Can't you do anything?" as I wept bitterly.

Bang, bang, bang on the door. "What are you doing in there?"

I turned on the tap quickly. "I'm washing my face."

"Well, how much longer are you going to take?"

"Not much."

---

[15] The Journal of Discourses, Vol. 9, p. 150.

"Well, hurry."

I splashed cold water on my face to try to remove the evidence of crying. Then I came out.

He grabbed me by the arm and shoved me into the bedroom.

"Bard, can't we go see Brother Mann and let him counsel us?"

"NO! It's none of Brother Mann's business how I run my family, and if you dare tell him anything, I'll just deny it. You'll be looked upon as a liar. The priesthood always sticks up for the man, not the woman."

"Do all men treat their wives the way you do?"

"That has nothing to do with it. Any man who would have you would treat you exactly the same way I do. You'll never get away from me," he repeated. "Never. Never. No never. So you'd better get over your hang-ups and bring yourself into submission or you're going to go into dissolution," as he raised his hand into the air, supposedly to the square. "I can promise you that in the name of the Lord."

I said nothing but I resented that damn lingo I had heard for so many years. I thought, "I don't believe it because I know that Joseph wouldn't treat me the way you do."

The next day Joseph came over to work on the boiler. As we sat down at the kitchen table in the office, I told Joseph about the horrible way Bard treated me at the time I had worked on the dedenter for two weeks and came in needing some rest. I described it to him in detail.

Joseph looked down at the floor, shook his head, and wept. He drew me close to him. We looked into each other's eyes. He had the most loving expression, then he spoke.

"I can't even imagine a man treating a woman as sweet as you are with such inconsideration." With tears still in his eyes as his broken voice continued, "I know what I would have done. I would have just held you in my arms while you slept."

I cannot explain this part--how I felt. I put my head on his chest with my arms around him. I thought what a beautiful spirit, as I wept with joy. Then I told him what Bard's attitude was to this day. He said, "May, you have got to do something. Can you make an appointment to see Brother Mann?"

"If I make an appointment and his wife Margaret happens to call and tell Nanas, I'm dead meat. But if we just sneak away and go see him, then nobody will be the wiser. OK?"

"You bet. I'll take you."

"Could you be here early tomorrow morning?"

"All right. How about 5:30?"

"Sounds perfect so we can be there by six o'clock."

CHAPTER 16

Early the next morning I met Joseph and he took me to see Brother Mann. When I knocked on the door, the girl that answered said, "He's not here right now. Can you come back later?"

"I can't come back later," I exclaimed. "But I'll tell you right now, if Brother Mann knew the reason why I came, he would want to see me."

"Just a moment," as she shut the door.

A few minutes later Brother Mann came to the door and invited us in. I introduced Joseph and Brother Mann and we sat down on the couch. I had not talked even five minutes to Brother Mann, explaining the way Bard treated me and the things he would say and the things he would do, when Brother Mann threw his hands in the air crying, "Stop! Stop! I've heard enough. I can't stand it anymore."

I asked, "What I want to know is if I can have a divorce?"

"If that's what you want, you certainly have grounds for a divorce. Yes. No man in his right mind should treat a woman in that manner."

"How soon could I get a divorce? Today maybe?"

"Well, I would recommend that you wait six months."

"Six months? I'll try. But what can I do to stop him from abusing me sexually?"

"Just stop having it with him."

"Just stop?"

"Yes. Stop. Don't do it anymore."

I smiled, "OK." I thought, "That sounds good. I'll surely see how it goes."

We talked a little about Bard's background. Then I said, "I'd like to ask you something. Bard has always told his family that you were behind him 100 percent in the things he teaches his family."

Mann shook his head while looking at the floor then raised his eyes to meet mine. In a casual voice he spoke, "That man is one of the biggest liars in the state."

"Why then did you marry me to him?"

"He said that you wanted to marry him and we feel that the woman should have her choice."

I looked at him as though I was stoned. I thought, "All this was an 18-year misunderstanding." I felt sick but regained my composure.

I said, "I appreciate your taking the time to see me."

"That's all right. Good luck. Let me know how you're doing."

"Thank you," as we shook his hand.

"And I'm pleased to meet you, Mr. Mandley."

Joseph replied, "I'm pleased to meet you, too."

While on our way home, I said to Joseph, "Boy, that will be the neatest thing that ever happened to me--to be free from that hell hole."

Joseph commented, "That was sure something that Brother Mann knew Bard's father and said that he was pretty much the same way."

"Bard always told me that when he was a little boy, his father would beat him up all the time. In fact, he said that his father wanted to kill him when he was two days old. He said that that was the reason for the scar across his forehead. His father took a razor blade to him. Bard's uncle took Bard to the hospital. He said that his father was always beating up and smacking his mother around all the time, too. I'd always felt so sorry for Bard. Anytime he had a dog or a rabbit or anything for a pet that he liked, and his father learned that he had something like that, his father would just go kill it. So considering a childhood like that, I've tried to understand him rather than condemn him. But I don't know, Joseph. It's been 18 years and I still don't understand him and I can't see where spending another 18 years would help him one ounce more."

Joseph let me off at the corner of the driveway. "Good luck, little darlin'," he said as he squeezed my hand.

"Yeah, I need it," then I stepped from his car and he left.

I went into the house. Bard was coming down the stairs to meet me. "Where have you been?"

"Uh. Joseph took me to see about getting in on a good deal with some cheese at one of the stores, but we got there too late and someone had bought it already. It was going for 50 cents a pound."

"I don't care about it," he snarled. "You had no business leaving on anything unless you have asked me and got my sanction."

"Well, Joseph heard about it last night and you were sleeping and I didn't want to disturb you. I knew it would only take a few minutes to run right there and back," I went on hoping to emphasize the change of subject. "Gee wouldn't it have been nice if we had got in on a deal like that? They even had bacon, too. But it was gone also." I knew Bard liked bacon.

"Well, next time you ask. I don't care if you do wake me up. You understand?"

I slapped at the wall, killing a cockroach, "Yes."

I hurried in and changed into my work clothes. Then I went to the shop. About 4 p.m. Bard came down, "Are you going to quit early so you can come up and take care of me? You left this morning without doing anything."

"No, I don't think so."

"What do you mean, 'no,' you don't think so?"

"Well, I'm tired of the battle, Bard. You won't go with me so we can talk it over with Brother Mann. Last Sunday at meeting Uncle Dan got up and said a woman's body is her own, and I don't want to do it. So, by that I'll take it that I don't have to."

"Oh, yeah? Well, your body is your own but you're supposed to serve me with it."

"Well, I don't look at it that way and I'm not going to. That's all there is to that."

He walked back to the house like he was in some big hurry. Some of the guys said that Bard walked like a penguin.

He brought back some of the "good books" again. I was cutting a piece of metal with the torch. He turned off the oxygen, "Now, you're going to listen to me and get this in your head." He read me the same stuff he had read to me time and time again about how I was supposed to submit and how I was supposed to believe and administer to his wants and his needs. As he read, he kept looking up from the book at my face to see if I was getting convinced or not. I purposely tried to express that he was boring me to death. His intensity picked up as he kept thumbing through the book, grabbing at any straw that he could find.

I leaned up against the tool shelf while sitting on the work table listening. I had a C-clamp in my hand that I was turning in and out. All of a sudden he said, "There now. Are you going to repent?"

"Repent of what?"

"Your damned disobedience to the laws of God. Here are the laws of God," as he shook the book in the air over my head. "Now, are you going to follow them?"

"Bard, that's your interpretation of the law."

"Well, you're to take care of me. It's not my fault I need a woman. You're the one with the crack between your legs. I can't take care of myself."

"Well, I don't know what you're going to do but I'm through with it."

"I could die with blood pressure and you'd be guilty of murder. You know that? What if I have to go to some whore on the street, the sin of adultery would be on your head, not mine because you're the one that drove me to it." He was poking me in the shoulder with his drilling finger.

This type of reasoning went on and on, Bard not allowing me to work, just standing in my way. I got up, turned the oxygen tank back on, and he turned it off. There was no point in trying to accomplish anything, so I went to the house. It was late anyway.

Later on that evening I lay there trying to sleep. He was hovering over me, shaking me, and holding onto the book in one hand while hollering at me. Needless to say, I got very little rest that night, perhaps two or maybe three hours.

215

For an entire week this same routine went on. Exhausted, I finally said, "OK. I'll give you 15 minutes."

"Fifteen minutes? I need more than that."

"Tough. It's 15 minutes or nothing."

"Well, OK."

So after 15 minutes was up, he asked, "How often do I get 15 minutes?"

"Once a day."

"I've got to have more than that!"

For three more days this went on. Then when I was at the shop, he said, "I want you to come upstairs in the office." I did.

He locked the door, pointed to the rug, "Now kneel down. I want to pray with you."

As we knelt there, he put both arms as to the square. His prayer was, "Eternal Father, in the name of Jesus Christ, and by the holy Melchizedek priesthood invested in me, I ask for the powers of heaven to bring a curse upon May that her back will come out of place so as to give her intense pain and that her friends, Joseph Mandley, Kevin Huntsley, and Jane Brooks, will have accidents even unto death, if necessary, to bring her into submission. This I ask in the name of Jesus Christ, amen. Now, you pray."

"If I pray, I'll pray the way I want to pray. I won't pray the way you want me to pray."

"Go ahead."

"Oh, God, my eternal Father in heaven. I humbly come before you at this time to give you thanks for all the blessings you have given me. I want to dedicate everything that I have unto you, including my life. And in exchange, I pray for guidance at this time that I may know the path that you would have me pursue that my course may be pleasing in thy sight. I pray for your spirit and ask for strength, mentally, physically and spiritually. I ask this humbly in the name of Jesus Christ, our Savior, amen."

We looked at each other and without speaking went downstairs. "Well, are you going to submit yourself now?"

I shook my head as I said, "Bard, I can't see why, even if I am in disobedience, how could that have anything to do with Joseph, Kevin and Jane? Why should they suffer for anything that I do or don't do? Why would the Lord punish them for a sin of mine?"

"Oh, don't worry. He would, if that's what it takes to bring you in submission to me."

The combination of every single thing that was upon me that I was suffering mentally, physically and spiritually at that time was so great every moment of the day, I felt so physically sick and weak. It was as if every step I took I knew not whether I would fall on my face. I

216

could not bring myself to do for him when I knew I did not have to. How could I go for another five months.

He refused to take me to Joseph's for a chiropractic treatment. I could hardly stand the pain. And although I only weighed 115 pounds, I lost 12 pounds. I looked and felt like a bag of bones.

When the pressure was so great, he came to me suspecting that my back was killing me though I had not said anything. "If you'll take care of me for three hours, I'll take you in to get a treatment." Bard had told Joseph not to come on the yard anymore and Joseph was trying to honor his wishes.

To think of having one glimpse of Joseph's sweet smile--oh, how blessed that would be. What a price I would have to pay. I cried inside. Bard had me where he wanted me. I hung my head and sought the support of a nearby tree.

"Well, do you want to go or not?"

"I left the welding tanks on. I'd better shut them off."

"Well, hurry and let me know what you're going to do."

I went straight to the shop bathroom and locked the door. "Oh, Father. If you're up there, I'm telling you. If I'm going to have some help or inspiration, I've got to have it in a hurry." My heart was so heavy. I walked to the house.

"Are we going?"

"I suppose," as I walked toward the car.

"Now, remember. You promised."

When we got there and I laid on the couch, it felt like heaven. Joseph's touch was sweet on my back. Later that night after we had returned home, as I entered the bedroom, I looked at Bard, his eyes beating upon me with the most sickening smile, as though to say, "I've won. Now, I'll get my way!" His hairy belly was protruding out from his dirty underwear. My mind was racing 100 miles an hour. If I had a way to run or a place to go without him ever catching me, God knows, I would have gone.

"Come on. Show yourself," he commanded.

My mind was petitioning heaven, "Oh, God. Please stop this," my mind was repeating. I stood there with my clothes on.

"Get undressed," he shouted. He fondled his privates as he reached over to turn on the red light. I felt the presence of evil spirits so thick in the blackness of that night. "Get your clothes off." He reached over and grabbed a handful of material from my blouse and shook it back and forth, accelerating my already trampled feelings.

"I will. For hell's sake, give me a minute," I hollered.

"What for?" he yelled.

I undid my clothes and stood there naked.

"Put on you black see-through robe." I took my time. "Come on.

217

Dance! Lift your legs. Show me your privates."

I looked at him and at that very moment, the red light shone on the left side of his face and the blackness of the night on the other. The look of agony was mixed with the triumph of hell. The exact same face I had seen in the dream when I was being abused at 15 years old. My feelings were exactly like those when I had that horrible nightmare. His face was an exact picture of the demon.

Artists throughout the ages have drawn their conceptions of what a devil looks like. But they have drawn a handsome man compared to this face before me. If I had been in the very depths of hell, naked, so that every freak, bastard and whoremonger there could see my body and fondle me, I would have not felt one speck worse.

The desperate need to escape consumed my being. Gritting my teeth as tears were streaming down my face, I said inside my mind, "Oh, God. I'm sorry but I can't wait any longer. I'd rather lose everything. I don't want to go against priesthood direction, but I cannot stand this. I would rather be dead. I'm going to get out from under this freaking oppression."

Just then, Bard's loud voice said, "Lay down now. I've seen enough."

I thought to myself as I laid down, "Do anything you want but it won't be for long."

Paper and pencil can never describe the horror of that night. As soon as he was satisfied enough so I could leave without being noticed, I quickly got dressed and ran down to the shop. I called Brother Mann as soon as I dared to. It was five o'clock in the morning. I let the phone ring about 65 times until his wife answered.

"Hello."

"Hello. This is May. It is urgent. I must speak to Brother Mann."

"Well, he's still asleep."

"I can't help it and I'm sorry. But I've got to talk to him right now. I can't wait. I'm sorry." I was shaking and crying.

"Well, let me see if I can wake him."

"Thank you."

"Hello."

"Hi. This is May. I'm sorry to bother you at this time of night. But I've got to tell you. I can't stand it here any longer. What do you suggest?"

"Well, I guess you'll need to stay there until he dies."

"Until he dies! I can't! I can't wait that long. I can hardly stand it another day."

"Well, what are you going to do?"

"I feel like running away."

"Well, there's nothing to stop you from doing that."

218

"Oh, yeah. The moment I do that, he will ask God to curse me."

Brother Mann said in a very jovial way, "Well, it won't have any effect."

I gasped, "It won't have any effect?"

"No," he said almost with a laugh in his voice. "It won't have any effect."

"Well, all right. That's what I'm going to do."

"OK. That's fine. Let me know where you run to."

"I will. Thank you. Bye."

As I sat there, I felt a heavy cement yoke I had carried on my shoulders lift straight up leaving me feeling so light, I felt as though I would float up and hit my head on the ceiling. Whew. I sat there for a long time with a blank stare on my face. Oh, that was the neatest thing. Oh.

I went over and knelt down on my rug. "Oh, God, my eternal Father in heaven. Thank you. That's the answer." I felt so good I could hardly contain myself. I was overcome with tears of joy. "Bless thy holy name forever."

I could never contemplate such a thing without knowing it would be with priesthood sanction. But now I felt I had finally received that sanction. My whole body tingled with joy, like little electric shocks all through my system.

I clapped my hands, "Thank you. Thank you. A million times thank you. I've got a lot to do. Now, let's see. Get my head on track. What have I got to do before I can run? Let's see, I must plan this really well. Uh, Kevin's got to be able to run this without me then I'll call in several times a day 'cause I don't know where I'm going or when I'll be back. Now, let's see."

I sat down and wrote out directions on everything I could think of that Kevin would need to know to keep things running without me. When Kevin arrived that morning, I told him the plan. I would leave one week from that day. It was perfect because I had just started my period. I would not have to have intercourse for this week. I worked with a zeal that would not quit.

During this time I imagined that maybe I would have to move to China and I could see myself working in the rice paddies. Or maybe I might move to some other far away city and get a job as a scrub woman cleaning a hotel or motel. Whatever or wherever, I had to go, and the "where" seemed irrelevant. I counted nearly every second until I could have my freedom.

CHAPTER 17

"Tonight is my last, May 13, 1982." This thought had been running through my mind over and over again. Bard was in the kitchen talking to Zosa. I thought, "I must hurry." I took a bag into Bard's room and very quickly lifted the mattress and shoved the things into the bag that I always had had to wear to please Bard, except for one pair of panties. I quickly went through the kitchen passing by Bard. "I forgot to turn off the compressors," I said. "I'll be right back."

I hurried out into the blackness of the night and went straight to the tool room and locked the door behind me. I put the clothes in a pile on the cement floor then quickly grabbed the torch and the striker and turned on the acetylene and oxygen tanks. Then I knelt down as a cool breeze chilled me through a crack in the door. With feelings of resentment and disgust, I said out loud, "This is what I think of all this damn stuff," as I lit the torch and threw the hot flames upon it until every speck was black ash. Then I turned off the torch and scooped up the ashes between two thin pieces of metal and then took the ashes to the mud holding tank where I threw them in, and said, "There. That's where you belong."

I hurried over to wash my hands and walked out proudly as I said to myself, "Tomorrow at this time I will be out of his clutches forever." Then I hurried into the house.

That night while doing Bard's bidding, my eyes kept focusing upon the clock each time a few more minutes had passed. That night seemed like a small eternity. While in my mind I was saying with teeth gritting and tears flowing, "Come morning, I will have the victory. You will never lay one finger on me ever again."

About a quarter to four in the morning, Bard looked as though he was asleep and I quietly got up and got dressed. I went to the shop with a feeling of exhilaration running through me as the fresh air kissed my face. "Thank God I made it through that hell for the last time. I'm coming down to the finish line now. Nothing can go wrong."

My mind was racing. I thought, "He must not know even the slightest of my plans," with a fear that something could go wrong but trusting that he would not know. I conducted business as usual to the best of my ability. I had everything I planned to take with me in a grocery bag: two skirts, two blouses, underwear, my patriarchal blessing along with my baby pictures, an old coin collection, a little money, my coat, and a Mosiah Hancock Journal my mother had given me, then I grabbed my cat.

Boyd Huntsley had offered to let me stay in a room in his

basement. I wrote a note to Bard and had Kevin take it to the mailbox. It read something like: "I have gone and I will never, ever return to stand your oppression. And if you want any of your children to stay with you, you had better learn to rule with something besides force and beatings." I had made previous arrangements for a man to come and get my little goats and take care of them. He was busy loading them at the time I left.

It was five o'clock in the afternoon. I had Boyd's other son who worked for me drive down the back alley to pick me up. I huddled down in the seat so I would not be seen.

Kevin was still working there at the shop when Bard came down and started hollering for me all around the yard. According to what Kevin told me later, he said that when Bard could not find me and the office door was locked, he flew into a rage, then broke out the shop kitchen window and asked his boy Skip to go in and unlock the door. After Skip had searched the office and upstairs, Kevin left.

I had arrived at Boyd's OK and Boyd had just shown me my room. As we stood there talking, the glass in one of the windows suddenly fell out and lay on the lawn unbroken. Somehow it seemed like a sign of bad things to come. Kevin arrived and Boyd asked him to go after putty to secure the window back in place.

We walked upstairs and were talking in the kitchen when a knock came on the front door. Someone answered it and there was Bard forcing his way through the front room toward the kitchen. In a flash I opened the door to the basement and stood behind it for a moment. My heart was pounding.

I heard Boyd and Bard outside the door. Boyd said, "You're not going down there."

"She's my wife and I demand that you turn her over to me. You're committing adultery by even having her in your home."

"I never even thought of such a thing. Why I haven't even had an affair with my own wife for six months!"

"You turn her over to me. She must answer for what she has done."

Hearing all this screaming, I began to shake.

"I don't know what you've done to her but she told me that she would rather rot in hell before she'd ever go back to you. So whatever you've done to the girl, it must be pretty bad."

Boyd later told me that Bard put his hands up to the square to try and put a curse on Boyd. I heard Boyd say, "Get your hands down. You're out of order."

I could not take it anymore and seeing the window was out, I grabbed my coat and sack with my little bit of money and took off out through the window. I crossed the lawn, over the fence, ran across the road and down through a subdivision. A couple of children were along the street and I asked them, "Do you live here close? Could I please use your phone?"

"Sure."

From there I called Boyd's and told Bertha, his wife, I was far away from there and that I knew Bard would not leave until they searched the place, then I called someone else to come get me to stay at their house. Bard called everyone's place that he knew I was familiar with, including where I was at. He called there seven times. They told him they had not seen me.

With all the disturbances of that night, I retired around 2 a.m. After a long, sound, uninterrupted sleep, I awakened to Freedom. My eyes glanced over the light yellow and white designs on the wallpaper and the lace curtains dancing from a gentle breeze. I yawned. The thought occurred to me, "What are you going to do today?" I smiled as I answered the thought, "Not a cotton pickin' thing!"

I reached for the pillow next to me propping myself up for a lazy day. I reached over into the sack I had brought. After fumbling through its contents, I pulled out a pink paperback book. Two dollars and fifty cents was scribbled in pencil in the upper righthand corner. I was holding The Mosiah Hancock Journal.

I closed my eyes as my mind wandered back several months. My sisters had brought Mother over to see me and she handed me this history saying, "May, as soon as you can, you need to take the time to read this story of your grandfather on your father's side."

I opened the cover to cast my eyes upon a faded photograph of a man who appeared as thought he had been through hell and back. A sense of gratitude that this picture had been preserved added to my feeling of wonderment as I snuggled into a comfortable position for a good reading session.

For hours I found myself entertained with an appreciation that grew stronger with every page. I came to a part where his poverty had kept him from having a pair of shoes even though his duties required him to go to the canyon through deep snow for firewood. His feet were badly frozen, he wrote. Who can imagine the pain and suffering of frozen feet. In three days' time every nail came off his toes. He wrote further, "Could I find fault with God or any of his servants or even my innocent brother who ran away and left me, not that I know it to be so."

I clasped the book, bringing it to my lips and kissing the lines he wrote. Then holding this precious record to my bosom, I lay with tears wetting my pillow. This is my ancestry. I could not help but notice that some of his experiences were similar to mine. But what would really disturb me was the way things turned out. Maybe he was helping me, I wondered. Who knows? But what a joy I felt to know I had come from his lineage.

The following Monday, I went to the West Jordan Police station and explained the situation briefly so they could understand what the circumstances were. They accompanied me to Reclaim and one officer went to the door.

"Is Mr. Kanderhosh home?" Bard came to the door. "Would you step out here, sir? We'd like to talk with you. May has been talking with us. Do you know what it is about?"

"No, I don't know. She won't even speak to me."

I said, "I'll tell you what it's about. I don't want to see you. I don't want to talk to you. I don't want you to come within 50 feet of me ever again. You no longer work for Reclaim Barrel Supply Company and I just want you to leave me alone."

The officer said, "Is that plain?"

Bard answered, "Yes."

The next day I was outside working with a plastic drum. Bard spotted me. As he walked toward me, I walked through the shop and outside over to where Boyd was working and stood by Boyd. Bard came through the building to the doorway. He saw me standing by Boyd. He stood looking at us and we looked at him, then he turned and left.

The next day was Wednesday. When Kevin and I came to work, there were police cars around the red house where Bard was staying. I wondered what was going on and could see that Olive, Nanas' sister who was Willy's mother, was there. We had always liked each other. She was standing on the lawn so I walked up to her and asked, "What in the world is going on?"

"Oh, May. It was horrible. Bard was praying in his room when Nanas came to the door. Bard's eyes were bloodshot and he was delirious--completely out of his head! When he saw Nanas, he thought she was you, and commanded her to come in. He yelled at her, 'Get in here. I'm your god! You have got to ATONE for what you have done to me.' Nanas was scared and ran over to her house and called Brother Mann to ask him what to do. Mann told her to call the police and then when the police arrived, they went into the house to get him and Bard said to one of the officers, 'Don't touch me or you'll freeze.' The officer said, 'It's plain to see you need help, Mr. Kanderhosh.' Two of them took hold of him. I think they took him to the hospital."

"I see. Well, how are you doing?"

"Oh, I'm just fine. But I've sure been wondering about you. Are things working OK for you?"

"Yeah. I'm all right."

"I sure hope so," she said as she leaned towards me. "I've always thought a lot of you, May."

I gave her a hug. "I've always liked you, too."

"I'm glad you left. I wouldn't tell them that, but I am glad."

"Thank you."

Will came up to my office about ten days after I had left and said, "Bard wants me to ask you a question. He wants to know if you're going to come back or are you going to be destroyed."

"I'm not coming back. Not now, not ever. And as far as going to hell is concerned, I've already been there and there's only one way to go and that's out."

"That's not the kind of answer I want."

"Well, that the only kind you're gonna get." He left.

I watched out the window as Will walked over to the red house and then Bard, along with all the members of the family, walked over to the white house. Just guessing, I suspected that some kind of ritual went on to bring curses on me because after that, Will would not drive my diesels. After three days of his lousy excuses, I fired him and hired a dependable truck driver.

Seeing Will in the yard, I went to him and said, "Will you ask them which house they want to live in--either the white one or the red one. Because if they want to live in the red one, then we can transfer Nanas' and Bard's life estate to that one."

He came back to me the next day. "Well, what did they decide?" I asked.

"We've decided we're going to have them both."

I sent them an eviction notice and in return I received a notice that I was being sued for half of all that I had for a settlement. Or they were asking that the court grant that I should have to return everything to them.

Even though I was away from there, my mind could not believe that I had finally gotten away safely. Every night for weeks I would have nightmares. I had a dream where I was in the bedroom by the door with my clothes on and my shoes off. I was thinking, "How do I get my shoes?" They were right by Bard. "I can't travel fast without them. Then I carefully walked over and slipped them on then walked back toward the door.

"Where are you going?" he yelled.

Just then I grabbed the doorknob and took off, running through the house and outside, across the driveway into a tall green wheat field. As I ran I was scared to death because his legs were longer than mine and maybe he would catch up. But I ran with all my might. I was so scared and sweaty that I would wake up.

Then the next night I dreamed that I was by the kitchen door, and Bard was in the kitchen. I was fidgety and nervous. My adrenalin was getting worked up as my strength increased for what I was about to attempt. Then I slipped out the door, hopefully without him knowing that I had left. Then I took off as fast as I could, running across a country-like area--trees, bushes, weeds.

After I had run for what seemed to be half an hour, I looked back and I could see Nanas and Bard running after me. I was near a canal so I jumped in. There was a heavy embankment and I burrowed in under the dirt and roots near some willows with only my head out of the water. I stayed as still as a mouse, hoping to God they would not have the slightest idea where I was. I heard them run pass but I stayed put because I was afraid to get out for I had no idea how close they might be. I woke up in a cold chill.

Another night I was running through a city or well populated area. As I ran through the city blocks and around buildings near apartment houses, I did not know where he was or how close. As I ran near a house where the window was open, I jumped in quickly. It was a little girl's bedroom. I quickly hid in her closet while she looked at me. I put my fingers up to my lips as if to say, "Shhh." I woke up.

I went to seek counsel from one of the priesthood brethren because I did not want to do anything that would not be according to the priesthood's approval. I sat there before him like a scared, whimpering child, not knowing what to do or if I dared to say anything. I could not keep my face from twisting from all the agony that was going through my soul.

This man sat me down, pulled up a chair in front of me, picked up my hands and put them in his, and said, "It's OK, sweetheart. Now just tell 'daddy' anything you want to."

I could not hold back my emotions any more and I burst into tears.

He said, "Just take all the time you need. It's OK."

So for three hours I gave him a brief description of the last 18 years.

He said, "Oh, my hell. I have never heard of anything that horrible going on even in Las Vegas."

I said, "What I would like to know is: according to the laws of God, what are my obligations to Bard or anyone in that situation?"

I explained to him all that was in my name so that I could carry on my business. He said, "Thank the Lord. It should be yours. You have earned it 20 times over."

I said, "They want a settlement."

"You owe him nothing. You have your own life to live now."

"If he would just admit even to any degree that he had done wrong in anything, my heart could be softened with compassion, but no. Not only all that he's stolen but now he wants more. He wants to force me to support him for the rest of his life. Did you know that?"

"Oh, that's ridiculous."

"But it's true. You know what though? I feel as if it would be worth $100 a month to me if he could bring himself to do one thing."

"What's that?"

"Well, the grapevine has it that Bard and Nanas are spreading it around that I'm having affairs with all the guys that work for me."

"Yes, I've heard that, too."

"They're not only insulting my integrity but also that of all the men that work there." Laughing, I added, "They don't just pick one guy. No. Hell, I'm supposed to be having it with all of 'em like I'm running a regular whorehouse up there or somethin'. I'm so sick of it. I'd just like to see him eat crow. If he wants anything out of me, let him come to you and to those people that he's spread those lies to and tell them there's no backing for it. Then perhaps I could consider giving him five cents."

"I doubt that he'd ever do that."

"If he doesn't, then I'll do nothing more for him. I'll hire an attorney and I'll just keep fighting it all the way to the Supreme Court, if I have to. I'm just thankful that the priesthood council isn't against me in this."

"Well, bless you. Do what you have to. I think the Lord's on your side. Let me know how it's going, OK?"

"You bet," I said, as I gave him a hug. "Thank you."

A few months went by. I made an appointment to see him at a later date to obtain a priesthood release of my marriage (divorce). When I arrived, Bard and Nanas were just leaving his house. Bard was approximately eight feet away. He turned to me and hollered, "You'll never get a divorce from me, and if he gives you one, it won't be binding in the heavens."

I stepped into the house and shut the door. "Yuck," I said. "He'd just love me to believe that shit."

"Oh, please. Don't talk that way in my home," he said excitedly.

"I'm sorry. But I just can't stand his lies."

"I understand."

We went to another room where an ordinance was performed to release me from Bard according to priesthood law. I was very happy and thanked the man then left.

I purchased a .38 revolver for security, also a Blue Heeler dog I called Miss Piggy. Although the business had an apartment where my office was in the shop, I did not have enough nerve to live there. The creepy feeling, combined with fear, would keep me paying rent and driving 15 miles to have a room to sleep at night where I would beg the Lord to let me have a night's rest without a nightmare.

These continued night after night for over a year, all different types of nightmares of my getting away. Then one night I dreamed I was running down a darkened street. There were only a few lights and I could just barely see the road ahead. I had my loaded .38 revolver and I was running as fast as I could. Bard was only 100 feet behind me. I was so fatigued that I felt I could not run much farther. I turned and commanded, "Stop, or I'll shoot. I mean it. I'll shoot." He kept coming and when he was about ten feet way, I shot him. As he was falling, I shot him again and again and again until I unloaded all six shots in him. Then I woke up. I have had fewer nightmares since.

After about a year and a half, I asked a friend to dedicate the office apartment to remove the evil spirits. He did, and I could feel a definite difference, so I then moved in.

After I moved in, however, I started having a whole new set of nightmares. It was like I ran away then I came back and then I was trying to run away again. I could not figure out why until it dawned on me, "Well, it's because you moved back here." Even though I was away from Bard and had the protection of a bolted door, my dog, and my loaded .38, I was still scared.

One day Will and Bardell came up to my apartment with their children and knocked on the door.

"Hello," I said.

"Hi. We come to let you know some good news."

"Oh?"

"Sherrie just had a baby. You knew she married Willy, didn't you?"

I had heard that she had.

"Well, we just wanted to tell you."

I was unable to fake a smile, feeling as though I was about to lose my lunch. "Whatever," was my only comment.

"OK. Well, we'll see ya' around." They left.

I thought to myself after they left, "What a waste of a life. The girl didn't have the chance of a snowball in hell." I shivered and again thanked the Lord that I was out of the mess.

I had taken a driver's training course and was now driving everywhere. I hired an attorney to fight my case, but he kept asking me, "What do you think is a fair settlement?"

I answered, "I don't think giving him anything is a fair settlement."

"Well, look, you walked out of there with everything and left them with a home and Will's farm, but no income from the business. What they want is so much a month out of your income."

The thought went through my mind as the attorney talked, "Bard wants a reward? After what he has stolen from Mother and made her suffer along with what I have suffered?" As I remembered Bard's words, "You'll never get away from me. Never, never, no never," these echoes went through my mind. I sat there sick.

Then my attorney said again, "Well, think about it. What are you prepared to offer them?"

"I can't reward them with anything and I don't feel I owe them anything. Not one dime. I tell ya', if I worked all day long to earn $50 and I thought I had to give Bard one dime, I'd feel so sick. I wouldn't be able to work."

"With all that you're making on Reclaim Barrel, don't you think it would better to offer even $100 per month and avoid a lawsuit of this magnitude rather than all the expense this is going to cost you? And even then, the judge might grant them so much of your income, or they might have the whole thing returned to them. You never know how it could go."

"Well, I can't help it. I can't reward him. I know I've earned everything I have."

"How can we prove that?"

I had been hedging about telling him very much but how could he possibly represent me if I did not tell him anything. Then I said, "I will go and give this some thought and I'll get back with you."

"OK."

On my way home I asked the Lord in my mind how to proceed. "I know nothing of these matters," I told the Lord, with a weak and sick feeling. "But I just cannot see rewarding them." I thought about this issue almost constantly.

I felt the necessity of preparing a document of explanation describing briefly those 18 years of my experience. I handed it to my attorney then said, "Maybe when you have read this, you might have some understanding as to where I'm coming from. All I am asking for is to be able to keep that which I have. Had I not earned it, they would not have put it in my name and I built Reclaim after that. I don't hate those people, but if I never had any encounter with them again, it would be too soon."

I sat there while he read the document. When he came to the part where Bard said he saved my life by killing a shit-eating dog that was headed my way, this attorney laughed and laughed in a hideous way. I thought, "And this man is representing me? Oh, no." Needless to say, I switched attorneys.

After several months with the second attorney, the case was ready to come to court and he kept hitting me with the idea, "What are you going to do for a settlement?" Saying, "Come on, now. We've got to give them something. Now, how much?" I looked at him and thought,

229

"Man, you're sick."

Three days before it was to appear before the judge, I went to see the judge to ask for an extension. He asked, "Why?"

"Because my attorney has been spending time on other people's cases and I feel like he's ready to wash me down the drain, and I want to hire another attorney that I can have more confidence in."

The judge said, "OK, kid. I'll give you a bite of the apple just this one time, but that's it."

"Thank you, Judge." Then I hired Brent Ryan.

The preparation for the case went on for many months. During that time, I went to pick up Mother on a lovely summer morning about 10 a.m. We had made plans to go to the canyon. We took off and as we came around the mountain at Parley's on our way to Oakley, I breathed a sigh, "Isn't this nice. Oh, yeah, this is why I came. Ummm. I love the fresh mountain air."

"Yes, this is nice," Mother commented.

When we arrived in Oakley on our way up to Mirror Lake, I stopped at a little store. "What would you like, Mom?"

She sat there thinking and finally said, "Let's see. I believe I'd like some ice cream and root beer. Do you think they have that?"

"Ice cream and root beer coming up!" I grinned as I skipped away into the little store. I felt so good about being able to give her these little treats. I returned with the goodies, and we sat there enjoying the warmth of the day and looking into the green pasture ahead of us.

"Life is so nice," I sighed, as I laid back in my seat with a slight breeze coming through while I ate a Fig Newton.

I looked at Mother as I asked, "Why did you stay there all those years? Heck, you weren't married to him. You could've left."

"Yeah, I know, but I felt that if you didn't have me to help you, you wouldn't have been able to endure under the load."

I sat there in silence and stared at the steering wheel. Tears came to my eyes, "I wouldn't have, either." I was so sorry about Mom's sufferings. "Mom, sometimes children are fools." I said, "Well, the love of a mother is as enduring as time."

I remembered how, even as a child, I had prayed for God to keep Mama alive because I felt I needed her for my strength. I said, "I'm glad that God chose a spirit like you to be my mother. I do love you. I hope I can live so that you and Daddy can be proud of me from here on out."

"Oh, May. I am proud of you."

I thought to myself as she said that, "That's just because you're so loving and so forgiving, but I'm not very proud of myself."

I said, "You know that book you gave me, <u>The Mosiah Hancock</u>

Journal? I've been reading that. And Mama, I'm so happy that he was my grandfather. I didn't know he was a bodyguard to the Prophet Joseph."

"Yeah. Your father was his last child and you're my last child," she said smiling, "so you just barely got in on that bandwagon."

I had a desire to sing a very fitting song that I had learned a long time ago.

I'll serve the Lord while I am young
And in my early days,
Devote the music of my tongue
To my Redeemer's praise.
I'll praise his name that he has given me,
Heritage and birth.
Amongst the most beloved of heaven
Who dwelled upon the earth."[16]

My eyes were wet and a lump arose in my throat.

"Oh how I love to hear you sing," Mom said.

I bent over and kissed her on the forehead. "We're going to have a good life." As I started up the car, I felt a warm, contented glow. "I just love to come to the canyons. It seems to me like it's God's home. I like to come up here to study the gospel."

We continued on our way and after a while we arrived at one of the beautiful lakes. I stopped the car and helped Mother out so we could sit under a shade tree by the lake. I saw a couple of little chipmunks dash out of sight.

"You know what, Mom? Joseph has a pet chipmunk."

"Oh, yeah?" she laughed.

"Yeah. And it comes right up and eats right out of his hand. He calls it Funny Face. I've seen it and it's really cute."

"How is Joseph anyway?"

"He's just fine."

"Is he ever going to marry you or what? How did that turn out?"

"Joseph knows that I love him very much but he told me that he had been praying for the Lord to send someone in my life that was younger that could for sure give me children. He said he didn't think he would be able to give me all the blessings that he wanted to see me have. I 'bout cried my eyes out. I begged him not to talk like that. He said, 'No, little darlin'. You deserve the best and even though it means my giving up something that's very precious to me, I want you

---

[16] (Make notation)

231

to have all that this life has to offer you.' Mama, I believe that Joseph was a Godsend to help me out of that prison. There's no way I could have ever done it without his help. I needed him to lean on. There will always be a deep love an appreciation. One little part of my heart that man will always have."

I turned to get my camera. "I'm going to get a picture of that cute little wild flower--right there."

I was gone for a few minutes taking a few pictures. When I returned, Mama said, "Well, May. What do you think of the priesthood work? Are you going to live the principle? Do you still believe it's the work of the Lord?"

"I do. But you know what? Alfredo said in meeting about the Holy Ghost being our guide. It seems to me that that's the most important thing right now. Because if I can't have the Lord's guidance in something, then I've failed already. One must know for herself and that's something that's so precious and sacred and secret--the convictions that a person has with their God. I can't see anybody being pushed into any type of marriage if they don't know that God is with them. Do you know what I mean?"

"Yeah, I know what you mean."

"Because you know, Mom," I said, as I reached over the seat to pick up a book I had in the back. "All that damn suffering we went through--that's not part of our religion." I was trying to find Section 121 of The Doctrine and Covenants. "Here, let me read what it says about a man's priesthood."

34. Behold, there are many called, but few are chosen. And why are they not chosen?

35. Because their hearts are set so much upon the things of this world, and aspire to the honors of men, that they do not learn this one lesson--

36. That the rights of the priesthood are inseparably connected with the powers of heaven, and that the powers of heaven cannot be controlled nor handled only upon the principles of righteousness.

37. That they may be conferred upon us, it is true; but when we undertake to cover our sins, or to gratify our pride, our vain ambition, or to exercise control or dominion or compulsion upon the souls of the children of men, in any degree of unrighteousness, behold, the heavens withdraw themselves; the Spirit of the Lord is grieved; and when it is withdrawn, Amen to the priesthood or the authority of that man.

38. Behold, ere he is aware, he is left unto himself, to

kick against the pricks, to persecute the saints, and to fight against God.

39. We have learned by sad experience that it is the nature and disposition of almost all men, as soon as they get a little authority, as they suppose, they will immediately begin to exercise unrighteous dominion.

40. Hence many are called, but few are chosen.

41. No power or influence can or ought to be maintained by virtue of the priesthood, only by persuasion, by long-suffering, by gentleness and meekness, and by love unfeigned;

42. By kindness, and pure knowledge, which shall greatly enlarge the soul without hypocrisy, and without guile--

43. Reproving betimes with sharpness, when moved upon by the Holy Ghost; and then showing forth afterwards an increase of love toward him whom thou hast reproved, lest he esteem thee to be his enemy;

44. That he may know that thy faithfulness is stronger than the cords of death.

45. Let thy bowels also be full of charity towards all men, and to the household of faith, let virtue garnish they thoughts unceasingly; then shall thy confidence wax strong in the presence of God; and the doctrine of the priesthood shall distil upon thy soul as the dews from heaven.

46. The Holy Ghost shall be thy constant companion, and thy scepter an unchanging scepter of righteousness and truth; and they dominion shall be an everlasting dominion, and without compulsory means it shall flow unto thee forever and ever.[17]

"Even though I love our religion and the priesthood brethren above any other, I don't think any religion has a franchise on God. I don't feel I have room to preach to anyone but because of the imperfectness that lies amongst us as a people, I have learned to appreciate good people, whatever their religion may be."

Then I remembered something sweet that had happened. "You know what I saw in the store the other day? There was a little boy over by the apples. His hair was combed nicely and he was in his little long-sleeved shirt and neat pants. Then I noticed a little girl with her hair done up nicely with her little waves and braids. She was wearing a

---

[17] The Doctrine and Covenants, Section 121:34-46.

long-sleeved dress that came below her knees. That brought a smile to my face as I thought, 'Oh, there is a mother somewhere here, too.' Then I spotted their mother over by the mushrooms. As my eyes dampened, I stood there watching her for a moment with joy as I thought, 'There's a little bit of heaven in this store.' Then I went about my business with a good feeling."

"The memory of the priesthood's teachings and the association of the Saints is sweet on my mind. I hope that if in some small way I can bless them here and there, even others that are not of the group, it makes my day to see them smile over some small thing I've done. I've not lost my faith, Mother. And I've not lost my testimony or my love but I feel I've got a lot of sorting out to do to separate the things that are true from that which is not. I feel weak but maybe in time the Lord will make me strong again."

My spirit was again overwhelmed with the desire to sing. I gave way with enthusiasm.

> I know that my Redeemer lives.
> What comfort this sweet sentence gives!
> He lives, he lives who once was dead.
> He lives my everliving head.
> He lives to bless me with his love.
> He lives to plead for me above.
> He lives my hungry soul to feed.
> He lives to bless in time of need.

Mother was now singing with me. Hearing Mom's sweet voice just made me feel good all over.

> He lives to grant me rich supply.
> He lives to guide me with his eye.
> He lives to comfort me when faint.
> He lives to hear my soul's complaint.
> He lives to silence all my fears.
> He lives to wipe away my tears.
> He lives to calm my troubled heart.
> He lives, all blessings to impart.
> He lives, my kind, wise, heav'nly friend.
> He lives and loves me to the end.
> He lives, and while he lives, I'll sing.
> He lives, my Prophet, Priest and King.
> He lives and grants me daily breath.
> He lives and I shall conquer death.
> He lives my mansion to prepare.

He lives to bring me safely there.
He lives, all glory to his name!
He lives, my Savior, still the same.
O sweet the joy this sentence gives:
I know that my Redeemer lives![18]

After two years of depositions and a great deal of expense, my case was scheduled to meet before a jury trial.

I was talking to Brent, my lawyer. "What their attorney is trying to emphasize for all it's worth is that I came in the family with just the clothes on my back. And seein' as how the original property on 5th East was Nanas', which she shared with Bard, they want it returned to her because that property, when it was sold, was used to buy the farm and the Reclaim Barrel property which was one and a half acres on Redwood Road. That is what I wound up with after 18 years. They're not denying that I built Reclaim Barrel.

Brent commented, "Yes, I can see what it is. Because you're the bread winner, they figure you're in the position that the man would be in wherein a wife would sue for support. That's why he's trying to claim disability and now they want you to support him."

"Right!" I exclaimed, "but more than that they're trying to say that just because I had food, clothing and shelter, I have had my pay." I sat there shaking my head while staring at the floor. "It's going to be a doozy--how to prove what I've told ya'. It's like one person over here could testify to one thing and another one over there could testify to another. The evidence is all over this whole cotton pickin' valley. But the most important thing is that it's recorded in the heavens where no one can erase or lie about the facts. We can only pray for heaven to help us win this case."

"Well, while you're praying, get me the names, addresses, and phone numbers of all the witnesses that you can think of and list the things they could testify to. Can you do that?"

"You got it!" I said as I sprang up off the chair. We shook hands. "I'll have that for you in the morning.

The months passed quickly while we gathered evidence to support my position. Three days before the court day, I met with a very close friend at his place of employment. The snow was falling heavily as he opened my car door to sit down. I began telling him about the court date.

---

[18] "I Know That My Redeemer Lives," words by Samuel Medley, music by Lewis D. Edwards, Hymns, p. 95.

I said, "I think maybe I should fast for these three days that we might have power from heaven to fight my battle."

He thought for a moment then picked up my hands and said, "No. I want you to be strong and valiant when you walk into that courtroom. I will fast for you."

I looked at him as I beheld the face of a true friend. Sweeter words I had never heard. "Bless you," I said, as I gave him a kiss on his cheek.

He looked at his watch. I must go now or I'll be late for work. But don't worry, OK?"

"Thank you." He got out and shut the door. I sat there pondering over the last two minutes as I thought of all my assets. My friends are the most precious.

The court day came. I met Mother in the hall. She kissed me and said, "I've been praying for you. We all have." We hugged.

"I wish you could come in, " I said.

"I wish I could, too, but they said I have to stay out here, so it's OK."

We took our positions. I sat next to Brent, my attorney, and Mary, his secretary. Mary bent over to whisper in my ear. She was looking over at Bard as she said, "You know, the first time I saw Bard a couple of months ago, when Brent was going to take his deposition-- when he walked in the room, no one needed to tell me who he was. I just knew. He looked like death warmed over with the most evil countenance. It sent a shiver through my whole body."

The judge stood up and court was in session.

PROCEEDINGS

THE COURT: THIS IS THE TIME SET FOR TRIAL IN THE MATTER OF J. BARD KANDERHOSH AND WIFE VS. MAY HANCOCK KANDERHOSH, CASE NO. C82-2576.

COUNSEL, STATE YOUR APPEARANCES FOR THE RECORD.

MR. FLANK: MARTIN FLANK, ATTORNEY FOR THE PLAINTIFFS.

MR. RYAN: BRENT RYAN, ATTORNEY FOR THE DEFENDANT AND THIRD-PARTY PLAINTIFF.

236

THE COURT: VERY WELL. MR. FLANK, YOU ARE APPEARING ON BEHALF OF THE THIRD-PARTY DEFENDANT?

MR. FLANK: THAT IS CORRECT. I'M ALSO ATTORNEY FOR THE THIRD-PARTY DEFENDANT, MR. DARDSON.

THE COURT: COUNSEL, IS THE PLAINTIFF READY TO PROCEED?

MR. FLANK: WE ARE READY.

THE COURT: AND THE DEFENDANT?

MR. RYAN: WE ARE, JUDGE.

THE COURT: VERY WELL. WILL YOU PLEASE CALL THE JURY.

(THE JURY WAS EMPANELED AND SWORN TO TRY THE CASE.)

THE COURT: AT THIS TIME, MR. FLANK, YOU MAY PROCEED WITH YOUR OPENING STATEMENT.

MR. FLANK: THANK YOU, YOUR HONOR.

LADIES AND GENTLEMEN, AS I STATED, I AM MARTIN FLANK, ATTORNEY FOR THE PLAINTIFFS, NANAS KANDERHOSH AND BARD KANDERHOSH, AS WELL AS THE THIRD-PARTY DEFENDANT, WILLER DARDSON. WHAT I AM GOING TO SAY AT THIS POINT IN TIME IS NOT TO BE CONSIDERED EVIDENCE BY YOU, BUT SIMPLY MY OPINION AS TO WHAT THE EVIDENCE IS GOING TO SHOW AND TRY TO DRAW YOU A PICTURE OF WHAT THIS PARTICULAR ACTION IS ABOUT.

THE STORY STARTS AND THE EVIDENCE WILL SHOW THAT IN 1974, NANAS KANDERHOSH BECAME A WIDOW. NANAS KANDERHOSH, THE LADY IN BLUE. HER HUSBAND HAD DIED. SHE HAD BELONGED AND HAD ALL HER LIFE

BELONGED TO A SPLINTER GROUP OF MORMONS WHO
BELIEVED IN POLYGAMY. MRS. KANDERHOSH INHERITED A
HOME HERE IN SALT LAKE COUNTY AND LIVED IN THAT
HOME UNTIL SHE MET MR. KANDERHOSH IN THE LATE
'50'S AND MARRIED MR. KANDERHOSH IN 1962, AT WHICH
TIME THEY MOVED INTO THEIR HOME IN SALT LAKE
COUNTY.

THEREAFTER, IN ABOUT 1965 OR THEREABOUTS, A
MR. WILLER DARDSON CAME TO THE HOME, WHO
COULDN'T GET ALONG WITH HIS PARENTS. HE WAS
ABOUT 17 YEARS OLD AT THAT TIME, AND THE
KANDERHOSHES TOOK HIM IN AS A FOSTER SON AND
TOOK CARE OF HIM. HE LIVED IN THE HOME. MR.
DARDSON FROM THEN ON BASICALLY LIVED AS A FAMILY
WITH THE KANDERHOSHES, ALTHOUGH HE LATER MARRIED
AND HAD CHILDREN AND HAD BEEN DIVORCED ABOUT THE
SAME TIME.

THE DEFENDANT, MAY KANDERHOSH, WHO WAS
HAVING PROBLEMS AT HOME AND WHO LIKEWISE
BELONGED TO THE SAME GROUP OF MORMONS WHO
BELIEVED IN POLYGAMY, CAME TO THE HOME OF THE
KANDERHOSHES. SHE WAS ABOUT 16 YEARS OF AGE AT
THAT TIME, AND SHE LIVED IN THAT HOME. LATER MR.
KANDERHOSH TOOK MAY KANDERHOSH, THE DEFENDANT,
AS ONE OF HIS WIVES. HE LIKEWISE TOOK ANOTHER
WOMAN AS HIS WIFE AND HAD FOUR CHILDREN BY HER.

IN 19--THIS WILL BE EVIDENCE ADMITTED BY
STIPULATION. THAT IN ABOUT 1962, NANAS KANDERHOSH
AS THE WIFE OF BARD KANDERHOSH PREPARED A DEED.
IT WAS HER HOME SOLELY UP TO ABOUT 1962, BUT IN

1962, SHE PREPARED A DEED WHEREBY SHE TURNED THAT HOME OVER TO MR. KANDERHOSH AND HERSELF IN JOINT TENANCY.

LATER IN 1972, AND THE EVIDENCE WILL SHOW COMPLETELY THAT ALL OF THE PROPERTY WE ARE GOING TO BE TALKING ABOUT CAME FROM THAT PROPERTY OWNED BY NANAS KANDERHOSH PRIOR TO HER MARRIAGE TO BARD KANDERHOSH. THERE WILL BE THEN ADMITTED INTO EVIDENCE BY STIPULATION CERTAIN DEEDS WHEREBY NANAS AND BARD KANDERHOSH TRADED THAT PROPERTY HERE IN SALT LAKE COUNTY FOR THREE LOTS IN WEST JORDAN.

ON THEIR THREE LOTS WAS AN OLD BUILDING WHICH LATER BECAME A FACTORY BY WHICH THE BUSINESS WAS OPERATED, AND IN ADDITION, ONE HOME. THAT IS DESCRIBED AS LOT 1, 19 AND 20 OF A HARTMAN SUBDIVISION, 19 AND 20 BEING THE FACTORY WHERE THEY HAD THEIR BUSINESS. LOT 1 BEING THE HOME WHERE THEY RESIDED.

THEY THEN PURCHASED LOT 2, WHICH WAS NEXT DOOR, WHICH HAD ANOTHER HOME ON IT. THE FAMILY ALSO RECEIVED SIX ACRES OF FARM GROUND WITH AN OLD HOME ON IT IN TRADE FOR THE PROPERTY THAT MRS. KANDERHOSH HAD OWNED PRIOR. SO IN TOTAL, THEY MADE A -- THEY HAD ENOUGH FOR A DOWN PAYMENT ON LOT 2 WHERE THERE WAS A HOME, LOT 1 WHERE THERE WAS A HOME, LOTS 19 AND 20 WHERE THE BARREL BUSINESS THAT WE ARE GOING TO TALK ABOUT WAS ESTABLISHED, AND SIX ACRES OF FARM GROUND. THE FAMILY LIVED IN THESE TWO HOMES.

239

NOW, WHEN I SAY THE FAMILY, WE ARE TALKING ABOUT A GROUP OF PEOPLE. THERE WAS BARD AND NANAS. THERE WAS MAY. THERE WAS AT ONE TIME WILLER DARDSON WITH HIS WIFE AND FIVE CHILDREN, AND THERE WAS ANOTHER WIFE OF BARD'S WITH ABOUT FOUR CHILDREN LIVING IN THOSE HOMES. AT THE PRESENT TIME ARE BARD AND NANAS, WILLER DARDSON, WHO HAS BEEN ILL AND HAS NOT BEEN ABLE -- HAD SOME MENTAL PROBLEMS AND OTHER THINGS, NOT BEEN ABLE TO WORK, AND THE OTHER WIFE, WHO HAS BEEN ILL AND JUST RECENTLY OUT OF THE HOSPITAL AND FOUR CHILDREN. THESE CHILDREN RUN IN AGE FROM 19 DOWN TO 14, ONE 14, 15, 17, AND 19. SOME OF THOSE CHILDREN YOU WILL HEAR TESTIMONY OF SOME PROBLEMS LIKEWISE.

THEN IN 1975 THE FAMILY DETERMINED THAT IT WOULD BE IN THE BEST INTEREST OF THE FAMILY IF THE PROPERTIES WERE CHANGED INTO THE YOUNGER MEMBERS OF THE FAMILY TO MAY KANDERHOSH'S NAME AND WILLER DARDSON'S. AND YOU WILL HAVE DEEDS IN EVIDENCE WHICH SHOW THAT BARD AND NANAS CONVEYED TO MAY KANDERHOSH AND WILLER DARDSON ALL OF THE PROPERTY, THAT BEING BOTH HOMES, THE BUSINESS PROPERTY, AND THE FARM.

THERE THEN BECOMES SOME PROBLEMS. A BUSINESS WAS STARTED, A CORPORATION WAS COMMENCED, AND INITIALLY THEY HAD A BOTTLE BUSINESS WHERE THEY CLEANED BOTTLES. THAT LATER TURNED INTO A BARREL BUSINESS WHERE THEY PICKED UP BARRELS AND RECONDITIONED THEM AND THEN TOOK THEM BACK. IN

THAT CORPORATION, MAY KANDERHOSH WAS NAMED THE PRESIDENT, WILLER DARDSON, VICE PRESIDENT, AND BARD KANDERHOSH, SECRETARY AND TREASURER.

THAT BUSINESS CONTINUED WITH ALL PEOPLE WORKING IN IT UNTIL ABOUT 1982 OR '81 WHEN ALL THE PROBLEMS COMMENCED. AT THAT TIME AND PRIOR TO THAT TIME, ALL INCOME, MONIES RECEIVED FROM THE BUSINESS WAS USED FOR THE ENTIRE FAMILY, INCLUDING NANAS, BARD, WILLER DARDSON, THE OTHER WIFE, THE CHILDREN, AND THEY LIVED IN THESE TWO HOMES.

AT THAT TIME, PRIOR TO 1982, NANAS KANDERHOSH RECEIVED $20 A DAY IN WHICH SHE PURCHASED GROCERIES, BOUGHT THE NECESSITIES FOR THE ENTIRE FAMILY. SHE, IN ESSENCE, WAS THE BASIC MOTHER OF THE GROUP. SHE IS 12 YEARS OLDER THAN BARD KANDERHOSH. BARD KANDERHOSH RECEIVED A CHECK. WILLER DARDSON RECEIVED A CHECK, AND MAY KANDERHOSH RECEIVED A CHECK. THE BUSINESS PAID ALL DEBTS AND OBLIGATIONS. THERE WAS STILL A BALANCE DUE ON LOT 2 WHERE THEY LIVED WITH A PAYMENT OF ABOUT $138, $150. THAT WAS PAID OUT OF THE BUSINESS. ALL UTILITIES WERE PAID OUT OF THE BUSINESS. IN ESSENCE, THEY LIVED AS ONE LARGE UNIT.

THEN THE PROBLEMS AROSE. IN FACT, MR. DARDSON AND MAY KANDERHOSH OPERATED THE PROPERTIES, MAY KANDERHOSH TENDING TO CONVEYING TO WILLER DARDSON THE FARM, AND WILLER DARDSON CONVEYING TO MAY KANDERHOSH THE BUSINESS PROPERTIES, LOT 19 AND 20, LOT 1, AND IN ADDITION LOT 2 WITH A LIFE ESTATE TO NANAS AND TO BARD KANDERHOSH.

241

SHE THEN DISCONTINUED PAYING ANY MONIES TO ANYONE. SHE ENTERED INTO AN AGREEMENT WITH MR. DARDSON WHEREBY SHE WOULD PAY SOME TAXES FOR HIS INTEREST IN THE BUSINESS.

AT THAT TIME, MR. DARDSON HAULED THE BARRELS. HE PICKED THEM UP AND DELIVERED THEM. MR. DARDSON IS NOT EDUCATED, BARELY ABLE TO READ AND WRITE, AND MAY KANDERHOSH WAS, IN FACT, THE BRAINS OF THE ORGANIZATION. THE EVIDENCE WILL SHOW THAT MAY KANDERHOSH MADE AN AGREEMENT WHEREBY THAT THE PROPERTY WOULD BE IN HER AND MR. DARDSON, WOULD BE IN HER NAME AND HIS NAME ON THE BASIS THAT THEY WOULD, IN FACT, TAKE CARE OF THE FAMILY DURING THEIR LIFETIME, AND THAT PEOPLE INCLUDING BARD, NANAS, THE OTHER WIFE, AND THE CHILDREN.

THAT TERMINATED IN APPROXIMATELY 1982; NO MORE MONIES WERE GIVEN TO THEM. EVIDENCE WILL SHOW THAT AT THAT TIME MAY KANDERHOSH TOOK OVER THE ENTIRE BUSINESS, USED THE MONEY ENTIRELY HERSELF, ALTHOUGH SHE DID CONTINUE TO PAY THE PAYMENT ON LOT 2 WHERE ONE OF THE HOMES WAS.

SHE THEN SERVED THE KANDERHOSHES WITH A NOTICE TO QUIT THE PREMISES ON ONE OF THE HOMES WHERE SOME OF THE FAMILIES LIVED, AND ADVISED THEM TO REMOVE THEMSELVES FROM THAT HOME. THIS LAWSUIT COMMENCED AT THAT TIME. BASICALLY THE EVIDENCE I HAVE SET FORTH WILL SHOW THESE FACTS.

I DON'T THINK THE QUESTION OF THE DEEDS ET CETERA WILL BE CONTROVERTED. WE ARE REQUESTING

THAT YOU BY REASON OF THE BREACH RETURN THE PROPERTY TO THE KANDERHOSHES.

WE'RE ALSO REQUESTING THAT THE CORPORATION BE DISSOLVED, AND THAT THE KANDERHOSHES RECEIVE ONE-HALF OF THE ASSETS OF THAT CORPORATION, AND THAT MAY KANDERHOSH RECEIVE THE OTHER HALF. ONE OTHER THING THE EVIDENCE WILL SHOW, AND THAT WILL BE THAT MAY KANDERHOSH, SINCE SHE, IN FACT, BREACHED THE AGREEMENT TO SUPPORT THE FAMILY, HAS PURCHASED TEN AND A HALF ACRES OF OTHER PROPERTY IN LEHI PAYING $2,200 FOR THAT PROPERTY INSTEAD OF HER AGREEMENT TO TAKE CARE OF THIS FAMILY. THANK YOU, LADIES AND GENTLEMEN.

THE COURT: THANK YOU, MR. FLANK. MR. RYAN?

MR. RYAN: MAY IT PLEASE THE COURT, LADIES AND GENTLEMEN. THIS CASE IS ABOUT A GENTLE, NAIVE, YOUNG GIRL WHO WAS NOT YET 16 YEARS OLD WHO PLEDGED HERSELF COMPLETELY TO A RELIGIOUS PRINCIPLE, THAT BEING THE PRINCIPLE OF PLURAL MARRIAGE AND ALL THAT GOES WITH IT TO A FAMILY. SHE WAS REWARDED FOR THAT UNSWERVING DEVOTION TO THAT FAMILY AND TO THAT PRINCIPLE BY BEING RUTHLESSLY VICTIMIZED BY THOSE WHOM SHE TRUSTED. MAY HANCOCK CAME TO LIVE WITH J. BARD KANDERHOSH, HIS WIFE, NANAS, AND WILLER DARDSON IN ABOUT 1963, LATE 1963 OR EARLY 1964, JUST PRIOR TO HER 16TH BIRTHDAY. SHE WENT THERE WITH THE EXPECTATION AND WITH THE UNDERSTANDING THAT AT THE TIME SHE REACHED HER MAJORITY AT THE AGE OF 18, THAT SHE

243

WOULD BECOME THE SECOND PLURAL WIFE OF J. BARD KANDERHOSH, AND THAT IN THAT CAPACITY, SHE WOULD HAVE A POSITION IN THAT FAMILY THAT SHE WOULD HAVE CHILDREN OF HER OWN, AND THAT AS OTHER WIVES WERE ADDED TO THAT FAMILY, THAT SHE WOULD HOLD THAT POSITION, A POSITION OF RESPECT AND OF RESPONSIBILITY.

NOW, IT WAS INTENDED THAT ALL PARTIES ENGAGED IN THIS ENTERPRISE OF PLURAL MARRIAGE, SUPPORT THE FAMILY, AND THAT WHATEVER THEY DID, IT WOULD BE FOR THE BETTERMENT OF THAT FAMILY. NOW, YOU WILL FIND AND THE EVIDENCE WILL SHOW THAT MAY WAS AN EXTREMELY, I SAY EXTREMELY, SHE WAS AN INCREDIBLY HARD WORKER, EXTREMELY DEDICATED, INCREDIBLY SO, TO RELIGIOUS PRINCIPLES AND UNSWERVING AND UNWAVERING IN HER DEVOTION TO THIS PRINCIPLE AND TO BARD KANDERHOSH.

NOW, MR. KANDERHOSH AT ALL TIMES, THE EVIDENCE WILL SHOW, RULED THIS FAMILY WITH THE PROVERBIAL IRON FIST. HE WAS ABOVE PEOPLE PHYSICALLY, AND THEY RESPECTED HIM, OR IF THEY OPPOSED HIS AUTHORITY IN ANY WAY, BUT THE KEY TO HIS AUTHORITY OVER ALL THESE PEOPLE, AS YOU WILL SEE, AND PARTICULARLY OVER MAY KANDERHOSH, WAS THE APPARENT RELIGIOUS AUTHORITY THAT HE PREACHED.

NOW, HE HAD A PECULIAR KEY TO MAY KANDERHOSH'S HEART, AND THAT WAS AGAIN HER DEVOTION TO THIS RELIGIOUS PRINCIPLE. BUT, HE CLAIMS AND HE TOLD MAY THAT HE WAS HER GOD,

244

THAT HE WAS HER LORD, AND THAT SHE WAS TO DO HIS WILL IN ALL THINGS, AND ON AT LEAST ONE OCCASION WHEN SHE REFUSED TO ENGAGE IN SOME REPREHENSIBLE CONDUCT HE REQUIRED OF HER, HE SAID THAT IF YOU REFUSE ME, I WILL PUT YOU DOWN AS THE LOWEST PERSON IN THIS FAMILY, LOWER THAN A CONCUBINE, AND YOU WILL BE MADE TO FEEL IT. SHE WAS NOT TO REFUSE ANYTHING, AND FOR MANY YEARS, SHE DID NOT.

NOW, MR. KANDERHOSH CEMENTED HIS AUTHORITY WITH STORIES TO MAY ABOUT HOW HE HAD 500 WIVES IN THE FIRST WORLD, HOW HE HAD TRANSFERRED HIMSELF FROM THIS LIFE TO THE OTHER LIFE AND HAD TALKED WITH PERPETUAL FIGURES ON THE OTHER SIDE, AND THAT HE HAD A KINGDOM WITH NUMEROUS WIVES IN IT, AND MAY BELIEVED THESE STORIES. SHE CAME AS A GIRL OF 15, AND ESSENTIALLY GREW UP UNDER THE TUTELAGE OF MR. KANDERHOSH AND THEIR FAMILY.

SHE HAD BEEN TAUGHT ABOUT FAITH AND OBEDIENCE TO THE NTH DEGREE PRIOR TO HER COMING THERE, AND WHEN SHE TELLS THE STORY OF WHAT HAPPENED TO HER, I AM CONFIDENT THAT YOU WILL BELIEVE HER STORY, BUT IT'S THE TRUTH.

NOW, MR. KANDERHOSH AND NANAS SAW AN OPPORTUNITY RIGHT OFF THE BAT WHEN MAY CAME TO WORK FOR HER BECAUSE SHE WORKED IN THE BOTTLE BUSINESS. AS MR. FLANK WAS DESCRIBING, THEY WASHED BOTTLES FOR TWO CENTS APIECE AND WERE MAKING ABOUT FOUR DOLLARS A DAY, AND IN 1963, WHEN MAY WENT TO WORK THERE, MRS. KANDERHOSH SHORTLY AFTER THAT TIME WAS HIT BY A CAR, AND FROM THAT

TIME UNTIL THIS, HAS NOT BEEN ABLE TO WORK, AND MAY TOOK OVER THAT BOTTLE BUSINESS.

IN ABOUT 1964, EVEN BEFORE SHE BECAME BARD'S WIFE AND WORKED AT THAT BUSINESS 14 TO 18 HOURS A DAY, SHE INCREASED THE PROFITABILITY OF THAT BOTTLE BUSINESS FROM FOUR DOLLARS A DAY TO TWENTY DOLLARS A DAY, FORTY DOLLARS A DAY, EIGHTY DOLLARS A DAY, PERFORMED VIRTUALLY ALL OF THE LABOR IN THAT BUSINESS BY HERSELF WITH VERY LITTLE, IF ANY, HELP FROM ANY OTHER MEMBERS OF THE FAMILY. YOU SEE, MR. KANDERHOSH HIMSELF WAS UNABLE TO WORK. MAY WAS THE ONLY ONE VIRTUALLY THERE WORKING WITH SOME HELP FROM MR. DARDSON.

NOW, MYRTA WAS JEALOUS OF MY CLIENT BECAUSE OF HER HARD WORK AND BECAUSE OF HER INTELLIGENCE, AND FOR WHATEVER REASON, WE DO NOT KNOW --

THE COURT: MR. RYAN, WHO IS MYRTA?

MR. RYAN: I'M SORRY, NANAS, MRS. KANDERHOSH. SHE'S KNOWN BOTH AS MYRTA AND NANAS. SO IF WE REFER TO MYRTA OR NANAS, THAT BEING MRS. KANDERHOSH. MAY KANDERHOSH, MR. FLANK REFERRED TO AS MAY HANCOCK. WHEN I SAY THAT, WE ARE TALKING ABOUT THE SAME PARTIES.

NOW, WITH REGARD TO THE PROPERTY SITUATION, IN 1975, MAY HAD WORKED FOR THIS FAMILY FOR NO REMUNERATION WHATSOEVER. HER PAY WAS A PLACE TO SLEEP, FOOD IN HER BELLY, AND THAT SOMETIMES, VERY, VERY SCARCE, AND RAGS ON HER BACK, AND VIRTUALLY NOTHING MORE FOR A PERIOD OF TEN YEARS. SHE

WORKED FOR THIS FAMILY AND RECEIVE NOTHING BUT WHAT I HAVE DESCRIBED TO YOU.

IN 1975 BARD KANDERHOSH CONVEYED HALF OF THE BUSINESS OR HALF OF THE PROPERTY WHICH MR. FLANK HAS DESCRIBED TO MAY, HALF OF IT TO MR. DARDSON, AND A FARM, A SIX-ACRE FARM, HALF OF THAT TO MR. DARDSON, HALF OF IT TO MAY, AND WE THINK THE TESTIMONY WILL SHOW AND THE EVIDENCE WILL PROVE THAT THIS WAS DONE BY MR. KANDERHOSH IN RECOGNITION OF AND IN CONSIDERATION OF SERVICES MAY HAD ALREADY PERFORMED FOR A PERIOD OF TEN YEARS.

NOW, MAY AND MR. DARDSON HAD PROBLEMS BECAUSE WILL, WILLER DARDSON, OWNED HALF OF THE BUSINESS. MAY, THIS BUSINESS WAS VIRTUALLY HER ENTIRE LIFE, AND YOU WILL SEE JUST HOW IMPORTANT THAT WAS TO HER AS THE TESTIMONY COMES OUT. SHE COULD NOT WORK UNDER THE CONDITIONS THAT EXISTED AT THAT TIME AND WENT TO BARD AND STATED THAT SHE COULD NOT. HE DECIDED THAT SHE WOULD RECEIVE THEN THE ENTIRE PIECE OF PROPERTY THERE AT APPROXIMATELY 8400 SOUTH REDWOOD ROAD. SHE WOULD THEN GIVE HER INTEREST IN THE FARM TO WILLER BECAUSE THIS WAS HIS. THAT WAS THE IMPORTANT PART OF HIS LIFE, AND THIS WAS DONE.

NOW, THEY SAY THAT THERE WAS AN AGREEMENT THAT MY CLIENT SUPPORT THEM FOR THE REST OF THEIR LIFE. THERE WAS NO AGREEMENT THAT MY CLIENT WOULD SUPPORT THEM FOR THE REST OF THEIR LIFE. SHE RECEIVED THAT PROPERTY FOR WORKING FOR THEM

247

FOR TEN YEARS. THE BUSINESS, RECLAIM BARREL SUPPLY, IS NOT AN EXTENSION OF THE BOTTLE BUSINESS. IN FACT, MR. KANDERHOSH DID VIRTUALLY EVERYTHING HE COULD TO STOP MAY FROM FOUNDING THAT BARREL BUSINESS. HE TRIED TO TALK HER OUT OF IT. HE DISCOURAGED HER. HE TRIED TO DO EVERYTHING HE POSSIBLY COULD TO KEEP HER FROM BUILDING THAT BARREL BUSINESS. NOTWITHSTANDING ANY OF THOSE ATTEMPTS ON HIS PART TO PUT HER DOWN, SHE, BY THE SHEER FORCE OF HER WILL AND HER DEDICATION TO HARD WORK AND TO THOSE PRINCIPLES THAT MOST OF US BELIEVE IN, OVERCAME THAT AND MADE THAT INTO A VERY, VERY SUCCESSFUL BUSINESS.

MR. FLANK WOULD HAVE YOU BELIEVE THAT IT WAS DONE WITH THE HELP OF THE FAMILY. IT WAS DONE IN SPITE OF THE FAMILY. NOW, WE BELIEVE THAT UNDER THOSE CIRCUMSTANCES THAT THAT BUSINESS, RECLAIM BARREL SUPPLY, INC., IS MAY'S. IT FOUND ITS GENESIS IN HER MIND. IT WAS PUT ON PAPER FROM HER MIND. IT WAS BUILT, IN FACT, YOU WILL FIND THAT SHE HERSELF WITH A LITTLE HELP FROM JOE MANDLEY CUT AND WELDED CUSTOM-MADE MACHINERY TO HANDLE THOSE BARRELS FOR THAT BARREL BUSINESS. WE THINK THAT'S HERS, AND WE THINK SHE OUGHT TO HAVE THAT AND CONTINUE TO HAVE THAT.

NOW, THERE IS ONE OTHER ASPECT TO THIS CASE, WHICH IS DIFFICULT. I THINK IT WILL BE DIFFICULT FOR ALL OF US TO HANDLE, AND THAT IS THE RELATIONSHIP BETWEEN MAY HANCOCK AND BARD KANDERHOSH. THE JUDGE HAS ALREADY INDICATED TO YOU THAT WE HAVE

248

CHARGED HIM WITH VARIOUS THINGS INCLUDING ASSAULT, BATTERY, INTENTIONAL INFLICTION OF EMOTIONAL DISTRESS AND FALSE IMPRISONMENT.

THE EVIDENCE WILL SHOW FROM MY CLIENT'S MOUTH THAT WHEN SHE HAD BEEN IN MR. KANDERHOSH'S RESIDENCE FOR A PERIOD OF LESS THAN ONE YEAR, HE SUCCESSFULLY SEDUCED HER SEXUALLY, AND ESSENTIALLY MADE HER HIS CONCUBINE, AND FROM THAT POINT UNTIL 1982 WHEN MY CLIENT FINALLY HAD THE WHEREWITHAL TO LEAVE, THAT MR. KANDERHOSH SEXUALLY ABUSED HER IN MANY UNMENTIONABLE WAYS. HE USED HIS AUTHORITY OVER HER AS HEAD OF THAT FAMILY TO COERCE HER INTO DEVIANT SEXUAL ACTS WHICH SHE DID NOT WANT TO ENGAGE IN.

HE MADE HER, FORCED HER TO WORK IN THE BUSINESS OR TO, BY THAT, I MEAN SHE COULD NOT STAND TO BE AROUND THE MAN. SHE WOULD PUT HER WHOLE HEART AND SOUL INTO THAT BUSINESS. SHE DID THAT FOR 14 TO 18 HOURS A DAY. WHEN SHE WAS FINISHED WITH WORK, HE WOULD FORCE HER TO PERFORM SEXUAL ACTS UPON HIM FOR A PERIOD OF A HALF HOUR TO THREE HOURS PER NIGHT. SHE GOT VERY, VERY LITTLE SLEEP. THERE ARE VERY FEW WITNESSES WHO WILL BE ABLE TO SUBSTANTIATE THIS BECAUSE OF THE NATURE OF IT, BUT YOU WILL HEAR THIS TESTIMONY FROM MAY'S MOUTH, AND I BELIEVE THAT YOU WILL BELIEVE HER, BECAUSE IT'S THE TRUTH.

HE KEPT HER A VIRTUAL PRISONER IN THE HOME. HE WOULD NOT ALLOW HER TO HAVE A DRIVER'S LICENSE. HE WOULD NOT ALLOW HER TO HAVE FRIENDS.

WHEN SHE ATTEMPTED TO CALL OUT OF THE HOME ON THE TELEPHONE, HE WOULD PICK UP THE PHONE OR WOULD TAKE THE PHONE OUT OF HER HAND AND WOULD NOT ALLOW HER TO HAVE ANY CONTACT, VIRTUALLY NO CONTACT WITH THE OUTSIDE WORLD.

IF SHE WANTED TO GO ANYWHERE TO BUY PARTS FOR THE BUSINESS OR WHATEVER, MR. KANDERHOSH WOULD TAKE HER. HE HELD SUCH A TIGHT GRIP AND CONTROL OVER HER THAT IT'S ALMOST UNBELIEVABLE. ALMOST, I SAY, IT'S BELIEVABLE BECAUSE IT'S THE TRUTH, AND THAT'S WHAT THE TESTIMONY WILL SHOW.

WE ARE ASKING ESSENTIALLY THAT THE JURY LEAVE US IN THE POSITION WE ARE WITH REGARD TO THE REAL PROPERTY. THAT PROPERTY WAS GIVEN BY DEED, WARRANTY DEED FROM THOSE PEOPLE TO MY CLIENT APPROXIMATELY SEVEN YEARS BEFORE SHE LEFT THAT ENVIRONMENT. WE THINK THAT THERE IS NO REASON WHATSOEVER IN THE WORLD THAT THEY HAVE ANY CLAIM TO IT. MY CLIENT HAS ALMOST SINGLE HANDEDLY SUPPORTED THAT ENTIRE FAMILY WHICH AT ONE TIME INCLUDING HERSELF, NUMBERED FOURTEEN PEOPLE, VIRTUALLY ALL BY HERSELF BECAUSE THESE PEOPLE REFUSED TO WORK.

WE ARE ASKING ALSO THAT YOU FIND THAT MR. KANDERHOSH HAS COMMITTED THESE TORTS, THESE TORTS AND ACTS UPON HER PERSON, AND WE ARE ASKING FOR COMPENSATION FOR THE DAMAGES THAT HE HAS DONE TO HER FOR THE PSYCHOLOGICAL DAMAGES.

SHE HAS ESSENTIALLY GIVEN HIM HER YOUTH, HER STRENGTH, BEAUTY OF HER YOUTH, AND VERY PROBABLY

250

HAS FOREGONE THE ABILITY TO HAVE CHILDREN. SHE'S 37 YEARS OF AGE NOW, WHICH SHE WAS PROMISED AND WAS NEVER FULFILLED, AND WE ARE ALSO ASKING FOR PUNITIVE DAMAGES AGAINST MR. KANDERHOSH, AND WE THINK THAT HIS CONDUCT IS SO REPREHENSIBLE THAT THIS JURY OUGHT TO FIND THAT HE DESERVES TO BE PUNISHED FOR THESE ACTS, AND WE ARE ASKING FOR PUNITIVE DAMAGES IN ADDITION TO THAT. THANK YOU.

THE COURT: ALL RIGHT, MR. RYAN. THANK YOU.

LADIES AND GENTLEMEN OF THE JURY, WE ARE GOING TO TAKE A BRIEF RECESS. I WILL ADMONISH YOU NOW NOT TO DISCUSS THIS CASE WITH ANYONE OR ALLOW ANYONE TO DISCUSS IT WITH YOU IN YOUR PRESENCE. PLEASE KEEP AN OPEN MIND UNTIL YOU HAVE HEARD ALL THE EVIDENCE IN THE CASE. THE COURT WILL BE IN RECESS FOR TEN MINUTES.

(A RECESS WAS TAKEN.)

THE COURT: THE JURY, PARTIES, AND COUNSEL ARE PRESENT. MR. FLANK, YOU MAY CALL YOUR FIRST WITNESS.

He called me to the stand. There was quite a long time during which their attorney asked me basic questions that I could answer pretty much with a "yes" or "no." Did I know them--Bard and Nanas? When did I come to live with them? Did I plan to marry Bard? Who was Zosa? Who had the children? And so on. Then he brought up the discussion at the time when the property was signed over to Will and me. He was trying to establish what I did to make Bard sign his share over to me.

Q   YOU SAID LIKEWISE YOU WEREN'T GOING TO
HAVE ANY FURTHER RELATIONSHIP WITH HIM SEXUALLY;
IS THAT CORRECT?

A   NOW, WAIT A MINUTE. LET'S DISCERN THAT
LAST QUESTION. YOU PUT IN TWO QUESTIONS, AND GOT
ONE ANSWER. THERE'S TWO DIFFERENT ANSWERS.

Q   WELL, YOUR ATTORNEY CAN WORK THAT OUT.

A   I DID NOT SAY THAT I WOULD LEAVE THE
FAMILY, BUT I DID NOT FEEL THE DESIRE TO CONTINUE
TO PUT ANY EFFORT AND THE HOURS THAT I WAS
WORKING UNDER THOSE CONDITIONS.

Q   DIDN'T YOU, IN FACT, TELL BARD YOU
WEREN'T GOING TO SLEEP WITH HIM ANY LONGER OR BE
HIS WIFE?

A   NO.

Q   YOU DID NOT?

A   NO, I DID NOT.

Q   DID YOU SAY, THOUGH, THAT YOU WERE NOT
GOING TO WORK ANY FURTHER? YOU WERE NOT GOING
TO DO IT AS A FAMILY; IS THAT CORRECT?

A   I TOLD HIM THAT I JUST COULD NOT BRING
MYSELF TO PUT DETERMINATION ENOUGH TO DO THE
WORK TO SUPPORT THE FAMILY UNDER THOSE
CONTENTIOUS CONDITIONS.

Q   DID YOU ENCOURAGE HIM TO DIVORCE NANAS?

A   NO.

Q   NANAS BY THAT TIME HAD MOVED OUT, HAD
SHE NOT? SHE WAS NOT LIVING WITH YOU AND BARD,
WAS SHE?

A   WELL, ANYBODY THAT WAS LIVING THERE WOULD FIND IT VERY DIFFICULT TO LIVE AROUND BARD.

Q   JUST YES OR NOT.

A   SO THE FACT SHE MOVED OUT DOESN'T SURPRISE ME, BUT I DON'T KNOW.

Q   SO IT WAS YOUR UNDERSTANDING THAT UNLESS BARD TRANSFERRED THIS PROPERTY OVER TO YOU AND WILL, YOU WERE NOT GOING TO WORK ANY FURTHER; IS THAT RIGHT? YOU WANTED THAT AS SECURITY?

MR. RYAN: OBJECTION. SHE HAS ALREADY ANSWERED THAT, AND THAT WAS NOT HER TESTIMONY.

THE COURT: THE OBJECTION IS OVERRULED. YOU MAY ANSWER THE QUESTION, MA'AM.

THE WITNESS: OKAY, SO WHAT ARE YOU GETTING AT?

Q   (BY MR. FLANK) JUST YES OR NOT, IS IT A FACT THAT IN 1975, WHEN YOU DEMANDED THAT BARD TRANSFER THAT PROPERTY TO YOU, YOU ADVISED HIM THAT UNLESS HE DID, YOU WERE NOT GOING TO WORK ANY LONGER FOR THE FAMILY?

A   I NEVER DID TALK THAT WAY OR IN THOSE WORDS.

Q   WELL, WAS THAT THE GENERAL THOUGHT?

A   THE GENERAL THOUGHT WAS THAT I WAS SO SICK OF THE WAY NAN THREATENED ME, I COULDN'T WORK.

Q   DID BARD MAKE DEMAND UPON NANAS FORCING HER TO SIGN THIS PROPERTY OVER TO YOU AND WILL?

A   NO, NOT THAT I KNOW OF. SHE SAID, WELL,
LOOK AT ALL THE YEARS THAT WILLY HAS WORKED.
MAY IS NOT THE ONLY ONE THAT'S DONE ANYTHING.
HE'S DONE THE TRUCK DRIVING AND THINGS, JUST
BECAUSE MAY HAS WORKED ALL THE BOTTLES, BUT
WILLY HAD TO GO GET THEM. SO SHE WAS STICKING UP
FOR WILLER AND BARD WAS STICKING UP FOR ME. SO
THEY DECIDED THAT THEY OUGHT TO PUT IT BETWEEN
THE TWO OF US.

Q   IT WAS NANAS' PROPERTY ORIGINALLY; IT WAS
NOT BARD'S?

A   YES, BUT I KNOW THAT I HAD SUPPORTED HER
FOR TEN YEARS AND BEEN A MAID AND EVERYTHING
ELSE TO EARN IT.

Q   THERE WERE OTHER MEMBERS OF THE FAMILY.
DID NANAS EVER TAKE ANYTHING FOR HERSELF? DID
SHE EVER BUY HERSELF A NEW CADILLAC OR NEW
CLOTHING?

A   HEY, SHE HAD WHATEVER JOY THAT ANYBODY
ELSE COULD HAVE IN THE HOME OF TREATING
EVERYBODY ELSE AS HER SUBJECTS, JUST LIKE ANIMALS.

Q   BUT SHE, NEVERTHELESS, REMAINED IN THE
FAMILY, HELPED CARE FOR ALL OF THE OTHER
CHILDREN, THE OTHER WIVES. IS THAT TRUE?

A   IF YOU CALL DEMANDING, COMMANDING AND
BEATING ZOSA A FORM OF HELPING TAKE CARE OF THE
KIDS, IF YOU CALL THAT THAT, THEN I GUESS THAT'S IT.

Q   TO THE BEST OF YOUR KNOWLEDGE, STILL,
ZOSA HAS SOME MENTAL PROBLEMS, DOES SHE NOT,
MAY?

254

A   IF YOU GOT BEAT THREE TIMES A DAY, I THINK YOU WOULD HAVE PROBLEMS, TOO.

THE COURT: MS. HANCOCK, SO WE CAN MOVE THIS MATTER ALONG, LISTEN CAREFULLY TO THE QUESTION AND ANSWER THE QUESTION ONLY. DON'T VOLUNTEER INFORMATION.

Q   (BY MR. FLANK) IS IT A FACT THAT MAY HAS SOME MENTAL PROBLEMS, JUST YES OR NO?

A   THAT WAS MY NAME YOU PUT THERE.

Q   I'M SORRY. ZOSA HAS SOME MENTAL PROBLEMS?

A   YES.

Q   AND THE CHILDREN HAVE SOME RETARDATION, LEARNING PROBLEMS ALSO, DO THEY NOT?

A   RIGHT.

Q   THESE INDIVIDUALS ARE STILL CARED FOR, TO YOUR KNOWLEDGE, RIGHT NOW BY NANAS. IS THAT TRUE?

A   I COULDN'T SAY BECAUSE I HAVE NO IDEA.

Q   YOU ARE LIVING RIGHT BEHIND THEM. ARE YOU NOT?

A   YES.

Q   YOU KNOW IF NANAS AND THOSE FOUR CHILDREN ARE STILL IN THOSE HOMES IN FRONT OF THAT BUSINESS, DO YOU NOT?

A   YES, BUT I DON'T KNOW IF ZOSA OR NAN IS TAKING CARE OF THEM.

Q   BUT YOU KNOW THAT WILL IS STILL IN THIS HOME, DO YOU NOT?

A   THIS MAY COME AS A SURPRISE, BUT I TRY TO
NOT LOOK IN THAT DIRECTION.

Q   SINCE 1982 WHEN YOU TOOK OVER THE
BUSINESS, OTHER THAN PAYING THE PAYMENTS ON LOT 2,
YOU HAVE NOT PROVIDED ANY FURTHER SUPPORT FOR
THEM, HAVE YOU?

A   THAT'S RIGHT.

Q   ALTHOUGH YOUR AGREEMENT WAS TO DO SO,
WAS IT NOT?

A   EXCUSE ME? THERE'S ONE THING ABOUT IT. I
HAVE BEEN PAYING THE TAXES ON THE RED HOUSE AND
ALSO THIS WATER LINE IS CONNECTED UP WITH THE SHOP
WATER LINE. SO I HAVE HAD TO TAKE CARE OF THIS,
TOO.

Q   SO YOU HAVE BEEN PAYING THE PAYMENTS ON
THE RED HOUSE, AND YOU HAVE BEEN PAYING THE
WATER BILL, AND YOU DISCONTINUED ANY FURTHER HELP
TOWARD THEM AND REFUSED TO ALLOW THEM TO
CONTINUE TO WORK IN THE BUSINESS, DID YOU NOT?

A   RIGHT.

Q   YOU TOOK OVER THE BUSINESS, CONTINUED TO
OPERATE IT, AND CONTINUED TO TAKE OF THE MONEY
THAT YOU RECEIVED FROM IT YOURSELF?

A   THAT'S RIGHT.

Q   YOU ALSO SERVED UPON THE KANDERHOSHES A
NOTICE THAT THE FAMILY WAS TO REMOVE FROM ONE
OF THE HOUSES, DID YOU NOT?

A   THAT'S RIGHT.

Q   IN NO WAY DID YOU EVER PAY ANY
CONSIDERATION OTHER THAN YOUR CLAIMED LABOR FOR

THE HOME OR THE PROPERTIES IN QUESTION, IS THAT TRUE? YOU DIDN'T EVER HAVE ANY MONEY, DID YOU, YOURSELF?

A   EXCEPT THE MONEY THAT WAS GIVEN TO ME, INHERITANCE MONEY, AND THAT WENT TO THEM, TOO.

Q   HOW MUCH WAS THAT?

A   WELL, THEY STOLE MY BROTHER'S SHARE, WHICH WAS 2,500, BUT I VOLUNTEERED MY 2,500.

Q   YOU PUT $2,500 IN?

A   UN-HUH (AFFIRMATIVE), JUST AS FAR AS MONEY GOES.

Q   I'M GOING TO SHOW YOU -- YOU DISCONTINUED HELPING THE FAMILY AND TOOK THE BUSINESS IN ABOUT JULY OF 1982; IS THAT CORRECT? WOULD THAT BE CLOSE?

A   I LEFT MAY 14, 1982.

Q   SO ON MAY 14, 1982, YOU TOOK THE BUSINESS, ALL MONIES FROM IT, SERVED THEM A NOTICE TO GET OUT OF THE ONE HOUSE. THEY NEVER DID GET OUT OF THE HOUSE. THEY ARE STILL LIVING THERE?

A   THAT'S RIGHT.

Q   BUT SINCE THIS TIME, YOU HAVE GIVEN THEM NOTHING OTHER THAN PAY THE HOUSE PAYMENT ON ONE OF THE HOMES THAT WAS BOUGHT ON CONTRACT AND PAY THE WATER BILL?

A   THAT'S RIGHT.

Q   I'LL SHOW YOU WHAT'S BEEN MARKED AS PLAINTIFF'S EXHIBIT 8. YOU MAKE GOOD MONEY IN THAT BUSINESS, DO YOU NOT?

A   SOMETIMES, YES, SOMETIMES, NO, DEPENDING
ON THE SEASON.

Q   I SHOW YOU WHAT'S BEEN MARKED AS
PLAINTIFF'S EXHIBIT 8, WHICH PURPORTS TO BE A TRUST
DEED AND A TRUST DEED NOTE. I ASK YOU IF YOU CAN
IDENTIFY THOSE DOCUMENTS.

A   SURE CAN.

Q   IS THAT A TRUST DEED AND TRUST DEED NOTE
DATED IN AUGUST 1982, AFTER YOU HAD TAKEN THE
BUSINESS?

A   UH-HUH (AFFIRMATIVE).

He produced a copy of the contract I singned for The purchase of
ten acres of land in Lehi. The attorney seemed determined to show that
I was making lots of money and buying land and goods rather than
spending the money from Reclaim to support Bard and his family. It
was as though their attorney was trying to send me on some grand guilt
trip or something. Then he brought up questions of my giving Boyd
and Kevin Huntsley each five percent of Reclaim.

Q   WHAT INTEREST DO THEY CLAIM?

A   EACH HAVE 5 PERCENT.

Q   AND YOU HAVE 90?

A   THAT'S RIGHT.

Q   SO WHAT YOU HAVE DONE, WOULD THIS BE A
TRUE STATEMENT, YOU HAVE SIMPLY SAID THAT Y(
OWN 100 PERCENT OF THE CORPORATION BECAUSE Y
HAVE RUN THE BUSINESS AND YOU HAVE NOW
TRANSFERRED 5 PERCENT TO EACH OF THE MRS. HUN
LEY. IS THAT TRUE?

258

A   I HAVE 100 PERCENT OF THE CORPORATION
BECAUSE I BUILT RECLAIM BARREL FROM SCRATCH.

Q   IT WAS IN THE FAMILY, WAS IT NOT, UP UNTIL
1982? IT WAS A FAMILY BUSINESS?

A   THE INCOME THAT WAS DERIVED WENT TO THE
FAMILY. THE WORK WAS NOT SHARED EQUALLY IN THE
FAMILY, NO.

Q   YOU WORKED HARDER AND WORKED LONGER,
AND YOU WERE THE BRAINS OF THE OUTFIT. IS THAT
TRUE?

A   THAT'S RIGHT. YOU BETTER BELIEVE IT.

Q   YOU, IN FACT, HAD ENOUGH BRAINS TO JUST
PUSH EVERYBODY ELSE IN THE FAMILY OUT AND
ASSUME AND TAKE CONTROL OF THE BUSINESS, YES OR
NOT?

A   THAT'S WHAT YOU WOULD LIKE TO SAY. NO,
THAT'S NOT TRUE.

Q   BUT YOU HAVE GOT ALL OF IT, YOU ARE
CLAIMING ALL OF IT?

A   YES, BUT THAT'S -- WHAT CAUSED ME --

MR. FLANK: THAT'S ALL, MS. HANCOCK.

THE COURT: MR. RYAN?

MR. RYAN: JUST ON THE ISSUE THAT MR.
FLANK BROUGHT UP, BECAUSE I WOULD LIKE TO
RESERVE MY DIRECT FOR WHEN I PUT ON MY CASE-IN
CHIEF.

CROSS EXAMINATION

BY MR. RYAN:

Q   MAY, GOING BACK TO WHEN MR. FLANK
STARTED EXAMINING YOU, WHEN YOU CAME TO THE

259

FAMILY, YOU INDICATED THAT THERE WAS A BOTTLE
BUSINESS THERE. IS THAT CORRECT?

A   RIGHT.

Q   TELL US WHAT SHAPE THAT BOTTLE BUSINESS
WAS IN, WOULD YOU PLEASE, JUST QUICKLY?

A   WELL, NANAS WAS WASHING APPROXIMATELY 35
CASES A DAY, OH, SAY, TWICE A WEEK, AND AT THE
PROFIT OF TWO CENTS A BOTTLE AT FOUR BOTTLES PER
CASE.

Q   HOW MUCH DID THAT PRODUCE A DAY
APPROXIMATELY?

A   OH, FOUR OR FIVE DOLLARS, BUT IT WAS
BETTER THAN THE WATKINS PRODUCT ROUTE THAT THEY
HAD WHERE BARD WOULD SAY SOMETIMES THEY WOULD
ONLY EARN 50 CENTS FOR A WHOLE DAY'S LABOR OR AT
LEAST IT WAS GOING TO FEED THEM.

Q   HOW MANY PEOPLE WORKED IN THAT BUSINESS,
THAT BOTTLE BUSINESS, RIGHT AT THE BEGINNING WHEN
YOU ARRIVED THERE, INCLUDING YOURSELF?

A   NANAS, BARD, WILLER, AND THEN WHEN I
CAME, ME.

Q   WHAT DID WILLER DO IN THE BUSINESS, IN THE
BOTTLE BUSINESS?

A   HE WOULD PICK UP THE BOTTLES FROM BEING
DIRTY AND BRING THEM THERE TO THE PLACE, AND WE
WOULD WASH THEM, AND THEY WOULD DELIVER THEM.

Q   HOW MUCH TIME DID THAT TAKE
APPROXIMATELY, ON THE AVERAGE?

A   I DON'T KNOW, BUT I CAN SURE PICK THEM UP
FASTER THAN WHAT WE COULD WASH THEM.

Q   DO YOU HAVE ANY IDEA HOW MUCH TIME HE
SPENT DOING THAT, IF YOU KNOW? IF YOU DON'T, JUST
SAY YOU DON'T KNOW.

A   I DON'T RECALL.

Q   HOW MUCH TIME DID YOU SPEND IN THE
BUSINESS TO BEGIN WITH WHEN YOU FIRST CAME
THERE?

A   ABOUT THREE HOURS A DAY MAYBE AT THE
MOST.

Q   DID THAT EVER CHANGE?

A   OH, YES.

Q   HOW DID IT CHANGE AND HOW MUCH?

A   WELL, WHEN NANAS GOT HIT IN THE
PEDESTRIAN LANE AND SHE SAID THAT SHE WAS IN TOO
MUCH PAIN TO EVER WORK ANOTHER BOTTLE, THEN BARD
TOLD ME THAT IF I DIDN'T TAKE OVER THE BOTTLE
BUSINESS, THAT THAT WOULD BE THE END OF IT. THERE
WASN'T ANYBODY TO WASH THEM.

Q   FROM THAT TIME THEN THAT NANAS WAS HIT
BY AN AUTOMOBILE, DID SHE EVER WORK IN THE
BOTTLE BUSINESS AGAIN?

A   NO.

Q   DID BARD WORK IN THE BOTTLE BUSINESS
AFTER THAT?

A   YES.

Q   DID WILL?

A   YES.

Q   WOULD YOU SAY THAT YOU AND WILL AND
BARD ALL PERFORMED ABOUT THE SAME PERCENTAGE OF
LABOR?

A NO, NO, BECAUSE HERE WE GET INTO THE TEACHINGS OF BARD WHEN I FIRST CAME INTO THE FAMILY.

Q LET'S NOT GET INTO THAT. JUST TELL ME APPROXIMATELY WHAT PERCENTAGE --

A HE SAID THAT HE DIDN'T HAVE TO WORK AS HARD AS I DID, BECAUSE HE SAID HE NEEDED FREE TIME TO GO OUT AND SOLICIT AND HAVE OTHER WOMEN COME INTO THE FAMILY. SO IT WAS MY DUTY TO PUT IN MY ALL AND TO NOT LET HIM BE BURDENED DOWN WITH A LOT OF WORK.

Q AND YOU BELIEVED THAT?

A YES, I DID.

Q APPROXIMATELY WHAT PERCENTAGE OF ALL WORK TO DO DID YOU DO IN THAT BOTTLE BUSINESS?

A I WOULD SAY APPROXIMATELY 70 PERCENT.

Q I BELIEVE THAT MR. FLANK SAID NOW, IT'S TRUE THAT NANAS WAS THE MOTHER, SO TO SPEAK, OF THE FAMILY. SHE WAS THE FIRST WIFE OF BARD, WASN'T SHE?

A RIGHT.

Q WHAT WERE HER DUTIES, DO YOU KNOW?

A EVERYBODY WAS TOLD THAT SHE WAS PRIVILEGED BECAUSE SHE WAS THE WIFE OF CLARENCE RITTLING, AND THAT WE SHOULD ALL HONOR HER AND OBEY HER IN ALL THINGS.

Q WHEN WERE YOU TOLD THAT AND BY WHOM?

A WHEN I FIRST CAME TO LIVE THERE.

Q WHO TOLD YOU THAT?

A BARD DID.

Q   AFTER SHE HAD HER ACCIDENT, WAS SHE EVER EMPLOYED IN ANY MONEY-MAKING ENTERPRISE, THAT YOU KNOW OF?

A   NO. SHE WOULD GO OUT AND BABYSIT ONCE IN A WHILE AFTER THAT.

Q   NOW, YOU INDICATED THAT YOUR MOTHER, WHEN SHE CAME TO LIVE IN THE FAMILY, BROUGHT SOME -- HAD SOME SOCIAL SECURITY; IS THAT CORRECT?

A   I DON'T KNOW IF SHE HAD IT AT THE TIME THAT SHE CAME TO LIVE THERE, BUT SHE WAS OLD ENOUGH THAT SHE COULD ACHIEVE IT SHORTLY AFTER.

Q   DID SHE RECEIVE THAT AT ANY TIME?

A   OH, YES.

Q   DID SHE RECEIVE IT HERSELF?

A   NO.

Q   WHAT HAPPENED TO IT?

A   NANAS AND BARD MADE MAMMA SIGN OVER HER LIFE ESTATE, AND THEN NANAS TOOK IT AND DONE WHATEVER.

Q   WHAT MAKES YOU SAY THAT THEY FORCED HER TO SIGN A LIFE ESTATE? YOU MEAN IN THE PAYMENTS, SOCIAL SECURITY PAYMENTS, DO YOU MEAN A LIFE ESTATE?

A   EXCUSE ME. I'M USING THE WRONG WORD, NOT LIFE ESTATE, POWER OF ATTORNEY. THAT'S WHAT I MEAN.

Q   WERE YOU PRESENT WHEN SHE WAS FORCED TO DO THAT?

A   YES, I WAS.

Q   WHAT HAPPENED? WHEN DID THAT HAPPEN, FIRST, MAY?

A   WELL, MOM AGREED TO LET NANAS TAKE HER CHECKS LONG BEFORE THEY MADE HER SIGN OVER POWER OF ATTORNEY.

Q   SO WHEN DID THE ACTUAL POWER OF ATTORNEY, WHEN DID THAT HAPPEN?

A   I THINK IT WAS ABOUT IN '79 OR '80.

Q   HOW LONG DID BARD AND NANAS RECEIVE THOSE SOCIAL SECURITY PAYMENTS?

A   CLEAR UP UNTIL THE TIME THAT MOTHER LEFT.

Q   AND THAT WAS JUST BEFORE YOU DID?

A   YES.

Q   HOW MUCH WERE THOSE PAYMENTS, DO YOU KNOW?

A   I DON'T KNOW. I THINK IT WAS ABOUT 120, BUT I'M NOT SURE.

Q   A MONTH?

A   UH-HUH (AFFIRMATIVE).

Q   DID IT EVER CHANGE BETWEEN THAT ENTIRE PERIOD?

A   WELL, OKAY, CAN I EXPLAIN?

Q   YES.

A   OKAY, AFTER THEY MADE MAMA SIGN OVER A POWER OF ATTORNEY, THEN MOM WENT TO LIVE WITH SOME FRIENDS OF THE FAMILY, AND DURING THAT TIME, IT WAS LIKE EIGHT OR NINE MONTHS, NANAS HAVING THE RIGHT THEN TO SIGN MOM'S CHECKS, SHE NEVER SENT THOSE CHECKS TO MOM WHERE SHE WAS STAYING OR THE MONEY.

Q HOW DO YOU KNOW THAT?

A BECAUSE THAT'S WHAT THE PEOPLE THAT MOM WAS STAYING WITH --

MR. FLANK: YOUR HONOR, I WILL OBJECT. SHE'S GOING TO SAY WHAT THEY SAID.

Q (BY MR. RYAN) DID NANAS EVER TELL YOU THAT SHE KEPT THE MONEY?

A OH, MY MOTHER DID, AND SO DID HAROLD AND CONNIE WHERE MOM WAS STAYING.

Q NOW, THE INCOME FROM THE BOTTLE BUSINESS, WHO CONTROLLED THE INCOME, MAY?

A NANAS AND BARD.

Q HOW WAS THE MONEY PAID FROM THESE CLIENTS, THE BOTTLES, THE PEOPLE THAT YOU WASHED THE BOTTLES FOR?

A THEY WOULD JUST SEND IN CHECKS, AND NANAS WOULD CASH THEM.

Q WAS THERE ANY BANK ACCOUNT?

A BOY, I DON'T EVEN KNOW. I DON'T THINK THERE WAS.

Q IF THERE WAS --

A WAIT A MINUTE. THERE WAS LATER ON, BUT I DON'T THINK THERE WAS TO BEGIN WITH.

Q WHEN WAS THERE FIRST A BANK ACCOUNT?

A I WOULD SAY APPROXIMATELY IN ABOUT '67, JUST A GUESS.

Q NOW, MR. FLANK ASKED YOU IF YOU HAD DEMANDED THAT YOU BE CONVEYED HALF OF THIS PROPERTY. WHOSE IDEA WAS THE TRANSFER OF THIS

PROPERTY INTO YOUR NAME FROM THE NAMES OF BARD
AND NANAS?

A   WELL, I TOLD BARD THAT I COULD NOT -- YOU
KNOW, I NEVER WAS, LIKE, HOW SHOULD I SAY, I
COULDN'T BE ENTHUSED OR HAVE THE STRENGTH OR THE
PUSH TO DO THE WORK IN THE BOTTLE BUSINESS WHEN
NANAS WAS CONTINUALLY TELLING LIES IN THE FAMILY,
SOWING DISCORD, DOING EVERY MISERABLE THING SHE
COULD TO TRY TO DRIVE ME OUT, AND BARD WAS
ALWAYS SAYING THAT HE WAS ON BORROWED TIME FROM
THE OTHER SIDE, AND THAT HE COULD DIE AT ANY TIME,
AND THAT I JUST TOLD HIM THAT IF YOU DIE, THEN I
KNOW I WILL BE KICKED OUT WITHOUT ONE DIME TO
SHOW FOR THE TEN YEARS OF LABOR THAT I HAVE PUT
INTO THIS FAMILY.

MR. FLANK: YOUR HONOR, I HAVE LET HER GO
ON. HE ASKED HER THE QUESTION, WHOSE IDEA WAS IT?
I THINK SHE MEANT TO SAY MINE, BUT I DON'T THINK IT
IS IN ANSWER TO THE QUESTION. I OBJECT TO ALL OF
THAT.

THE COURT: WELL, THE OBJECTION IS
SUSTAINED. LET'S JUST LISTEN TO THE QUESTION AND
ANSWER THE QUESTION ONLY, MA'AM.

THE WITNESS: OKAY.

Q   (BY MR. RYAN) WHOSE IDEA WAS THE
TRANSFER OF THE PROPERTY, MAY?

A   MINE AND BARD AGREED.

Q   WHO SUGGESTED IT FIRST, DO YOU RECALL?

MR. FLANK: YOUR HONOR, IT THINK SHE'S

ANSWERED THAT QUESTION. IT WAS HER IDEA, AND BARD
AGREED TO IT. I DON'T KNOW WHAT MORE ANSWER WE
COULD HAVE HOPED TO GET FROM HER.

MR. RYAN: THAT ISN'T WHAT SHE SAID.

THE COURT: WELL, THE ANSWER IS OF
RECORD. THE OBJECTION AS TO THE NEXT QUESTION IS
OVERRULED. YOU MAY ANSWER IT, IF YOU ARE ABLE.

THE WITNESS: OKAY.

MR. RYAN: JUST A MINUTE. COULD YOU READ
BACK THE QUESTION?

(THE LAST PENDING QUESTION WAS READ BACK BY
THE REPORTER.)

THE WITNESS: WHAT I SUGGESTED TO HIM WAS
THAT I HAD TO HAVE SOMETHING FOR SECURITY, AND HE
SUGGESTED THE PROPERTY, BUT JUST SOMETHING TO
MAKE ME FEEL LIKE I WASN'T JUST WORKING AND
WORKING AND BURNING MY LIFE AWAY.

MR. RYAN: I HAVE NO FURTHER QUESTIONS AT
THIS TIME.

THE COURT: ALL RIGHT, ANYTHING FURTHER?

MR. FLANK: JUST A COUPLE OF QUESTIONS.

REDIRECT EXAMINATION
BY MR. FLANK:

Q   MAY, WOULD 1965 STICK IN YOUR MIND AS
BEING THE YEAR THAT YOU MARRIED BARD
KANDERHOSH?

A   I DON'T KNOW WHAT YEAR I MARRIED HIM, BUT
IT WAS WHEN I WAS 18.

Q   YOU SAID THAT BARD WOULDN'T WORK, AND HE
SAID HE HAD TO GO OUT AND LOOK FOR OTHER WOMEN.

DID HE EVER FIND ANY OTHER WOMEN TO MARRY AFTER
YOU?

A   NO, BUT HE WOULD GO OUT LOOKING.

MR. FLANK: THAT'S ALL.

THE COURT: ANYTHING FURTHER?

MR. RYAN: JUST ONE QUESTION.

RECROSS EXAMINATION

BY MR. RYAN:

Q   DO YOU KNOW OF ANY ATTEMPTS THAT HE
MADE?

A   OH, YES.

Q   TELL US HOW MANY, WHEN, AND WHAT HE DID.

A   YOU WANT TO KNOW MY VERSION OF IT?

Q   NO. I WANT TO KNOW WHAT YOU OBSERVED OR
HEARD OR SAW, WHATEVER YOU SAW OR HEARD, I WANT
YOU TO TELL US.

A   HE WOULD GO OUT TO CAFES TO TAKE NAN,
AND THEY WOULD GO AND EAT, AND HE WOULD FLIRT
WITH THE WAITRESSES, AND EVERY ONCE IN A WHILE --

MR. FLANK: YOUR HONOR, I WILL OBJECT TO
THIS. HE SAID WHAT HE WOULD DO. SHE DIDN'T --
THERE WOULD BE FOUNDATION WHEN SHE WAS PRESENT.

THE COURT: THE OBJECTION AS TO
FOUNDATION IS SUSTAINED.

Q   (BY MR. RYAN) HOW DID YOU KNOW THIS, MAY?

A   BECAUSE SOMETIMES THE GIRL WOULD GET FAR
ENOUGH ALONG TO COME TO THE PLACE.

Q   LISTEN TO MY QUESTION. HOW DID YOU KNOW
THAT HE WAS DOING THIS? DID HE TELL YOU THIS, OR
DID SOMEONE ELSE TELL YOU THIS?

A   YES. HE WOULD TELL ME.

Q   GO AHEAD THEN. WHAT DID HE TELL YOU?

A   OKAY, HE WOULD SAY, WELL, I NEED TIME. THERE'S THIS ONE GIRL OVER HERE AT THIS CERTAIN CAFE THAT -- HER NAME IS SUCH AND SUCH, AND THIS IS BASICALLY HER BACKGROUND, AND I THINK THAT I HAVE A CHANCE. I HAVE GOT TO CONTINUALLY GO THERE AND TALK TO HER AND SEE IF I CAN GET HER TO COME ALONG, AND EVERY ONCE IN A WHILE, HE WOULD GET ONE OF THE GIRLS TO COME OVER AND MEET THE REST OF US, AND THAT'S ABOUT AS FAR AS IT WOULD GO.

Q   HOW OFTEN DID HE DO THIS DURING THE LAST FIVE YEARS THAT YOU WERE THERE?

A   THE LAST FIVE YEARS I WAS THERE, ALL THE WOMEN THAT HE ATTEMPTED, THAT I KNOW OF, AT THAT TIME JUST LOOKED AT HIM LIKE HE WAS SICK, AND THEY WOULDN'T HAVE NOTHING TO DO WITH HIM.

MR. FLANK: YOUR HONOR, I THINK SHE'S ANSWERED.

MR. RYAN: JUST A MINUTE.

THE COURT: MS. HANCOCK, I WILL TELL YOU ONE LAST TIME, LISTEN TO THE QUESTION AND ANSWER THE QUESTION ONLY. DON'T VOLUNTEER INFORMATION. NOW, THE QUESTION WAS, HOW MANY TIMES IN THE LAST FOUR YEARS DID HE DO THIS?

Q   (BY MR RYAN) HOW MANY TIMES IN THE LAST FIVE YEARS, I BELIEVE.

THE COURT: FIVE YEARS.

269

THE WITNESS: WHAT SPECIFICALLY IS HE
SUPPOSED TO HAVE DONE? IF YOU ARE GOING TO
DEFINE IT THAT FAR?

Q   (BY MR. RYAN) HOW MANY TIMES DURING THE
LAST FIVE YEARS YOU WERE THERE FROM
APPROXIMATELY 1977 THROUGH 1982 DID BARD GO OUT
AND ATTEMPT TO GET OTHER WOMEN TO COME INTO THE
FAMILY AS ADDITIONAL WIVES?

A   DURING THAT TIME, I DON'T THINK THAT --
THERE WERE SEVERAL PEOPLE THAT THEY APPROACHED,
BUT I WASN'T FILLED IN ON WHAT EXTENT OR HOW FAR
ALONG IT WENT.

Q   SO YOU DIDN'T KNOW THEN?

A   I DON'T KNOW.

Q   HOW ABOUT BEFORE, THE INSTANCE THAT YOU
HAVE JUST RELATED TO US THAT HE TOLD YOU ABOUT,
WHEN DID THAT HAPPEN?

A   THAT WAS BEFORE THEN.

Q   DURING WHAT TIME PERIOD?

A   OH SAY, FROM '65 ON TO SAY, '75.

Q   FOR ABOUT THE FIRST TEN YEARS?

A   YEAH.

Q   HOW MANY TIMES DID HE GO ATTEMPT TO FIND
OTHER WOMEN DURING THAT TEN YEARS, IF YOU KNOW?

A   I THINK IT WAS ABOUT FOUR TIMES THAT I
KNOW OF.

Q   ABOUT FOUR TIMES?

A   UH-HUH (AFFIRMATIVE).

MR. RYAN: NO FURTHER QUESTIONS.

THE COURT: ANYTHING FURTHER?

MR. FLANK: NOTHING FURTHER.

THE COURT: YOU MAY STEP DOWN, MS. HANCOCK. CALL YOUR NEXT WITNESS.

MR. FLANK: I CALL NANAS KANDERHOSH.

THE COURT: COME FORWARD, MS. KANDERHOSH, AND BE SWORN.

MYRTA NANAS KANDERHOSH, CALLED AS A WITNESS BY AND ON BEHALF OF THE PLAINTIFFS, BEING FIRST DULY SWORN, WAS EXAMINED AND TESTIFIED AS FOLLOWS:

DIRECT EXAMINATION BY MR. FLANK:

Q   WOULD YOU STATE YOUR NAME AND SPELL IT?

A   MYRTA, M-Y-R-T-A, NANAS, N-A-N-A-S AND THEN RITTLING, R-I-T-T-L-I-N-G AND THEN KANDERHOSH, K-A-N-D-E-R-H-O-S-H.

Q   YOU GO BY MYRTA KANDERHOSH, IS THAT TRUE?

A   YES, AND NANAS.

Q   PRIOR TO 1954, YOU WERE MARRIED TO MR. RITTLING?

A   YES. MR. RITTLING DIED JULY 13, 1954.

Q   IN ORDER TO KIND OF SPEED THIS UP, AND WE HAVE ALREADY GONE THROUGH, JUST KIND OF, IF YOU CAN, ANSWER THE QUESTION. LISTEN TO IT, AND ANSWER IT. YOU MARRIED MR. KANDERHOSH IN 1962?

A   YES.

Q   YOU WERE HIS FIRST WIFE?

A   YES.

Q   HOW OLD ARE YOU NOW?

A   I'M 67.

Her attorney questioned her on a lot of basic questions--her own history, also about the children and the living circumstances of the home. She said that Will had signed his share of the property back to her.

Then he asked what animals they had on the farm at the present time.

A WE HAD COWS. LET'S SEE. TWO MILK COWS AND SOME STEERS.

Q WHY DID YOU SELL THEM?

A WILL GOT IN A WRECK, AND I COULDN'T TAKE CARE OF THEM.

Q THEY HAVE ALL BEEN SOLD?

A YES.

Q THE FAMILY -- STRIKE THAT. WHAT INCOME THERE IS FROM THAT FARM RENT GOES INTO THE FAMILY?

A IT GOES FOR TAXES, EVERY BIT OF IT. I JUST PUT IT OVER. THE TAXES IS TWO THOUSAND SOMETHING DOLLARS A YEAR.

Q IS THERE A HOME ON THAT? IS THAT WHERE YOU GET YOUR $300 A MONTH FROM?

A RIGHT.

Q THAT'S FOR RENT?

A RIGHT.

Q YOU HAVE REQUESTED THAT THAT PROPERTY BE TRANSFERRED BACK TO YOU, IS THAT TRUE?

A YES.

Q LOTS 19 AND 20 AND LOTS 1 AND 2?

A YES.

Q WHY IS THAT?

A   WELL, WE NEED HOMES, AND I FEEL LIKE I CAN USE THE BACK LAND FOR SOME THINGS THAT I NEED, MAYBE TO RENT THE APARTMENT UP THERE AND GET A LITTLE INCOME OFF OF IT FOR MYSELF FOR MY LIVING TO PAY THE TAXES.

Q   IS WILL OR BARD WORKING AT THE PRESENT TIME?

A   NO, THEY ARE NOT.

Q   ANYONE WORKING IN THE FAMILY? IS ZOSA WORKING?

A   ZOSA HAS BLOOD POISON IN HER LEGS. SHE HAS THEM UP, AND THE DOCTOR WON'T LET HER. SHE JUST CAME FROM THE HOSPITAL.

Q   YOU ARE REQUESTING AN ACCOUNTING AS FAR AS THE BUSINESS IS CONCERNED, IS THAT TRUE?

A   IF I CAN, YES.

MR. FLANK: THAT'S ALL I HAVE.

CROSS EXAMINATION

BY MR. RYAN:

Q   MRS. KANDERHOSH, WHY DID YOU GIVE BARD HALF OF YOUR LAND WHEN YOU MARRIED HIM?

A   WELL, I FELT LIKE HE WAS MY HUSBAND, IF ANYTHING HAPPENED TO ME, THEN HE WOULD BE ABLE TO TAKE CARE OF IT.

Q   THAT'S RIGHT, BECAUSE YOU FELT LIKE HE WAS PART OF YOUR FAMILY, AND HE OUGHT TO HAVE AN INTEREST IN THAT LAND, SHOULDN'T HE?

A   I FELT LIKE HE WAS THE HEAD OF THE FAMILY, YES.

273

Q   AND HE SHOULD HAVE AN INTEREST IN THE
LAND BY VIRTUE OF THAT FACT AND NON OTHER?

A   I LOVED HIM.

Q   BUT THAT WASN'T MY QUESTION. HE SHOULD
HAVE AN INTEREST IN THAT LAND BY VIRTUE OF THE
FACT THAT HE WAS YOUR HUSBAND AND YOU LOVED HIM,
AND NO OTHER, NO OTHER REASON, IS THAT CORRECT?

A   WELL, YES. IF HE EVER HAD -- IF WE EVER
HAD -- WE HAD WILL, AND WILL WAS AT THAT TIME
THERE, AND I FELT LIKE WILL NEEDED SOMETHING, AND
HE SAID HE WAS GOING TO SUPPORT ME, TOO.

Q   WHEN YOU SAID YOU HAD WILL, NOW, WILL
ISN'T YOUR SON, IS HE?

A   I HAVE HAD HIM SINCE HE WAS 14.

Q   BUT HE'S NOT YOUR SON, IS HE?

A   NO. HE'S MY SISTER'S BOY.

Q   AND HE'S BEEN AROUND THERE AND HAS
HELPED YOU AND BARD AND HAS BEEN VERY LOYAL TO
YOU, HASN'T HE?

A   THATS WHAT HIS STEP-FATHER TOLD HIM TO
DO.

Q   BUT HE HAS BEEN LOYAL, HASN'T HE?

A   YES, HE HAS.

Q   NOW, HAS YOUR HUSBAND BEEN EMPLOYED
SINCE YOU MARRIED HIM?

A   BARD?

Q   YES.

A   HE WORKED ON THE BRICKYARD BEFORE, YES.
HE WAS WORKING FOR CABINET, WHAT WAS THE NAME,
CABINET, 1-A CABINET.

Q   WHEN DID YOU GET MARRIED? PLEASE REMIND ME OF THAT DATE.

A   1962, JUNE THE 27TH.

Q   1962?

A   ELKO, NEVADA.

Q   SO THAT'S 23 YEARS AGO; IS THAT CORRECT?

A   YES, BUT I MET BARD IN '57, WAY BEFORE THAT, BEFORE MY HUSBAND DIED.

Q   SO FROM 1962 UNTIL NOW, YOU HAVE BEEN MARRIED? WHEN WAS THE FIRST JOB THAT MR. KANDERHOSH HAD SINCE YOU MARRIED HIM IN 1962?

Q   WELL, WE WORKED ON THE BOTTLES, AND WE WORKED AT WATKINS PRODUCTS TOGETHER, TOO.

Q   NOW, THE BOTTLE BUSINESS STARTED IN ABOUT 1962, DIDN'T IT, WHEN YOU GOT MARRIED?

A   NO, THAT WAS BEFORE THAT, BECAUSE WILL WAS WORKING AT THE UTAH THEATRE, AND CURT JENSEN TOLD WILL TO GO TAKE THE BOTTLES DOWN, AND YOU WILL GET SOME MONEY OUT OF THEM, AND THAT'S WHERE THE BOTTLE BUSINESS STARTED.

Q   WHEN WAS THAT, WHAT YEAR?

A   OH, HEAVENS, THAT WAS FIVE OR SIX YEARS BEFORE.

Q   BEFORE 1962?

A   WELL, HE WORKED AT THE UTAH THEATRE. I THINK IT WAS THREE YEARS BEFORE ANYWAY.

Q   THREE YEARS BEFORE 1962?

A   THAT HE WAS WORKING AT THE UTAH THEATRE AS A JANITOR.

Q   SO YOU ARE SAYING THAT THE BOTTLE
BUSINESS WAS FIVE YEARS OLD WHEN MAY CAME?

A   IT COULD HAVE BEEN.

Q   IS THAT RIGHT OR NOT?

A   IT COULD HAVE BEEN, BECAUSE I WENT ALL
THROUGH THE PROCESS OF GETTING IT STARTED AND UP
ON ITS FEET.

Q   NOW, THIS WATKINS PRODUCTS THING WAS A
DOOR-TO-DOOR SALES PROJECT, WASN'T IT?

A   YES.

Q   YOU AND BARD DID THIS TOGETHER?

A   TOGETHER.

Q   HOW MANY MONTHS OR YEARS DID YOU DO
THAT?

A   SEVEN YEARS.

Q   SEVEN YEARS?

A   WE DONE THAT SEVEN YEARS TOGETHER.

Q   WHEN DID YOU START THAT?

A   '57, '57 OR '56, IN THERE.

Q   DECEMBER OF 1957?

A   NO. IT WAS AUGUST.

Q   OF 1957?

A   YES, '57.

Q   BUT THAT'S FIVE YEARS BEFORE YOU MARRIED
HIM?

A   WHAT?

Q   THAT'S FIVE YEARS BEFORE YOU AND BARD
WERE MARRIED, WASN'T IT?

A   YES. I KNOW BARD BEFORE MY FIRST
HUSBAND DIED, WAY BEFORE.

Q   WELL, MS. KANDERHOSH, THE FACT OF THE MATTER IS THAT OTHER THAN THE BOTTLE BUSINESS, YOUR HUSBAND, BARD KANDERHOSH, HAS NOT BEEN EMPLOYED AT ANYTHING SINCE YOU MARRIED HIM, HAS HE?

A   WELL, ONLY THAT, THE BOTTLE BUSINESS -- LET'S SEE. THE WATKINS, AND THEN THE BOTTLES, AND THEN WE STARTED THE BARRELS.

Q   BUT OTHER THAN THOSE THINGS, HE HASN'T BEEN EMPLOYED FOR ANYBODY AT ANY TIME, HAS HE?

A   WELL, WE WERE IN OUR OWN SELF-EMPLOYMENT.

Q   YES OR NO?

A   YES -- NO.

Q   OTHER THAN THOSE TWO, NO? NOW, WHEN YOU MARRIED MR. KANDERHOSH, YOU INDICATED HIS AGE PRESENTLY IS WHAT? HE'S 54, ISN'T HE?

A   WELL, YES, RIGHT NOW, HE WILL BE -- YES, 55 IN MARCH.

Q   IF HE WAS 54 NOW AND YOU MARRIED HIM 23 YEARS AGO, HE WAS 31 YEARS OLD WHEN YOU MARRIED HIM, WASN'T HE?

A   YES.

Q   HAS MR. KANDERHOSH BEEN ON WELFARE AT ANY TIME SINCE 1962?

A   NO, JUST THIS.

Q   HE'S NEVER BEEN ON WELFARE?

A   NOT THAT I KNOW.

Q   YOU WOULD KNOW, I ASSUME, SINCE YOU

HAVE BEEN LIVING WITH HIM ALL THIS TIME, WOULDN'T
YOU?

    A   I GUESS I WOULD.

    Q   NOW, IS THERE ANYTHING PHYSICALLY WRONG
WITH MR. KANDERHOSH THAT WOULD MAKE IT
IMPOSSIBLE FOR HIM TO HOLD A JOB?

    A   YES.

    Q   THAT YOU KNOW OF?

    A   YES.

    Q   WHAT IS THAT?

    A   HE'S HANDICAPPED.

    Q   HOW IS HE HANDICAPPED?

    A   WELL, HE WAS WORKING ON THE BARRELS, AND
A BARREL FELL DOWN ON HIM HERE (INDICATING), AND
HE HAD TO GO HAVE AN OPERATION.

    Q   WHEN DID THAT HAPPEN?

    A   OH, GLORY, I CAN'T TELL YOU THE YEAR OR
THE TIME, BUT HE WENT INTO THE HOSPITAL AND HAD
THIS OPERATION. I WENT WITH HIM.

    Q   WELL, YOU CAN REMEMBER BACK TO 1957 IN
WATKINS PRODUCTS. THIS MUST HAVE BEEN 20 YEARS
BEFORE THAT.

    A   WELL, I WAS MARRIED TO HIM WHEN IT
HAPPENED. BUT, OH, I GUESS ABOUT '76, SOMEWHERE IN
THERE.

    Q   SO JUST AFTER THE BOTTLE BUSINESS
STARTED, WAS IT?

    A   IT WAS AFTER THE BARREL BUSINESS HAD
STARTED, ABOUT TWO YEARS AFTER, SOMETHING LIKE
THAT.

Q   WAS HE IN THE HOSPITAL?

A   YES. HE HAD THE OPERATION.

Q   WHAT KIND OF AN OPERATION WAS IT, DO YOU KNOW?

A   WELL, DR. WILKINSON SAID IT WAS --

Q   IF YOU KNOW.

A   I CAN'T TELL YOU EXACTLY WHAT HE MEANT.

Q   WHAT WAS --

A   WELL, IT WAS THE HERNIA ALONG WITH THE BOWELS THAT HAD COME UP OVER THE TOP OF IT.

Q   AND HE'S UNABLE TO WORK BECAUSE OF THAT?

A   NO. HE HAS AN ARM THAT'S BEEN CRUSHED IN A WRECK.

Q.   HE HAS A CRUSHED ARM, TOO?

A   YES. IT WAS CRUSHED, AND IT WENT PARALYZED.

Q   WHEN DID THAT HAPPEN?

Q   THAT'S JUST THE YEAR THAT -- IT WAS AFTER I HAD LEFT HIM AND BEEN OVER AT THE OTHER HOUSE. I HAD AN OPERATION.

Q   ABOUT 1980, WAS IT?

A   NO. I BELIEVE IT WAS AFTER THAT.

Q   ABOUT 1982?

A   IT WAS A LITTLE WHILE BEFORE MAY LEFT.

Q   '81 OR '82?

A   SOMEWHERE IN THERE.

Q   IS THERE ANYTHING ELSE WRONG WITH HIM THAT WOULD PRECLUDE HIM?

279

A   YES. HE'S GOT DIABETES. HE'S GOT A NERVE PROBLEM.

Q   WHAT KIND OF A NERVE PROBLEM IS THAT?

A   HIGH BLOOD PRESSURE. I DON'T KNOW WHAT THE NERVE PROBLEM IS, BUT IT WAS NERVES.

Q   HIGH BLOOD PRESSURE?

A   HIGH BLOOD PRESSURE, DIABETES, AND HE HAS TO HAVE A SPECIAL DIET. I HAVE TO HAVE A SPECIALTY. I HAVE SUGAR DIABETES.

Q   IS THERE ANYTHING ELSE THAT'S WRONG WITH HIM THAT WOULD PRECLUDE HIM FROM HOLDING A JOB?

A   HE'S GOT AN EQUILIBRIUM, BECAUSE HE WAS CRUSHED PRETTY BAD IN THAT ACCIDENT.

Q   DOES THAT MEAN THAT HE TOPPLES OVER?

A   YES. HE FALLS VERY EASILY, ESPECIALLY ON ICE AND STUFF.

Q   HOW OFTEN DOES HE FALL?

A   ESPECIALLY ON THE MUD AND ICE.

Q   HOW OFTEN DOES THAT HAPPEN?

A   OH, JUST ONCE IN A WHILE, I GUESS, JUST GOES DOWN.

Q   WELL, AS WE LEFT COURT EARLIER TODAY, I NOTICED YOU AND MR. KANDERHOSH WALKING TOGETHER OUT IN THE ICE AND SNOW. I DIDN'T SEE ANYBODY FALL. DID ANYONE FALL?

A   NO. I GO ALONG AND BALANCE. WE BALANCE TOGETHER.

Q   NOW, YOU INDICATED YOU TALKED ABOUT A TIME WHEN YOU AND YOUR HUSBAND AND MAY WERE IN

280

THE YARD TALKING ABOUT CONVEYING PROPERTY TO
MAY; IS THAT CORRECT?

A   UH-HUH (AFFIRMATIVE).

Q   NOW, WILL WAS PART OF THAT PROGRAM,
WASN'T HE?

A   YES.

Q   WHY WASN'T HE THERE?

A   HE WAS OUT PICKING UP BARRELS.

Q   SO YOU AND BARD AND MAY HAD A MEETING?

A   HAD AN ARGUMENT.

Q   YOU HAD AN ARGUMENT?

A   RIGHT.

Q   HOW DID THAT START?

A   WELL, MAY JUST COME UP, AND SHE SAID, I'M
NOT GOING TO DO -- I'M NOT GOING TO DO IT. THAT'S
IT.

Q   NOT GOING TO DO WHAT?

A   SHE WASN'T GOING TO DO NOTHING FOR ME.
SHE MADE IT UP.

Q   WHY WAS THAT, MRS. KANDERHOSH?

A   WELL, SHE SAYS THAT I ARGUED WITH HER. I
WILL TELL YOU, SHE WAS ONE OF THE BIGGEST ARGUERS
HERSELF.

Nanas came off her chair and began whirling her fist in
the air, gritting her teeth as she hollered out wild
accusations.   For all the years I had tried to figure her out
and had never been successful, I was still dumbfounded.   She
had not changed a lick.   I bowed my head and closed my eyes
as my mind drifted into the past.   Many times her attitude had
contributed to my inferiority complex as I wondered if there
was something that I should be doing for her that perhaps I
was not doing.   That might somehow have caused her

281

disposition because to look at her children, they were really a nice bunch of kids. I liked them all, and her sisters also-- Collette, Olive, Sandra. And she had as sweet a husband in Clarence as a woman could hope for. At one time I had wanted to make her happy but had long since given up in hopeless despair.

Q WASN'T IT BECAUSE ---

A AND MEAN.

Q WASN'T IT BECAUSE YOU TOLD STORIES TO BARD BEHIND HER BACK TO GET HER IN TROUBLE?

A NO, I DID NOT.

Q WASN'T IT ALSO THAT YOU CONTROLLED ALL THE MONEY OUT OF THE BOTTLE BUSINESS?

A OH, I PAY THE BILLS, THE SAME THAT I EXPECTED HER TO DO.

Q AND ESSENTIALLY SHE WAS TREATED SO BADLY THAT SHE COULDN'T STAND TO WORK IN THE BUSINESS ANY MORE? THAT'S WHY SHE WAS MAD, WASN'T SHE?

A HOW SHE WAS TREATING ME, SHE SCRATCHED MY HEAD OPEN WITH HER HAND LIKE A TIGER. I HAD TO BE GONE TO THE HOSPITAL. MR. REYNOLD AND HIS WIFE TOOK ME TO THE HOSPITAL BECAUSE SHE DID, SHE TORE MY HEAD WIDE OPEN.

Q WHEN DID THAT HAPPEN?

A YOU TELL ME THAT SHE WASN'T MEAN?

Q WHEN DID THAT HAPPEN?

A MR. REYNOLD, BARD, AND WILL HAD GONE TO A MEETING.

Q WHEN DID THAT HAPPEN, MRS. KANDERHOSH?

A WHEN WE WERE OVER TO 4118, SHE STARTED THAT RIGHT THERE.

282

Q   THAT WAS 5TH EAST?

A   THAT WAS 5TH EAST.

Q   THAT WAS BACK IN '63 OR '64?

A   RIGHT, WHEN SHE FIRST CAME. SHE STARTED
ALL THESE THINGS. SHE WAS THE BIGGEST QUARRELER,
BIGGEST SCRATCHER, THE BIGGEST TORTURER YOU EVER
SAW IN YOUR LIFE.

Q   YOU DIDN'T GET ALONG WITH HER?

A   SHE TORTURED THE WHOLE FAMILY. SHE
WOULD TAKE THOSE CHILDREN OUT THERE AND BURN
THEIR HANDS, BURN THEM. I HAD TO TAKE THEM TO
THE HOSPITAL TO GET THEM TREATED FOR INFECTION,
AND YOU DON'T -- IF YOU DON'T BELIEVE ME, WILLER
DARDSON, BECAUSE HIS CHILD HAD INFECTION IN HIS
HANDS FROM THOSE MATCHES MAY BURNED.

Q   JUST A SECOND. YOU SAY MAY BURNED THOSE
--

A   BURNED THOSE CHILDREN'S HANDS AND
FINGERS.

Q   DID YOU SEE HER DO IT?

A   DID I HEAR THOSE KIDS SCREAM IN THEIR
SHOP?

Q   NO, DID YOU SEE MAY?

A   SHE WOULDN'T OPEN THE DOOR.

Q   DID YOU SEE HER DO IT, MA'AM?

A   I SAW THE RESULTS, BECAUSE I HAD TO TAKE
THEM TO THE HOSPITAL.

Q   WHAT I ASKED YOU WAS, DID YOU SEE HER
BURN THEIR HANDS?

A   SHE BURNED DAVID'S HANDS RIGHT OVER THE
FLAME. I SAW THAT, AND IT HUNG WITH A BLISTER ON
IT.

Q   DID YOU TELL STORIES ALL ROUND THE
FAMILY THAT -- A   NO, I DID NOT.

Q   DID YOU TELL EVERYBODY IN THE FAMILY THAT
MAY HAD DONE THIS WITH THE CHILDREN'S HANDS?

A   THEY KNOW IT. THE KIDS KNOW IT. THEY
COULD TESTIFY ON IT, THAT SHE BURNED THEM. SHE
BEAT THEM BLACK AND BLUE.

Q   DID YOU TELL OTHER MEMBERS OF THE
FAMILY OTHER THINGS THAT MAY HAD DONE?

A   NO.

Q   THAT WEREN'T GOOD?

A   NO, BECAUSE SHE DID.

Q   WHAT ELSE DID MAY DO THAT YOU DIDN'T
LIKE, MRS. KANDERHOSH?

A   I DIDN'T LIKE HER TORTURING PEOPLE.

Q   HOW DID SHE TORTURE PEOPLE?

A   TORTURED THEM.

Q   HOW DID SHE DO THAT?

A   HOW DID SHE TORTURE PEOPLE? SHE TOOK
ZOSA. ZOSA HAD THESE VARICOSE VEINS, VERY BAD
ONES. SHE TOOK THAT WOMAN AND PUT HER FEET IN
HOT WATER OVER A FLAMING BURNER, AND I SAW IT
MYSELF. I SAID, MAY, YOU ARE GOING TO COOK HER
FEET. HER FEET CAME OUT IN BLISTERS. I HAD TO
HOLD THEM UP. SHE TOOK HER MOTHER AND BEAT HER
MOTHER OVER THE HEAD WITH A CLUB UNTIL HER HEAD

WAS BLEEDING ALL DOWN HERE. WHO DOCTORED IT? I
DID TWICE.

Q   THIS WAS THE LADY THAT WAS HERE TODAY?

A   THAT IS MAY RIGHT HERE.

Q   BUT THIS LADY THAT WAS SITTING HERE
TODAY WAS MAY'S MOTHER? THAT'S THE ONE --

A   THAT'S THE ONE SHE HIT OVER THE HEAD WITH
A CLUB AND BROKE HER HEAD OPEN. I WAS THE ONE
THAT HAD TO DOCTOR THE SORES TWICE. THEN I TOLD
HER IF SHE DONE IT ONCE MORE, SHE WOULD DO THE
DOCTORING HERSELF, AND SHE DID IT ONCE MORE, AND
SHE HAD TO DO THE DOCTORING.

Q   MRS. KANDERHOSH --

A   PUT DIRTY CLOTHES ON THE HEAD AND
EVERYTHING AND GOT INFECTION.

Q   LET ME ASK YOU A QUESTION. YOU WERE TO
HAVE BEEN LOOKED UPON IN THE FAMILY AS THE FIRST
WIFE, IS THAT CORRECT?

A   WELL, YES.

Q   AND THAT CARRIES WITH IT A GREAT DEAL OF
--

A   I WAS A MOTHER.

Q   THAT'S RIGHT, AND YOU WERE HEAD OF THE
FAMILY?

        MR. FLANK: MRS. KANDERHOSH, JUST ANSWER
THE QUESTION.

        THE WITNESS: OH, YES.

Q   (BY MR. RYAN) YOU WERE HEAD OF THE
FAMILY, THE MATRIARCH OF THE FAMILY, WEREN'T YOU?

A   I TRIED TO DO MY BEST.

285

Q   NOW, MRS. KANDERHOSH, IS IT TRUE THAT MAY FOR A PERIOD OF YEARS PUT YOU TO BED AS A MAIDEN VIRTUALLY ALMOST EVERY NIGHT FOR A PERIOD OF YEARS?

A   NO, NOT FOR YEARS.

Q   SHE BATHED YOU, DIDN'T SHE?

A   VERY LITTLE.

Q   SHE BATHED YOU AND SHE DRESSED YOU?

A   SOME OF THE OTHER FAMILY DID, TOO.

Q   BUT SHE DID, DIDN'T SHE?

A   NOT ALL THE TIME.

Q   BUT SHE DRESSED YOU?

A   NOT ALL THE TIME.

Q   SHE RUBBED YOUR LEGS DOWN?

A   NOT ALL THE TIME. ZOSA DONE THAT.

Q   AND PUT LOTION ON YOU?

A   ZOSA DONE MOST OF THAT HERSELF, ZOSA. THAT'S WHY I LOVE ZOSA TODAY. I LOVE THAT GIRL VERY DEARLY.

MR. FLANK: MRS. KANDERHOSH, JUST LISTEN TO THE QUESTION AND DON'T FILL IN. WE WILL BE HERE A WEEK.

Q   (BY MR. RYAN) NOW, MRS. KANDERHOSH, IS THERE A MORTGAGE ON THAT FARM?

A   OH, WHEN I PURCHASED THAT --

THE COURT: JUST A MINUTE. MR. RYAN, WE ARE GOING TO HAVE TO TAKE RECESS FOR THE REPORTER.

LADIES AND GENTLEMEN OF THE JURY, WE WILL

BE IN RECESS FOR TEN MINUTES. REMEMBER THE
ADMONITION I HAVE GIVEN.

(A RECESS WAS TAKEN.)

THE COURT: THE JURY, PARTIES, AND
COUNSEL ARE PRESENT. YOU MAY CONTINUE, MR. RYAN.

MR. RYAN: THANK YOU, JUDGE.

Q   (BY MR. RYAN) MRS. KANDERHOSH, WE WERE
JUST COMMENCING TO TALK ABOUT A MEETING OR AN
ARGUMENT BETWEEN YOURSELF, YOUR HUSBAND, BARD,
AND MAY HANCOCK. DO YOU RECALL WHEN THAT
OCCURRED?

A   LET'S SEE. ABOUT IN '76.

Q   1976?

A   SOMEWHERE AROUND THERE.

Nanas began to calm down and they entered into a lengthy
examination as to the transfer of deeds and the timing. Nanas
claimed there was some kind of quit claim deed that was
supposed to transfer the property back to Bard and Nanas that
was to be brought to light if Will and I defaulted in serving
them according to their expectations. There was no evidence
of such a deed so the proceedings continued.

Will was called to the stand. He was questioned by Mr.
Flank on this same subject.

Q   NOW IS IT A FACT THAT IN 1982 YOU
TRANSFERRED TO MAY SAID PROPERTY, AND SHE
TRANSFERRED PROPERTY TO YOU, SO YOU'VE BECOME
THE SOLE OWNER OF THE FARM, AND SHE HAD THE TITLE
TO THE OTHER PROPERTY PURSUANT TO THESE DEEDS?

A   THIS HERE --

Q   WAS THAT TRUE?

A   THIS IS TRUE.

Q   YOU HAVE SINCE CONVEYED THE FARM BACK
TO THE FAMILY, HAVE YOU NOT?

A   THAT'S TRUE.

Q   YOU DON'T OWN ANYTHING?

A   THAT'S TRUE.

Q   ARE YOU STILL LIVING AT THE HOME OF THE
FAMILY?

A   YES, I AM.

Q   STILL EATING THERE?

A   YES.

Q   DO YOU HAVE ANY INCOME AT ALL?

A   NONE WHATSOEVER.

Q   HAVE YOU HAD ANY EMOTIONAL MENTAL
PROBLEMS IN THE LAST FEW YEARS?

MR. RYAN: EXCUSE ME. I HAVE TO OBJECT
AT THIS POINT. HE'S LEADING THE WITNESS, YOUR
HONOR.

MR. FLANK: I AM, YOUR HONOR. I WILL
WITHDRAW.

Q   (BY MR. FLANK) HAVE YOU HAD SOME
PHYSICAL PROBLEMS?

A   YES, I HAVE.

Q   MENTAL PROBLEMS?

A   YES.

Q   YOU MAKE NO CLAIM TO ANY OF THE
PROPERTY OTHER THAN A FAMILY MONEY OF THAT YOU
HAVE DEEDED BACK TO THE FAMILY?

A   THAT'S TRUE.

Q   DO YOU REMEMBER IN 1975 OR DO YOU

RECALL ANYTHING IN REGARD TO SIGNING SOME DEEDS
AT A MEETING AT MR. JEFFS'?

A   YES, I DO.

Q   TELL US WHO WAS PRESENT THEN?

A   THERE WAS MYSELF, MAY HANCOCK, NANAS
KANDERHOSH, AND BARD KANDERHOSH AND MR. JEFFS.

Q   HE PREPARED SOME DOCUMENTS?

A   YES, HE DID.

Q   DID BARD AND MRS. KANDERHOSH, NANAS
KANDERHOSH, SIGN THOSE DEEDS?

A   YES.

A   WERE THERE SOME OTHER DEEDS PREPARED?

A   THERE WAS.

Q   WHAT WERE THEY?

A   THERE WERE SOME QUIT CLAIM DEEDS TO BE --
THAT IF THERE WAS ANY DISPUTE BETWEEN MAY OR I,
OR IF THERE WAS ANY DISPUTE BETWEEN MR.
KANDERHOSH AND MRS. KANDERHOSH, BETWEEN MAY AND
I, IF THERE WAS A DISPUTE, THAT THE LAND DEEDS
WHICH WERE QUIT CLAIM DEEDS, AS I UNDERSTOOD,
WERE TO BE IN -- WAS TO BE IN GARY L. JEFFS' FILES.
NOW THEY WERE --

Q   OKAY, WHO WERE THEY BACK TO? DID YOU
SIGN THOSE?

A   YES, I SIGNED THOSE. THEY WERE TO GO
BACK TO J. BARD KANDERHOSH AND MRS. KANDERHOSH.

Q   SO YOU SIGNED SOME DEEDS TO PUT THE
PROPERTY BACK IN THEIR NAMES. DO YOU KNOW
WHATEVER HAPPENED TO THOSE?

A   FROM WHAT I UNDERSTAND --

Q   DO YOU KNOW YOURSELF?

A   NO, I DON'T.

Q   BUT YOU SIGNED THOSE?

A   YES.

Q   SINCE YOU HAVE NO INCOME, YOU ARE BASICALLY LIVING BY REASON OF NANAS' HELP, IS THAT TRUE?

A   THAT'S TRUE.

Q   WHAT LITTLE INCOME SHE HAS, SHE SHARES WITH YOU AND THE REST OF THE FAMILY MEMBERS?

A   THAT'S TRUE, ALONG WITH WHAT BARD HAS, TOO.

Q   WITH WHAT BARD HAS AND NANAS HAS AND WHAT LITTLE RENT YOU GET OFF THE FARM?

A   RIGHT.

Q   THAT'S WHAT THE ENTIRE FAMILY LIVES ON?

A   YES.

MR. FLANK: THAT'S ALL I HAVE.

THE COURT: YOU MAY CROSS EXAMINE.

MR. FLANK: I'M SORRY. LET ME ASK HIM ONE MORE QUESTION.

Q   (BY MR. FLANK) AT THE TIME THIS PROPERTY WAS PUT IN JOINT TENANCY IN YOUR NAME AND MAY'S NAME, DID YOU MAKE ANY AGREEMENT WITH MAY TOWARDS MR. AND MRS. KANDERHOSH?

A   I DON'T KNOW WHAT YOU ARE TALKING ABOUT.

Q   WAS THERE ANY AGREEMENT IN REGARD TO CARING FOR THEM?

A   YES, THERE WAS.

Q   WHAT WAS THAT AGREEMENT?

A   THAT SHE WAS TO TAKE CARE OF THEM FOR
THE REST OF THEIR LIFE, AND FOR ME TO, FOR US, MAY
AND I, TO DO THE BEST WE COULD WITH WHAT WE HAD
TO MAKE SURE THAT THEY CAME FIRST. THEN AFTER
THEIR DEATH, THEN THAT WAS TO BE -- THEN WE WOULD
BE SENIORITIES IN THE COMPANY, AND THE BUSINESS
WAS TO BE DEALT AS WAS THE FINANCES WAS TO BE 50-
50 PERCENT, AND THIS IS THE REASON WHY I HAVE NOT
HAD A JOB, IS BECAUSE I HAVE BEEN HOPING THAT THIS
WOULD COME TO COURT SO THAT THIS HERE, SO YOU
COULD PAY OFF THIS $10,000 THAT I OWE THE STATE
FOR BACK WAGES AS CHILD SUPPORT.

Q   WELL, JUST ANSWER YOUR QUESTION. YOU
AGREED TO TAKE CARE OF NANAS AND BARD DURING
THEIR LIFETIME?

A   YES, I DID.

Q   AND PROVIDE FOR THE FAMILY?

A   YES.

Q   INCLUDING ZOSA AND THE FOUR CHILDREN?

A   THAT'S TRUE.

A   HAVE YOU DONE THE BEST YOU COULD WITH
THAT?

A   I HAVE DONE THE BEST I COULD.

Q   YOU HAVE DEEDED THE PROPERTY BACK TO
THEM THAT YOU OBTAINED?

A   YES, I HAVE.

Q   DID YOU WORK IN THE BUSINESS FROM THE
TIME YOU COMMENCED LIVING WITH NANAS UP UNTIL
MAY TOOK OVER THE BUSINESS?

A   WELL, NOW, WHAT DO YOU MEAN BY --

A DID YOU WORK IN THE BUSINESS FROM THE TIME, THE BOTTLE BUSINESS, FROM THE TIME IT WAS COMMENCED, AND DID YOU WORK IN THE BOTTLE BUSINESS AND BARREL BUSINESS UP UNTIL MAY TOOK OVER THE BUSINESS?

A YES. I WAS THE FOUNDER OF THE BOTTLE BUSINESS, YES.

Q WHAT DID YOU DO IN REGARD TO THOSE BUSINESSES?

A I DID THE TRUCK DRIVING. I DID THE LIFTING. I DID THE STREET WALKING. I WENT TO ONE CAFE, TO THE OTHER CAFE TO GET THE CONTRACTS, AND THEN AS IT GOT BIGGER, THEN MAY CALLED UP A FEW DRIVE-INS.

Q HOW MANY HOURS WOULD YOU WORK A DAY?

A I WOULD WORK BEGINNING TO END. I WAS WORKING THREE JOBS WHEN I FIRST STARTED OUT. I WAS WORKING AS A COOK AT VILLAGE INN PANCAKE HOUSE. I WAS WORKING AS A COOK AT FRED AND KELLY'S. THAT WAS DOWN ON STATE STREET AND ABOUT 1000 SOUTH, AND THEN AT NIGHT, LIKE AT ABOUT 10:30 OR 11:30, EXCUSE ME, I WOULD GO TO THE CAPITOL THEATRE AND I WOULD DO JANITORIAL WORK THERE. NOW, THIS WAS --

Q NOW, DID ALL YOUR MONEY FROM THOSE JOBS GO INTO THE FAMILY?

A YES.

Q THEN WHEN THE BUSINESS STARTED, HOW MANY HOURS DID YOU WORK IN THE BUSINESS?

A WELL --

Q JUST GIVE ME A ROUND NUMBER.

A   WELL, WHEN I FIRST STARTED, I JUST WORKED ON IT PART-TIME BECAUSE I WAS PULLING THREE JOBS AT THE TIME.

Q   YOU WORKED PART-TIME BESIDES YOUR OTHER JOBS?

A   AND I WAS RIDING A BICYCLE. SO I HAD -- I RODE A BICYCLE FROM 4500 SOUTH UP HERE TO 3RD SOUTH, AND I WOULD RIDE IT THROUGH THE WINTER YEAR ROUND, AND I WAS RIDING IT FOR ALMOST FIVE YEARS.

Q   IN THE BARREL BUSINESS, WHAT DID YOU DO?

A   IN THE BARREL BUSINESS, I WAS THE TRUCK DRIVER. I WAS DRIVING THE DIESELS. WELL, WE FIRST STARTED OUT WITH GASOLINE RIGS, AND I TOLD THEM, I SAYS, I THINK WE WOULD BE A LOT BETTER ECONOMY-WISE TO GO DIESEL.

Q   DID YOU DRIVE A DIESEL TRUCK?

A   YES.

Q   HOW MANY HOURS A DAY WOULD YOU WORK OR HOW MANY HOURS A WEEK WOULD YOU WORK IN THE BUSINESS?

A   I WAS WORKING APPROXIMATELY -- WELL, I WAS WORKING SOMETIMES I WOULD WORK 12 HOURS, AND SOMETIMES I WOULD WORK 22 HOURS A DAY. SO I WAS ONLY GETTING TWO HOURS SLEEP SOMETIMES.

Q   ALL THE MONEY THAT YOU RECEIVED FROM THAT COMPANY WENT INTO THE FAMILY?

A   THAT'S TRUE, AND TO BUILD UP THE COMPANY ITSELF.

Q   BUY EQUIPMENT AND BUY TRUCKS?

293

A   TRUE.

Q   YOU RECEIVED NOTHING BASICALLY FOR YOURSELF TO BUY YOURSELF A PERSONAL AUTOMOBILE OR CLOTHING OR THAT TYPE OF THING?

A   NONE WHATSOEVER.

MR. FLANK: THAT'S ALL I HAVE.

CROSS EXAMINATION

BY MR. RYAN:

Q   MR. DARDSON. YOU CONVEYED YOUR INTEREST IN THAT FARM BACK TO THE CORPORATION CONTROLLED BY NANAS, DIDN'T YOU?

A   THAT'S TRUE.

Q   WHAT WAS THE REASON FOR THAT?

A   THAT THERE WAS A REASON, BECAUSE I WAS -- THE PROPERTY BELONGED TO HER, AND THAT WAS THE FOUNDATION AGREEMENT ON WHICH WE -- WHEN WHICH I RECEIVED IT FROM HER.

Q   WAS THAT THE REAL REASON SO YOU COULD AVOID YOUR WIFE, BARDELL DARDSON, GETTING ANY PART OF YOUR PROPERTY IN A DIVORCE SETTLEMENT?

A   YES AND NO ON THAT.

When Will answered he slipped a smile, then he regained a sober expression.

Q   WELL, THAT WAS THE REAL REASON, WASN'T IT?

A   NO. THE REAL REASON WAS NOT THAT. THE REAL REASON WAS BECAUSE THAT LAND BELONGED TO MRS. KANDERHOSH, AND IT DID NOT BELONG TO ME JUST BECAUSE YOU BRING OVER YOUR CHILD FOR ME TO TAKE

294

CARE OF, THAT DOES NOT BRAND THAT CHILD MY CHILD.
THEY WOULD GET ME FOR KIDNAPPING.

Q   SO YOU WERE CONCERNED THAT BARDELL
WOULD GET PART OF THAT PROPERTY?

A   NO, I WAS NOT.

Q   I THOUGHT YOU SAID IN ANSWER TO MY
QUESTION, YES AND NO. DIDN'T YOU SAY THAT TO MY
QUESTION?

A   I DID, BUT I SAID AT THAT TIME, THE LAND
WAS ALREADY IN DEBT TO THE BANK WHEN I RECEIVED
IT, WHICH HAD A $7,000 NET ON IT.

Q   YOU COULDN'T PAY FOR IT?

A   THAT'S TRUE.

Q   SO YOU GAVE IT BACK? NOW, I'M GOING TO
SHOW YOU WHAT'S BEEN MARKED AS DEFENDANT'S
EXHIBIT 15, AND ASK YOU IF YOU RECOGNIZE THIS
DOCUMENT, MR. DARDSON?

A   YES. I THINK THIS IS SOME DEEDS THAT
MARTIN FLANK FIXED OUT FOR US.

Q   IN FACT, THAT'S A DEED CONVEYING THAT
FARM FOR THE SECOND TIME, ISN'T IT, TO CLARKE
TAYLOR, JR., ISN'T IT?

Q   YOU DID NOT EVEN OWN THE PROPERTY AT
THAT TIME, BECAUSE YOU HAD ALREADY CONVEYED AND
RECORDED THE SAME PROPERTY TO NAN'S FLOWERS AND
GIFTS IN JANUARY OF 1983, DIDN'T YOU?

A   THAT'S BECAUSE THIS HERE PROPERTY WAS
STILL IN MY NAME AT THAT TIME, AND AT THE PRESENT
TIME, IT HAD THAT INDEBTEDNESS, AND I DID NOT WANT
CLARKE TAYLOR TO HAVE ANY INDEBTEDNESS. SO WHEN

THE INDEBTEDNESS WAS OFF, I TURNED OVER TO HIM WITH NANAS' CONSENT.

Q   SO NANAS TOLD YOU IT WAS OKAY TO EXECUTE A SECOND WARRANTY DEED, DID SHE, TO CLARKE TAYLOR? IS THAT WHAT HAPPENED?

A   THAT WAS TAKEN UNDER ADVISEMENT OF MR. FLANK. WE DON'T DO ANYTHING BECAUSE WE WANT TO DO IT.

Q   WHY DID YOU CONVEY THAT PROPERTY TO MR. TAYLOR WHEN YOU DID NOT EVEN OWN IT, MR. DARDSON?

A   BECAUSE I WAS EITHER GOING TO LOSE IT THROUGH THE BANK, WOULD EITHER TAKE IT, OR ELSE MR. CLARKE TAYLOR WOULD TAKE IT.

Q   SO THAT'S THE REASON YOU CONVEYED IT BACK TO NANAS, IS THAT CORRECT?

A   THAT'S RIGHT.

My thoughts on the whole situation were the same as always. They not only were protecting themselves from Bardell but also so they could manipulate favors out of Clarke Taylor and still have Social Services or Welfare support them because they all refused to work.

My attorney asked Will if he worked in the barrel business after 1981.

A   WHAT I'M REFERRING TO --

Q   JUST ANSWER MY QUESTION. DID YOU OR DID YOU NOT WORK IN THE BARREL BUSINESS AFTER SEPTEMBER 29, 1981?

A   I DON'T KNOW WHEN MAY FIRED ME FROM THE BARREL BUSINESS.

MR. RYAN: I HAVE NO FURTHER QUESTIONS.

REDIRECT EXAMINATION

BY MR. FLANK:

Q   DID SHE REFUSE TO LET YOU WORK ANY
LONGER IN THE BARREL BUSINESS?

A   YES, SHE DID.

Q   YOU HAVE HAD AN EMOTIONAL BREAKDOWN?

A   YES, I HAVE.

MR. RYAN: OBJECTION, YOUR HONOR. THESE
ARE ALL LEADING QUESTIONS. I WOULD ASK THAT THE
ANSWER BE STRICKEN.

THE COURT: THE OBJECTION IS SUSTAINED.

MR. RYAN: I ASKED THAT 14 BE ADMITTED,
DID I NOT?

THE COURT: YOU DID, AND IT'S BEEN
RECEIVED.

Q   (BY MR. FLANK) WHO IS MR. TAYLOR?

A   CLARKE TAYLOR. HE'S JUST A FRIEND OF
MINE.

Q   I SHOW YOU WHAT'S BEEN MARKED AS
PLAINTIFF'S EXHIBIT 16, AS A GROUP, AND ASK YOU IF
YOU HAVE SEEN THOSE BEFORE?

A   YES. THESE WAS SIGNED IN YOUR OFFICE.

Q   WHAT ARE THEY?

A   THEY ARE WARRANTY DEEDS.

Q   FROM WHOM TO WHOM?

A   FROM NANAS. LET'S SEE. FROM WILLER
DARDSON.

Q   DOES IT SHOW GRANTOR, WHO THE GRANTOR IS
ON EACH OF THOSE?

A   NO. NO, CLARKE TAYLOR.

Q   IS THERE ONE TO YOU?

A   YES.

Q   IS THERE ONE TO --

A   J. BARD KANDERHOSH AND NANAS KANDERHOSH.

Q   SO DEEDS WERE PREPARED BACK FROM MR. TAYLOR TO ONE FOR EACH OF YOU?

A   RIGHT.

MR. FLANK: ANY OBJECTION?

MR. RYAN: LET ME TAKE A LOOK AT IT. I WOULD LIKE TO VOIR DIRE THE WITNESS ABOUT THESE DEEDS, IF I MAY.

THE COURT: WELL, YOU WILL HAVE AN OPPORTUNITY TO CROSS EXAMINE. THERE HASN'T BEEN AN OFFER.

Mr. Ryan called Bard Kanderhosh to the stand and began to question him.

DIRECT EXAMINATION

BY MR. RYAN:

Q   MR. KANDERHOSH, PLEASE STATE YOUR FULL NAME.

A   J. BARD KANDERHOSH.

Q   WHERE DO YOU RESIDE?

A   8487 SOUTH REDWOOD ROAD.

Q   IS THAT IN THE RED HOUSE THAT'S BEEN DISCUSSED?

A   AFFIRMATIVE.

Q   WITH WHOM DO YOU LIVE?

298

A   WITH ZOSA AND SKIP AND LEE AND WILL.

Q   SKIP AND WHO?

A   LEE.

Q   AND WILL?

A   UH-HUH (AFFIRMATIVE).

Q   NOW IS WILL WILLER DARDSON?

A   WILLER DARDSON.

Q   AND SKIP AND LEE ARE YOUR CHILDREN, ARE THEY NOT?

A   UH-HUH (AFFIRMATIVE).

Q   SO THERE ARE FOUR PEOPLE LIVING IN THE HOME?

A   THAT'S RIGHT.

Q   NOW, MR. KANDERHOSH, IN THAT RED HOUSE, HOW MANY ROOMS ARE THERE?

A   THERE'S FIVE.

Q   FIVE ROOMS?

A   FIVE BEDROOMS.

THE COURT: IS THERE SOME COMPELLING RELEVANCE TO HOW MANY ROOMS ARE IN THE HOUSE?

MR. RYAN: YES, VERY MUCH SO.

THE COURT: WHY DON'T YOU PROFFER?

MR. RYAN: THE PROFFER IS, NUMBER ONE, IN THE DEPOSITION HE WOULD NOT ANSWER THAT QUESTION.

THE COURT: BESIDES THAT, WHAT IS THE RELEVANCE TO THIS LINE OF INQUIRY?

MR. RYAN: THE FACT THAT MY CLIENT HAD NO OTHER PLACE TO SLEEP BUT IN HIS BEDROOM.

MR. FLANK: I WOULD OBJECT. I DON'T KNOW WHAT THIS HAS TO DO WITH IT, WITH EITHER THE ELEMENTS OF OUR COMPLAINTS AND/OR HIS COUNTERCLAIM.

THE COURT: WELL, I AM GOING TO ALLOW YOU TO PURSUE THE LINE OF QUESTIONING, BUT I DON'T SEE HOW THE DEMAND THAT SHE SLEEP IN HIS BEDROOM HAS ANY RELEVANCE WITH THE NUMBER OF ROOMS IN THE HOUSE. LET'S LIMIT THAT QUESTION DIRECTLY SO WE CAN GET ON WITH IT.

Q (BY MR. RYAN) SO THERE ARE FIVE BEDROOMS?

A UH-HUH (AFFIRMATIVE).

Q HOW MANY OTHER MAJOR ROOMS?

A THE FRONT ROOM AND KITCHEN AND BATH AND A HALF.

Q FRONT ROOM, KITCHEN, AND FIVE BEDROOMS, IS THAT CORRECT?

A UH-HUH (AFFIRMATIVE).

Q ANY OTHERS, ANY OTHER ROOMS?

A NO.

Q NOW, GOING BACK TO APPROXIMATELY 1963 OR '64, YOU DISCUSSED WITH MAY THE PROSPECTS OF HER BECOMING YOUR THIRD POLYGAMIST WIFE?

A YES.

Q WHEN DID YOU DO THAT?

A I DON'T RECALL.

Q WAS IT JUST SEVERAL MONTHS PRIOR TO HER COMING TO LIVE WITH YOU IN LATE '63; IS THAT CORRECT?

A   I DON'T UNDERSTAND YOUR QUESTION.

Q   DID YOU START DISCUSSING THIS, HER COMING TO LIVE WITH YOU AS YOUR THIRD POLYGAMIST WIFE, JUST PRIOR TO THE TIME THAT SHE DID COME IN LATE 1963?

A   I DIDN'T DISCUSS IT.

Q   YOU DIDN'T DISCUSS IT WITH HER BEFORE SHE CAME?

A   NO.

Q   YOU TOLD MAY, DIDN'T YOU, THAT SHE WAS MEANT FOR YOU AS YOUR THIRD WIFE?

A   UH-HUH (AFFIRMATIVE).

Q   YOU DID?

A   YES.

Q   YOU TOLD HER THAT ONE OF THE MEMBERS OF YOUR RELIGIOUS GROUP HAD TOLD YOU THAT, DIDN'T YOU?

A   UH-HUH (AFFIRMATIVE).

Q   THAT WAS BROTHER MANN?

A   YES.

Q   YOU KNEW THAT MAY HAD A GREAT DEAL OF RESPECT FOR BROTHER MANN, DIDN'T YOU?

A   YES.

Q   YOU KNEW THAT MAY WAS VERY NAIVE AND INEXPERIENCED, TOO, DID YOU NOT?

A   WELL, I WOULDN'T SAY THAT.

Q   YOU DIDN'T KNOW THAT SHE WAS NAIVE AND INEXPERIENCED?

A   (SHOOK HEAD NEGATIVELY.)

Q   SHE WAS ONLY 16 YEARS OLD. YOU KNEW
THAT?

A   YES, BUT SHE HAD ALL HER FACULTIES.

Q   YOU KNEW SHE WAS A HARD WORKER?

A   NOT AT FIRST, SHE WASN'T.

Q   NOT AT FIRST, SHE WASN'T? YOU TOLD HER
THAT SHE WAS TO BE YOUR THIRD WIFE WHEN SHE
REACHED 18, DIDN'T YOU?

A   YES.

Q   DID YOU DISCUSS WITH HER WHAT HER DUTIES
WOULD BE AS A MEMBER OF YOUR FAMILY WHEN YOU
MARRIED HER?

A   NO, OUTSIDE THAT SHE WAS TO TAKE CARE OF
THE BOTTLE BUSINESS.

Q   NOW, SHE CAME TO LIVER THERE
APPROXIMATELY TWO YEARS BEFORE YOU MARRIED HER,
DIDN'T SHE?

A   HUH?

Q   SHE CAME TO LIVE WITH YOU ABOUT TWO
YEARS BEFORE YOU ACTUALLY MARRIED HER, DIDN'T
SHE?

A   YES.

Q   NOW, THERE CAME A TIME WHEN SHORTLY
AFTER SHE CAME THERE THAT YOU AND SHE STARTED TO
SLEEP TOGETHER, IS THAT CORRECT?

MR. FLANK: YOUR HONOR, I WOULD OBJECT,
AND I WOULD REQUEST I APPROACH THE WITNESS.

THE COURT: APPROACH THE WITNESS?

MR. FLANK: RIGHT. I WOULD OBJECT ON THE

BASIS OF THE FIFTH AMENDMENT. IF, IN FACT, HE ANSWERS, IT MAY INCRIMINATE HIM IF SHE WERE 16.

THE COURT: LADIES AND GENTLEMEN OF THE JURY, WE ARE NOW AT ANOTHER POINT IN THIS TRIAL WHEN I HAVE TO DISCUSS A MATTER WITH COUNSEL OUTSIDE YOUR HEARING. I WILL ASK YOU, PLEASE, TO WAIT OUTSIDE. THE JURY IS EXCUSED FOR THE MOMENT.

(THE FOLLOWING PROCEEDINGS WERE HAD IN OPEN COURT OUTSIDE THE PRESENCE OF THE JURY:)

THE COURT: THE JURY HAS NOT EXITED THE COURTROOM.

STATE THE BASIS FOR YOUR OBJECTION, MR. FLANK.

MR. FLANK: IT'S MY OPINION, YOUR HONOR, THAT IF MY CLIENT ANSWERS, THAT HE'S, IN FACT, HAD SEXUAL RELATIONS WITH A SECOND WIFE, THAT IS A CRIME IN THE STATE OF UTAH, AND SUCH ADMISSION COULD REQUIRE HIM TO BE PUNISHED FOR THAT CRIME. SHE WAS LIKEWISE 16 YEARS OF AGE AT THAT TIME, A MINOR, AND COULD BE LIKEWISE A CRIME FOR CONTRIBUTING TO THE DELINQUENCY OF A MINOR. I BELIEVE AT THAT TIME, IT WOULD HAVE BEEN CARNAL KNOWLEDGE, ALSO A CRIME AS I RECALL THE LAW AT THAT POINT IN TIME, ANYONE UNDER 17, AND I OBVIOUSLY KNOW WHAT HIS ANSWER IS GOING TO BE.

THE COURT: MR. RYAN, DO YOU WISH TO RESPOND TO THAT?

MR. RYAN: ONLY TO SAY THAT I FEEL THAT THIS ENTIRE LINE OF QUESTIONING IS VERY RELEVANT TO OUR CASE, THE EMOTIONAL DISTRESS.

THE COURT: THE QUESTION ISN'T IF IT'S RELEVANT; THE QUESTION IS IF YOU HAVE A RESPONSE TO THE FIFTH AMENDMENT CLAIM, TO THE FIFTH AMENDMENT RESPONSE TO ANSWER IN ANSWER TO YOUR QUESTION. IT IS TRUE THAT UNLAWFUL SEXUAL INTERCOURSE OF A FEMALE UNDER THE AGE OF 16 YEARS IS, IN FACT, A THIRD DEGREE FELONY. THE PRIVILEGE OF SELF-INCRIMINATION SET FORTH IN TITLE 78-24-09 WHEREIN IT ALLOWS A WITNESS TO ASSERT THE FIFTH AMENDMENT PRIVILEGE WHEN, IN FACT, THE CONDUCT COMPLAINED OF WOULD POTENTIALLY OR TEND TO SUBJECT THE WITNESS TO PUNISHMENT FOR A FELONY.

TO THE EXTENT THAT THERE IS ELICITED FROM THIS WITNESS TESTIMONY REGARDING INTERCOURSE WITH A FEMALE UNDER THE AGE OF 16, 16 OR YOUNGER, CERTAINLY THE ASSERTIONS AS TO QUESTIONS RELATING TO THAT CONDUCT, I RULE WOULD BE APPROPRIATELY ASSERTED.

THE QUESTION, HOWEVER, AS TO POTENTIALLY FORNICATION OR MORE LIKELY ADULTERY, ADULTERY IS A CLASS A MISDEMEANOR OR UNDER 76-7-103, I AM LOOKING AT THE MOMENT, POLYGAMY --

MR. FLANK: BOTH OF WHICH ARE FELONIES.

THE COURT: WHY DON'T YOU ASK YOUR WITNESS WHILE I'M LOOKING HERE, MR. FLANK, IF, INDEED, IT IS HIS DESIRE TO ASSERT THE PRIVILEGE OF SELF-INCRIMINATION.

MR. FLANK: IS IT YOUR DESIRE TO ASSERT

YOUR PRIVILEGE OF SELF-INCRIMINATION WITH REGARD
TO THE QUESTIONS?

THE WITNESS: YES.

THE COURT: ALL RIGHT, GENTLEMEN, THIS MAY
BE AN APPROPRIATE TIME FOR US TO TAKE ANOTHER
SHORT RECESS. IN THE MEANTIME I NOTE, MR. FLANK,
YOU HAVE RECEIVED A COPY OF THE CASE THAT HAS TO
DO WITH THE ISSUE THAT WAS PREVIOUSLY DISCUSSED.
LET'S TAKE A BRIEF RECESS, COUNSEL.

(A RECESS WAS TAKEN.)

THE COURT: THE JURY AND PARTIES AND
COUNSEL ARE PRESENT. YOU MAY CONTINUE, MR. RYAN.

MR. RYAN: THANK YOU. WOULD YOU READ
BACK THE LAST QUESTION, PLEASE?

(THE LAST PENDING QUESTION WAS READ BACK BY
THE REPORTER.)

Q   (BY MR. RYAN) I WILL JUST RESTATE THE
QUESTION. MR. KANDERHOSH, YOU SEDUCED MAY
HANCOCK APPROXIMATELY NINE MONTHS AFTER SHE
CAME TO LIVE WITH YOU IN APPROXIMATELY 1964, DIDN'T
YOU?

A   I REFUSE TO ANSWER ON THE GROUNDS OF THE
FIFTH AMENDMENT.

Q   IN FACT, FROM THAT TIME FORWARD, YOU
ENGAGED IN AN ONGOING SEXUAL RELATIONSHIP WITH
HER UNTIL --

A   STAND ON THE FIFTH.

Q   -- UNTIL YOU WERE MARRIED TO HER AT
APPROXIMATELY THE AGE OF 18. IS THAT CORRECT?

A   I REFUSE TO ANSWER THAT ON THE GROUNDS
IT MAY INCRIMINATE ME.

Q   NOW, YOU DID GO THROUGH A MARRIAGE
CEREMONY WITH MAY HANCOCK, DID YOU NOT, MR.
KANDERHOSH?

A   I REJECT ON THE FIFTH AMENDMENT.

Q   THAT WAS AT APPROXIMATELY THE AGE OF 18?
MAY HANCOCK WAS 18 YEARS OLD, IS THAT CORRECT?

A   I REFUSE TO ANSWER.

Q   FROM THAT POINT FORWARD, YOU LIVED WITH
MAY HANCOCK AS HER HUSBAND UNTIL 1982 WHEN SHE
LEFT, DID YOU NOT?

A   I REFUSE TO ANSWER ON THE FIFTH.

Q   NOW, MR. KANDERHOSH, IT'S TRUE, ISN'T IT,
THAT YOU HAD AS FAR AS MAY WAS CONCERNED, A
VORACIOUS SEXUAL APPETITE. IS THAT CORRECT?

A   I REFUSE TO ANSWER.

Q   IN FACT, YOU REQUIRED THAT SHE SATISFY
YOU SEXUALLY FOR A PERIOD FROM APPROXIMATELY
ONE-HALF HOUR TO THREE HOURS EACH AND EVERY
NIGHT. IS THAT CORRECT?

A   NO.

Q   FROM THE TIME THAT YOU MARRIED HER
UNTIL SHE LEFT IN 1982, IS THAT CORRECT?

A   I REJECT ON THE FIFTH.

Q   WHEN SHE ATTEMPTED TO REFUSE YOUR
ADVANCES, YOU TOLD HER THAT YOU WOULD PUT HER
DOWN TO THE LOWEST LEVEL OF YOUR FAMILY, LOWER
THAN A CONCUBINE, AND SHE WOULD BE MADE TO FEEL
IT, DIDN'T YOU?

A   NOT TRUE.

Q   YOU DID NOT EVER SAY THAT?

A   NO.

Q   DID YOU SAY ANYTHING LIKE THAT?

A   NO.

Q   DID YOU THREATEN HER IN ANY WAY, MR. KANDERHOSH?

A   NO.

Q   YOU TOLD HER THAT YOU HAD COMMUNICATIONS WITH PEOPLE ON THE OTHER SIDE, I MEAN, IN THE SPIRIT WORLD, DIDN'T YOU?

A   THAT'S UNTRUE. THAT'S UNTRUE.

Q   YOU BELONG TO A FUNDAMENTALIST SECT, DO YOU NOT, MR. KANDERHOSH?

A   I REFUSE TO ANSWER.

Q   DO YOU HOLD A PRIESTHOOD OFFICE IN THAT SECT?

A   REFUSE TO ANSWER.

Q   ISN'T ONE OF THE TENETS OF THAT SECT THAT THE WOMAN IS SUBSERVIENT TO THE MAN?

A   REFUSE TO ANSWER.

Q   THAT THE WOMAN IS REQUIRED TO DO ALL THINGS THAT HER HUSBAND TELLS HER TO DO? THAT'S CORRECT, ISN'T IT, MR. KANDERHOSH?

A   REFUSE TO ANSWER.

Q   IN FACT, YOU TOLD MAY THAT YOU HAD SO MUCH POWER THAT YOU HAD THE RIGHT TO DETERMINE WHETHER THE COUNCIL, THE HIGH COUNCIL HAD TOLD THE PEOPLE THE TRUTH OR NOT, DIDN'T YOU?

A   NO.

307

Q   YOU NEVER TOLD HER THAT?

A   (NO RESPONSE.)

Q   IN FACT, YOU TOLD HER THAT YOU WERE SO FAVORED IN THE SIGHT OF GOD THAT YOUR PATRIARCHAL BLESSING COULDN'T EVEN BE WRITTEN, DIDN'T YOU?

A   THAT'S UNTRUE.

Q   YOU TOLD HER ALSO THAT YOU HAD 500 WIVES IN THE SPIRIT WORLD WAITING FOR YOU?

A   UNTRUE.

Q   IN FACT, YOU TOLD MAY THAT YOU WERE HER GOD, IS THAT CORRECT?

A   THAT'S UNTRUE.

Q   AND THAT YOUR LITTLE KINGDOM THERE MADE UP OF NANAS AND ZOSA AND MAY THAT IS YOUR LITTLE KINGDOM, WASN'T IT?

MR. FLANK: YOUR HONOR, I OBJECT.

THE WITNESS: REFUSE TO ANSWER.

MR. FLANK: I OBJECT. I DON'T KNOW IF THAT'S A QUESTION.

THE COURT: WELL, HE'S REFUSED TO ANSWER.

Q   (BY MR. RYAN) NOW, YOU TOLD MAY THAT SHE WAS GIVEN TO YOU TO SATISFY YOUR SEXUAL NEEDS, DIDN'T YOU?

A   UNTRUE.

Q   THAT GOD GAVE HER TO YOU FOR THAT PURPOSE, DIDN'T YOU?

A   UNTRUE.

Q   YOU ALSO TOLD HER THAT SHE WOULD BE

DESTROYED IF SHE DIDN'T PERFORM THOSE FUNCTIONS FOR YOU?

A   UNTRUE.

Q   YOU ALSO TOLD HER THAT THE HIGH COUNCIL WOULD KICK HER OUT OF THE CHURCH IF SHE DIDN'T ACCEDE TO YOUR EVERY REQUEST?

A   UNTRUE.

Q   YOU TOLD HER THAT YOU HAD THE SAME POWERS THAT JOSEPH SMITH HAD, DIDN'T YOU?

A   UNTRUE.

Q   THAT WHATEVER YOU CURSED WOULD BE CURSED, AND THAT WHATEVER YOU BLESSED WOULD BE BLESSED, IS THAT CORRECT?

A   NO.

Q   YOU NEVER SAID THAT?

A   THAT'S UNTRUE.

Q   THAT'S UNTRUE? NOW, WHERE DID MAY SLEEP IN THE HOUSE, THE RED HOUSE?

A   I OBJECT ON THE FIFTH.

Q   SHE SLEPT IN YOUR BEDROOM, DIDN'T SHE, MR. KANDERHOSH?

A   I REJECT.

Q   IN YOUR BED, DIDN'T SHE?

A   REJECT ON THE FIFTH.

Q   EACH EVERY NIGHT VIRTUALLY, EACH AND EVERY NIGHT FOR A PERIOD OF APPROXIMATELY 18 YEARS, ISN'T THAT CORRECT?

A   UNTRUE.

Q   IN FACT, YOU CAUSED HER AND REQUIRED HER

TO PERFORM ALL KINDS OF ACTIVITIES THAT PLEASED
YOU, DIDN'T YOU?

A   NO.

Q   LIKE YOU MADE HER DANCE FOR YOU?

A   NO.

Q   YOU FORCED HER TO PERFORM FELLATIO UPON
YOU?

A   NO.

Q   YOU SHOWED HER PICTURES IN PORNOGRAPHIC
BOOKS AND REQUIRED HER TO DO THE ACTS THAT WERE
PHOTOGRAPHED IN THESE BOOKS, DIDN'T YOU?

A   NO.

Q   YOU DID THIS OVER A PERIOD ALMOST THE
ENTIRE PERIOD THAT MAY KANDERHOSH LIVED IN YOUR
HOME, DIDN'T YOU?

A   NO.

Q   YOU WOULD OFTEN WAKE HER IN THE MIDDLE
OF THE NIGHT, WOULDN'T YOU, MR. KANDERHOSH, BY
PULLING HER HAIR OR PULLING HER NOSE?

A   NO.

Q   AND FORCING HER TO ENGAGE IN SEXUAL
INTERCOURSE OR OTHER SEXUAL ACTIVITIES WITH YOU?

A   NO.

Q   YOU TOLD HER THAT PERFORMING SEXUALLY
FOR YOU WAS MUCH MORE IMPORTANT THAN HER
WORKING IN THE BUSINESS, DIDN'T YOU?

A   NO.

Q   YOU KNEW SHE HAD A BACK PROBLEM, DIDN'T
YOU?

A   YES.

Q   YOU KNOW HOW SHE GOT THAT BACK
PROBLEM, TOO, DON'T YOU, MR. KANDERHOSH?

A   SHE HAD IT WHEN SHE CAME.

Q   SHE DEVELOPED IT OVER TIME, DIDN'T SHE,
BECAUSE IN SLEEPING IN YOUR BED, YOU WOULD
REQUIRE THAT SHE SLEEP ONLY IN ONE SPECIFIC
POSITION AND OVER A PERIOD OF YEARS, THAT
DEVELOPED INTO A SEVERE BACK PROBLEM FOR HER?

A   UNTRUE.

Q   THAT'S ALL TRUE, ISN'T IT, MR. KANDERHOSH?

A   NO, IT ISN'T.

Q   YOU ALSO TOLD MAY THAT WHEN SHE
REFUSED AT TIMES TO ENGAGE IN THESE SEXUAL
ACTIVITIES WITH YOU, THAT IF YOU WERE UNSATISFIED
AND THEN WENT TO COMMIT ADULTERY WITH ANOTHER
WOMAN, THAT THAT ADULTERY WOULD BE ON MAY'S
HEAD. IS THAT CORRECT?

A   UNTRUE.

Q   YOU DIDN'T ALLOW MAY TO HAVE ANY
ASSOCIATION WITH ANY FRIENDS, DID YOU?

A   SHE HAD ALL KINDS OF ASSOCIATIONS.

Q   WITH WHOM, MR. KANDERHOSH?

A   JUST A LIST OF WITNESSES.

Q   JOSEPH MANDLEY?

A   YES.

Q   IN FACT, HE WAS HIRED TO COME AND WORK
OVER THERE ON THE BUSINESS, WASN'T HE?

A   UH-HUH (AFFIRMATIVE).

Q   BUT SHE DIDN'T SEE ANYBODY SOCIALLY, DID
SHE?

A   YES. SHE SAW JANE, JOSEPH ALL SHE WANTED
TO.

Q   SHE SAW HIM ANY TIME SHE WANTED?

A   UH-HUH (AFFIRMATIVE).

Q   YOU DIDN'T THREATEN HER THAT IF SHE WENT
OUT AND SAW THESE PEOPLE, THAT SHE WOULD BE
KICKED OUT OF THE FAMILY, DID YOU, MR.
KANDERHOSH?

A   NO.

Q   IN FACT, YOU WOULDN'T EVEN LET MAY GO TO
THE SYMPHONY WITH JANE? AT ONE TIME SHE ASKED
DURING A PERIOD OF ABOUT TEN YEARS, AND THAT WAS
THE ONLY THING SHE ASKED TO DO, WASN'T IT?

A   SHE ASKED IF SHE COULD HELP HER REMODEL
HER HOUSE. I LET HER DO IT.

Q   MAY DIDN'T HAVE A DRIVER'S LICENSE, DID
SHE, MR. KANDERHOSH?

A   NO.

Q   WHY WAS THAT?

A   IT WASN'T NECESSARY, AND SHE DIDN'T ASK
FOR ONE.

Q   SHE DID NOT ASK FOR ONE? ISN'T IT TRUE
THAT YOU SPECIFICALLY FORBID HER FROM HAVING A
DRIVER'S LICENSE?

A   NO, I DID NOT.

Q   AND THAT IS THE REASON FOR THAT, WAS SO
SHE WOULD NOT BE ABLE TO SEE WHAT THE OUTSIDE
LIFE WAS LIKE?

A   UNTRUE.

Q   YOU TOLD MAY THAT SHE WAS A SERVANT TO NANAS, DIDN'T YOU? DID YOU TELL MAY THAT?

A   YES.

Q   IN FACT, YOU TREATED HER LIKE A SERVANT TO NANAS, DIDN'T YOU?

A   YES.

Q   YOU REQUIRED HER TO BATHE AND PREPARE FOR BED NANAS VIRTUALLY EVERY NIGHT, DIDN'T YOU?

A   NOT EVERY NIGHT, NO.

Q   HOW OFTEN?

A   IT WASN'T VERY LONG. SHE ONLY DONE IT ABOUT TWO MONTHS.

Q   ONLY FOR TWO MONTHS? WHAT DID THIS ENTAIL?

A   HELPING TO BATHE AND STUFF OF THIS NATURE.

Q   RUBBING HER LEGS DOWN?

A   PUTTING ON HER SOCKS.

Q   HOW LONG DID THAT TAKE WHEN MAY PERFORMED THAT?

A   ABOUT AN HOUR.

Q   IN FACT, IT TOOK SOMETIMES AS LONG AS TWO OR THREE HOURS, DIDN'T IT, MR. KANDERHOSH?

A   I WOULDN'T SAY THAT.

Q   SOMETIMES IT DID, DIDN'T IT?

A   NOT TO MY RECALL.

Q   MR. KANDERHOSH, DO YOU RECALL WHEN THE BARREL BUSINESS COMMENCED? DO YOU REMEMBER WHEN IT STARTED?

A   I THINK IT STARTED AROUND '74.

313

Q DO YOU RECALL TELLING MAY THAT YOU THOUGHT IT WAS A BAD IDEA, THE BARREL BUSINESS?

A NO.

Q AND THAT SHE SHOULD NOT WASTE HER TIME ON IT?

A NO.

Q YOU NEVER TOLD HER THAT? YOU TOLD HER THAT YOU DIDN'T WANT ANYTHING TO DO WITH THE BARREL BUSINESS, DIDN'T YOU?

A NO, I DIDN'T.

Q AND THAT IF SHE DID ANYTHING AND MADE ANYTHING OUT OF IT, IT WAS HERS?

A I DIDN'T SAY THAT.

Q IF SHE FELL ON HER FACE, THAT THAT WAS HER PROBLEM. IS THAT CORRECT?

A THAT'S UNCORRECT.

Q NOW, DO YOU RECALL THE TESTIMONY OF MAY, THAT SHE SAID THAT IF SHE DIDN'T DO THE BOTTLES, I'M GOING BACK TO THE BOTTLE BUSINESS NOW, THAT THERE WOULD BE NO BOTTLE BUSINESS? DID YOU SAY THAT?

A YES, I DID.

Q THE REASON FOR THAT WAS THAT THERE WASN'T ANYBODY ELSE THERE TO WASH THESE BOTTLES, IS THAT RIGHT?

A THAT'S RIGHT.

Q AND MAY TOOK THAT BOTTLE BUSINESS OVER, DIDN'T SHE?

A YES, WITH THE HELP OF OTHERS.

Q FROM THAT POINT ONWARD, SHE DID APPROXIMATELY THREE-FOURTHS OF THE WORK THAT

314

WAS DONE IN THE BOTTLE BUSINESS, DIDN'T SHE?

A   NO.

Q   SHE DIDN'T? DID YOU HELP HER IN THAT
BUSINESS?

A   YES, I DID.

Q   I THOUGHT YOU WERE INCAPACITATED.

A   NOT AT THAT TIME.

Q   HOW WERE YOU ABLE TO HELP HER?

A   NOT AT THAT TIME, I WASN'T.

Q   WHO ELSE HELPED IN THE BUSINESS?

A   EDITH HELPED HER.

Q   THAT'S HER MOTHER, RIGHT?

A   YES.

Q   ANYONE ELSE?

A   WILL HELPED HER AT TIMES.

Q   WILL HELPED HER AT TIMES? HE BASICALLY
WAS OUT DRIVING THE TRUCK THOUGH, WASN'T HE?

A   AND NANAS HELPED HER TAKE OFF RINGS AND
LIDS.

Q   NOW, DO YOU RECALL EVER SAYING THAT IF IT
WEREN'T FOR MAY'S DILIGENCE IN THE BARREL
BUSINESS, AND I'M GOING BACK TO THE BARREL
BUSINESS NOW, THAT THERE WOULD BE NO BARREL
BUSINESS, THAT THE BARREL BUSINESS WOULD FOLD?

A   NO.

Q   IN FACT, YOU SAID THAT MANY, MANY TIMES
OVER A PERIOD OF ABOUT FIVE YEARS, DIDN'T YOU,
BEFORE SHE LEFT?

A   NO, I DIDN'T.

Q   YOU NEVER SAID THAT?

A   I SAID THAT AFTER I LEFT.

Q   YOU WERE VERY CONCERNED, WEREN'T YOU, ABOUT THE BARREL BUSINESS?

A   YES, I WAS CONCERNED.

Q   THE REASON YOU WERE CONCERNED IS BECAUSE YOU KNEW IT WOULD NOT RUN WITHOUT MAY, WEREN'T YOU?

A   WELL, POSSIBLY WE COULD TAKE CARE OF IT. WE COULD HAVE DONE AT THAT TIME, BUT NOT NOW.

Q   POSSIBLY YOU COULD TAKE CARE OF IT? WHO DO YOU MEAN?

A   WILL AND NANAS AND I.

Q   IN FACT, WILL HADN'T HAD ANYTHING TO DO WITH THE BARREL BUSINESS FOR YEARS, HAD HE?

A   HE WORKED QUITE A LONG WHILE AS A TRUCK DRIVER FOR HER.

Q   HOW MANY EMPLOYEES WERE IN THE BARREL BUSINESS IN 1982 WHEN MAY LEFT, DO YOU KNOW?

A   I THINK ABOUT SIX.

Q   DO YOU KNOW WHAT THE GROSS INCOME OF THAT BUSINESS WAS AT THAT TIME?

A   AROUND $80,000.

Q   DO YOU KNOW WHAT THE LABOR COSTS WERE ABOUT THAT TIME?

A   NO, I DON'T.

Q   DO YOU KNOW WHAT THE COSTS OF THE OTHER FIXED COSTS OF DOING BUSINESS WERE?

A   NO. I DIDN'T GET INTO IT.

Q   BUT YOU FELT LIKE YOU COULD STEP RIGHT IN THERE AND TAKE IT OVER AND RUN IT?

A   I FELT WILL WAS CAPABLE OF TAKING CARE OF
THE FINANCIAL END OF IT.

Q   NOW, DO YOU RECALL SAYING IN ABOUT 1980
OR '81 TO MAY, YOU HAVE EARNED EVERY BIT OF WHAT
YOU HAVE AND MORE, FAR MORE THAN I CAN EVER GIVE
YOU?

A   NO, THAT'S UNTRUE.

Q   YOU NEVER SAID THAT? I SUPPOSE IF I BRING
SOMEBODY IN TO SAY THAT YOU SAID THAT, THEN YOU
WOULD STILL PERSIST IN YOUR ANSWER?

THE COURT: WELL, THE QUESTION OF
CREDIBILITY OF ONE IS A JURY ISSUE, MR. RYAN, NOT
FOR THIS WITNESS TO COMMENT ON THE CREDIBILITY OF
THIS OTHER WITNESS.

MR. RYAN: IF I COULD TAKE JUST A MINUTE,
YOUR HONOR.

Q   (BY MR. RYAN) MR. KANDERHOSH, AT THE TIME
THAT MAY CAME TO LIVE IN YOUR FAMILY, AS SHE'S
TESTIFIED, IN 1964, DID YOU DISCUSS HER HAVING
CHILDREN?

A   NO.

Q   DID YOU AT ANY TIME FROM THAT TIME UNTIL
1982 DISCUSS HER HAVING CHILDREN WITH YOU?

A   NO.

Q   DID MAY EVER TELL YOU THAT SHE WISHED TO
HAVE CHILDREN?

A   NO.

Q   DID YOU EVER KEEP MAY FROM LEAVING THE
HOUSE SO YOU COULD FORCE HER TO ENGAGE IN
SEXUAL ACTIVITY WITH YOU?

A   NO.

Q   DO YOU RECALL REQUIRING MAY TO ENGAGE IN THESE DANCING AND OTHER ACTIVITIES THAT I HAVE PREVIOUSLY MENTIONED, AND THAT YOU WOULD MAKE HER DO IT OVER AND OVER AND OVER AGAIN UNTIL SHE GOT IT JUST RIGHT, AS YOU SAID?

MR. FLANK: YOUR HONOR, I WILL OBJECT. I THINK HE'S BEEN THROUGH THIS ABOUT 20 TIMES. HE'S EITHER OBJECTED ON THE FIFTH. IT'S EXACTLY THE SAME QUESTION HE'S ASKED BEFORE.

THE COURT: THE QUESTION REGARDING DANCING IS SUSTAINED.

Q   (BY MR. RYAN) AS TO ALL OTHER PARTS OF THE QUESTION, MR. KANDERHOSH, WHAT IS YOUR RESPONSE?

A   STAND ON THE FIFTH.

Q   ISN'T IT TRUE, MR. KANDERHOSH, THAT WITH REGARD TO THE BARREL BUSINESS THAT MAY GOT THE FIRST BARREL ACCOUNTS?

A   YES, I THINK SO.

Q   IN FACT, ALL OF THE NEW ACCOUNTS THAT WERE DEVELOPED THEREAFTER WERE DONE BY MAY AND MAY ALONE?

A   MOSTLY.

Q   ISN'T IT TRUE THAT SHE DESIGNED HERSELF AND MADE ALL OF THE EQUIPMENT IN THE BARREL BUSINESS, VIRTUALLY ALL OF IT?

A   WITH THE HELP OF ME AND JOSEPH MANDLEY.

Q   WITH THE HELP OF YOU AND JOE MANDLEY. WHAT DID YOU DO TO HELP, MR. KANDERHOSH?

318

A   HELPED IN THE DESIGN OF IT, OF THE
EQUIPMENT.

Q   NOW, YOU HAVE HEARD THE TESTIMONY ABOUT
THE CONVEYANCE OF THE PROPERTY TO MAY AND TO
WILL, HAVE YOU NOT?

A   YES.

Q   YOU WERE INVOLVED IN CONVERSATIONS
LEADING UP TO THAT, WERE YOU?

A   UH-HUH (AFFIRMATIVE).

Q   NOW, ISN'T IT TRUE, MR. KANDERHOSH, THAT
THE REASON THAT MAY WAS GIVEN THAT PROPERTY WAS
IN RECOGNITION OF TEN YEARS OF WORK THAT SHE HAD
GIVEN TO YOU AND YOUR FAMILY?

A   NO.

Q   WELL, WHY DID YOU GIVE IT TO HER THEN?

A   BECAUSE I LOVED HER, FOR ONE REASON, AND
THAT SHE SAID SHE WOULD TAKE CARE OF US FOR THE
REST OF OUR LIVES.

Q   NOW, MR. DARDSON HAS TESTIFIED ABOUT SOME
DEEDS THAT WERE MADE AT THE TIME MAY RECEIVED
HER DEEDS TO THE PROPERTY?

A   THAT'S TRUE.

Q   WHERE ARE THOSE, DO YOU KNOW?

A   I DON'T KNOW WHAT HAPPENED TO THEM.

Q   DO YOU KNOW IF THEY WERE EVER SIGNED?

A   YES, I SIGNED THEM.

Q   YOU SIGNED THE QUIT CLAIM DEEDS?

A   NO. MAY SIGNED THEM, AND WILL SIGNED
THEM.

Q   OH, MAY SIGNED THEM, BUT YOU DON'T KNOW

319

WHERE THEY ARE?

A   NO.

MR. RYAN: I HAVE NO FURTHER QUESTIONS AT
THIS TIME.

MR. FLANK: JUST A FEW.

<u>CROSS EXAMINATION</u>

<u>BY MR. FLANK:</u>

Q   MR. KANDERHOSH, DURING THE PERIOD FROM
THE TIME THE BOTTLE BUSINESS COMMENCED UNTIL MAY
LEFT, DID YOU WORK IN THE BUSINESS?

A   YES.

Q   WHAT DID YOU DO?

A   WELL, I ROLLED BARRELS AND STUFF LIKE THAT
WHEN THEY ARE PAINTING, MAINLY.

Q   DID YOU WORK RIGHT ALONG WITH MAY AND
WITH WILL AND WITH THE REST OF THE EMPLOYEES?

A   RIGHT ALONG WITH MAY.

Q   DID YOU WORK AS MANY HOURS AS MAY?

A   PRETTY CLOSE.

MR. RYAN: EXCUSE ME, YOUR HONOR. I
THINK THAT SINCE THIS IS HIS WITNESS, THAT HE
CANNOT LEAD THE WITNESS. AM I INCORRECT IN THAT?

THE COURT: WELL, HE IS CROSS EXAMINING
THE WITNESS THAT YOU CALLED.

MR. RYAN: OF COURSE, HE'S ADVERSE TO ME.

THE COURT: THAT IS TRUE. YOU CALLED HIM,
HOWEVER. YOU MAY CONTINUE, MR. FLANK.

Q   (BY MR. FLANK) BUT YOU WORKED IN THE
BUSINESS UP UNTIL SHE LEFT?

A   THAT'S RIGHT.

Q   DID SHE THEN SAY THAT YOU COULD NOT COME
BACK?

A   NO.

Q   YOU HAVE NOT WORKED IN THE BUSINESS
SINCE '82?

A   THAT'S RIGHT.

Q   YOU HAVE NOT RECEIVED ANY MONIES FROM
THAT BUSINESS SINCE MAY OF 1982?

A   THAT'S RIGHT.

Q   DID YOU ATTEMPT TO FIND THOSE QUIT CLAIM
DEEDS THAT HAD BEEN SIGNED BY MAY AND MR.
DARDSON WHEN SHE NO LONGER GAVE THE FAMILY
MONEY?

A   WE TRIED TO FIND THEM, BUT GARY THOUGHT
HE GAVE THEM TO MAY, BUT HE WASN'T SURE.

Q   YOU COULD NOT FIND THEM?

A   UNH-UNH (NEGATIVE).

Q   SO FROM THAT POINT, THE PROPERTY, SINCE
1975, HAS BEEN IN MAY'S NAME AND WILL'S NAME?

A   THAT'S CORRECT.

Q   BUT UP UNTIL '82, ALL MONIES FROM THE
PROPERTIES AND THE BUSINESS WENT INTO THE FAMILY?

A   THAT'S RIGHT.

Q   YOU HAVE NO INCOME AT THE PRESENT TIME?

A   I HAVE SOCIAL SECURITY.

Q   HOW MUCH DO YOU RECEIVE IN SOCIAL
SECURITY?

A   I DON'T KNOW EXACTLY WHAT IT IS.

Q   YOU DO GET SOME SOCIAL SECURITY?

A   YES.

321

Q   YOU HAVE HEARD THE TESTIMONY IN REGARD TO WHERE THE PROPERTY CAME, AND AT THE TIME YOU MARRIED NANAS, YOU HAD NOTHING, DID YOU?

A   THAT'S RIGHT.

Q   SHE OWNED ALL PROPERTY?

A   THAT'S RIGHT.

Q   SHE PUT THIS OVER IN YOUR NAME WITH HERS IN JOINT TENANCY?

A   YES, SIR.

Q   WAS THAT AT YOUR DEMAND? DID YOU TELL HER TO DO THAT?

A   NO.

Q   BUT SHE DID IT FOR YOU?

A   YES.

Q   DID YOU DEMAND THAT SHE TRANSFER THE PROPERTY TO WILL AND MAY?

A   YES.

Q   WHY?

A   BECAUSE THEY WERE YOUNGER AND THEY PROMISED TO TAKE CARE OF US.

MR. FLANK: THAT'S ALL I HAVE.

THE COURT: ANYTHING FURTHER, MR. RYAN?

MR. RYAN: VERY QUICKLY, JUDGE. NO, NOTHING FURTHER. I HAVE NOTHING FURTHER.

THE COURT: YOU MAY STEP DOWN, MR. KANDERHOSH. YOU MAY CALL YOUR NEXT WITNESS.

MR. RYAN: I CALL MAY HANCOCK.

THE COURT: MS. HANCOCK, YOU ARE STILL UNDER OATH.

MAY HANCOCK KANDERHOSH

CALLED AS A WITNESS BY AND ON BEHALF OF THE

DEFENDANT, HAVING BEEN PREVIOUSLY DULY SWORN,

WAS EXAMINED AND TESTIFIED FURTHER AS FOLLOWS:

DIRECT EXAMINATION

BY MR. RYAN:

Q   MAY, ARE YOU KNOWN BY ANY OTHER NAMES

THAN MAY?

A   YES, KAZIAH.

Q   DO PEOPLE CALL YOU KAZIAH?

A   I HAVE BEEN DOING SOME ART WORK SINCE I

LEFT, AND ALL MY ART WORK I HAVE BEEN SIGNING

KAZIAH.

Q   WHAT EDUCATIONAL BACKGROUND DO YOU

HAVE, MAY?

A   WELL, I DIDN'T FINISH THE EIGHTH GRADE.

Q   DID YOU FINISH THE SEVENTH?

A   YEAH.

Q   WHERE WAS THAT?

A   I DON'T KNOW WHAT THE NAME OF THE

SCHOOL WAS, BUT IT WAS IN MIDVALE.

Q   HAVE YOU TAKEN ANY OTHER COURSES FROM

ANY INSTITUTIONS SINCE THAT TIME?

A   (SHOOK HEAD NEGATIVELY.)

Q   YOU HAVE TO SPEAK. SHAKING YOUR HEAD

DOESN'T COME OUT. YOU HAVE TO SPEAK AUDIBLY.

A   I STARTED TO TAKE A HOME STUDY COURSE

FROM JORDAN HIGH SCHOOL, BUT BARD AND NANAS

TALKED ME INTO THE IDEA OF HELPING THEM IN THE

323

BUSINESS, AND HE TOLD ME THAT EDUCATION WAS A
BUNCH OF BALONEY.

MR. FLANK: YOUR HONOR, I WILL OBJECT
WITHOUT SOME FOUNDATION AS TO JUST GENERAL
REMARKS.

THE COURT: SUSTAIN.

Q   (BY MR. RYAN) ARE YOU PRESENTLY A
MEMBER OF ANY RELIGIOUS, ORGANIZED RELIGIOUS
GROUP?

A   YES.

Q   WHAT GROUP IS THAT?

A   THE DELRED GROUP.

Q   IS THAT A MORMON FUNDAMENTALIST GROUP?

A   YES.

Q   ARE MR. AND MRS. KANDERHOSH ALSO
MEMBERS OF THAT GROUP?

A   NO.

Q   ARE THEY MEMBERS OF ANY OTHER ORGANIZED
RELIGIOUS GROUP?

A   YES.

Q   WHAT GROUP?

A   I THINK PART OF THE TEASONDRITES.

Q   IS THAT ALSO A MORMON FUNDAMENTALIST
GROUP?

A   YES. THERE'S BEEN A LOT OF BREAK-OFFS.

Q   WERE YOUR PARENTS FUNDAMENTALISTS?

A   YES.

Q   WHAT IS YOUR PARTICULAR RELIGIOUS BELIEF
WITH REGARD TO PLURAL MARRIAGE?

324

A   WELL, I BELIEVE THAT IT'S A LAW OF GOD, AND
I BELIEVE THAT IT'S VERY IMPORTANT THAT IT BE
CONSIDERED IN A PERSON'S LIFE, AND THAT THEY DO
ALL THAT THEY CAN TO TRY TO LIVE ACCORDING TO THE
LAWS OF GOD THAT ARE TAUGHT THAT WAY.

Q   HOW LONG HAVE YOU BEEN TAUGHT THAT
PRINCIPLE?

A   SINCE THE DAY I WAS BORN.

Q   HOW IMPORTANT IS THAT TO YOU IN LIFE?

A   AS IMPORTANT AS LIFE ITSELF.

Q   WAS THERE EVER A TIME IN YOUR LIFE, SAY,
SINCE 1964, THAT IT WAS NOT THAT IMPORTANT?

A   SINCE 1964?

Q   HAS IT ALWAYS BEEN AS IMPORTANT SINCE
1964?

A   YES.

Q   DO YOU HAVE ANY BELIEFS WITH REGARD TO
AUTHORITIES OF A HUSBAND, FOR INSTANCE?

A   ARE YOU TALKING ABOUT THE WAY I BELIEVE
NOW OR THE WAY I BELIEVED THEN?

Q   THEN.

A   WELL, I --

Q   LET'S BE EVEN MORE SPECIFIC. AT THE TIME
YOU WENT TO LIVE IN MR. KANDERHOSH'S FAMILY, LET'S
TALK ABOUT YOUR BELIEFS THEN. WHAT ABOUT
AUTHORITY?

A   I BELIEVED THAT WHEN I WOULD GO TO
CHURCH, THEY WOULD TEACH THAT A MAN WAS
SUPPOSED TO BE THE RULER OF THE HOME, AND THAT
THE WOMAN WAS SUPPOSED TO OBEY THEM IN ALL

325

THINGS, AND THAT IF THEY WERE TAUGHT WRONG OR
ASKED TO DO SOMETHING WRONG, THAT AT THAT POINT,
ANY PUNISHMENT FROM GOD WOULD THEN COME UPON
THEIR HEAD FOR REQUIRING YOU TO DO IT, AND IF YOU
ARE IN OBEYANCE, THEN YOU WOULD GAIN YOUR
EXALTATION BY BEING OBEDIENT NO MATTER WHAT YOU
DO.

Q   DID YOU HAVE ANY DISCUSSIONS WITH MR.
KANDERHOSH BEFORE YOU WENT TO LIVE THERE IN 1964
ABOUT ANY OF THESE PRINCIPLES?

A   OH, YES.

Q   CAN YOU JUST GIVE US IN A VERY BRIEF WAY
WHAT WAS DISCUSSED?

A   THAT HE WAS TO BE THEIR RULER OF THE
HOME, THE LAW GIVER IN ALL THINGS, AND THAT I WAS
TO HAND ALL MY MONEY OVER TO HIM AND DO
WHATEVER WORK OR ANY TYPE OF A DUTY THAT HE
WOULD PLACE UPON ME.

Q   WHAT WERE YOU TO RECEIVE IN RETURN, IF
ANYTHING?

A   WELL, I HOPED THAT THROUGH IT ALL, THAT
GOD WOULD SEE THAT I HAD MORE DEVOTION FOR HIM
AND HIS PRINCIPLES THAN I DID FOR MY OWN SELF AND
MY OWN LIFE, AND I HOPED TO GAIN MY CALLING AND
ELECTION.

Q   DID YOU DISCUSS HAVING CHILDREN WITH MR.
KANDERHOSH?

A   OH, YES.

Q   WHEN DID YOU FIRST DISCUSS HAVING
CHILDREN?

326

A   WHEN WE FIRST DISCUSSED MARRIAGE.

Q   YOU WERE STILL 16 AT THE TIME?

A   YES.

Q   NOW, IF I UNDERSTAND THE PREVIOUS TESTIMONY, AND I WILL TRY TO CUT SOME OF THIS SHORT, YOU WENT TO LIVE THERE JUST BEFORE YOUR 16TH BIRTHDAY. IS THAT CORRECT?

A   RIGHT.

Q   BUT ACTUALLY WENT THROUGH A MARRIAGE CEREMONY WITH MR. KANDERHOSH NEAR YOUR 18TH BIRTHDAY, CORRECT?

A   RIGHT.

Q   NOW, WHAT HAPPENED WITH REGARD TO YOUR RELATIONSHIP WITH MR. KANDERHOSH BETWEEN THE TIME THAT YOU WENT TO LIVE THERE AND WHEN YOU ACTUALLY GOT MARRIED?

A   WELL, THROUGH HIS INFLUENCE, HE PERSUADED ME AND I WENT ALONG WITH THE IDEA OF HAVING PRE-MARITAL SEX, AND, OF COURSE, THERE WASN'T ANY CHILDREN TO DERIVE FROM THAT, BUT HE WANTED TO KEEP IT AWAY FROM THE REST OF THE FAMILY THAT HE WAS DOING THIS.

Q   HOW WOULD HE ACCOMPLISH THIS? WHERE DID YOU SLEEP AT THE TIME?

A   WELL, NAN DID NOT CARE IF WE SLEPT TOGETHER.

Q   WELL, WHERE DID YOU SLEEP? DID YOU HAVE YOUR OWN BEDROOM?

A   NO.

Q   WHERE DID YOU SLEEP? WHAT BEDROOM?

A   IN HIS BED. WHEREVER HE WAS AT, THAT'S
WHERE I SLEPT.

Q   WAS THAT SOMETIMES DIFFERENT BEDS? WAS
THAT ALWAYS IN THE SAME BEDROOM?

A   UNTIL HIS ROOM WAS CHANGED, LIKE
SOMETIMES DURING A PERIOD OF SO MANY YEARS, HIS
ROOM WOULD BE CHANGED FROM ONE ROOM TO
ANOTHER, BUT IT WAS DESIGNATED HIS BEDROOM, AND
THAT'S THE ONLY BED THAT I HAD TO SLEEP IN.

Q   NOW, WHEN YOU MARRIED MR. KANDERHOSH IN
ABOUT 1965, I GUESS, DID ANYTHING CHANGE? DID YOUR
RELATIONSHIP WITH HIM CHANGE IN ANY WAY?

A   NO, BUT HE WOULD PUT ME INTO WORKING IN
THE BUSINESS BEFORE THEN, BUT I WAS TO GO DO
HOUSEHOLD CHORES WHEN I FIRST CAME THERE, BUT
THEN LATER ON, AFTER WE WERE MARRIED, THEN HE
TOLD ME THAT IT WAS EXTREMELY NECESSARY THAT I
CONCENTRATE MY TIME AND MY EFFORTS IN THE
BUSINESS TO BRING IN THE INCOME, AND THAT IF I DID
NOT QUIT DOING HOUSEWORK, THAT I WOULD GO INTO
DISSOLUTION FOR DISOBEDIENCE, AND THERE WAS --

Q   WHAT'S DISSOLUTION?

A   WELL, THE WAY I UNDERSTOOD IT, IT WAS LIKE
WHERE SOMEONE HAS THE RIGHT OR THE POWER TO SEND
YOU INTO THE CONDITION OF DESTRUCTION OF THE BODY
AND SOUL.

Q   NOW, DID BARD SAY THAT HE HAD THE POWER
TO DO THIS?

A   OH, YES.

Q   DID BARD MAKE ANY OTHER STATEMENTS TO

328

YOU ABOUT HIS AUTHORITY, HIS RELIGIOUS
AUTHORITIES?

A   OH, YES.

Q   CAN YOU GIVE US AN IDEA OF WHEN HE
STARTED THOSE AND HOW LONG THEY WENT ON?

A   WELL, LIKE I SAID, HE SAID THAT HE WAS SUCH
A VALIANT PERSON THAT IN THE WORK OF THE LORD,
THAT HIS PATRIARCHAL BLESSING WAS SO PRECIOUS THAT
IT COULD NOT EVEN BE WRITTEN, AND HE SAID THAT HE
HAD AUTHORITY AND A POSITION IN GOD'S WORK THAT
WAS LIKE UNTO THAT OF THE PRIESTHOOD COUNCIL
THAT WOULD GIVE THE MEETING TO US ON SUNDAY,
ONLY HE SAID WHICH HE LOOKED AT AS APOSTLES, ONLY
HE SAID THAT HIS POSITION WAS OF THE NATURE THAT
HE COULD DETECT EVEN IF THEY WERE TEACHING WRONG
DOCTRINE, AND FOR US TO GET IT STRAIGHT WHAT THE
TRUTH WAS, WE WOULD HAVE TO GET HIS
INTERPRETATION WHEN WE GOT HOME FROM MEETING.

Q   DID YOU BELIEVE ALL THIS?

A   SORRY TO SAY, YES.

Q   WHEN DID HE START TELLING YOU THESE
THINGS ABOUT HIS AUTHORITY?

A   OH, WHEN I JUST INITIALLY FIRST MET HIM.

Q   HOW LONG DID THEY GO ON?

A   LIKE IN?

Q   THE STATEMENTS THAT HE WOULD MAKE
ABOUT RELIGIOUS AUTHORITY?

A   ON AND ON AND ON FOR YEARS. I MEAN, ALL
THE TIME.

Q   DID THEY GO UP UNTIL 1982 WHEN YOU LEFT?

A   OH, YES.

Q   WHAT ELSE DID HE TELL YOU ABOUT HIS AUTHORITY, HIS RELIGIOUS AUTHORITY?

A   WELL, HE TOLD ME THAT HE HAD A GIFT GIVEN HIM THAT'S LIKE UNTO THE GIFT THAT THE PROPHET JOSEPH SMITH HAD, THAT ANYTHING HE WOULD CURSE, GOD WOULD CURSE, ANYTHING HE WOULD BLESS, GOD WOULD BLESS, AND IT WOULD EXTEND THROUGH ALL ETERNITY.

Q   DID YOU BELIEVE THIS, MAY?

A   YES, I DID. I WAS AFRAID TO CROSS IT, BECAUSE THAT TO ME SOUNDED LIKE A LOT OF POWER.

MR. FLANK: YOUR HONOR, I OBJECT. SHE'S ANSWERED YES.

THE COURT: THE OBJECTION IS SUSTAINED. REMEMBER, MA'AM, ANSWER THE QUESTION ONLY.

Q   (BY MR. RYAN) WHAT ELSE DID HE STATE ABOUT HIS RELIGIOUS AUTHORITY? DID HE SAY HE HAD ANY OTHER POWERS?

MR. FLANK: YOUR HONOR, THAT'S LEADING.

THE COURT: IT IS LEADING. SUSTAINED.

Q   (BY MR. RYAN) DID HE SAY ANYTHING ABOUT BEING RELIGIOUS WISE? DID HE SAY ANYTHING ELSE HE HAD THE POWER TO DO?

A   HE SAID THAT HE IS MY LORD AND MASTER, AND THAT HE WOULD BE THE MAN THAT WOULD HOLD THE KEYS OF WHEN IF I GOT INTO MY ETERNAL EXALTATION OR NOT.

Q   DID YOU BELIEVE THAT?

A   YES.

330

Q   DID HE SAY ANYTHING ELSE?

A   HE SAID THAT I WAS TO DO WHATEVER HE WANTED NO MATTER WHAT IT WAS, AND THAT IF IT WAS WRONG, IT WOULD BE UPON HIS HEAD.

Q   DID HE PUT ANY LIMIT ON WHAT YOU WERE TO DO?

A   NO.

Q   NOW, YOU SLEPT IN HIS BED, YOU HAVE STATED. HOW LONG DID THIS GO ON?

A   FOR 18 YEARS.

Q   FOR 18 YEARS? DID YOU EVER TRY TO GET OUT OF THAT ARRANGEMENT AND SLEEP SOMEWHERE ELSE?

A   OH, YES.

Q   HOW OFTEN DID YOU DO THAT?

A   WELL, WHEN I HAD FIRST GOT MARRIED, I MEAN, BEFORE I EVEN GOT MARRIED, ONE NIGHT, I CAN'T REMEMBER THE REASON, BUT I SAID, WELL, I WOULD LIKE TO SLEEP IN SOME OTHER BED THAT WAS IN THE HOUSE, AND HE TOLD ME, HE SAYS, WHY? AND I SAID, I JUST WOULD LIKE TO, AND HE SAYS, WELL, ANYTIME THAT YOU GET TO WHERE YOU DON'T WANT TO SLEEP WITH ME, I WIL PUT YOU DOWN AS THE LOWEST PERSON IN MY FAMILY, AND YOU WILL BE MADE TO FEEL IT.

Q   WHEN DID THAT HAPPEN, MAY?

A   THAT WAS RIGHT AROUND THE TIME WE GOT MARRIED.

Q   DID MR. KANDERHOSH PUT MANY DEMANDS ON
YOU OF A SEXUAL NATURE?

A   OH, YES.

Q   GIVE US AN IDEA OF WHAT KIND OF DEMANDS
HE MADE UPON YOU.

A   OKAY, HE TOLD ME THAT BECAUSE I HAD A
BEAUTIFUL BODY, THAT IT WAS MY DUTY AND MISSION IN
LIFE TO TAKE CARE OF HIM SEXUALLY, AND THAT I
WOULD GET JUST AS HIGH A REWARD ON THE OTHER
SIDE AS IF I HAD CHILDREN. DO YOU WANT MORE?

Q   YES. I WANT YOU TO TELL ME WHAT OTHER
DEMANDS HE MADE UPON YOU.

A   AND I ASKED, BUT WHEN WILL I HAVE MY
CHILDREN, BECAUSE I LOVE CHILDREN --

MR. FLANK: YOUR HONOR, I WILL OBJECT, NOT
BY REASON, SHE'S NOT ANSWERING THE QUESTION. SHE
IS JUST RAMBLING.

THE COURT: WELL, IS YOUR OBJECTION
FOUNDATION OR WHAT?

MR. FLANK: YES, IT IS FOUNDATION AND
SIMPLY NO FOUNDATION WHATSOEVER WITH REGARD TO
WHEN THIS HAPPENED, WHO, WHY --

THE COURT: THE OBJECTION IS SUSTAINED.

Q   (BY MR. RYAN) WHEN DID THIS HAPPEN, MAY?
THE INCIDENT YOU ARE JUST DESCRIBING?

A   ABOUT WHEN I WANTED CHILDREN OR WHAT?

Q   YES.

Q   I WOULD ASK AT DIFFERENT PERIODS ALL THE
TIME, AND HE WOULD TELL ME THAT I HAD TO WAIT
UNTIL HE COULD BRING MORE WOMEN IN THE FAMILY TO

DO THE WORK IN THE BUSINESS SO I COULD GET
PREGNANT.

Q   WHEN DID THAT START?

A   IT WOULD PROBABLY BE RIGHT AFTER THE TIME
WE WERE MARRIED.

Q   HOW LONG DID IT GO ON?

A   UNTIL I LEFT.

Q   NOW, LISTEN TO MY QUESTION, WHAT KIND OF
DEMANDS, SEXUAL DEMANDS, DID HE MAKE ON YOU
DURING YOUR MARRIAGE?

A   SO YOU WANT A DESCRIPTION HERE AND NOW?

Q   YES.

A   OKAY, WHEN I WOULD FIRST COME IN THE
BEDROOM, HE SAYS, OKAY, WHEN YOU WALK IN THE
DOOR, I WANT YOU TO WALK IN AND COME OVER AND
PUT ON SOME FANCY PANTS. OKAY, THEN -- HOW FAR
OF A DETAILED DESCRIPTION DO YOU WANT?

Q   I WANT YOU TO JUST DESCRIBE WHAT
HAPPENED, MAY. IT'S IMPORTANT.

A   COULD WE MAYBE TAKE A BREAK FOR A FEW
MOMENTS?

THE COURT: COUNSEL APPROACH THE BENCH.

(A BENCH CONFERENCE WAS HELD, NOT REPORTED.)

Q   (BY MR. RYAN) MAY, DID BARD REQUIRE
ANYTHING OF YOU THAT WAS DEVIANT IN NATURE? DO
YOU KNOW WHAT I MEAN BY DEVIANT?

A   YES. THAT'S PUTTING IT MILD.

Q   TELL ME WHAT HE REQUIRED OF YOU THAT WAS
DEVIANT.

A   WELL, HE WOULD GET PICTURES FROM THESE GIRLIE BOOKS, AND HE WOULD SHOW THEM TO ME AND SAY, OKAY, THIS IS WHAT I WANT YOU TO DO FOR ME, AND I WOULD LOOK AT THAT AND SAY, WELL, I DON'T WANT TO DO THAT, AND HE WOULD SAY, WELL, THAT'S WHAT YOU HAVE TO DO. THAT'S WHAT YOU HAVE TO DO BEFORE I AM SATISFIED.

Q   DID YOU THEN DO THAT FOR HIM?

A   NOT RIGHT OFF, NO.

Q   HOW DID IT MAKE YOU FEEL BEING FORCED OR REQUESTED TO DO THAT?

A   LOWER THAN THE WORST SCUM OR SLIME ON THE GROUND.

Q   WHEN DID THIS FIRST START?

A   HE MAINLY GOT INTO REALLY DEMANDS AFTER I HAD STARTED THE BARREL BUSINESS ABOUT HIM NOT HELPING ME. HE HAD MORE TIME TO JUST --

THE COURT: THE QUESTION, MA'AM, WAS WHEN DID IT START. THAT WAS ABOUT --

THE WITNESS: OKAY, LET ME ASK THIS QUESTION, WHEN DID WHAT START?

Q   (BY MR. RYAN) WHEN DID THIS REQUEST FOR DEVIANT SEXUAL BEHAVIOR START?

A   IT WAS MAINLY AT THE TIME AFTER I STARTED THE BARREL BUSINESS THAT IT AS REALLY OPPRESSIVE AND EXTREMELY WICKED IN ITS NATURE.

Q   THAT WAS IN WHAT YEAR?

A   APPROXIMATELY '77, '78.

Q   HOW LONG DID IT CONTINUE?

A   UNTIL I LEFT.

Q   OTHER THAN WHAT YOU HAVE DESCRIBED, WERE
ANY OTHER DEMANDS OF A DEVIANT SEXUAL NATURE
MADE OF YOU BY BARD?

A   OH, YES.

Q   WHAT WERE THOSE?

A   THERE'S SOME STUFF THAT I AIN'T NEVER
TELLING NOBODY, NOT EVEN MY BEST FRIENDS.

Q   WELL, TELL WHAT YOU CAN.

A   OKAY, WELL -- I CAN'T TELL YOU.

The thought of exposing what I had gone through in front of the
whole courtroom full of people was greater than I could bear. I looked
around me and felt such shame, as though someone was about to dump
a bucket of black tar upon me. I sat trembling. My mouth could not
speak to reveal the offenses that were of such a nature that I had
never told anyone. Some things are not even written in this book. I
fought to control myself. Drying my eyes and steadying my voice, I
proceeded to utter words from a tormented soul.

Q   JUST TRY TO ANSWER MY QUESTION.

A   WELL, THIS HERE WHERE HE WOULD SAY, OKAY,
YOU COME IN THE ROOM A CERTAIN WAY. YOU LIFT
YOUR DRESS A CERTAIN WAY. YOU PUT ON YOUR PANTS
A CERTAIN WAY. YOU TURN AROUND, AND YOU LIFT
YOUR LEGS A CERTAIN WAY WHILE I'M WATCHING YOU,
AND HE WOULD BE LAYING THERE MANIPULATING HIS
BODY, AND HE WOULD SAY, OKAY, LAY DOWN, AND THEN
WE WOULD HAVE INTERCOURSE, AND HE WOULD SAY,
OKAY, GET UP AGAIN, AND HE WOULD SAY, NOW, I WANT
YOU TO -- IT WOULD BE ALMOST THE SAME TYPE OF A
RITUAL TYPE THING ON AND ON AND ON. I WOULD HAVE
TO DO THIS, AND THEN I WOULD HAVE TO LAY DOWN
AND THEN HAVE AN AFFAIR, AND THEN HE WOULD PULL

335

OUT, AND THEN HE WOULD RELAX, AND THEN HE WOULD
SAY, NOW, GET UP AND WORK ME UP AGAIN. ON AND ON
AND ON.

Q   NOW, THIS WENT ON FOR A PERIOD OF ABOUT
'77 UNTIL YOU LEFT?

A   THIS HAPPENED AFTER OUR MARRIAGE, BUT IT
GOT TO WHERE IT WAS TREMENDOUSLY OBSESSIVE
DURING THAT TIME OF '77 UNTIL I LEFT, YES.

Q   NOW, IS THERE ANY WAY OF STATING APPROX-
IMATELY HOW LONG THIS WENT ON DURING REGULAR
ROUTINE NIGHT OR DAY?

A   OKAY, NOW, LIKE WHEN THE ALARM WOULD
RING AND THAT WOULD WAKE HIM UP, SO I WOULD HAVE
TO DO THIS FOR ABOUT ANYWHERE FROM A HALF AN
HOUR TO AN HOUR AND A HALF IN THE MORNING. MOST
OF THE TIME, IT WAS LIKE A HALF AN HOUR, AND THEN
AT NIGHT WHEN I WOULD COME IN, I WOULD HAVE TO GO
THROUGH THIS, AND THIS WOULD BE THE TIME -- IT
WOULD BE MORE LIKE AN HOUR TO AN HOUR AND A
HALF, AND THEN HE WOULD WAKE ME UP THEN AROUND
2:00 OR 3:00 IN THE MORNING TO GET UP AND DO THE
THINGS FOR ABOUT A HALF AN HOUR, AND YOU BET, I
WOULD HAVE TO WAKE UP.

Q   IF YOU WOULDN'T WAKE, UP, WHAT WOULD
HAPPEN?

A   HE WOULD KICK ME, AND HE WOULD KEEP
KICKING ME AND YANKING ON MY NOSE AND SHAKING MY
ARM, SAYING, COME ON, GET. YOU GOT TO GET UP AND
TAKE CARE OF ME. WHO COULD SLEEP? YOU GET SO
DEAD TIRED, JUST NOTHING --

336

MR. FLANK: YOUR HONOR, I WILL OBJECT. SHE'S --

THE COURT: THE OBJECTION IS SUSTAINED. MA'AM, JUST ANSWER THE QUESTION. TRY NOT TO VOLUNTEER.

Q (BY MR. RYAN) DID THESE THINGS HAVE ANY EFFECT ON YOUR EMOTIONAL WELL-BEING, MAY?

A OH, YEAH.

Q TELL ME WHAT EFFECT, AND TRY TO BE AS SUCCINCT AS POSSIBLE. TELL ME WHAT EFFECTS THIS HAD ON YOU.

A IT MADE ME FEEL LIKE I WAS JUST THE MOST DISGRACED DEGRADABLE DESECRATED, JUST LIKE MY BODY WAS JUST NOTHING, LIKE I HAD NOT PRIDE, NO-- WHAT'S THE WORD, VIRTUE, PRIDE, SELF -- WHAT DO YOU CALL IT?

Q RESPECT?

A YES, RESPECT.

Q NOW, YOU WERE WORKING IN THE BARREL BUSINESS AT THIS TIME, WERE YOU NOT?

A YES.

Q HOW MUCH TIME DID YOU ROUTINELY SPEND EVERY DAY IN THE BARREL BUSINESS, MAY?

A WELL, I WOULD GET UP AT 5:00 O'CLOCK IN THE MORNING, AND I WOULD WORK UNTIL 10:00 O'CLOCK AT NIGHT.

Q LET ME GO BACK TO THE BOTTLE BUSINESS SO I CAN ESTABLISH A COUPLE OF THINGS THERE. YOU HAVE HEARD THE TESTIMONY THAT'S HERE, THAT'S BEEN MADE PREVIOUSLY. HOW MUCH MONEY WAS BEING MADE

337

IN THE BOTTLE BUSINESS WHEN YOU ARRIVED THERE IN ABOUT 1964?

A   ABOUT FOUR TO FIVE DOLLARS A DAY.

Q   DID THAT CHANGE ANY DURING THE NEXT TIME PERIOD?

A   OH, YEAH, BECAUSE WHEN NANAS GOT HIT, AND THEN I HAD TO TAKE IT OVER, SHE WASHED BOTTLES UP UNTIL THE TIME SHE GOT HIT, EVEN IF IT WAS ONLY 100 CASES A WEEK, SHE STILL DID IT.

Q   DID THERE COME A TIME WHEN THE BOTTLE BUSINESS STARTED TO PRODUCE SUBSTANTIALLY MORE INCOME?

A   OH, YES.

Q   WHEN WAS THAT?

A   BECAUSE, SEE --

Q   NO, WHEN WAS IT?

A   ABOUT A MONTH AFTER I HAD STARTED WASHING THEM.

Q   WHY WAS THAT INCREASE IN INCOME?

A   BECAUSE I HAD A YOUNGER BODY AND COULD DO MORE.

Q   HOW MANY BOTTLES DID YOU WASH A DAY?

A   A HUNDRED CASES.

Q   A HUNDRED CASES OF BOTTLES? WHAT IS A CASE?

A   IT'S FOUR GALLON JUGS.

Q   FOUR HUNDRED BOTTLES IS A HUNDRED CASES?

A   YES.

Q   HOW LONG WOULD IT TAKE YOU TO DO A HUNDRED CASES?

A   APPROXIMATELY FIVE HOURS.

Q   NOW, DID THERE COME A POINT -- WHAT'S THE METHOD THAT YOU DID IN THE BARREL BUSINESS OR IN THE BOTTLE BUSINESS, EXCUSE ME?

A   WELL, ARE YOU TALKING TIME PERIODS AGAIN NOW?

Q   WELL, YES, AT ANYTIME, I JUST WANT TO KNOW WHAT WAS THE HIGHEST INCOME --

A   OKAY, THE HIGHEST WAS WHEN THEY CONTACTED A COMPANY NAMED SPRING HILLS DISTILLED WATER, AND WITH THAT COMPANY, THE WHOLE TERM OF THE DEAL WAS THAT WE WERE TO PICK UP THE LOAD, BRING IT TO OUR PLACE, RETURN THE BOTTLES WHEN WE WERE THROUGH, JUST THE WATER TO REMOVE THE LABEL AND ANYTHING THAT WAS REALLY OF A FILTHY NATURE THAT WOULDN'T WASH OFF JUST WITH HOT WATER OR CAUSTIC RINSE AFTER THAT, BECAUSE, SEE, THEY WOULD WASH THEM AFTERWARD. WE WOULD JUST MAINLY REMOVE THE LID, THE RING, THE LABEL, AND ANYTHING THAT WAS OBVIOUSLY BAD.

Q   NOW, HOW MUCH INCOME WAS THE BUSINESS PRODUCING UNDER THAT HILLS CONTRACT?

A $32 A DAY.

Q   THAT'S WHAT, TWO HUNDRED CASES?

A   YES.

Q   IS THERE ANY WAY OF STATING HOW MUCH PERCENTAGEWISE WORK WAS BEING DONE BY YOU AS

OPPOSED TO WILL, AS OPPOSED TO BARD IN THAT BOTTLE
BUSINESS?

A   WELL, WILL WOULD DO SOME OF THE PICK-UP
AND DELIVERY ON SPRING HILLS, BUT HE HAD THE OTHER
BOTTLES --

THE COURT: MA'AM, THE QUESTION IS, CAN
YOU STATE A PERCENTAGE? IF YOU CAN'T, SAY SO.

THE WITNESS: OKAY, LET ME THINK.

Q   (BY MR. RYAN) WOULD IT BE EASIER TO STATE
THE NUMBER OF HOURS PER DAY WORKED BY
EVERYBODY ON A ROUTINE DAY?

A   OH, CAN I THINK?

Q   SURE.

A   OKAY, I WOULD SAY THAT I WAS DOING
APPROXIMATELY 60 PERCENT OF ALL LABOR IN THE
BOTTLE BUSINESS DURING THAT PERIOD OF TIME.

Q   WHO WAS PERFORMING THE OTHER 40?

A   WILLER WAS PERFORMING THE OTHER. HE
WOULD PERFORM ABOUT 25, AND BARD ABOUT 15.

Q   NOW, YOU WORKED IN THE BARREL BUSINESS
FOR ABOUT TEN YEARS, DID YOU NOT?

A   BARREL BUSINESS?

Q   OR THE BOTTLE BUSINESS?

A   YES.

Q   NOW, DURING THAT TIME, WERE YOU PAID ANY
WAGES?

A   NO.

Q   DID YOU RECEIVE ANYTHING FOR YOUR
LABORS IN THE BOTTLE BUSINESS? HOW ABOUT
CLOTHING?

340

A   MY CLOTHES WERE BOUGHT AT D.I.

Q   BY WHOM?

A   WELL, I WOULD GET TO GO AND PICK OUT MY CLOTHES AT DESERET INDUSTRIES, YEAH.

Q   DID YOU RECEIVE ANYTHING ELSE FOR WORKING THERE?

A   NO, BUT EVENTUALLY I GOT TO BUY NEW BOOTS INSTEAD OF JUST WEARING STUFF I WOULD FIND OUT TO THE DUMP.

Q   SO YOU DID NOT RECEIVE ANYTHING OTHER THAN CLOTHING? I MEAN, I ASSUME YOU ATE MEALS IN THE HOUSE?

A   YEAH, RIGHT.

Q   WERE YOU PAID ANY AMOUNTS IN CASH AT ALL?

A   NO.

Q   NOT FOR THAT ENTIRE TEN YEARS?

A   NO.

Q   NOW, YOU HAVE HEARD THE TESTIMONY THAT'S GONE ON PREVIOUSLY RELATING TO THE PROPERTY, THE DIVISION OF PROPERTY, HAVE YOU NOT?

A   OH, YES.

Q   DID YOU HAVE ANY DISCUSSIONS WITH BARD ABOUT THAT, ABOUT ACQUIRING PROPERTY, GETTING THAT PROPERTY FROM NANAS AND BARD?

MR. FLANK: YOUR HONOR, I WOULD OBJECT. I THINK THIS SAME THING WAS GONE OVER THIS MORNING. SHE HAS ALREADY ANSWERED THOSE EXACT SAME QUESTIONS THIS MORNING. SHE SAID IT WAS HER IDEA, EXACTLY THE SAME QUESTION THIS MORNING.

THE COURT: MR. RYAN, DO YOU WISH TO RESPOND TO THAT?

MR. RYAN: WELL, I DON'T RECALL IF I HAD GONE OVER THIS OR NOT. IF I HAVE, I APOLOGIZE TO THE COURT. I DON'T RECALL.

THE COURT: WELL, BECAUSE OF THE PROCEDURE, THAT IS, THIS WITNESS BEING CALLED TWICE NOW, IT SEEMS TO ME THAT COUNSEL'S OBJECTION IS FAIRLY WELL TAKEN, AND IT SHOULD BE SUSTAINED. I THINK WE HAVE CROSSED THIS GROUND BEFORE.

MR. RYAN: I WILL AVOID THAT, JUDGE.

Q (BY MR. RYAN) MAY, NOW, I'M TALKING ABOUT THE ENTIRE TIME PERIOD THAT YOU HAVE LIVED WITH MR. KANDERHOSH UP UNTIL 1982, AND PARTICULARLY FROM THE TIME THE BARREL BUSINESS WAS INCORPORATED UNTIL 1982. WHAT KIND OF FREEDOMS DID YOU HAVE IN THE HOME?

A I HAD THE RIGHT TO CONTACT COMPANIES AND TO WORK IN THE BUSINESS AND TO DO STUFF FOR THE FAMILY, LIKE COOKING AND THAT, AND TAKE CARE OF NAN IN THE MORNING AND EVENING AND TAKE CARE OF HIM SEXUALLY, AND THAT'S ABOUT IT.

Q NOW, YOU TOOK, YOU SAY, CARE OF NAN?

A YES.

Q WHAT DO YOU MEAN BY THAT?

Q OKAY, I MEAN THAT IT WAS MY DUTY AFTER SHE HAD HER ACCIDENT.

Q THIS IS IN 1964?

342

A   YEAH. OKAY, SHE CAME HOME FROM THE
HOSPITAL, AND SHE HAD TO HAVE SOMEBODY TO HELP
HER DRESS AND UNDRESS IN THE MORNING AND NIGHT.
LET'S PUT IT THIS WAY, OKAY, LIKE IN THE EVENING,
UNDRESS, OKAY, PUT ON HER NIGHT CLOTHES, MASSAGE
HER ON HER HIP AND HER BRUISE ON HER LEG AND
MASSAGE HER FEET AND LEGS AND MASSAGE HER BACK.
I LEARNED HOW TO BE A PRETTY GOOD CHIROPRACTOR,
AND SHE ENJOYED THAT. SO THAT WAS MY NIGHT
DUTIES ON THAT, TO PUT HER TO BED, AND THEN IN THE
MORNING, IT WAS MY DUTY TO, WHEN SHE GOT UP,
HELP GIVE HER A BATH AND THEN DRESS HER, AND
THEN THAT'S IT.

Q   THIS STARTED IN 1964?

A   YES.

Q   HOW LONG DID IT GO ON?

A   THIRTEEN YEARS.

Q   THIRTEEN YEARS? YOUR TESTIMONY IS THAT
YOU DID IT DAY AND NIGHT EVERY DAY FOR 13 YEARS?

A   IF THERE WAS EVEN FIVE DAYS IN 13 YEARS
THAT I DIDN'T DO IT, THAT WOULD BE STRETCHING IT.

Q   HOW MUCH TIME WOULD THIS TAKE ON YOUR
ROUTINE OR REGULAR EVENING?

A   THIS WOULD TAKE ANYWHERE FROM 45
MINUTES TO AN HOUR AND A HALF.

Q   HOW ABOUT IN THE MORNING?

A   BUT IT WOULDN'T TAKE THAT MUCH EVERY
NIGHT.

Q   HOW ABOUT IN THE MORNING?

A   APPROXIMATELY A HALF AN HOUR, 45

MINUTES.

Q   DID YOU HAVE ANY FRIENDS OUTSIDE OF THE
FAMILY?

A   ONE.

Q   WHO WAS THIS?

A   JANE.

Q   WHAT'S JANE'S LAST NAME?

A   BROOKS.

Q   DID YOU HAVE MUCH CONTACT WITH HER?

A   NO, BECAUSE WHEN I WOULD BE TALKING TO
HER AND BARD WOULD FIND OUT IT WAS TALKING TO
HER, HE WOULD HANG UP, JUST HANG UP.

MR. FLANK: YOUR HONOR, I OBJECT. SHE'S
NOT ANSWERING THE QUESTION.

THE COURT: MS. HANCOCK, WHEN AN
OBJECTION IS MADE, YOU MUST STOP TALKING. THE
REPORTER CAN HEAR ONE AT A TIME.

THE OBJECTION IS SUSTAINED.

Q   (BY MR. RYAN) DID ANYONE DO ANYTHING TO
STOP YOU FROM HAVING A RELATIONSHIP WITH JANE?

A   OH, YES.

Q   WHO?

A   BARD.

Q   WHAT DID HE DO?

A   HE TOLD HER THAT IF I COULD NOT BE MORE
OBEDIENT TO HIM, THAT --

MR. FLANK: YOUR HONOR, I WOULD OBJECT.
IT'S SOMETHING THAT WOULD BE HEARSAY, SOMETHING
HE TOLD JANE. I WOULD WANT FOUNDATION.

THE COURT: THE OBJECTION AS TO

FOUNDATION IS SUSTAINED.

Q (BY MR. RYAN) WERE YOU PRESENT DURING
ANY CONVERSATIONS WHERE BARD TOLD JANE WHAT --

A YES, I WAS.

Q PLEASE TELL US WHEN THAT CONVERSATION-
OCCURRED, WHEN ONE OF THEM, THE FIRST ONE DID.

A HE TOLD HER THAT BECAUSE --

Q WHEN?

A OH, WHEN?

Q YES.

A WHAT YEAR? APPROXIMATELY '81.

Q WHO WAS PRESENT DURING THE
CONVERSATION?

A BARD, JANE AND MYSELF.

Q WHAT WAS SAID AND BY WHOM?

A BARD TOLD HER THAT IF I COULDN'T SHOW
MORE OBEDIENCE TO HIM, THAT HE WOULD RATHER THAT
SHE DID NOT COME ON THE PLACE, THAT HE FELT LIKE
SHE WAS A BAD INFLUENCE ON ME, TO OFFEND HER TO
WHERE SHE WOULDN'T COME AND SEE ME, SO JUST IN A
CONTENTION FEELING THERE.

Q DID THAT HAPPEN MORE THAN ONCE?

A OH, YES.

Q HOW MANY TIMES DID IT HAPPEN DURING THE
NEXT SEVERAL YEARS, SAY?

A WELL, LIKE WHEN SHE CAME AND ASKED ME IF
I COULD GO IN --

Q NO, HOW MANY TIMES DID IT HAPPEN DURING
THE NEXT SEVERAL YEARS?

A OH, GUESSING, I WOULD SAY THREE OR FOUR,

FIVE TIMES, SOMEWHERE IN THERE.

Q   DID YOU HAVE A DRIVER'S LICENSE PRIOR TO 1982?

A   NO.

Q   DID YOU ASK FOR A DRIVER'S LICENSE?

A   OH, YES.

Q   WHOM DID YOU ASK FOR THE DRIVER'S LICENSE?

A   BARD.

Q   WHAT WAS HIS RESPONSE?

A   HE SAYS, NO. HE SAYS, I CAN TAKE YOU OR WILL OR I CAN TAKE YOU ANYWHERE YOU NEED TO GO. YOU DON'T NEED ONE.

Q   WHEN DID YOU FIRST ASK FOR A DRIVER'S LICENSE?

A   THAT WOULD BE HARD TO SAY.

Q   WHAT'S YOUR BEST ESTIMATE OF WHEN THAT WAS? WAS IT WHEN YOU WERE 16 --

MR. FLANK: IT'S LEADING.

THE WITNESS: PROBABLY NOT.

THE COURT: WELL, IT IS LEADING, QUITE FRANKLY. I THINK YOU HAVE GOTTEN ALL YOU CAN OUT OF THAT. LET'S MOVE ON.

MR. RYAN: EXCUSE ME JUST A MINUTE, JUDGE.

THE WITNESS: EXCUSE ME. CAN I SAY ONE ANSWER TO THAT, THOUGH?

THE COURT: NO, MA'AM. WAIT UNTIL THERE'S A QUESTION PENDING.

Q   (BY MR. RYAN) MAY, WHOSE IDEA WAS THE

BARREL BUSINESS?

    A   IT WAS MINE.

    Q   WHY DO YOU SAY THAT?

    A   BECAUSE AFTER THE PROPERTY HAD BEEN TURNED OVER TO WILL AND I, I WAS TRYING TO DO EVERYTHING THAT I COULD TO GENERATE THE BUSINESS, AND I MADE MASSIVE CALLS ON ALL KINDS OF ACCOUNTS THAT MIGHT BE POSSIBLE BOTTLES, AND IT WAS JUST A DRY RUN, JUST GOING OUT THERE TO FIND WHAT I COULD FIND. I WOULD GO LOOKING DESPERATELY FOR SOMETHING TO DO IN THE WAY OF THIS TYPE OF A CLEANING OF SOMETHING.

    Q   WHAT DID YOU FIND, IF ANYTHING?

    A   ONE OF THE COMPANIES THAT I WASHED BOTTLES FOR YEARS, HE ASKED ME, HE SAID, MAY, DO YOU KNOW WHERE I CAN GET ANY --

    MR. FLANK: YOUR HONOR, I WILL OBJECT. THIS IS HEARSAY.

    MR. RYAN: IT'S NOT OFFERED FOR THE TRUTH OF IT.

    MR. FLANK: WELL, IT IS --

    THE COURT: WELL, IT'S TIME FOR US TO TAKE OUR RECESS. HOW MUCH MORE TIME DO YOU ANTICIPATE, MR. RYAN, ON DIRECT EXAMINATION?

    MR. RYAN: NOT MORE THAN 15 MINUTES, I WOULD SAY.

    THE COURT: ALL RIGHT, LADIES AND GENTLEMEN, WE WILL TAKE UP WHERE WE LEFT OFF IN THE MORNING AT 9:30. I WILL ASK YOU ALL TO BE BACK HERE AT 9:30 IN THE MORNING. REMEMBER THE

347

ADMONITION I HAVE GIVEN YOU TO KEEP AN OPEN MIND
UNTIL YOU HAVE HEARD ALL THE EVIDENCE.

COURT WILL BE IN RECESS UNTIL 9:30 IN THE
MORNING.

After the first day of trial, my attorney said, "I need to talk with you." So we met where we could be in private and he said, "Do you realize that if the jury decides in their behalf, you stand a chance of losing everything? I think you ought to consider a settlement because the way it stands, you could lose everything."

"Well, I'll think about it and pray about it and let you know in the morning."

"Yes, you do that. Think real hard, won't ya'?"

So I went home and thought about it and prayed about it and a cold chill ran through me. Give them more besides what they have stolen from Mother and me? I could never sanction that.

I went back to Brent's office the next morning. He said, "Well, did you think about it?"

"Yes, I did. I can't do it."

"May, what the hell do you think you hired an attorney for if you won't even listen to him?"

"Oh, but I do listen to you. I've heard everything you've said. I've considered it and now I'm telling you. I've made my decision. In all good conscience, as far as I can see it's like aiding and abetting a criminal, to say the least. The answer is 'no.'"

"Well, the problem is that Martin (Bard's attorney) gets you up on the stand and has you for lunch. He keeps asking questions that are half true and then because it's half true, he works you around to answer 'yes.' He's just leading you right down the tube. What you've got to do, if it's not altogether true, is say 'no, that's not the way it is,' then maybe we'll stand a chance. But just remember, if the jury goes for them, you stand to lose it all."

"What you don't realize, Brent, is that this matter is in the hands of the Lord. And after we've given it our best, then whatever way it turns out is the way He wants it to go. OK? I'll recognize His hand in it and love Him anyway. If they're granted Reclaim, I don't think they will even get five cents on the dollar what it's worth because everything would be sold for scrap prices. And if I did lose it, I'll do something else. I still have a brain and two hands and a willingness to use them."

"May, God's got more important things to do than worry about little things like this."

348

I could not believe my ears! I quickly made the statement, "Well, if you don't think that God has a hand in these matters, then you don't understand the religion that you profess to believe in."

"You might wish you'd made a settlement before you're through."

"Brent, you're handling my case and I appreciate your efforts and what you're trying to do for me. But even you don't comprehend what it is about or you would never suggest such a thing. I would rather lose it all trying than to make a concession to reward him."

"Well, let's go give 'em hell, then," he said, as he picked up his briefcase and we left.

(ADJOURNED AT 5:00 UNTIL 9:30 A.M. NEXT DAY.)

THE COURT: THE MEMBERS OF THE JURY ARE PRESENT. THE PARTIES AND COUNSEL ARE PRESENT.

MR. RYAN, YOU MAY CONTINUE WITH YOUR EXAMINATION OF MS. HANCOCK.

MR. RYAN: THANK YOU.

Q (BY MR. RYAN) MS. HANCOCK, AT THE TIME YOU ENTERED INTO A MARRIAGE WITH MR. KANDERHOSH IN 1965, DID YOU HAVE ANY AGREEMENT ABOUT WHAT YOU WOULD EXPECT OR RECEIVE IN THAT MARRIAGE AND WHAT YOU WOULD GIVE?

A YES.

Q WHAT WAS THAT AGREEMENT?

A THAT --

MR. FLANK: YOUR HONOR, I WOULD OBJECT AS TO FOUNDATION, WHEN WAS THIS CONVERSATION, WHERE IT TOOK PLACE, WHO WAS PRESENT.

THE COURT: SUSTAINED.

Q (BY MR. RYAN) DID YOU HAVE CONVERSATIONS WITH MR. KANDERHOSH ABOUT THAT AGREEMENT?

349

A   YES.

Q   WHERE DID THESE TAKE PLACE AND WHEN?

A   AT 5TH EAST WHEN I WAS JUST AFTER I TURNED 16, WHEN WE STARTED DISCUSSING MARRIAGE PRETTY HEAVY.

Q   WHAT WAS SAID DURING THOSE CONVERSATIONS AND BY WHOM?

A   OKAY, IT WAS DISCUSSED AND AGREED BY BOTH BARD AND I THAT I WAS TO BE ABLE TO HAVE CHILDREN, AND TO WORK IN THE FAMILY AND HAVE THE WORK EQUALLY SHARED, THAT NO GREAT BURDEN WOULD BE ON MY PARTICULAR PARTY AND THAT, AND THAT I WAS TO BE TREATED WITH RESPECT.

Q   HOW, IN FACT, WERE YOU TREATED THEREAFTER, MS. HANCOCK, BY MR. KANDERHOSH?

A   WELL, I WAS TREATED AS A SUBJECT AND NOT A PERSON.

A   WHEN DID THIS COMMENCE?

A   AFTER WE WERE MARRIED.

Q   HOW LONG DID IT CONTINUE?

Q   UNTIL I LEFT.

Q   HOW ELSE WERE YOU TREATED?

A   I WAS DEPRIVED FROM HAVING CHILDREN. HE REFUSED TO GET ME PREGNANT.

Q   WHEN DID THAT COMMENCE?

A   WELL, LIKE I ASKED HIM, I SAID, WHAT IF I TRICK YOU SO I COULD GET PREGNANT? HE LOOKED AT ME AND HE SAID, DON'T YOU EVER, EVER DO A THING LIKE THAT.

Q   HOW LONG DID THIS FAILURE TO CAUSE YOU

350

TO GET PREGNANT GO ON?

    A   UNTIL I LEFT.

    Q   HOW ELSE WERE YOU TREATED?

    A   WITH DISRESPECT.

    Q   HOW?

    A   OH, INSULTS AND LIKE HE WOULD TELL THE CHILDREN AND THE FAMILY THAT IF I WOULDN'T BE SUBMISSIVE TO HIM IN ALL THINGS, THAT I WAS NOT A RIGHTEOUS WOMAN, AND I WAS GOING TO GO INTO DISSOLUTION UNLESS I REPENT.

    Q   HOW LONG DID HE SAY THAT?

    A   WHENEVER I REFUSED TO GIVE HIM THE SEXUAL DEMANDS THAT HE WOULD PERSIST ON.

    Q   HOW LONG DID THAT GO ON?

    A   UNTIL I LEFT.

    Q   WHEN DID IT START?

    A   IT STARTED MAINLY AROUND THE TIME THAT I ESTABLISHED THE BARREL BUSINESS.

    Q   IN APPROXIMATELY 1976?

    A   YES.

    Q   HOW ELSE WERE YOU TREATED DURING THE TIME YOU LIVED WITH MR. KANDERHOSH?

    A   LIKE EVERY MINUTE OF MY DAY AND NIGHT BELONGED TO HIM.

    Q   CAN YOU EXPLAIN THAT A LITTLE IN MORE DETAIL FOR US, PLEASE?

    A   THAT I DIDN'T HAVE THE RIGHT TO LAY DOWN OR REST NOT IN THE TRUCK, NOT IN ANY ROOM IN THE HOUSE, NOT IN THE OFFICE, NOWHERE, EXCEPT IN HIS BED, AND THEN WHEN I WOULD LAY IN HIS BED TO

REST, THEN HE WOULDN'T ALLOW ME TO REST.

Q   NOW, WHEN DID THIS COMMENCE?

A   MAINLY AROUND THE TIME IN '76.

Q   HOW LONG DID IT GO ON?

A   UNTIL I LEFT.

Q   HOW ELSE WERE YOU TREATED IN THE FAMILY
BY MR. KANDERHOSH?

A   WELL, WHEN I WAS GIVEN COUNSEL BY ONE OF
THE AUTHORITIES, THAT I SHOULD JUST FLAT OUT
REFUSE TO COMMIT TO HIS --

MR. FLANK: YOUR HONOR, I WILL OBJECT AS
BEING HEARSAY, AND IT'S NOT RESPONSIVE TO HIS
QUESTION.

THE COURT: THE OBJECTION AS TO HEARSAY
IS SUSTAINED.

THE WITNESS: EXCUSE ME, THE QUESTION
AGAIN?

Q   (BY MR. RYAN) JUST TELL US HOW YOU WERE
TREATED OTHER THAN WHAT YOU HAVE ALREADY TOLD
US. DON'T TELL US WHAT SOMEBODY ELSE TOLD YOU,
JUST TELL US HOW YOU WERE TREATED BY MR.
KANDERHOSH.

A   OKAY, HE TOLD ME, HE SAYS, COME ON
UPSTAIRS. HE SAYS, I WANT TO PRAY WITH YOU.
OKAY, SO WE BOTH KNELT DOWN.

Q   WHEN DID THIS HAPPEN?

A   THIS HAPPENED APPROXIMATELY SIX MONTHS
BEFORE I LEFT.

Q   CONTINUE, PLEASE.

A   SO WE KNELT DOWN, AND HE RAISED HIS

352

HANDS TO THE SQUARE, AND HE ASKED GOD TO CURSE ME.

Q HOW DID HE ASK GOD TO CURSE YOU, MAY?

A THAT I WOULD HAVE POOR HEALTH, AND THAT MY BACK WOULD COME OUT OF PLACE, AND THAT MY FRIENDS WOULD HAVE ACCIDENTS, EVEN UNTO DEATH, THE WAY HE WORDED IT, WHATEVER WAS NECESSARY TO BRING ME INTO SUBJECTION TO HIM.

Q DID HE TELL YOU WHY HE CURSED YOU IN THAT FASHION?

A YES. HE SAYS, WHATEVER IS NECESSARY TO MAKE YOU BE SUBMISSIVE TO ME.

Q NOW, OTHER THAN WHAT YOU HAVE TOLD US, HOW ELSE DID HE TREAT YOU TO THE FAMILY, MAY?

A BY NOT ALLOWING ME TO HAVE A DRIVER'S LICENSE LIKE I ASKED HIM MANY TIMES, IF YOU WILL JUST LET ME LEARN HOW TO DRIVE, I WILL GLADLY TAKE MYSELF AROUND TO GET PARTS FOR THE BUSINESS. HE SAID, NO, I WILL TAKE YOU.

MR. FLANK: YOUR HONOR, I THINK WE HAVE BEEN OVER THIS THREE OR FOUR TIMES. HIS QUESTIONS ARE REPETITIVE AND SIMPLY STATEMENTS THAT WE HAVE ALREADY HEARD.

THE COURT: WE HAVE BEEN OVER THIS GROUND. SUSTAINED.

Q (BY MR. RYAN) NOW, MAY, THE BUSINESS, YOU HAVE HEARD TESTIMONY THAT THE BUSINESS WAS ESTABLISHED IN APPROXIMATELY 1976 OR '77, THE BARREL BUSINESS, IS THAT CORRECT?

A YES.

Q   NOW, ALL THESE QUESTIONS THAT I AM GOING TO ASK YOU WILL HAVE ONLY TO DO WITH THE BARREL BUSINESS, IF THAT CAN BE UNDERSTOOD.

IS THERE AT THE PRESENT TIME EQUIPMENT - NECESSARY TO RUN THE BARREL BUSINESS?

A   YES.

Q   WHAT KIND OF EQUIPMENT IS NECESSARY IN THE BUSINESS?

A   DEDENTER TO TAKE OUT THE DENTS.

Q   OF THE OLD BARRELS?

A   YES, AND A CHAINER THAT HOLDS SIX DRUMS WITH CHAINS IN THAT TILT FROM THEIR TOP TO BOTTOM WHILE THEY ARE ROLLING SIDEWAYS WITH APPROXIMATELY 50 POUNDS OF CHAIN IN IT THAT SCOURS OUT THE RUST AND DIRT AND THAT TYPE OF THING.

Q   ANYTHING ELSE NECESSARY?

A   YES, A SPRAYING SETUP TO SPRAY OFF THE OUTSIDE OF THE DRUMS AND A VAT THAT HAS A PUMP SETUP IN THERE FOR A HOT CAUSTIC WASH AND THEN THEY GET A CLEAR WATER RINSE, AND THEY GET A HIGH POWERED VACUUM THAT I MADE SPECIAL TO SUCK OUT THE ROCKS AND THE WATER AND THAT, AND THEN --

Q   EXCUSE ME, GO AHEAD.

A   AND THEN A SPECIAL SPEED AIR DRYING SYSTEM THAT DRIES THE BARREL IMMEDIATELY SO THEY DON'T HAVE RUST, AND THEN AFTER THEY ARE INSPECTED, THEN THEY GET PUT ON A STRAIGHTENER, AND THIS SEALS AND STRAIGHTENS THE CHIME ON THE

354

TOP AND THE BOTTOM OF THE DRUMS, AND THEN THEY GET THE PLUGS REPLACED IN THEM, WHICH ALSO, THERE'S A BUNG WASHER THAT WE RECONDITION THE OLD BUNGS AND CLEAN THEM UP JUST LIKE NEW AND REPLACE THE GASKETS, AND THEY ARE REPLACED IN THE DRUMS, AND THEN THEY GO OVER AND GET AN AIR HOSE PUT IN THERE AND SUBMERGED UNDER WATER TO TEST FOR LEAKS, AND THEN MARKED ACCORDINGLY, AND THEN IF THEY NEED TO BE WELDED, THEY WILL GO OVER TO HAVE THAT DONE, AND IF THEY ARE PLAIN WORN OUT, LIKE A ROTTEN SPOT LIKE A PINHOLE, THEN THAT GOES OUT AND GETS CONVERTED, AND THEY ROLL DOWN THE RAMP AND GO IN THE PAINT SHED, AND WE GO OVER THE SIDES OF THEM WITH A HEAVY BRUSH ON A AIR GRINDER WHILE ONE BOY IS SPINNING THE DRUM AND THE OTHER ONE WILL GO ALONG AND REMOVE THE LOOSE RUST AND PAINT AND THAT, AND THEN --

Q   OKAY, LET ME ASK YOU, AT THIS POINT, HAVE THESE ITEMS OF EQUIPMENT THAT YOU HAVE DESCRIBED, HAVE THEY BEEN IN THE BUSINESS SINCE 1976 OR '77?

A   NO.

Q   WHEN WERE THESE ITEMS OF EQUIPMENT ADDED, AND HOW WERE THEY ADDED?

A   WELL, AS FAST AS I COULD GENERATE ENOUGH MONEY TO PUT BACK IN THE BUSINESS AND ALSO FIGURE OUT HOW TO BUILD SOMETHING THAT WOULD DO THE JOB.

MR. FLANK: YOUR HONOR, AGAIN, I THINK THE QUESTION WAS WHEN WERE THEY DONE. SHE IS NOT

RESPONSIVE AGAIN TO THE QUESTION. I THINK ALL HE
WANTED WAS A TIME PERIOD.

THE COURT: SUSTAINED.

Q   (BY MR. RYAN) CAN YOU EXPLAIN WHEN EACH
OF THESE ITEMS OF EQUIPMENT WAS ADDED, WHEN,
WHAT YEAR?

A   OKAY, THE DEDENTER WAS MADE IN
APPROXIMATELY '77 TO '78, AND THE CHAINER, I WAS
ACQUIRING THE PARTS --

Q   JUST TELL US WHEN.

A   DURING '79 AND IT DIDN'T ACTUALLY GET
FABRICATED UNTIL 1980.

Q   HOW ABOUT THE DRUM DRYER?

A   WE MADE A DRUM DRYER BACK IN
APPROXIMATELY '77, BUT IT BURNED OUT, AND I HAD TO
MAKE ANOTHER ONE.

Q   WHEN WAS THAT INSTALLED?

A   APPROXIMATELY IN '81.

Q   HOW ABOUT THE WASHER?

A   THAT WAS MADE IN ABOUT '76 OR '77.

Q   WERE ANY OF THESE ITEMS OF EQUIPMENT
THAT YOU DESCRIBED PURCHASED ON THE MARKET
SPECIALLY?

A   A FEW OF THEM.

Q   WHICH ONES WERE?

A   THE CHIME STRAIGHTENER SEALS THE TOP AND
THE BOTTOM CHIMES.

Q   WHAT ELSE?

A   AN OPEN HEAD CONVERTER.

Q   WHERE DID YOU GET THE OTHER ITEMS OF

356

EQUIPMENT?

    A   I MADE THEM.

    Q   WHEN YOU SAY YOU MADE THEM, WHAT DO YOU MEAN BY THAT?

    A   I MEAN THAT I GOT TOGETHER WITH JOSEPH MANDLEY, AND WE DREW OUT THE PLANS, AND I TOOK THE BEST IDEAS FROM HIS PLANS AND THE BEST IDEAS FROM MY PLANS AND PUT THEM TOGETHER IN A MASTER PLAN, AND I LEARNED HOW TO WELD AND USE A TORCH, AND I MADE THEM.

    Q   NOW, THERE'S BEEN TESTIMONY PREVIOUSLY ABOUT THE INVOLVEMENT OF OTHER MEMBERS OF THE FAMILY IN THE BARREL BUSINESS. SINCE 1976 UNTIL 1982, WAS MRS. KANDERHOSH EMPLOYED IN THE BARREL BUSINESS AT ALL?

    A   NO.

    Q   HOW ABOUT MR. WILLER DARDSON?

    A   FOR TRUCK DRIVING ONLY.

    Q   DURING WHAT TIME PERIOD?

    A   FROM THE TIME THE BARREL BUSINESS COMMENCED UNTIL THE TIME OF 1982 WHEN I ENDED UP FIRING HIM.

    Q   WHY DID YOU FIRE HIM?

    A   BECAUSE HE WOULD DICTATE TO ME THE TIME WHEN HE WANTED TO WORK, NOT THE TIME THE DELIVERIES NEEDED TO BE MADE, AND I WAS LOSING CUSTOMERS AN ACCOUNTS, THAT TYPE OF THING.

    Q   DID MR. BARD KANDERHOSH WORK IN THE BARREL BUSINESS AT ALL SINCE 1976?

    A   HE WOULD DO A LITTLE BIT TOWARDS WHEN

357

WE WERE BUFFING AND PAINTING. HE WOULDN'T DO
MUCH IN THE BUFFING, BUT WHEN WE WERE PAINTING,
HE WOULD ROLL THE DRUM OVER NEXT TO THE PAINT
TABLE SO THAT THE MAN THAT WAS PUTTING THE
DRUMS ON AND OFF WOULD HAVE THE DRUM THERE
HANDY FOR HIM.

    Q   NOW, WHO PRESENTLY RUNS THE BUSINESS,
MAY?

    A   WELL, A MANAGER THAT TAKES OVER WHEN
I'M NOT THERE.

    Q   WHEN YOU ARE THERE, THOUGH, WHO RUNS
THE BUSINESS?

    A   OH, YES, I DO.

    Q   WHO RAN THE BUSINESS IN 1976?

    A   I DID.

    Q   NOW, IN 1976, WHO DECIDED WHAT CONTRACTS
TO ACCEPT?

    A   I DID.

    Q   WHO DECIDED WHAT EMPLOYEES, IF ANY, TO
HIRE?

    A   I DID.

    Q   WHO DECIDED WHO TO FIRE?

    A   I DID.

    Q   NOW, IN 1982, APPROXIMATELY HOW MANY
HOURS PER DAY DID YOU SPENT IN THE BUSINESS?

    A   WHAT TIME PERIOD NOW?

    Q   IN 1982 BEFORE YOU LEFT THE BARD
KANDERHOSH RESIDENCE.

    A   I WOULD SAY APPROXIMATELY 12 HOURS A
DAY.

Q   HOW MUCH TIME HAD YOU SPENT PREVIOUS TO THAT, FROM 1976? IS THERE ANY WAY OF GENERALIZING HOW MUCH TIME YOU SPENT IN THE BUSINESS FROM THE TIME IT WAS FOUNDED UNTIL 1982?

A   WELL, I WOULD GET UP EVERY MORNING BY 5:00 O'CLOCK, AND I WOULD BE DOWN THERE TO WORK BY 5:30, AND I GENERALLY WORKED UNTIL 10:00 TO 10:30.

Q   WHY SO LONG?

A   WELL, BECAUSE CUSTOMERS WANT WHAT THEY WANT WHEN THEY WANT IT, AND IF YOU DON'T, THEY DON'T WANT TO HEAR AN EXCUSE; THEY WANT SERVICE, AND THAT'S IT, AND IF YOU DON'T COMPLY WITH THAT, THEN THEY JUST WON'T DEAL WITH YOU.

Q   ANY OTHER REASON YOU SPENT SUCH LONG HOURS AT THE BUSINESS?

A   YES, BECAUSE I LOVED TO USE THAT FOR A GOOD EXCUSE TO STAY OUT OF BARD'S BEDROOM.

Q   SO YOU DID USE IT FOR THAT PURPOSE?

THE COURT: THAT'S WHAT SHE SAID, COUNSEL. LET'S MOVE ON.

Q   (BY MR. RYAN) WHAT EFFECT, IF ANY, DID THESE LONG HOURS HAVE ON YOU?

A   OH, JUST BEING EXCEEDINGLY TIRED EVERY DAY, JUST LIKE I COULD FALL OVER IN MY TRACKS ANY MINUTE, JUST EVERY DAY.

MR. RYAN: NO FURTHER QUESTIONS.

THE COURT: ALL RIGHT, MR. FLANK?

CROSS EXAMINATION

BY MR. FLANK:

Q   I WON'T BE VERY LONG WITH YOU, MAY. I

359

DON'T UNDERSTAND RELIGION VERY WELL. I'M JUST GOING TO ASK YOU SOME QUESTIONS ABOUT YOURSELF. THIS FUNDAMENTALIST GROUP THAT YOU HAVE NOW JOINED, I THINK YOU CALLED IT THE DELRED GROUP?

A   YES.

Q   DO THEY HAVE THE SAME FUNDAMENTAL BELIEFS AS THE GROUP YOU WERE WITH WHEN YOU WERE WITH MR. KANDERHOSH?

A   NO.

Q   DO THEY BASICALLY -- AGAIN, I DON'T KNOW MUCH ABOUT IT, FOLLOW THE FUNDAMENTALIST BELIEFS OF THE MORMON RELIGION?

A   WELL, THE FUNDAMENTALS OF MORMON RELIGION.

Q   JUST YES OR NO, DO THEY? DO YOU RECOGNIZE JOSEPH SMITH?

A   OH, YES.

Q   AS I UNDERSTAND A LITTLE BIT ABOUT THE - MORMON RELIGION, WHEN YOU MARRY, DO YOU MARRY FOR TIME AND ETERNITY?

A   OH, YES.

Q   IN THE RELIGION, WHEN YOU CLAIM YOU MARRIED MR. KANDERHOSH, DID YOU MARRY HIM FOR TIME AND ETERNITY?

A   YES.

Q   DURING THAT PERIOD OF TIME, YOU CONSIDER YOURSELF AT LEAST RELIGIOUSLY OR SPIRITUALLY AS HIS WIFE?

A   OH, YES.

Q   DO YOU STILL?

A   NO.

Q   SO DURING THAT PARTICULAR 18 YEARS THAT
YOU DID CONSIDER YOURSELF HIS WIFE, BASED ON
WHATEVER RELIGIOUS BELIEF YOU HAD, YOU FELT THAT
YOU SHOULD OBEY HIS COUNSELING, IS THAT TRUE?

A   OH, YES.

Q   SO THAT, IN FACT, AS FAR AS THE BUSINESS
WAS CONCERNED OR YOUR WORK WAS CONCERNED OR
YOUR LIFESTYLE WAS CONCERNED, THAT WAS BASED ON
THE GENERAL LIFESTYLE OF THE REST OF THE FAMILY,
WAS IT NOT? WHAT I'M SAYING IS, THEY DIDN'T GO
OUT AND HAVE FRIENDS OR THEY DIDN'T DO OTHER
THINGS, JUST THE SAME AS YOU DID NOT?

A   OH, YOU BET THEY DID. THEY DID. THEY DID.

Q   WERE YOU EVER CHAINED SO YOU COULD NOT
LEAVE,MAY? I MEAN, WERE YOU LOCKED IN A ROOM?

A   AT TIMES, YES.

Q   BY MR. KANDERHOSH?

A   RIGHT.

Q   MS. HANCOCK, ISN'T IT A FACT THAT YOU
CONSIDER YOURSELF TO BE FAR MORE INTELLIGENT AND
COMPETENT AND CAPABLE THAN MR. KANDERHOSH, YES
OR NOT?

A   NOW, WHAT TIME PERIOD ARE YOU TALKING
ABOUT, LIKE RIGHT NOW OR WHEN?

Q   THE LAST TEN YEARS. DO YOU FEEL
YOURSELF TO BE FAR MORE INTELLIGENT THAN MR.
KANDERHOSH?

A   WELL, I FEEL THAT I HAVE BEEN FAR MORE
WILLING TO PROVIDE BUSINESS AND TO ACCOMPLISH

361

SOMETHING THAN HE EVER HAS BEEN, YES, SIR.

Q   YOU FEEL HE DID NOT HAVE THE
WHEREWITHAL TO DO A LOT OF THINGS MENTALLY. IS
THAT TRUE?

A   WELL, I FELT HE HAD THE MENTAL CAPACITY
IF HE WOULD USE IT, BUT HE JUST HAD ALL THESE
EXCUSES OF WHY HE WOULDN'T USE IT.

Q   ISN'T IT A FACT,MAY, THAT YOU HAVE REALLY
BEEN THE CONTROLLING FACTOR IN THAT FAMILY, THAT
YOU ARE THE MOST INTELLIGENT, THAT YOU ARE THE
CONTROL OF THE ENTIRE FAMILY, YES OR NO?

A   WELL, I REALIZE THAT I WAS THE BRAINS OF
THE BUSINESS, BUT I DIDN'T WANT TO ELEVATE MYSELF
TO FEEL LIKE I WAS SUPERIOR TO PEOPLE IN THE
FAMILY. THAT'S NOT A RIGHTEOUS ATTITUDE.

Q   ISN'T IT A FACT THAT YOU PRETTY WELL CON-
TROLLED THE ENTIRE FAMILY, TOLD THEM WHAT TO DO,
WHEN TO DO IT?

A   NO.

Q   YOU DID NOT TELL THEM WHEN TO GO TO
WORK? DID YOU TELL WILL WHEN TO GO TO WORK,
WHEN NOT TO GO TO WORK?

A   IT WOULDN'T HAVE DONE ME ANY GOOD.

Q   BUT YOU TRIED?

A   HEY, I TOLD HIM WHEN DELIVERIES WERE TO
BE MADE, BUT THIS DIDN'T MEAN HE WAS THERE TO
MAKE THEM.

Q   ISN'T IT A FACT ALSO, MAY, THAT AS FAR AS
YOUR CLAIMED SEXUAL DEMANDS BY MR. BARD
KANDERHOSH, THAT YOU WERE THE ONE THAT, IN FACT,

MADE THE SEXUAL DEMANDS ON HIM, NOT HIM ON YOU?

A   THAT IS A LIE.

Q   YOU SAY THAT'S NOT TRUE?

A   THAT'S NOT TRUE.

Q   EVEN IN THE LAST FEW YEARS WHEN HE HAD HIGH BLOOD PRESSURE AND ALL THESE THINGS, YOU ARE CLAIMING THAT HE MADE ALL THESE DEMANDS ON YOU?

A   THAT IS RIGHT.

Q   YOU HAVE HAD THREE ATTORNEYS IN REGARD TO THIS ACTION, HAVE YOU NOT, MS. HANCOCK?

A   YES.

Q   AT NO TIME UNTIL THE LAST ATTORNEY WAS ANY CLAIM EVERY MADE, ANY SEXUAL CLAIMS OR DEMANDS, ET CETERA, IS THAT TRUE, ONLY IN THE LAST YEAR, ALTHOUGH THIS CASE HAS BEEN GOING ON THREE YEARS?

A   NO, THAT'S NOT TRUE.

Q   ISN'T IT A FACT THAT YOUR DEFENSES PREVIOUSLY ONLY HAD TO DO WITH THE FACT OF THE AMOUNT OF MONEY ISSUED TO THEM DURING THEIR LIFETIME SHOULD BE ESTABLISHED?

A   THIS IS ACCORDING TO WHAT THEY WANTED TO APPROACH THE DAYS, NOT FROM INFORMATION I GAVE THEM.

Q   BUT YOU NEVER MADE ANY CLAIM UNTIL NOW, DID YOU?

A   WHEN YOU GO TO AN ATTORNEY, HE DOES IT HIS WAY --   Q   YES OR NO?

A   WELL, I WOULD HAVE TO LOOK BACK AT THE -

- IF THEY HAVEN'T BEEN CLAIMED, THERE'S CERTAINLY NO REASON WHY THEY SHOULDN'T HAVE BEEN.

Q   PREVIOUS TO NOW, YOU FELT DURING THIS ENTIRE PERIOD YOU WERE THE WIFE OF MR. KANDERHOSH, DID YOU NOT?

A   THE SLAVE OF MR. KANDERHOSH.

Q   RELIGIOUSLY, YOU FELT HE WAS -- YOU WERE A WIFE?

A   A SUBJECT.

Q   SPIRITUALLY?

A   SUBJECT FOR THE PURPORTED -- YES, SUPPOSED TO BE A WIFE.

Q   YOU SAY YOU WANTED CHILDREN?

A   OH, YES.

Q   YOU BEING MORE INTELLIGENT THAN HIM, YOU COULDN'T FIND A WAY OF CHILDREN, YES OR NO?

A   I WAS AFRAID TO DO ANYTHING AGAINST HIS WILL BECAUSE OF THIS GRAND AUTHORITY HE CLAIMED TO HAVE WITH THE HEAVENS, AND I KNEW I NEVER HAD NO SUCH AUTHORITY.

Q   ISN'T IT A FACT THAT IN ABOUT 1979 OR 1980, YOU INSISTED AND FORCED NANAS KANDERHOSH FROM THE HOME TO MOVE INTO ANOTHER HOME?

A   NO.

MR. RYAN: OBJECTION, YOUR HONOR. THAT'S BEEN ASKED AND ANSWERED AT LEAST FIVE DIFFERENT TIMES IN THE PAST.

THE WITNESS: NO, THAT'S NOT TRUE.

THE COURT: WELL, THE ANSWER IS ALREADY IN.

Q   (BY MR. FLANK) MS. KANDERHOSH, DID YOU
EVER DESTROY THE DEEDS THAT WERE MADE OUT WHICH
WOULD HAVE TRANSFERRED THE PROPERTY BACK TO MR.
AND MRS. KANDERHOSH?

A   THERE WAS NO DEEDS TO BE DESTROYED.

Q   YOU DID NOT DESTROY THEM, YES OR NO?

A   NO. THAT'S A MYTH THAT THEY EVER
EXISTED.

Q   NOW, ABOUT THE BUSINESS, THE BARREL
BUSINESS. IT'S TRUE, IS IT NOT, THAT THE BARREL
BUSINESS WAS COMMENCED IN ABOUT 1976, ALL
EQUIPMENT THEREIN WAS PURCHASED BY THE FAMILY?

A   NO.

Q   WHERE DID THE MONEY COME FROM TO
PURCHASE THE BUSINESS OR THE BUSINESS EQUIPMENT
STARTING IN 1976?

A   RIGHT HERE IN MY RIGHT ARM.

Q   DID IT COME FROM THE BUSINESS INCOME?
WHERE DID YOU GET THE MONEY?

A   WHERE DID I GET THE MONEY? I STARTED
OUT WITH THREE BARRELS A WEEK, AND I WASHED THEM
OUT ON THE FLOOR WITH SOME TIDE AND A HOSE, IF
YOU CALL THAT EQUIPMENT.

Q   ALL I'M ASKING IS, DID YOU HAVE ANY INDE-
PENDENT MONEY, OR DID IT COME FROM THE FACT
THAT YOU HAD SOME PROPERTY, YOU HAD A FACTORY
THAT HAD BEEN TRADED FOR BY NANAS, AND ON THAT
FACTORY, YOU PURCHASED, BEGAN TO PURCHASE
PROPERTY OR EQUIPMENT, AND YOU BUILT UP A
BUSINESS IN 1976, FROM 1976 TO THE PRESENT TIME, IS

365

THAT TRUE? YOU DIDN'T HAVE ANY INDEPENDENT
MONEY, DID YOU?

A   BECAUSE I DIDN'T GET PAID ANY INDEPENDENT
MONEY OFF OF EVERYTHING OFF MY LABORERS.

Q   DID ANYBODY INVEST ANY MONEY IN THIS
BUSINESS, BY OUTSIDERS, OR DID IT ALL COME IN FROM
FAMILY RESOURCES?

A   ALL COME FROM FAMILY RESOURCES, IF
THAT'S THE WAY YOU WANT TO PUT IT.

Q   NOW, IN ADDITION TO THE ITEMS YOU HAVE
ALREADY TESTIFIED ABOUT, THAT EQUIPMENT, THERE
WAS ALSO TRUCKS, WAS THERE NOT, SOME SEMIS OR
SOME DIESELS?

A   NO.

Q   YOU HAVE NO RECOLLECTION AT THE PRESENT
TIME?

A   THAT CAME LATER.

Q   WILL TESTIFIED THAT HE DROVE A DIESEL
TRUCK. DO YOU STILL HAVE THAT DIESEL TRUCK?

A   NO. I DON'T HAVE THAT ONE.

Q   DO YOU HAVE ANOTHER ONE? HAS THAT BEEN
TRADED IN?

A   YES.

Q   HOW MANY TRUCKS DO YOU HAVE AT THE
PRESENT TIME?

A   TWO.

Q   ARE THEY DIESELS?

A   UH-HUH (AFFIRMATIVE).

Q   ARE THEY PAID FOR?

A   NO.

Q   HOW MUCH MONEY IS OWED ON THEM?

A $10,000.

Q   BETWEEN THE TWO OF THEM?

A   UH-HUH (AFFIRMATIVE).

Q   ARE YOU PAYING PAYMENTS ON THOSE?

A   YES.

Q   THAT'S COMING FROM THE BUSINESS?

A   UH-HUH (AFFIRMATIVE).

Q   HAVE YOU BOUGHT ANY OTHER EQUIPMENT SINCE 1980 WHEN YOU REMOVED YOURSELF FROM THE FAMILY, BESIDES THE TWO TRUCKS? LET ME ASK YOU THIS: WHAT DID YOU PAY FOR THOSE TWO TRUCKS? HOW MUCH HAVE YOU INVESTED IN THEM?

A   OKAY, I PAID $5,000 FOR ONE, AND THEN I PAID 1,500 FOR THAT ONE TRAILER, AND I PAID $3,000 FOR THE OTHER TRAILER, AND $10,000 FOR THE OTHER DIESEL.

Q   SO APPROXIMATELY $16,000 TOTAL, AND YOU STILL OWE TEN?

A   YES, I STILL OWE TEN.

Q   HOW MUCH ARE THE PAYMENTS ON THOSE?

A   IT'S ABOUT 500 A MONTH.

Q   ALL OF THOSE PAYMENTS HAVE BEEN COMING FROM THE INCOME FROM THE BUSINESS?

A   RIGHT.

Q   DO YOU HAVE ANY OTHER PAYMENTS THAT COMES FROM THE INCOME OF THE BUSINESS?

A   THAT'S GOING TO WHAT?

Q   YOU ARE PRESENTLY MAKING. ARE YOU MAKING ANY OTHER PAYMENTS FROM THE BUSINESS AT

367

THE PRESENT TIME?

A   ON EQUIPMENT, I DON'T THINK SO.

Q   NOR PAYMENTS ON ANYTHING, ANY PROPERTY,
ANYTHING?

A   WELL, EXCEPT THAT I'M IN DEBT
PERMANENTLY, BUT THAT DOES NOT HAVE ANYTHING TO
DO WITH THE BUSINESS.

Q   YOU PAY $200 ON THE LEHI PROPERTY. WHAT
HAPPENS TO THAT $200 THAT YOU WERE PAYING A
MONTH ON THAT?

A   OKAY, I HAD TO BORROW SOME MONEY SO I
COULD PAY OFF MY FARM SO I COULD GET CLEAR TITLE
TO IT TO SETTLE THE FENCE LINE BOUNDARY LINE
FIGHT THAT I HAVE GOT DOWN THERE IN LEHI WITH THE
NEIGHBOR.

Q   YOU STILL OWE MONEY ON THAT?

A   YES.

Q   ABOUT HOW MUCH IS THAT?

A   I OWE JUST ABOUT $30,000.

Q   YOU ARE PAYING THAT OUT WHAT A MONTH?

A   1,400.

Q   IT'S TRUE, IS IT NOT, MAY, THAT AS FAR AS
THE ENTIRE FAMILY WAS CONCERNED, TAKING INTO
CONSIDERATION NANAS, WILL, BARD, ZOSA, THERE WAS
NO OTHER MEMBER IN THE FAMILY WHO COULD
OPERATE THAT BUSINESS. IS THAT TRUE, IN YOUR
OPINION?

A   THAT'S RIGHT.

Q   YOU WERE THE ONLY ONE WITH THE BRAINS
AND INTELLIGENCE TO DO THAT?

368

A   YES, AND YOU MAKE IT SOUND LIKE THAT'S A CRIME.

Q   NO, I DON'T.

A   LIKE I SHOULD BE PUNISHED BECAUSE I'M THE ONLY ONE THAT WOULD BE WILLING TO DO IT.

Q   BUT YOU WERE THE ONE WHO COULD DO IT. YOU WERE THE ONLY FAMILY MEMBER THAT WAS CAPABLE AND COMPETENT OF DOING THAT, WERE YOU NOT?

A   SO SHOULD I BE PUNISHED? I HOPE NOT.

Q   THAT'S TRUE.

A   THAT'S TRUE.

THE COURT: MA'AM, JUST ANSWER THE QUESTION.

Q   (BY MR. FLANK) AS A PRACTICAL MATTER, UP UNTIL 1982, BEING THE SPIRITUAL WIFE OF BARD KANDERHOSH, YOU FELT IT WAS YOUR RESPONSIBILITY AND OBLIGATION TO ASSIST THAT FAMILY THE BEST YOU COULD. IS THAT TRUE?

A   WELL --

Q   YES OR NOT?

A   YES. I HAD LOVE FOR THE FAMILY AND TRIED TO DO WHAT I COULD FOR THEM. I LOVED THE CHILDREN AND FELT SORRY FOR ZOSA.

MR. FLANK: THAT'S ALL I HAVE, YOUR HONOR.

THE COURT: ANYTHING FURTHER, MR. RYAN?

MR. RYAN: JUST ONE VERY QUICK THING.

REDIRECT EXAMINATION

BY MR. RYAN:

Q   MAY, WHERE DO YOU LIVE?

A   IN THE APARTMENT ABOVE THE BUSINESS.

Q   LET ME SHOW YOU WHAT'S BEEN MARKED AS
DEFENDANT'S EXHIBIT 17, AND ASK YOU IF YOU
RECOGNIZE THAT PHOTOGRAPH?

A   YES. THAT'S MY APARTMENT RIGHT THERE.

Q   DID YOU TAKE THIS PICTURE?

A   YES.

A   WHEN?

A   LAST WEEK.

A   DOES THIS ACCURATELY REFLECT WHAT YOUR
HOME LOOKS LIKE?

A   YES.

Q   WHAT ELSE IS IN THAT BUILDING, IF
ANYTHING?

A   OKAY, MY APARTMENT GOES BACK THE FIRST
HALF, AND THEN THE REST IS JUST A STORAGE AREA
FOR BUSINESS ITEMS.

Q   IS ANY PART OF THE BARREL BUSINESS IN
THAT BUILDING?

A   OH, SURE, DOWN, THE BOTTOM FLOOR.

Q   NOW, IS THAT THE FACTORY THAT MR. FLANK
HAS REFERRED TO?

A   YES.

MR. RYAN: NOTHING FURTHER. I WOULD
MOVE THAT THAT BE ADMITTED.

MR. FLANK: MAY I SEE IT? I HAVE NO
OBJECTION, YOUR HONOR.

THE COURT: 17 IS RECEIVED. ANY FURTHER
EXAMINATION?

MR. RYAN: NOTHING.

MR. FLANK: I HAVE NOTHING FURTHER.

THE COURT: YOU MAY STEP DOWN, MS. HANCOCK. CALL YOUR NEXT WITNESS.

MR. RYAN: JOSEPH MANDLEY.

JOSEPH MANDLEY

CALLED AS A WITNESS BY AND ON BEHALF OF THE DEFENDANT, BEING FIRST DULY SWORN, WAS EXAMINED AND TESTIFIED AS FOLLOWS:

DIRECT EXAMINATION

BY MR. RYAN:

Q   WOULD YOU PLEASE STATE YOUR FULL NAME AND ADDRESS.

A   JOSEPH C. MANDLEY.

Q   ARE YOU IN BUSINESS, MR. MANDLEY?

A   I WAS UNTIL I RETIRED, YES.

Q   WHEN DID YOU RETIRE?

A   ABOUT FOUR OR FIVE YEARS AGO. WELL, IT WAS REALLY SIX YEARS AGO.

Q   APPROXIMATELY 1979?

A   YES.

Q   WHAT BUSINESS WERE YOU ENGAGED IN PRIOR TO YOUR RETIREMENT?

A   HEATING.

Q   WHAT?

A   PLUMBING AND HEATING.

Q   ANYTHING ELSE?

A   NO. I WAS CONNECTED WITH THE SHERIFF'S DEPARTMENT, SEARCH AND RESCUE.

Q   WHAT KIND OF EDUCATION DO YOU HAVE, MR. MANDLEY?   371

A   HIGH SCHOOL.

Q   ANYTHING BEYOND THAT?

A   NO.

Q   APPROXIMATELY HOW MANY YEARS EXPERIENCE IN PLUMBING AND HEATING DO YOU HAVE?

A   ABOUT 45.

Q   ARE YOU FAMILIAR WITH MAY HANCOCK?

A   YES, I AM.

Q   WHEN DID YOU FIRST MEET HER?

A   WELL, IT HAS BEEN QUITE A FEW YEARS. IT WAS WHEN THEY WERE LIVING UP ON 5TH EAST AND ABOUT 40TH SOUTH, SOMEWHERE RIGHT ALONG IN THAT AREA.

Q   NOW, I WILL REPRESENT TO YOU THAT THERE'S BEEN TESTIMONY ESTABLISHING THAT AT APPROXIMATELY 1963 OR '64, IS THAT ABOUT RIGHT?

A   THAT'S ABOUT CORRECT.

Q   WHAT KIND OF ASSOCIATION DID YOU HAVE WITH HER AND/OR THE FAMILY SHE WAS LIVING WITH AT THAT TIME?

A   I DIDN'T HAVE ANY ASSOCIATION WITH HER OUTSIDE OF SEEING HER AND WILL'S WIFE OUT LATER THAT WAS WHO WAS WORKING ON WASHING BOTTLES, BUT I WAS CALLED DOWN THERE TO MAKE A REPAIR ON THE BOILER THAT WAS IN VERY BAD CONDITION AT THAT TIME.

Q   ARE YOU FAMILIAR WITH A BUSINESS KNOWN AS RECLAIM BARREL SUPPLY?

A   YES, SIR, I AM.

Q   WHEN DID YOU FIRST BECOME ACQUAINTED

372

WITH THAT BUSINESS?

A   THAT'S BEEN ABOUT NINE, TEN YEARS AGO,
SOMETHING LIKE THAT.

Q   WOULD THAT BE APPROXIMATELY 1976?

A   I BELIEVE IT WOULD BE APPROXIMATELY.

Q   WHAT WAS THE NATURE OF YOUR
INVOLVEMENT OR YOUR KNOWLEDGE OF THEIR
BUSINESS?

A   WELL, I WAS CALLED DOWN THERE TO MAKE
REPAIRS ON DIFFERENT TYPES OF EQUIPMENT THAT
THEY HAD THERE.

Q   WHO CALLED YOU DOWN?

A   MAY CALLED ME.

Q   DID ANYONE ELSE EVER CALL YOU DOWN?

A   NO, I DON'T BELIEVE THEY DID. WELL, THERE
IS A POSSIBILITY THAT MAYBE BARD DID, AND THERE'S A
POSSIBILITY THAT WILLER, THAT HIS WIFE CALLED ME.

Q   DO YOU RECALL THOSE SPECIFICALLY?

A   NO. I WOULD HAVE TO GO BACK ON
HUNDREDS AND HUNDREDS OF INVOICES TO FIND OUT,
TO KNOW WHO CALLED.

Q   NOW, WHAT KIND OF WORK THEN DID YOU
PERFORM AT THAT BUSINESS?

A   IT WAS REPAIR ON -- WHEN I FIRST WENT
DOWN THERE, IT WAS MAKING REPAIRS ON THE BOILER
THAT THEY HAD IN THE RED BRICK HOUSE AND ON THE
GAS FURNACE OVER THE WHITE HOUSE ON THE SOUTH
SIDE OF THE RED BRICK. I THINK THIS WAS THE FIRST
WORK THAT I DID DOWN THERE ON THAT PLACE.

Q   WERE YOU CALLED AT TIMES AFTER THAT?

373

A   AFTER THAT, WHEN THERE WAS TROUBLE THAT CAME UP, YOU KNOW, DOWN ON THE EQUIPMENT THAT THEY WERE TRYING TO BUILD TO WASH BARRELS OR ONE THING AND ANOTHER LIKE THAT THERE, THEY WAS ALWAYS WASHING BOTTLES AT THE TIME THAT I FIRST WENT IN THERE. THEY WAS WASHING BOTTLES, TOO, AS WELL AS DRUMS.

Q   WHEN YOU FIRST STARTED GOING DOWN THERE TO HELP IN 1976, HOW LONG DID THIS GO ON, YOUR INVOLVEMENT IN HELPING DOWN THERE?

A   IT WENT ON FOR SEVERAL YEARS.

Q   HOW MANY, DO YOU RECALL?

A   WELL, UNTIL ABOUT, I WOULD SAY, ABOUT 1980 IS WHEN I -- ABOUT THE LAST TIME I WAS DOWN THERE, IF I REMEMBER CORRECTLY.

Q   SO FROM APPROXIMATELY '76 UNTIL '80, YOU WERE INVOLVED THERE?

A   YES.

Q   HAVE YOU HAD ANY CONTACTS WITH THE BUSINESS SINCE 1980?

A   NO.

Q   NOW, DURING THIS APPROXIMATELY FOUR-YEAR PERIOD, AND I WAS GETTING TO THAT WITH MY PREVIOUS QUESTIONS, WHAT OTHER KINDS OF SERVICES DID YOU PERFORM THERE?

A   BESIDES THE WORK THAT WAS IN MY FIELD?

Q   WELL, PARTICULARLY THE WORK THAT WAS IN YOUR FIELD?

A   WELL, I HELPED BUILD AND MAINTAIN AND HELPED DESIGN THE DIFFERENT PIECES OF EQUIPMENT

374

THAT WAS USED ALONG WITH MAY AND BARD. WE
SPENT MANY, MANY HOURS GOING OVER CONCERNS, HAD
MADE BLUEPRINTS. MAY WAS THE ONE THAT MADE UP
THE PLANS, THAT IS, GOING TO READ. THAT'S NOT MY
DIRECTIONS, AND THAT'S WHAT HELPED BUILD THE
BARREL WORK TO THE POSITION IT IS IN TODAY.

Q   BUT DID I HEAR YOU RIGHT, YOU SAID THAT
MAY MADE THE DESIGNS?

A   YES. SHE WAS THE -- SHE'S AN EXPERT AT
DRAWING. I SHOULD GIVE HER A LOT OF CREDIT IN
THAT DEPARTMENT, I WILL TELL YOU.

Q   DURING THAT FOUR-YEAR PERIOD,
APPROXIMATELY HOW MUCH TIME, SAY, ON A WEEKLY
BASIS OR HOW MANY HOURS WOULD YOU SPEND THERE
ON AN AVERAGE DURING AN AVERAGE WEEK?

A   OH, IT VARIES. IT VARIED A LOT, ACCORDING
TO THE TIME THAT I COULD PUT IN DOWN THERE UNTIL
WE GOT TO BUILDING THE CHAINER AND BUILDING HOT
AIR FURNACES FOR DRYING THE DRUMS AND FOR
BUILDING THE PAINT MACHINES AND THINGS LIKE THAT.
THEN UP UNTIL THAT TIME, WHY, IT WAS JUST
PERIODICAL, BUT THEN FROM THAT PERIOD ON, WHY,
THERE WAS CONSIDERABLE TIME PUT IN DOWN THERE
EACH WEEK.

Q   WHAT DID YOU MEAN BY CONSIDERABLE TIME?

A   APPROXIMATELY MAYBE ANYWHERE FROM 30
TO 40 HOURS A WEEK.

Q   A WEEK?

A   YES.

Q   HOW LONG DID THAT GO ON?

A   IT WENT ON FOR APPROXIMATELY, I WOULD
SAY, TWO YEARS.

Q   SO YOU WOULD SPEND APPROXIMATELY 30 TO
40 HOURS A WEEK FOR TWO YEARS STRAIGHT?

A   WELL, PROBABLY NOT THAT MANY EACH WEEK,
BECAUSE THERE'S OTHER WORK THAT I HAD TO DO
BESIDES DOWN THERE, BUT ON THE AVERAGE, IT WOULD
AVERAGE OUT CLOSE TO THAT.

Q   NOW, WHEN YOU WERE SPENDING ALL THIS
TIME THERE, WHEN WOULD YOU ARRIVE IN THE
MORNING NORMALLY?

A   WE WOULD BE RIGHT AROUND 7:00 OR 7:30,
UNLESS THERE WAS A BREAKDOWN IN THERE THAT WE
HAD TO GET TAKEN CARE OF, YOU KNOW, SO THAT
THEY COULD RUN THE BARRELS, YOU KNOW, AS QUICK
AS POSSIBLE, BECAUSE THEY HAD CONTRACTS, YOU
KNOW, TO PUT OUT DRUMS, AND THEN SOMETIMES IF
THE MACHINERY BROKE, WHY, THEY WOULD GET DOWN
THERE, GET THERE AS EARLY AS 4:00, 3:30, 4:00 O'CLOCK
IN THE MORNING.

Q   WERE YOU ABLE TO OBSERVE DURING THE
TIME THAT YOU WERE THERE WHO WAS RUNNING THE
BUSINESS?

A   WELL, MAY WAS THE ONE THAT WAS TAKING
THE RESPONSIBILITY OF IT. BARD WAS, WHAT I WOULD
CALL, THE ASSISTANT SUPERINTENDENT OF THE
COMPANY, BECAUSE HE WAS THERE THE MAJORITY OF
THE TIME.

Q   WHAT DID HE DO WHILE HE WAS THERE, THAT
YOU OBSERVED?

A   WELL, HE WAS, MORE OR LESS, IN WHAT I WOULD SAY KIND OF A BOSSING POSITION.

Q   WOULD YOU EXPLAIN THAT FURTHER, PLEASE.

A   WELL, HE WAS HELPING TO SUPERVISE.

Q   DID HE DO ANY OF THE ACTUAL LABOR?

A   VERY LITTLE.

Q   WHAT LITTLE BIT DID HE DO?

A   WELL, THE MOST WORK THAT I SEEN BARD DO DOWN THERE IS WHEN THEY WERE PAINTING DRUMS, THEN HE WOULD GET OVER THERE AND HELP ON THE DRUMS, MOVING THEM FROM ONE POSITION TO ANOTHER SO THEY COULD GO THROUGH THE PAINT MACHINES.

Q   DID YOU OBSERVE MR. KANDERHOSH'S RELATIONSHIP WITH ANY EMPLOYEES OTHER THAN MAY?

A   WELL, YES. THERE WAS SOME THINGS WITH OTHER PEOPLE THAT HAD BEEN EMPLOYEES. IF BARD WOULD SEE THEM, YOU KNOW, STANDING AROUND FOR A FEW MINUTES, HE WAS AFTER THEM TO KEEP THEM WORKING. HE WAS WATCHING THAT SITUATION PRETTY CLOSE.

Q   DID YOU KNOW OF ANY OF THE EFFECTS THAT THIS MIGHT HAVE HAD ON THE BUSINESS OR THE EMPLOYEES?

A   WHAT EFFECTS, YOU SAY? HIS BOSSING THE EMPLOYEES AROUND?

Q   YES.

A   QUITE A FEW OF THE EMPLOYEES QUIT BECAUSE MAY WAS GIVING ORDERS, AND BARD WAS GIVING ORDERS, AND THAT CAUSED A CONFLICT OF INTEREST BETWEEN THE TWO. THAT'S A FACT, TOO. I

377

SEEN IT A LOT OF TIMES.

Q WERE YOU AWARE THAT MAY GOT A DEED TO THE PROPERTY ON WHICH THE BUSINESS SITS?

A YES.

Q WAS THAT DURING THE TIME YOU WERE INVOLVED WITH THE BUSINESS?

A YES, IT WAS.

Q DID YOU EVER HAVE ANY DISCUSSIONS WITH MR. BARD KANDERHOSH REGARDING THE DEEDS OR BUSINESS ACQUISITIONS OF THAT PROPERTY?

A YES, I DID.

Q DO YOU RECALL WHEN THESE CONVERSATIONS TOOK PLACE?

A NO. EXACT DATES ON THEM, I CAN'T REMEMBER.

Q WOULD THIS HAVE BEEN DURING THAT FOUR-YEAR PERIOD?

A YES, THEY WOULD HAVE BEEN.

Q WOULD YOU PLEASE TELL US WHO WAS PRESENT DURING THOSE CONVERSATIONS AND WHAT WAS SAID AND BY WHOM?

A MAY WAS ALSO PRESENT, AND BARD WHEN WE WERE TALKING ABOUT BARD ABOUT THE -- WAS WHEN MAY WAS HAVING PROBLEMS WITH WILL ON MISAPPROPRIATING FUNDS AND THINGS LIKE THAT. SO AT THAT TIME, AND I DIDN'T SEE ANY OF THAT.

Q WE DON'T WANT YOU TO SAY THAT UNLESS IT WAS SAID DURING A CONVERSATION.

A SOME OF THESE THINGS WERE SAID DURING A CONVERSATION, BUT I COUNSELED BARD, AND I

378

COUNSELED MAY WITH THESE INSTRUCTIONS, AND THE WAY THAT I UNDERSTAND BUSINESS, YOU CANNOT RUN A BUSINESS WITH TWO OR THREE HEADS UNLESS ONE HEAD IS OVER THE REST. TWO OR THREE MORE BOSSES, IT WILL NOT WORK, AND BECAUSE OF THE CONFLICTS, YOU KNOW, THAT ARISEN, BETWEEN MAY AND WILL, BUT EACH OF THEM HAD A HALF INTEREST IN THE PROPERTY AND THE BUSINESS. THE WAY I UNDERSTOOD IT, THE WAY THAT IT WAS EXPLAINED TO ME, SO I SUGGESTED TO BARD AND TO MAY BOTH AND WILL WAS THERE, I HEARD THE SAME THING, THAT THEY DIVIDE THE PROPERTY UP, THAT IS, MAY TAKE OVER THE BARREL BUSINESS, AND WILL TAKE OVER THE FARM, THAT SHE WOULD GIVE WILL HER HALF OF THE FARM, WHICH THEY OWNED HALF OF, ACCORDING TO THE WAY THE DEEDS WERE MADE OUT.

I DIDN'T SEE THE DEEDS. THEY WERE JUST -- THIS IS HEARSAY AGAIN, BUT I DID NOT SEE THEM. BUT I MADE THAT SUGGESTION, AND THEY HIRED AN ATTORNEY, AND THEY GOT THOSE DEEDS AND THINGS RIGHT ENDS UP, AND THE PROPERTY WAS DIVIDED EQUALLY BETWEEN MAY AND WILL.

Q   DID MR. KANDERHOSH EVER TELL YOU ANY OF HIS FEELINGS ABOUT GIVING THAT PROPERTY TO MAY?

A   HE DID JUST AFTER IT WAS COMPLETED.

Q   WHAT DID HE SAY?

A   HE MADE THE STATEMENT, HE WAS WALKING FROM THE PAINT SHOP TO WHAT THE OFFICE --

MR. FLANK: YOUR HONOR, I'M GOING TO OBJECT. I DON'T KNOW WHEN IT WAS COMPLETED, WHAT

379

TIME WE ARE TALKING ABOUT. I DON'T REMEMBER OR
WHERE, WERE THE DEEDS IN -- WHEN THEY
TRANSFERRED BACK AND FORTH.

THE COURT: WELL, THE RECORDS,I THINK,
ALREADY ESTABLISH WHEN THIS TRANSACTION WAS
CONCLUDED BY THE TERM OF THE DEEDS.

MR. FLANK: BUT I THINK HE'S TALKING ABOUT
WHERE THE DEEDS WHEN THEY TRANSFERRED THEM, AND
I WANT TO MAKE THAT CLEAR.

THE COURT: I DON'T KNOW OF ANY PRIOR
CHANGE OF DEEDS. THE ONLY INFORMATION I HAVE OF
MY OWN IS WHEN IT WAS CONTRACTED BETWEEN MAY,
BARD, AND THE ENTIRE FAMILY.

MR. FLANK: THAT'S FINE THEN.

Q   (BY MR. RYAN) WAS THIS THEIR
CONVERSATION THAT YOU ARE TALKING ABOUT? WHAT
YEAR WAS IT, TO THE BEST OF YOUR KNOWLEDGE?

THE COURT: WE HAVE BASICALLY ALREADY
ESTABLISHED THAT.

THE WITNESS: THE EXACT DATE ON THAT, I
COULDN'T SWEAR TO IT.

Q   (BY MR. RYAN) GO AHEAD AND TELL US WHAT
THE CONVERSATION WAS.

A   WE WERE TALKING FROM THE PAINT -- WE HAD
BEEN OVER THERE PAINTING, AND THEN I WAS OVER
THERE FOR, TO FIX SOME PIECE OF EQUIPMENT OR
SOMETHING IN THERE. I DON'T KNOW JUST WHAT IT
WAS AT THAT TIME, BACK UP TO WHAT WAS THE
OFFICE, AND WE WERE TALKING ABOUT THE DEEDS
BEING STRAIGHTENED UP, AND ONE THING AND ANOTHER

LIKE THAT BETWEEN MAY AND WILL, AND AS THINGS
SEEMED TO BE RUNNING A LOT IN THE BUILDING, BARD
MADE THIS STATEMENT, THEY WERE TALKING ABOUT IT,
YOU KNOW, ABOUT MAY WORKING ALL THE YEARS, YOU
KNOW, IN THE BUSINESS, AND IN THE BOTTLE BUSINESS,
AND GRADUATING INTO THE BARREL BUSINESS, AND HE
MADE THIS STATEMENT, THAT HE WAS SORRY THAT HE
DIDN'T HAVE MORE TO GIVE HER, BUT HE FIGURED THAT
THAT WOULD BE A BIG HELP TO HER AT THAT TIME IN
TRANSFERRING THE PROPERTY OVER TO HER.

 Q DID HE MAKE ANY OTHER STATEMENTS AT
THAT TIME?

 A YES,THERE WAS, BUT THE EXACT CONTENT, I
CANNOT SWEAR TO.

 Q CAN YOU TELL US WHAT YOUR RECOLLECTION
OF THE CONVERSATION WAS?

 A THE ONLY THING I CAN RECALL WOULD BE
PUTTING IT TO THE SITUATION WAS THAT THIS LIFE
ESTATE, YOU KNOW, THAT WAS GIVEN TO, THAT MAY
AGREED TO ON THE WHITE HOUSE OF NANAS LIVING IN,
THAT THAT WAS THE RESPONSIBILITY THAT MAY HAD
TAKEN ON HERSELF WHEN THE PLACE WAS DIVIDED, AND
SHE AGREED TO THAT, AND I THINK SHE KEPT IT UP
SINCE.

 Q SINCE THIS CONVERSATION YOU HAVE JUST
DESCRIBED, HAD YOU HAD PRIOR CONVERSATIONS WITH
MR. BARD KANDERHOSH REGARDING HIS FEELINGS ABOUT
GIVING THAT PROPERTY TO MAY?

 A NO, I HAVEN'T.

 Q YOU INDICATED THAT SOMETIMES YOU CAME

TO THE BUSINESS AT 4:00 O'CLOCK IN THE MORNING. IS
THAT CORRECT?

A   YES.

Q   DID YOU EVER FIND ANYONE THERE WORKING
AT THAT HOUR?

A   MAY.

Q   HOW OFTEN?

A   EVERY TIME I WENT DOWN THERE THAT EARLY
IN THE MORNING OR ANYTIME, SHE WAS THERE.

Q   DO YOU HAVE ANY RECOLLECTION DURING THE
PERIOD FROM 1976 TO 1980 OF HOW MANY HOURS IN A
DAY MR. BARD KANDERHOSH WOULD SPEND IN THE
BUSINESS?

MR. FLANK: YOUR HONOR, I THINK HE'S
ALREADY TESTIFIED HE WAS THERE MOST OF THE TIME
THAT MAY WAS THERE.

THE WITNESS: NO.

MR. FLANK: GO AHEAD. I WITHDRAW THE
OBJECTION.

THE WITNESS: BARD USUALLY SHOWED UP
AROUND 8:00, 9:00, 10:00 O'CLOCK IN THE MORNING IS
WHEN HE WOULD COME DOWN TO SEE WHAT WAS GOING
ON.

Q   (BY MR. RYAN) DID HE STAY THERE ALL DAY?

A   NO. HE WOULD COME AND GO.

Q   WERE YOU ABLE TO OBSERVE THE
RELATIONSHIP BETWEEN MR. BARD KANDERHOSH AND
MAY HANCOCK DURING THE TIME THAT YOU WERE
THERE?

A   ONLY IN THIS RESPECT, YOU KNOW, THAT

382

SOMETIMES ALONG ABOUT, SOMETIMES 2:30, 3:00 O'CLOCK IN THE AFTERNOON, THAT HE WOULD GET AFTER MAY, YOU KNOW, TO COME UP THERE AND GET TO BED SO SHE COULD GET SOME SLEEP WHEN WE WERE RIGHT IN THE MIDDLE, YOU KNOW, OF WORKING ON PROJECTS.

Q   ANYTHING ELSE?

A   NO, BUT I KNOW AT THAT TIME THAT WHENEVER MAY WOULD STOP FOR A VERY FEW MINUTES, SHE WAS SOUND ASLEEP.

Q   HOW MANY TIMES DID YOU OBSERVE THIS?

A   WELL, I WOULD SAY QUITE A FEW DOZEN TIMES.

Q   WHAT, IF ANYTHING, WOULD MR. KANDERHOSH DO WHEN MAY WOULD GO TO SLEEP?

A   THEN HE WOULD GO ON UP TO THE HOUSE.

Q   WOULD SHE BE ALLOWED TO SLEEP?

A   WHAT?

Q   WOULD MAY BE ALLOWED TO SLEEP?

A   NO, NOT DOWN ON THE JOB, NO WAY.

Q   WHERE WOULD SHE GO TO SLEEP?

A   BACK UP TO THE HOUSE.

Q   BUT WHEN SHE WENT TO SLEEP ON THE JOB, WHERE WOULD SHE SLEEP?

A   SHE WOULD BE UP IN THE OFFICE UP IN THERE OR SOMETHING LIKE THAT. WE WOULD BE TALKING OR SOMETHING LIKE THAT, AND, YOU KNOW, AND OVER CHANGES IN EQUIPMENT OR PLANS THAT WERE BEING DRAWN, AND A LOT OF TIME LIKE THAT, SHE WOULD DROP OFF TO SLEEP.

Q   DID YOU HAVE ANY CONVERSATIONS AT ALL
WITH MR. KANDERHOSH REGARDING THE RUNNING OF
THE BUSINESS?

A   WELL, YES, ONLY IN AN ADVISORY SITUATION
WAS ALL.

Q   DID HE MAKE ANY STATEMENTS ABOUT MAY'S
RUNNING OF THE BUSINESS DURING THOSE
CONVERSATIONS?

A   YES, HE DID. NOW THE EXACT WORDS THAT
HE USED ON THEM, I DON'T REMEMBER. THAT WOULD
BE HARD FOR ME TO SAY.

Q   WHAT IS YOUR BEST RECOLLECTION?

A   THAT, WELL, HE SAID SEVERAL TIMES THAT
MAY WAS THE ONE THAT HAD THE ABILITY TO RUN IT,
TO TAKE CARE OF IT.

MR. RYAN: I HAVE NOTHING FURTHER AT THIS
TIME.

THE COURT: BEFORE YOU CROSS EXAMINE,
MR. FLANK, LET'S TAKE A BRIEF RECESS. WE HAVE
BEEN IN SESSION NOW FOR SOME TIME.

LADIES AND GENTLEMEN, REMEMBER THE
ADMONITION I HAVE GIVEN YOU. WE WILL BE IN RECESS
FOR TEN MINUTES.

(A RECESS WAS TAKEN.)

THE COURT: THE JURY IS PRESENT. THE
PARTIES AND COUNSEL ARE PRESENT.

YOU MAY PROCEED WITH YOUR CROSS
EXAMINATION,MR. FLANK.

<u>CROSS EXAMINATION</u>

BY MR. FLANK:

Q   I JUST HAVE A COUPLE OF QUESTIONS, MR. MANDLEY. I THINK YOU TESTIFIED THAT AFTER 1980, YOU HAVEN'T BEEN BACK ON THE PROPERTY. IS THAT TRUE?

A   NO, THAT'S NOT TRUE. I DIDN'T SAY I HAVEN'T BEEN BACK ON THE PROPERTY, BUT I HAVEN'T BEEN BACK TO WORK.

Q   HAVE YOU BEEN BACK THERE SINCE '82, SINCE MAY LEFT THE FAMILY?

A   SINCE '82, ONCE, I THINK.

Q   NOW, I THINK YOU TESTIFIED THAT YOU WERE INVOLVED IN A CONVERSATION ABOUT WILL TRANSFERRING PROPERTY AND MAY TRANSFERRING PROPERTY. IS THAT TRUE?

A   YES.

Q   I BELIEVE THE RECORD SHOWS THAT OCCURRED SOMETIME IN 1982 OR '81, AND SO YOU MIGHT HAVE BEEN THERE SOMETIME IN '81?

A   YES, DEFINITELY.

Q   IT WAS PRIOR TO THIS COMING DOWN OR AFTER?

A   NO, IN '81.

Q   WAS IT PRIOR TO THEM PREPARING THE DEEDS, TRANSFERRING THE PROPERTY BACK AND FORTH OR WAS IT AFTER THEY HAD ALREADY DONE IT?

A   I THINK IT WAS AFTER.

Q   SO IT WOULD BE SOMETIME AFTER THE DATES SHOWN ON THIS PARTICULAR DEED?

A   I WOULD THINK SO, YES.

A   YOU WERE NOT WORKING DOWN THERE? YOU

385

WERE JUST DOWN VISITING MAY AT THAT TIME?

A   NO. THERE WAS SOME WORK I WAS DOING AT
THAT TIME.

Q   YOU ASSISTED IN THAT WORK, IS THAT
CORRECT?

A   THAT'S RIGHT.

Q   IN CONSTRUCTING THE EQUIPMENT FOR THAT
OPERATION?

A   YES, SOME OF IT. THE HEATING SYSTEM, YOU
KNOW, FOR DRYING THE DRUMS. I DESIGNED IT, AND I
HELPED BUILD IT.

Q   YOU KNEW DURING THE ENTIRE PERIOD FROM
'76 ON THAT MAY WAS BARD'S WIFE, I SUPPOSE?

A   NO, I DID NOT.

Q   YOU DID NOT KNOW THAT?

A   NO, SIR, I DID NOT.

Q   YOU HAD JUST BEEN CALLED DOWN AS AN
EMPLOYEE? WHEN DID YOU FIRST FIND THAT OUT?

A   I WAS CALLED -- HE ALWAYS CALLED HER HIS
DAUGHTER.

Q   WHEN DID YOU DISCOVER SHE WAS HIS WIFE?

A   OH, I DON'T KNOW WHETHER THAT WAS IN '80
OR JUST BEFORE THAT, BUT IT WAS RIGHT ABOUT '80,
1980.

Q   AS A PRACTICAL MATTER, YOU WELL
UNDERSTOOD, BEING AROUND MAY AND BEING AROUND
BARD, THAT MAY WAS THE MORE INTELLIGENT, WAS THE
OPERATOR OF THE BUSINESS. IS THAT TRUE? I THINK
YOU TESTIFIED TO THAT?

A   WELL, YES, TO A BIG EXTENT.

Q   YOU TESTIFIED THAT BARD HAD SAID THAT IF
SHE COULD OPERATE THE BUSINESS, SOMEBODY ELSE
COULD; IS THAT TRUE?

A   I DIDN'T SAY IT JUST IN EXACTLY THOSE
WORDS.

Q   WELL, IS THAT YOUR UNDERSTANDING?

A   WELL, I WOULD THINK SO, YES.

Q   IN FACT, THAT WAS YOUR BELIEF, THAT MAY
WAS MORE INTELLIGENT, HAD MORE ABILITY TO DO
THOSE THINGS THAN BARD DID?

A   WELL, SHE HAD THE EXPERTISE THAT SHE
COULD MEET PEOPLE AND TALK WITH THEM THAT BARD
DIDN'T HAVE.

Q   DID YOU FEEL BARD TO BE OF MORE
INTELLIGENCE THAN MAY?

A   NO, I DID NOT.

Q   HAD YOU EVER KNOWN BARD PRIOR? DID YOU
HAVE ANY ACQUAINTANCE WITH HIM DURING THE
PERIOD FROM '67 WHEN YOU FIRST WENT TO THEIR
HOME UNTIL 1976?

A   I HAD CONTACT WITH THEM, YES. HE USED TO
COME UP AND VISIT WITH THEM, YES, UP TO MY PLACE
OF BUSINESS.

Q   YOU HAD THIS PLUMBING BUSINESS AND
HEATING?

A   YES

MR. FLANK: THAT'S ALL I HAVE.

THE COURT: ANYTHING FURTHER, MR. RYAN?

MR. RYAN: NOTHING FURTHER, JUDGE.

THE COURT: ALL RIGHT, MR. MANDLEY, YOU

387

ARE FREE TO GO. THANK YOU, SIR.

MR. MANDLEY: THANK YOU.

MR. RYAN: I JUST HAVE ONE OTHER WITNESS
TO CALL BACK FOR A COUPLE OF QUESTIONS. J. BARD
KANDERHOSH.

MR. FLANK: DID YOU WANT TO PROFFER YOUR
--

MR. RYAN: BEFORE THAT, JUDGE, WE HAVE A
PROFFER, IF WE MAY PRESENT THAT TO THE COURT.

THE COURT: YOU MAY.

MR. RYAN: I HAD PLANNED ON CALLING AS A
WITNESS BARDELL DARDSON. IF BARDELL DARDSON
WERE CALLED TO TESTIFY, SHE WOULD TESTIFY THAT
SHE WAS MARRIED TO WILLER DARDSON AND LIVED IN
THE FAMILY FROM 1968 THROUGH 1982, AND THAT
DURING THAT TIME, MAY SLEPT EACH NIGHT IN BARD
KANDERHOSH'S BEDROOM, THAT SHE DID NOT HAVE HER
OWN BEDROOM.

MR. FLANK: I WOULD STIPULATE THAT IF SHE
WERE CALLED TO TESTIFY, SHE WOULD TESTIFY THAT
UNTIL THE TIME SHE SUPPORTED THE FAMILY UNTIL SHE
WAS DIVORCED FROM MR. DARDSON, THAT WAS TRUE
THAT SHE -- I THINK THE DIVORCE OCCURRED IN ABOUT
1980 OR THEREABOUTS WHEN SHE LEFT, NOT '82.

MR. RYAN: WELL, I UNDERSTOOD IT WAS '82.

MR. FLANK: IT WAS '80 INSTEAD OF '82.

THE COURT: YOU HAVE NO OBJECTION TO THE
PROFFER?

MR. FLANK: I HAVE NO OBJECTION IF SHE
WERE CALLED TO TESTIFY, SHE WOULD TESTIFY TO

388

THAT.

THE COURT: THE PROFFER IS ACCEPTED.

MR. RYAN: NOW THE, OTHER PROFFER I HAD WOULD COME FROM MR. KEVIN HUNTSLEY AND MR. BOYD HUNTSLEY. MR. KEVIN HUNTSLEY IS THE SON OF BOYD HUNTSLEY. MR. BOYD HUNTSLEY HAS BEEN EMPLOYED AT RECLAIM BARREL SUPPLY SINCE THE INCEPTION IN 1976. MR. KEVIN HUNTSLEY HAS BEEN EMPLOYED SINCE APPROXIMATELY 1979. THEY WOULD JOINTLY AND SEVERALLY TESTIFY THAT DURING THAT TIME PERIOD, THAT MAY KANDERHOSH WAS PRIMARILY THE ONE RESPONSIBLE FOR THE RUNNING OF THE BUSINESS, AND THE MAKING OF DECISIONS, AND THAT MR. BARD KANDERHOSH HAD VERY LITTLE, IF ANY, INVOLVEMENT IN THE DAY-TO-DAY RUNNING OF THE BUSINESS. THAT'S THE PROFFER.

MR. FLANK: I WOULD AGREE THAT IF THEY WERE CALLED TO TESTIFY, THAT WOULD BE THEIR TESTIMONY, THAT MAY KANDERHOSH WAS, IN FACT, THE OPERATOR OF THE BUSINESS, THE BRAINS, WHO MADE DECISIONS FOR THE BUSINESS.

THE COURT: VERY WELL, GENTLEMEN. I WILL ACCEPT THAT PROFFER LIKEWISE.

YOU NOW HAVE ONE LAST WITNESS, MR. RYAN?

MR. RYAN: THAT IS CORRECT, MR. BARD KANDERHOSH.

THE COURT: MR. KANDERHOSH, COME FORWARD, PLEASE. YOU ARE STILL UNDER OATH.

<u>J. BARD KANDERHOSH</u>

CALLED AS A WITNESS BY AND ON BEHALF OF THE

DEFENDANT, HAVING BEEN PREVIOUSLY DULY SWORN, WAS EXAMINED AND TESTIFIED FURTHER AS FOLLOWS:

DIRECT EXAMINATION

BY MR. RYAN:

Q MR. KANDERHOSH, DO YOU RECALL YESTERDAY WHEN YOUR WIFE TESTIFIED THAT SHE KNEW OF NO TIME THAT YOU RECEIVED ANY PAYMENTS FROM WELFARE?

A SHE SAID THAT, BUT --

Q THAT'S NOT TRUE, IS IT?

A NO.

Q IN FACT, YOU HAVE RECEIVED WELFARE PAYMENTS IN THE PAST, HAVE YOU NOT?

A YES.

Q IN FACT, IN 1983 YOU WERE RECEIVING $505 A MONTH?

A I DON'T KNOW WHAT THE FIGURE WAS.

Q LET ME REFRESH YOUR MEMORY, IF I MAY. DO YOU RECALL YOUR DEPOSITION TAKEN ON APRIL 11, 1983? THIS WAS BY MR. LARRY HANSEN?

A UN-HUH (AFFIRMATIVE).

MR. RYAN: MAY I READ FROM THIS?

THE COURT: WELL, FIRST IF YOU ARE GOING TO READ FROM IT, LET'S HAVE THE DEPOSITION FILED.

MR. RYAN: MAY I ASK THAT THE DEPOSITION OF J. BARD KANDERHOSH BE PUBLISHED, DATED APRIL 11TH OF 1983?

THE COURT: IS IT FILED? ANY OBJECTION?

MR. FLANK: NO OBJECTION.

THE COURT: VERY WELL. THE DEPOSITION OF

MR. KANDERHOSH IS PUBLISHED. LET'S GIVE MR. RYAN THAT ORIGINAL SO THAT MR. KANDERHOSH CAN FOLLOW ALONG.

Q (BY MR. RYAN) COULD I GET YOU TO TURN TO PAGE 27, MR. KANDERHOSH.

I'M SORRY, THAT'S THE DEPOSITION TAKEN ON APRIL 11TH. THAT'S THE MOST RECENT ONE.

POSSIBLY, MR. FLANK, WOULD YOU STIPULATE THAT THE DEPOSITION WAS TAKEN, HE WAS PRESENT AT THE TIME, AND WE COULD USE A COPY POSSIBLY TO SAVE TIME?

THE COURT: DO YOU HAVE A COPY OF THAT DEPOSITION, MR. FLANK?

MR. FLANK: I'M JUST LOOKING, YOUR HONOR. EACH OF THE ATTORNEYS TOOK A COPY. LET'S SEE IF THIS IS THE ONE.

MR. RYAN: THAT'S THE ONE.

MR. FLANK: I DO.

MR. RYAN: IN FACT, HE HAS THE ORIGINAL.

MR. FLANK: I DO.

THE COURT: YOU HAVE THE ORIGINAL?

MR. FLANK: I DO.

THE COURT: ALL RIGHT. LET'S USE THAT.

Q (BY MR. RYAN) NOW, YOU ARE ON PAGE 27. I DIRECT YOU TO LINE 22, THE QUESTION, "WHAT SOURCES OF INCOME HAVE YOU HAD TO SUPPORT YOUR FAMILY DURING THE YEAR 1983?" AND ANSWER, "I HAVE BEEN ON WELFARE." DO YOU RECALL THOSE?

A YES.

Q THEN ON PAGE 28, THE QUESTION ON PAGE 5 -

391

- OR EXCUSE ME, LINE 5, "HOW MUCH DO YOU RECEIVE FROM THAT SOURCE?" ANSWER, "$575." DO YOU RECALL THAT TESTIMONY?

A   YES.

Q   IS THAT CORRECT?

A   YES.

Q   THAT WAS THE AMOUNT THAT YOU RECEIVED AT THAT TIME?

A   I BELIEVE SO.

Q   HOW LONG AFTER THAT DID YOU RECEIVE THOSE PAYMENTS, MR. KANDERHOSH?

A   I DON'T KNOW.

A   DO YOU STILL RECEIVE THEM?

A   NO.

Q   SO THEY TERMINATED AT SOME POINT?

A   SINCE I GOT ON THIS SOCIAL SECURITY, THEY CUT IT DOWN QUITE A WAYS BUT STILL RECEIVE SOME AMOUNT. I RECEIVE SOME AMOUNT.

Q   BUT YOU DON'T KNOW WHAT THAT AMOUNT IS?

A   NO. MY WIFE COULD TESTIFY TO THAT AMOUNT.

Q   I BELIEVE SHE TESTIFIED THAT YOU DID NOT RECEIVE ANY, DIDN'T SHE, JUST YESTERDAY?

A   I DON'T KNOW IF SHE UNDERSTOOD YOUR QUESTION.

MR. RYAN: I HAVE NO FURTHER QUESTIONS.

CROSS EXAMINATION

BY MR. FLANK:

Q   THAT IS THE COMPENSATION THAT YOU RECEIVED AFTER MAY QUIT, YOU APPLIED FOR AFTER

392

YOU DISCONTINUED RECEIVING MONEY FROM THE
BUSINESS. IS THAT TRUE?

A   THAT'S TRUE.

Q   THAT'S BASICALLY WHAT YOU HAD TO LIVE ON,
YOU AND THE CHILDREN?

A   YES.

A   AND NANAS?

A   UH-HUH (AFFIRMATIVE).

Q   OR ZOSA, I'M SORRY.

A   YES.

MR. FLANK: THAT'S ALL. I HAVE NOTHING
FURTHER.

MR. RYAN: I HAVE NOTHING FURTHER, JUDGE.

THE COURT: MR. KANDERHOSH, YOU MAY STEP
DOWN AGAIN.

DO YOU NOW REST, MR. RYAN?

MR. RYAN: THE DEFENDANT RESTS.

THE COURT: ANY REBUTTAL?

MR. FLANK: WE HAVE NONE.

THE COURT: LADIES AND GENTLEMEN OF THE
JURY, THE EVIDENCE IN THIS CASE IS NOW CONCLUDED.
IT IS NECESSARY FOR MYSELF AND THE ATTORNEYS
INVOLVED IN THIS CASE NOW TO PREPARE THE
INSTRUCTIONS REGARDING THE LAW THAT WILL BE
GIVEN TO YOU ON THIS CASE FOR YOUR
CONSIDERATION. IT WILL TAKE US TIME TO DO THAT,
AND ACCORDINGLY, WHAT I WANT TO DO IS RECESS YOU
FOLKS UNTIL THIS AFTERNOON AT 2:00 O'CLOCK.
ACTUALLY, I THINK IT WOULD BE WISER FOR YOU TO
RETURN HER AT 1:30. I AM OPTIMISTIC THAT WE CAN

HAVE THE INSTRUCTIONS READY FOR YOU AT THAT
TIME, AT WHICH TIME WE WILL GIVE YOU THE
INSTRUCTIONS, THE LAWYERS WILL ARGUE THEIR CASE,
AND THEN YOU WILL BE ALLOWED TO DELIBERATE TO
ARRIVE AT YOUR DECISION. REMEMBER THE ADMONI-
TION THAT I HAVE GIVEN YOU NOT TO DISCUSS THE
CASE WITH ANYONE.

YOU HAVE NOW HEARD ALL OF THE EVIDENCE,
AND SO PLEASE KEEP AN OPEN MIND UNTIL YOU HAVE
HEARD THE ARGUMENTS OF COUNSEL AND THE CASE IS
DELIVERED TO YOU. RETURN HERE THIS AFTERNOON AT
1:30, AND THE COURT WILL BE IN RECESS. I WANT TO
SEE COUNSEL IN CHAMBERS.

(A RECESS WAS TAKEN.)

THE COURT: THE JURY, PARTIES, AND
COUNSEL ARE PRESENT.

(THE JURY WAS INSTRUCTED BY THE COURT.)

THE COURT: AS I HAVE INDICATED, LADIES
AND GENTLEMEN, I AM SUBMITTING TO YOU A SPECIAL
VERDICT FORM WHICH CONSISTS OF TWELVE QUESTIONS,
NOT NECESSARILY ALL OF WHICH MUST BE ANSWERED,
BUT THAT WILL BECOME APPARENT TO YOU AS YOU
READ THROUGH THE VERDICT FORM, AND AS I HAVE
STATED TO YOU, THE QUESTIONS ARE PRINCIPALLY YES,
NO ANSWERS, AND IT TAKES THE AGREEMENT OF SIX
JURORS TO ARRIVE AT AN ANSWER ON EACH OF THE
QUESTIONS. THAT NEED NOT, HOWEVER, BE THE SAME
SIX ON ALL QUESTIONS.

COUNSEL, YOU MAY PRESENT YOUR CLOSING
ARGUMENTS. I FIRST, THOUGH, WANT TO GET A TIME

394

COMMITMENT. MR. FLANK?

MR. FLANK: I WILL TAKE TEN MINUTES INITIALLY AND FIVE MINUTES ON REBUTTAL, YOUR HONOR.

THE COURT: VERY WELL. I WILL WARN YOU AT TWO MINUTES.

MR. RYAN?

MR. RYAN: I WILL TAKE FIFTEEN MINUTES.

THE COURT: SAME WARNING. YOU MAY PROCEED.

MR. FLANK: LADIES AND GENTLEMEN, YOUR HONOR, I NOW HAVE AN OPPORTUNITY TO BASICALLY TELL YOU WHAT I THINK THOSE INSTRUCTIONS SAY AND WHAT I THINK THE EVIDENCE WAS AND HOW I BELIEVE YOU SHOULD DETERMINE THIS CASE. YOU HAVE HEARD AN INSTRUCTION THAT WHAT I SAY TO YOU IS NOT EVI-DENCE, ONLY ARGUMENT. YOU SHOULD KEEP THAT IN MIND WHEN I SPEAK, AS WELL AS MR. RYAN SPEAKS. WE ARE SIMPLY TRYING NOW, THE INITIAL OPENING STATEMENT, SPECIFICALLY ATTEMPTED TO SET OUT THE PICTURE BY WHICH I HOPE THAT YOU EVENTUALLY GOT THE PICTURE. I'M NOW GOING TO TRY AND PUT IT BACK TOGETHER AGAIN AS TO WHAT I BELIEVE THE EVIDENCE SHOWED.

NOW, THERE'S NO QUESTION AS TO CERTAIN FACTS, TOTALLY UNCONTROVERTED. THOSE FACTS WERE BASICALLY THESE, AND I THINK THESE ARE IMPORTANT. I'M GOING TO TRY AND GIVE YOU THE FIRES, NOT THE SMOKE.

WHAT THE FIRE SHOWED WAS THAT NANAS

395

KANDERHOSH WAS A WIDOW WHO MARRIED BARD
KANDERHOSH IN 1962 WHO OWNED PROPERTY. THAT
PROPERTY WAS LATER TRADED FOR THE PROPERTY WE
ARE NOW CONSIDERING. NO ONE ELSE PUT ANY MONEY
INTO IT. IT WAS ALL PAID. THE LOTS 1, 19 AND 20
WERE PAID IN FULL BY THAT TRADE WITH THE FARM,
WHICH WE ARE NOT CONCERNED WITH. THE EVIDENCE
WAS THAT THE FARM WAS TURNED OVER TO WILLER
WHO LATER TURNED IT BACK TO THE FAMILY.

THE END RESULT BASICALLY THEN IS THIS:
THAT NANAS KANDERHOSH IN FACT, OWNED PROPERTY
WHICH WAS TRADED FOR LOTS 1, 19, 20 AND 2. 2, THERE
REMAINED A MORTGAGE ON IT. IT WAS BOUGHT A YEAR
LATER. THERE STILL REMAINS A MORTGAGE ON THAT
PROPERTY. WE ARE ASKING YOU TO RETURN THAT
PROPERTY, LOTS 1 AND 2, 1 BEING THE -- OR LOT 2
BEING THE WHITE HOUSE, LOT 1 BEING THE RED HOUSE,
AND LOTS 19 AND 20 WE ARE ASKING YOU TO RETURN
THAT PROPERTY TO NANAS KANDERHOSH.

NOW, WHAT YOU HAVE TO FIND TO COME TO
THAT CONCLUSION, NUMBER ONE, YOU HAVE JUST
HEARD AN INSTRUCTION, AND THIS WAS LISTED AS
INSTRUCTION NO. 11, BUT PLAINTIFFS AND DEFENDANTS
ENTERED INTO AN AGREEMENT WHEREBY PLAINTIFF
AGREED TO CONVEY CERTAIN REAL PROPERTY, AND
DEFENDANT AGREED TO ALLOW PLAINTIFF TO REMAIN
AND USE THAT PROPERTY, AND IT GOES ON, AND YOU
CAN READ IT, YOU WILL HAVE THESE INSTRUCTIONS. 11
IS THE IMPORTANT ONE, AND IF YOU BELIEVE THAT SHE
ORDERED THEM OFF OF THE PROPERTY, WHICH SHE

396

TESTIFIED SHE DID, AND IF YOU BELIEVE THAT SHE
AGREED TO SUPPORT AND HELP THAT FAMILY IN
REGARD TO THE BUSINESS, AND SHE BREACHED THAT,
WHICH SHE SAYS SHE DID. THEN YOU SHOULD AWARD
THE PROPERTY BACK TO NANAS.

THE EVIDENCE BASICALLY WAS THIS: THAT
SHE SPECIFICALLY STATED, AND YOU HEARD HER READ
IN HER OWN ACTION AGAINST WILLER THAT IN
CONSIDERATION FOR THE TRANSFER OF THAT PROPERTY
TO HER AND WILLER, THEY AGREED EQUALLY TO PAY
ONE-HALF OF THE SUPPORT AND MAINTENANCE OF
NANAS AND BARD AND THE FAMILY, THE BEST THEY
COULD. SHE HAS ADMITTED THAT FACT, DURING THAT
PERIOD OF TIME, THAT DURING THAT PERIOD OF TIME,
SHE DID, IN FACT, DO WHAT SHE HAD AGREED TO FROM
1975 TO 1982, AND IN 1982, SHE TERMINATED THAT
AGREEMENT.

NOT ONLY DID SHE DISCONTINUE AT THAT
POINT IN TIME OF ASSISTING THE FAMILY AND
PURSUANT TO HER AGREEMENT, SHE SERVED A NOTICE
FOR THEM TO REMOVE FROM THE HOME.

ALL YOU HAVE TO DO, IF YOU BELIEVE THAT'S
WHAT OCCURRED, THEN SHE BREACHED THE AGREEMENT
THAT SHE ENTERED INTO WHEN THE PROPERTY WAS
TRANSFERRED, AND YOU SHOULD HAVE THE PROPERTY
RETURNED TO NANAS. THE END RESULT THEN WOULD
BE, AND YOU HEARD THE TESTIMONY OF NANAS, SHE
GOT $203 FROM AN OIL PAYMENT AND SOME SOCIAL
SECURITY. NANAS, IN FACT, ASSISTS THE ENTIRE
FAMILY IN PROVIDING THEIR INCOME.

397

WHAT YOU HAVE TO LOOK AT, AND FROM THE
EVIDENCE YOU HEARD, THERE ARE OTHER SIDES
INVOLVED, FOUR CHILDREN, ANOTHER SICK WOMAN.
NANAS SPENDS ALL HER PROCEEDS, EVERYTHING SHE
HAS TO TAKE CARE OF THAT FAMILY. SHE'S DOWN THE
BEST SHE CAN. YOU HAVE EVEN HEARD THAT THEY
HAVE HAD WELFARE SINCE SHE DISCONTINUED ASSISTING
IN '82.

NOW, WHAT HAS MAY DONE? MAY HAS, IN
FACT, TESTIFIED THAT SHE HAS EARNED $3,000, A
MINIMUM OF $3,000 PER MONTH INCOME FROM THE
BUSINESS. SHE BOUGHT A PIECE OF PROPERTY IN LEHI,
PAID $2,200 A MONTH FOR IT, A FARM. SHE HAS PUT A
WELL ON IT. SHE'S BOUGHT SOME LOGS TO BUILD A
HOUSE ON IT. BASICALLY, WHERE DOES THE EQUITY
LIE? YOU HEARD MAY TESTIFY, AND I WAS QUITE
SURPRISED THAT SHE ESCAPED FROM THE SITUATION IN
MAY OF 1982 BECAUSE IT WAS INTOLERABLE, THAT HERE
SHE BELIEVES IN A RELIGION THAT BELIEVES IN
POLYGAMY, THAT BELIEVES THAT SHE SHOULD BE
MARRIED TO A MAN WITH MORE THAN ONE WIFE, AND
YET SHE TESTIFIED THAT SHE CONTINUES TO BELIEVE
THAT, THAT, IN FACT, SHE BELIEVES AND HAS JOINED
ANOTHER GROUP WHO BELIEVES THE SAME THING, AND
SHE TESTIFIED THAT SHE BELIEVES PURSUANT TO THE
TENETS OF THOSE CHURCHES THAT A WOMAN SHOULD
OBEY HER HUSBAND, AND THAT SHE, IN FACT, DURING
THE 18-YEAR PERIOD OF TIME LIVED WITH THAT BELIEF.

SHE BELIEVED THAT SHE WAS LEGALLY AND
RELIGIOUSLY MARRIED TO -- SPIRITUALLY, SPIRITUALLY

398

MARRIED TO BARD. SHE BELIEVED AND STILL BELIEVES, AND I THINK THAT'S IMPORTANT THAT SHE STILL BELIEVES THESE SAME THINGS, THAT, IN FACT, SHE DID NOT ESCAPE FROM ANYTHING. THE ONLY THING SHE DID WAS CREATE A SITUATION WHEREBY SHE SAW A BUSINESS PROSPER. SHE SAW THAT MONEY WAS TO BE MADE. SHE SAW A BETTER LIFE FOR HERSELF FINANCIALLY, NOT SPIRITUALLY, NOTHING TO DO WITH WHAT SHE BELIEVED AS FAR AS HER LIFE WAS CON-CERNED, BUT MONEY. THAT GREED BECAME THE MASTER, NO LONGER HER TOTAL BELIEF IN THE SPIRITUAL AND RELIGION OF THE SECT THAT SHE BELONGED TO.

THE COURT: TWO MINUTES, MR. FLANK.

MR. FLANK: THE END RESULT OF HER CLAIMS OF ASSAULT, FALSE IMPRISONMENT AND BATTERY AND EMOTIONAL HARM HAD TO DO WITH THINKING ABOUT THIS SOME YEARS AFTER, NOT AT THE TIME SHE LEFT AND SERVED NOTICE FOR THEM TO GET OUT OF THE HOUSE ON THE BASIS OF GREED.

MR. BARD KANDERHOSH, I DON'T KNOW, I HAVE NO COMPREHENSION ABOUT PLURAL MARRIAGE OR OTHERWISE, BUT MR. BARD KANDERHOSH BELIEVES THAT SAME TENET. YOU HAVE HEARD HIM TESTIFY, AND YOU HAVE HEARD MAY TESTIFY. YOU HAVE HEARD MAY TESTIFY THAT SHE BELIEVED HERSELF TO BE THE INTELLIGENT MEMBER OF THE FAMILY, TO BE THE CONTROLLER OF THE FAMILY, AND YOU HAVE HEARD THEM EACH. YOU MAKE UP YOUR MIND.

DOES BARD APPEAR TO YOU TO BE A

399

FORCEFUL PUSHY MAN? DON'T YOU THINK MAY COULD
HAVE DONE EXACTLY WHAT SHE WANTED TO ANYTIME
SHE WANTED TO DO IT? YOU HAVE HEARD HER
TESTIFY, AND I'M SURE YOUR BELIEFS ARE AS MINE
ARE, THAT SHE CERTAINLY COULD. IF YOU AWARD
DAMAGES TO HER AS AGAINST BARD, WHAT HAVE YOU
DONE? WHAT DOES HE HAVE? NOTHING.

WE ARE NOT ASKING THAT YOU RETURN THAT
HOUSE TO BARD, THOSE HOUSES OR THE BUSINESS
PROPERTY. WE ARE ASKING YOU TO RETURN THOSE TO
NANAS.

NOW, THE QUESTION OF THE BUSINESS, AND I
WILL BE VERY SHORT, MY TIME IS UP. WE DO REQUEST
THAT YOU GIVE NANAS AND BARD A PORTION OF THAT
BUSINESS. WHAT PERCENTAGE, I FEEL, WOULD BE A 50
PERCENT AND HER A 50 PERCENT, AND THERE WILL BE A
PROVISION IN THE VERDICT THAT YOU CAN MAKE THAT
DETERMINATION. WE REQUEST YOU TO DO SO. THANK
YOU, LADIES AND GENTLEMEN.

THE COURT: THANK YOU, MR. FLANK.

MR. RYAN?

MR. RYAN: THANK YOU. MAY IT PLEASE THE
COURT, OPPOSING COUNSEL, LADIES AND GENTLEMEN OF
THE JURY: I APPRECIATE HAVING THE OPPORTUNITY AT
THIS POINT TO ADDRESS YOU AND WOULD SUGGEST TO
YOU THAT AT LEAST ONE TIME IN YOUR LIVES, YOU
WILL HAVE AN OPPORTUNITY TO DO JUSTICE IF YOU SO
DESIRE, AND I THINK IN MY EIGHT-SOME YEARS IN THE
LAW PRACTICE, I HAVE BECOME SOMEWHAT JADED TO
THE QUESTION OF WHAT IS RIGHT IN THAT WAY. WHAT

400

DOES JUSTICE MEAN?

IN THIS CASE, HOWEVER,I THINK YOU HAVE THAT OPPORTUNITY. YOU HAVE SAT HERE, AND I APOLOGIZE FOR THE LENGTHINESS OF SOME OF THE TESTIMONY TO WHICH YOU HAVE BEEN SUBJECTED AND ALSO FOR THE CONTENTS OF IT, BUT I AM CONFIDENT THAT YOU AS IMPARTIAL MEMBERS OF THIS COMMUNITY WILL HAVE DISCERNED VISUALLY, WHO WAS TELLING THE TRUTH FROM THAT STAND, AND I THINK THAT YOU WILL RENDER A JUST VERDICT BASED UPON THAT.

NOW, I WOULD LIKE TO JUST SORT OF MAKE THIS IN TWO DIFFERENT APPROACHES, AND ONE IS HAVING TO DO WITH THE SITUATION THAT MS. HANCOCK FOUND HERSELF IN IN 1963. THIS TESTIMONY WAS UNCONTROVERTED. SHE WENT INTO THIS MARRIAGE RELATIONSHIP WITH MR. KANDERHOSH BELIEVING THAT SHE WAS TO BE A MEMBER OF THAT FAMILY, THAT SHE WOULD HAVE CHILDREN, THAT SHE WOULD HAVE AN EQUAL SHARE OF THE LABOR, AND THAT SHE WOULD BE TREATED WITH RESPECT.

IF YOU BELIEVE WHAT SHE HAS TOLD YOU FROM THAT STAND, YOU CAN SEE THAT HER ANTICIPATION AND HER AGREEMENT WAS VIOLATED INSIDIOUSLY IN EVERY CONCEIVABLE WAY. YET THROUGH ALL OF THAT, SHE STAYED 18 YEARS. SHE WENT THERE AS A YOUNG GIRL OF 16, CAME BACK AT APPROXIMATELY THE AGE OF 34 AFTER THIS IS ALL OVER.

AT THAT TIME, SHE HAD VIRTUALLY LOST ALL OF THE OPPORTUNITY TIME-WISE OF HAVING CHILDREN

401

AND TOLD YOU SHE DIDN'T EVEN HAVE ANY CLOTHING, THAT SHE HADN'T BOUGHT AT DESERET INDUSTRIES.

NOW, DURING THIS TIME, SHE TOOK THIS BUSINESS AND TURNED IT INTO A PAYING PROPOSITION, AND THROUGH HER OWN EFFORTS, NOT THE EFFORTS AND HELP OF ANYBODY ELSE. IN FACT, DESPITE THE OTHER MEMBERS OF THE FAMILY, SHE TURNED THAT BARREL BUSINESS INTO A PAYING PROPOSITION AS WELL.

NOW, LET'S CONSIDER WHAT THE OPPOSITION IS ASKING FOR. NOW, MR. KANDERHOSH IS AN INDIVIDUAL. HE'S BEEN MARRIED SINCE APPROXIMATELY THE AGE OF 33 OR 34 TO MRS. KANDERHOSH, AND SINCE THAT TIME, BY THEIR OWN TESTIMONY, HAS NOT HAD ONE EMPLOYMENT, SAVE IT BE WITH PRODUCTS GOING DOOR TO DOOR AND WORKING IN THE BOTTLE BUSINESS, AND A LITTLE BIT IN THE BARREL BUSINESS.

NOW, THAT IS A LONG TIME TO BE WITHOUT A JOB, AND HE'S ONLY 54 YEARS OLD AT THIS TIME. NOW, I DON'T THINK THAT PEOPLE OUGHT TO BE REWARDED FOR NOT DOING ANYTHING.

NOW, THIS WAS BUILT ON THE PRINCIPLES OF THE PROTESTANT WORK ETHIC, AND I WANT YOU, IF YOU WILL, TO MEASURE MY CLIENT BY THAT SAME STANDARD, AND MEASURE THESE PEOPLE BY THIS SAME STANDARD. THEY DID NOTHING FOR HER ESSENTIALLY EXCEPT PROVIDE HER A PLACE TO LIVE AND TOOK ADVANTAGE OF HER AT EVERY CONCEIVABLE WAY, AT EVERY CONCEIVABLE TURN, AND NOW THEY WANT HER OUT OF THE BUSINESS.

NOW, THE TESTIMONY HAS BEEN UNCONTROVERTED

402

EXCEPT BY MR. KANDERHOSH HIMSELF, AND THAT MAY WAS THE FOUNDER OF THE BUSINESS. SHE WORKED AT THE BUSINESS. SHE'S THE ONE THAT DID THE CONTRACT. SHE EVEN MADE, SHE DESIGNED, AND MADE HERSELF WITH HER OWN HANDS THE ITEMS OF MACHINERY IN THERE, AND NOW THEY WANT TO TAKE THAT FROM HER. I DON'T THINK THAT YOU AS THESE LADIES' PEERS ARE GOING TO ALLOW THEM TO DO THAT, AND I URGE YOU NOT TO. IN OTHER WORDS, DO I THINK THAT YOU WILL GIVE BACK TO MRS. KANDERHOSH AND MRS. KANDERHOSH THE REAL PROPERTY UPON WHICH THAT BUSINESS SITS.

NOW, I WON'T GO THROUGH ALL OF THE THINGS WE HAVE TALKED ABOUT, BUT WITH REGARD TO THE FACT THESE PEOPLE HAVE HAD NO REMUNERATIVE EMPLOYMENT DURING VIRTUALLY THEIR ENTIRE LIVES. I HAVE HEARD NO TESTIMONY FROM ANY DOCTOR ABOUT ANY PHYSICAL IMPAIRMENT. THERE WAS NO DOCTOR ON THAT STAND TO SAY THAT MR. KANDERHOSH WAS UNABLE TO FIND WORK OR THAT NANAS KANDERHOSH WAS UNABLE TO HOLD A JOB. THERE'S NO TESTIMONY TO THAT.

NOW, LET ME JUST TELL YOU THAT YOU WILL HAVE ACCESS TO THESE DOCUMENTS WHEN YOU GET IN THE JURY ROOM. THESE ARE DEEDS WHICH TRANSFERRED THIS PROPERTY ABOUT, AS YOU HAVE HEARD SOME TESTIMONY. THESE PEOPLE WERE VERY METICULOUS ABOUT DEEDS AND ABOUT THE DOCUMENTS THEY DID.

NOW, MR. FLANK AND HIS CLIENTS ARE TRYING

403

TO CONVINCE YOU THAT MY CLIENT RECEIVED THIS PROPERTY, AND AT THE SAME TIME SHE RECEIVED IT, SHE EXECUTED QUIT CLAIM DEEDS BACK TO THEM TO SECURE HER SUPPOSED PROPERTY TO TAKE CARE OF THEM FOR THE REST OF HER LIFE. I ASK YOU WHAT ARE THESE DEEDS? THEY WERE SUPPOSEDLY PREPARED BY -- I DON'T REMEMBER HIS NAME RIGHT NOW. THE QUESTION, WHERE WAS HE, WHY DIDN'T HE COME AND TESTIFY THAT HE PREPARED THOSE DEEDS, AND THAT MY CLIENT SIGNED THEM? MY CLIENT DENIES THEY EXIST. THE ONLY PEOPLE THAT SAY THEY EXIST ARE MR. AND MRS. KANDERHOSH AND WILLER DARDSON, AND THERE'S NO COPY OF ANY DEEDS. THOSE COULD BE ADMISSIBLE IF THE ORIGINALS WERE GONE.

I SUBMIT TO YOU THAT THERE ARE NO DEEDS, THAT THE ENTIRE CONCEPT THAT THERE WERE DEEDS RETURNING THE LAND IS A FIGMENT OF THEIR IMAGINATION, WHICH THEY CONJURED UP TO SUPPORT THEIR POSITION THAT MY CLIENT WAS GOING TO SUPPORT THEM FOR THE REST OF THEIR LIVES. IMAGINE THAT. I DON'T THINK THAT YOU HAVE BEEN TALKED INTO BELIEVING THAT.

NOW, THEY HAVE ASSERTED THAT MRS. KANDERHOSH OWNED THIS PROPERTY, WHICH IS TRUE. SHE PAID $35,000 ON THAT PROPERTY, LOT 2, EXCUSE ME, LOT 1, LOT 19 AND LOT 20. NOW, IN RETURN FOR THIS, MRS. KANDERHOSH HAS TESTIFIED, MY CLIENT TESTIFIED, THIS WAS CONTROVERTED. MY CLIENT BASICALLY SERVED HER AS A HAND MAIDEN FOR SOME 13 YEARS. MY CLIENT SUPPORTED THAT FAMILY

404

ALMOST BY HERSELF, THAT ENTIRE FAMILY FOR 18 YEARS.

NOW, IF YOU DIVIDE THAT $35,000 BY 18, YOU WILL COME UP WITH LESS THAN $2,000 PER YEAR, WHICH I THINK IS REALLY A SMALL WAGE FOR HER TO HAVE RECEIVED DURING THE ENTIRE TIME OF THAT CONTRACT, OR THE ENTIRE TIME THAT SHE WAS IN THAT FAMILY.

NOW, WE ARE ASKING, FIRST, THAT YOU LEAVE THE REAL PROPERTY AS IT IS. MY CLIENT GAVE NANAS KANDERHOSH A LIFE ESTATE IN THAT HOUSE. SHE SHOULD HAVE THAT. SHE SHOULD STAY THERE. MY CLIENT SHOULD PAY THAT. THAT'S WHAT SHE AGREED TO DO. SHE SHOULD ALSO BE ABLE TO KEEP THE REAL PROPERTY THAT SHE WAS GIVEN IN CONSIDERATION OF THE TEN YEARS OF SERVICE THAT SHE HAD GIVEN TO THIS FAMILY PRIOR TO THIS TIME, AND WE ARE ASKING THAT THOSE REMAIN THERE, THAT YOU FIND THAT THERE WAS NO ENFORCEABLE AGREEMENT FOR ANY CLIENT TO SUPPORT THESE PEOPLE FOR THE REST OF THEIR LIVES, BUT WE ARE ALSO ASKING, AND YOU WILL SEE THESE INSTRUCTIONS AGAIN AS THE COURT HAS GIVEN THEM TO YOU, THAT MY CLIENT HAD INFLICTED UPON HER THE SEVERE EMOTIONAL DISTRESS,AND YOU HAVE HEARD ALL THE TESTIMONY.

I DON'T WANT TO GO AND BELABOR THIS ANY MORE, BUT I AM CONFIDENT THAT YOU WILL FIND THAT MR. KANDERHOSH'S ACTIONS VIS-A-VIS HER WERE INTENTIONALLY, MALICIOUSLY WITH A MOST MALICIOUS HEART DONE TO HER. SHE WAS PUT IN SUCH A

POSITION. IMAGINE BEING THAT AGE AND NOT HAVING A DRIVER'S LICENSE. IMAGINE NEVER HAVING ANY CLOTHES OTHER THAN FROM D.I. AND WORKING ALL THIS TIME. IMAGINE WORKING 14 TO 18 HOURS A DAY. IMAGINE GETTING UP AT 4:30 IN THE MORNING AND WORKING ALL DAY IN THIS BUSINESS. APPARENTLY A GIRL LIKE HER, A YOUNG WOMAN CREATING ALL THIS EQUIPMENT AND RUNNING THIS BUSINESS.

IMAGINE WHAT THIS LADY HAS BEEN THROUGH. IMAGINE NOT BEING ABLE TO SLEEP IN A BED WITHOUT BEING AWAKENED TWO OR THREE TIMES AT NIGHT TO PERFORM SOME CRAZY SEXUAL THING ON MR. KANDERHOSH. I TELL YOU, IT'S AMAZING TO ME THAT SHE IS IN AS GOOD OF A MIND AS SHE IS.

WE ARE ASKING, AND WHETHER OR NOT MR. KANDERHOSH HAS THE ABILITY TO PAY, WERE YOU TO AWARD DAMAGES AGAINST HIM, IS TOTALLY IRRELEVANT TO WHETHER YOU SHOULD OR NOT. WE ARE ASKING THAT YOU COMPENSATE HER IN SOME REASONABLE AMOUNT. I'M NOT GOING TO SUGGEST O YOU ANY AMOUNT. I'M GOING TO LEAVE THAT TO YOUR DISCRETION, BUT I THINK THAT SHE SHOULD BE COM-PENSATED IN SOME WAY. WHETHER SHE CAN COLLECT THAT OR NOT, SHE OUGHT TO HAVE THE SATISFACTION OF HAVING CONVINCED YOU FROM THIS STAND THAT SHE IS ENTITLED TO SOME COMPENSATION FOR UNSPEAKABLE TREATMENT THAT SHE HAS RECEIVED AT THE HANDS OF THIS MAN.

NOW, YES, MY CLIENT BELIEVES IN POLYGAMY. MY CLIENT DID NOT SIGN UP TO BE A THING FOR ANY

406

PERSON AT ALL. SHE SIGNED UP TO BE A PERSON, TO BE A PART OF THE FAMILY. THAT AGREEMENT WAS BREACHED IN THE WORST CONCEIVABLE WAY, AND SHE JUST OUGHT TO BE COMPENSATED FOR THAT.

MRS. KANDERHOSH, YOU HAVE ALREADY HEARD HER TESTIMONY, THAT THEY RECONVEYED THE FARM PROPERTY. SHE HAS A LIFE ESTATE IN THE WHITE HOUSE. IT SEEMS TO ME THAT THAT MORE THAN COMPENSATES HER FOR THE ORIGINAL INVESTMENT IN THIS PROPERTY. SHE HAS ONE OF THE HOUSES. SHE HAS THE FARM. CERTAINLY THERE IS NO REASON TO REWARD HER OR MR. KANDERHOSH FOR ANYTHING THEY HAVE DONE. I ALSO POINT OUT THAT MY CLIENT, ALTHOUGH SHE HAS BOUGHT THIS PIECE OF PROPERTY THAT'S BEEN MENTIONED, SHE OWES APPROXIMATELY $30,000 ON IT, TO WHICH SHE TESTIFIED.

THIS ALMOST DOES NOT MERIT TALKING ABOUT, BUT I WILL ANYWAY, TO SUGGEST THAT MY CLIENT WAS THE CONTROLLING FORCE IN THIS FAMILY IS COMPLETELY WITHOUT MERIT, AND I SUGGEST THAT YOU REJECT THAT OUT OF HAND. YOU HAVE HEARD MY POSITION. YOU HAVE HEARD THE POSITION OF MY CLIENT. YOU HAVE HEARD THE TESTIMONY. I URGE YOU TO AGAIN USE YOUR VISCERAL ABILITIES TO DETERMINE THE OUTCOME OF THIS CASE, AND I PERSONALLY WOULD LIKE TO SAY THAT I APPRECIATE VERY MUCH THE FACT THAT YOU HAVE GIVEN THIS THE ATTENTION THAT YOU HAVE. I APPRECIATE YOUR CONCERN AND WHATEVER THAT YOU WILL DO ON BEHALF OF MY CLIENT. THANK YOU.

407

THE COURT: THANK YOU, MR. RYAN.

MR. FLANK?

MR. FLANK: I NOW GET ANOTHER FIVE MINUTES. I SPLIT MINE UP, BECAUSE BASICALLY I'M THE PLAINTIFF, AND THE BURDEN OF PROOF IS ON ME IN REGARD TO THIS CASE. I JUST HAVE A VERY FEW STATEMENTS IN REGARD TO WHAT MR. RYAN SAID. YOU SEE, MR. RYAN WOULD HAVE YOU BELIEVE THAT MAY HANCOCK WAS DIFFERENT THAN THE REST OF THE FAMILY, THAT BARD KANDERHOSH AND NANAS KANDE-RHOSH SHOPPED AT NEIMAN MARCUS. WHERE DO YOU THINK THEY SHOPPED? NOW, WHERE DO YOU THINK THEY HAVE ALWAYS SHOPPED? YOU SEE POVERTY IN MY CLIENTS. THEY HAVE NO MONEY, BUT POVERTY, THEY HAVE TOTAL POVERTY. THERE ISN'T ANY QUESTION ABOUT IT, THAT MAY WAS A DUTIFUL WIFE AND MEMBER OF THE FAMILY, IS NANAS' RESPONSE.

SHOULD NANAS SUFFER BY REASON OF THE FACT THAT MAY NOW SAYS, I WANT IT ALL? I HAVE GOT IT ALL, AND I'M GOING TO KEEP IT ALL? MR. RYAN SAID HE'S PRACTICED EIGHT YEARS, AND HE WANTS JUSTICE. I HAVE PRACTICED TWENTY-SEVEN, AND THAT'S ALL I WANT. I SIMPLY WANT YOU TO TAKE THE EVIDENCE AS YOU HEAR IT.

WHAT DID SHE AGREE TO DO? SHE WAS A MEMBER OF THE FAMILY. NANAS IS 67 YEARS OLD, AND SHE IS STILL TRYING TO HELP. I AM NOT ASKING THAT YOU GIVE THAT PROPERTY BACK TO BARD. I'M ASKING YOU TO GIVE IT BACK TO NANAS WHO HAD IT. IT WAS

HERS. IT WAS HERS INITIALLY, AND IT WAS HERS WHEN SHE TRADED IT, AND FROM NO OTHER SOURCE. MAY HAD NOTHING TO DO WITH THAT. IT WAS NANAS'.

NOW, AS TO THE BUSINESS. YOU HEARD THAT ALL THE EQUIPMENT PURCHASED, BOUGHT, ET CETERA, FROM THE BUSINESS. BARD WORKED -- THERE ON THE WITNESS STAND, HE SAID BARD WAS THERE MOST OF THE TIME. WILLER WAS THERE. YOU HAVE HEARD HIM TESTIFY. GOD KNOWS, THEY MIGHT NOT BE LIKE YOU AND I. THEY MIGHT NOT HAVE THE INTELLIGENCE AS YOU AND I. THEY MIGHT NOT BE ABLE TO DO THE SAME THINGS AS YOU AND I, BUT THEY ARE HUMAN. THEY HAVE A RIGHT TO BE TREATED AS HUMANS, AND THE ADMISSION BY MAY, WELL, SURE, I WAS SMARTER. SURE, MORE INTELLIGENT, SURE I WAS THE ONE THAT SUGGESTED AND DEMANDED I GET THE TITLE TO THE PROPERTY AND HE HAD A READY, WILLING, AND ABLE LEGAL PARTY IN READING AND INSISTING THAT NANAS SIGN THAT OVER.

THE COURT: TWO MINUTES, MR. FLANK.

MR. FLANK: MY FEELINGS, OF COURSE, ARE FOR NANAS. MY FEELINGS ARE FOR ZOSA. MY FEELINGS ARE FOR THOSE FOUR CHILDREN. IF YOU, IN FACT, DETERMINE THAT MAY IS ENTITLED TO THOSE HOUSES, THEN YOU DECIDE THAT MAY REMOVE THEM FROM ONE OF THE HOMES. IF YOU DETERMINE THAT SHE IS ENTITLED TO LOT 19 AND 20, THAT NANAS SHOULD NOT RECEIVE ANY RENT OR OTHER COMPEN-SATION FOR THAT, THEN NANAS WILL REMAIN IN

409

POVERTY TOTALLY. YOU HEARD NANAS TESTIFY WHAT MONEY SHE GOT. YOU HEARD NANAS TESTIFY AS TO WHAT SHE DID WITH THAT MONEY. SHE HAS NEVER BEEN ANYTHING BUT IN POVERTY.

THE FACT THAT SHE LIKEWISE MARRIED IN THIS GROUP SHOULD NOT LIKEWISE SET HER TO POVERTY. HE SAID SHE WORKED TEN YEARS. SHE SHOULD HAVE $2,000. THEY TRADED IT FOR $35,000 BACK IN 1972. WHAT SHOULD NANAS HAVE? SHE'S BEEN WORKING AND STRUGGLING FOR 25, 30 YEARS, I BELIEVE. YOU SEE THE SITUATION AND WHERE JUSTICE LIES, AND I ASK YOU SIMPLY TO FOLLOW YOUR HEART AND THE EVIDENCE IN THIS CASE. THANK YOU.

THE COURT: THANK YOU, MR. FLANK.

(THE BAILIFF WAS SWORN TO TAKE CHARGE OF THE JURY DURING ITS DELIBERATIONS.)

THE COURT: LADIES AND GENTLEMEN OF THE JURY, THE BAILIFF WILL GIVE YOU NO INSTRUCTIONS. YOU MUST REPORT TO THE COURT WHEN YOU HAVE ANY QUESTIONS OR INQUIRIES. NO MATERIALS ARE TO BE TAKEN INTO THE JURY ROOM WITH YOU WITH THE EXCEPTION OF THE COURT'S WRITTEN INSTRUCTIONS, EXHIBITS RECEIVED IN EVIDENCE, AND YOUR OWN PERSONAL NOTES AND EFFECTS. YOU ARE NOW RELEASED TO GO TO THE JURY ROOM.

WE WILL BE IN INFORMAL RECESS UNTIL THE JURY RETURNS. I WANT COUNSEL TO STAY IN THE AREA.

(AT 2:20 P.M. THE JURY RETIRED TO THE JURY ROOM TO COMMENCE DELIBERATIONS.)

THE COURT: LET'S GO ON THE RECORD.
GENTLEMEN, I HAVE RECEIVED A NOTE FROM THE JURY
WHICH READS AS FOLLOWS: WE SEEM TO BE MISSING
EXHIBIT NO. 15. IN LOOKING AT MY NOTES AS WELL AS
THE CLERK'S LIST OF EXHIBITS, IT APPEARS THAT
EXHIBIT NO. 15, WHICH IS THE DEED FROM DARDSON TO
TAYLOR OF APRIL 27, 1984, WAS DISCUSSED, AND
IDENTIFIED, BUT NEVER OFFERED OR RECEIVED.
CONSEQUENTLY, BY VIRTUE OF THAT OVERSIGHT, IT IS
MY SUGGESTION THAT WE MERELY RECEIVE BY STIPULA-
TION THE EXHIBIT, AND THEN PROVIDE IT TO THE JURY
SO THEY HAVE A COMPLETE PACKET OF EXHIBITS.

MR. FLANK, ANY OBJECTION?

MR. FLANK: I HAVE NO OBJECTION.

THE COURT: MR. RYAN?

MR. RYAN: NO OBJECTION.

THE COURT: VERY WELL, GENTLEMEN. THANK
YOU. I WILL DO SO.

(EXHIBIT 15 WAS RECEIVED AND A RECESS TAKEN.)

THE COURT: WE ARE NOW IN SESSION, AND
AGAIN, I UNDERSTAND THAT THE JURY HAS ARRIVED AT
A VERDICT. THE PARTIES ARE PRESENT WITH COUNSEL.

MR. BAILIFF, WILL YOU BRING THEM IN,
PLEASE?

(AT 5:30 THE JURY REPORTED TO THE COURTROOM
WITH THE FOLLOWING VERDICT.)

THE COURT: THE MEMBERS OF THE JURY
HAVE NOW RETURNED TO THE COURTROOM. MS.
PEDLER, ARE YOU THE FOREMAN OF THE JURY?

MS. PEDLER: YES, YOUR HONOR, I AM.

411

THE COURT: YOU HAVE ARRIVED AT A VERDICT?

MS. PEDLER: WE HAVE ARRIVED.

THE COURT: WILL YOU PLEASE GIVE THE VERDICT FORM TO THE BAILIFF?

BEFORE I READ THE VERDICT, LADIES AND GENTLEMEN OF THE JURY, I WANT TO SAY TO YOU NOW THAT I, ON BEHALF OF MYSELF AND THE PARTIES IN THIS CASE, EXPRESS MY APPRECIATION FOR YOUR CLOSE ATTENTION AND YOUR DILIGENT SERVICE IN THIS MATTER. I SAY THAT BEFORE THE VERDICT IS READ BECAUSE I KNOW THAT WHATEVER THE VERDICT IS, IT WILL BE A TRUE AND JUST VERDICT IN WHICH YOU HAVE PUT YOUR SERIOUS EFFORT AT RESOLVING THIS DISPUTE.

WILL YOU PLEASE READ THE VERDICT?

THE CLERK: J. BARD KANDERHOSH AND NANAS KANDERHOSH, HIS WIFE, VS. MAY HANCOCK KANDERHOSH SPECIAL VERDICT NO. C-82-2576.

(THE VERDICT WAS READ BY THE CLERK.)

THE COURT: DO YOU WISH, COUNSEL, TO HAVE THE JURY POLLED?

MR. FLANK: I WOULD, YOUR HONOR.

THE COURT: LADIES AND GENTLEMEN OF THE JURY, I WILL ASK YOU ONE QUESTION AND ONE QUESTION ONLY, TO WHICH YOU WILL ANSWER EITHER YES OR NO. THE QUESTION IS, WAS THIS AN IS THIS YOUR VERDICT? MRS. SMITH?

MRS. SMITH: YES.

THE COURT: MR. KOSOVICH?

MR. KOSOVICH: YES.

THE COURT: MS. PEDLER?

MS. PEDLER: YES.

THE COURT: MS. SKILLCORN?

MS. SKILLCORN: YES.

THE COURT: MS. RUSSELL?

MS. RUSSELL: NOT ENTIRELY.

THE COURT: MR. FERGUSON?

MR. FERGUSON: YES.

THE COURT: MR. WHITE?

MR. WHITE: NO, NOT ALL THE WAY.

THE COURT: MR. HOLMAN?

MR. HOLMAN: YES.

THE COURT: VERY WELL. LADIES AND GENTLEMEN OF THE JURY, YOUR SERVICE IN THIS CASE IS NOW CONCLUDED. YOU ARE FREE TO GO. OF COURSE, THE ADMONITION I HAVE GIVEN YOU ABOUT NOT DISCUSSING THE CASE IS NOW LIFTED. YOU CAN DISCUSS IT WITH WHOMEVER YOU CHOOSE. THAT IS NOT TO SAY, HOWEVER, THAT YOU MUST DISCUSS IT IF YOU CHOOSE NOT TO. THAT'S ENTIRELY YOUR DECISION. I THANK YOU FOR YOUR SERVICES, AND YOU ARE FREE TO GO.

MR. RYAN, YOU PREPARE THE JUDGMENT ON THE VERDICT.

MR. RYAN: I WILL, JUDGE. THANK YOU.

(PROCEEDINGS CONCLUDED.)

The verdict was read on December 11, 1985:

    1.   That the Defendant . . . retains full right to . . . the following described real property located in Salt Lake County, Utah: [Reclaim Barrel property and red house]. Plantiffs' claim for transfer is denied.

    2.   That full title and all rights to the described property are retained by the Defendant . . . with regard to the following real property located in Salt Lake County, Utah: [white house]
SUBJECT TO the conditions set forth on that certain Warranty Deed recorded . . . of the records of the Recorder of Salt Lake County, Utah.

    3.   That neither of the Plaintiffs owns any portion of or interest in Reclaim Barrel Supply, Inc., a Utah corporation.

    4.   That neither of the Plaintiffs is entitled to a distribution of any of the profits of Reclaim Barrel Supply, Inc., from May 17, 1982 to the present time.

    5.   That Plaintiff, Bard Kanderhosh, committed the tort of intentional infliction of emotional distress upon Defendant.

    6.   That Plaintiff, Bard Kanderhosh, committed the tort of battery upon Defendant.

    7.   That Plaintiff, Bard Kanderhosh, committed the tort of assault upon Defendant.

    8.   That no compensatory or punitive damages are awarded to Defendant by reason of the foregoing described tortious conduct of Plaintiff.

Thank you, God. There is justice. As I looked at the judge and the jury, tears streaming down my face, I felt such gratitude that they had compassion upon me.

I stood in the courtroom with a steady stream of tears running down my face as the ladies and gentlemen of the jury came up and each one shook my hand. A little dark-haired woman patted me on the hand and said, "Whatever is to be done right for Nanas, I know you will do it."

I appreciated that remark with all my soul. Then another woman shook my hand and said, "Bless you. You deserve all that you have." Then a man commented, "Good luck." And so on.

On the way home I could not help but notice my whole body felt exceptionally light, almost like I could float. For truly an iron yoke had been lifted, like the door to a prison being unlocked and opened where I had been chained for 20 long years.

I was free to go at last--to be--to think--to create--to love. My life was now just beginning. A thrill of joy radiated through me. As I looked out over the sunset, the sky was on fire.

"God is alive and well," I uttered with a trembling voice. "Thank you forever."

I am a free spirit!

Kaziah May Hancock

PROLOGUE

The years have rolled by. I have continued to keep Reclaim going, now with the capacity of over 200 drums per day. Most of my income goes to paying the ten employees who work for me.

My brother, Rod, has spent his entire life in the care of a mental institution. Mother has now remarried and is very happy.

I, too, am very happy because the prayers of Joseph Mandley have been answered. I look forward to a married life with someone I truly love with joy and contemplation of children. I have also picked up my long-lost love of sketching and am trying to be an artist. How that will turn out is anyone's guess.